BEASTARS

Volume 2

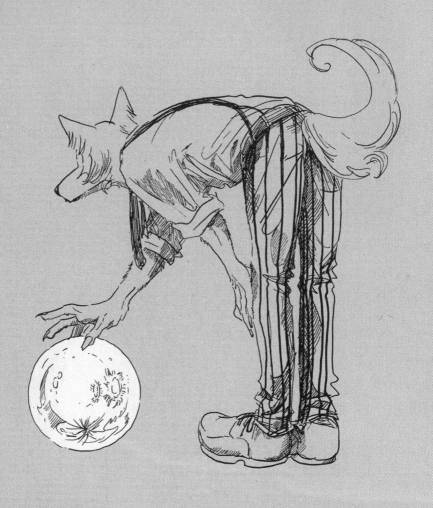

Story & Art by
Paru Itagaki

Plot Treatment...

BEASTARS

Cherryton Academy is an integrated boarding school for a diverse group of carnivores and herbivores. Recently, Tem, an alpaca member of the Drama Club, was slain on campus. The murderer has yet to be identified, and everyone's nerves are on edge.

The Drama Club is hard at work rehearsing to perform the play *Adler* to welcome new students. Louis, the head of the actors pool, plays the titular role. For Louis, his herbivore identity is critical to his representation of the character.

One night, while rehearsing with Tem's replacement, Louis seriously injures his leg. Meanwhile, Legoshi—who is standing guard outside because they are breaking curfew—scents a female rabbit. When his predatory instincts almost take over, he is filled with self-loathing.

Now Legoshi has been sent on a Drama Club errand to the Gardening Club on the school rooftop, only to come face-to-face with that same cute rabbit from the other night...

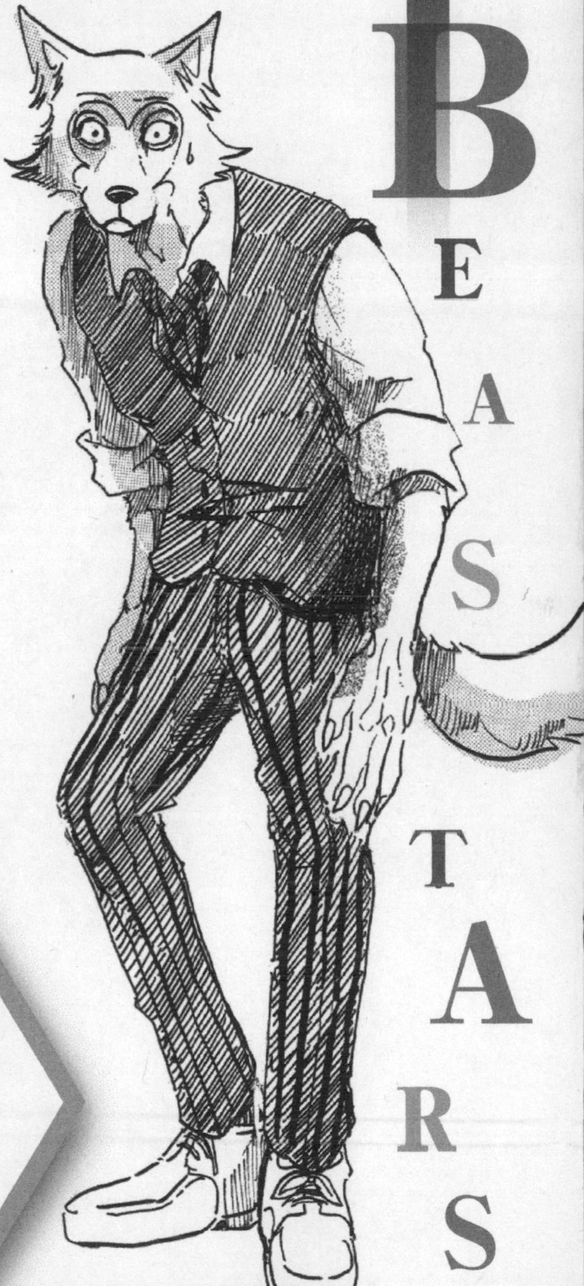

Legoshi

★Gray wolf ♂
★High school second-year
★Member of the Drama Club production crew
★Physically powerful yet emotionally sensitive
★Struggles with his identity as a carnivore

CAST OF CHARACTERS

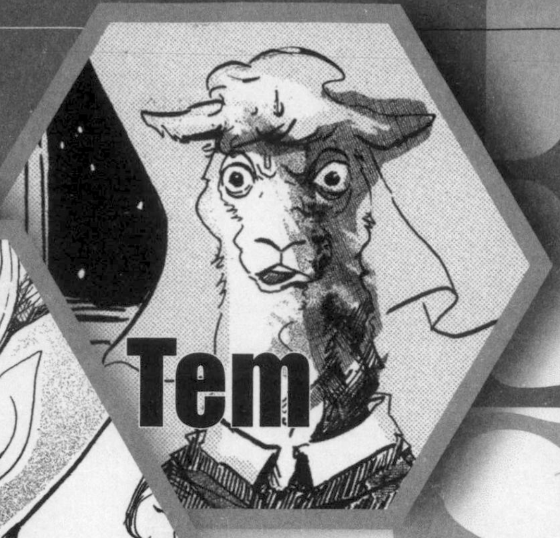
Tem

★Alpaca ♂
★Murdered by an unknown assailant

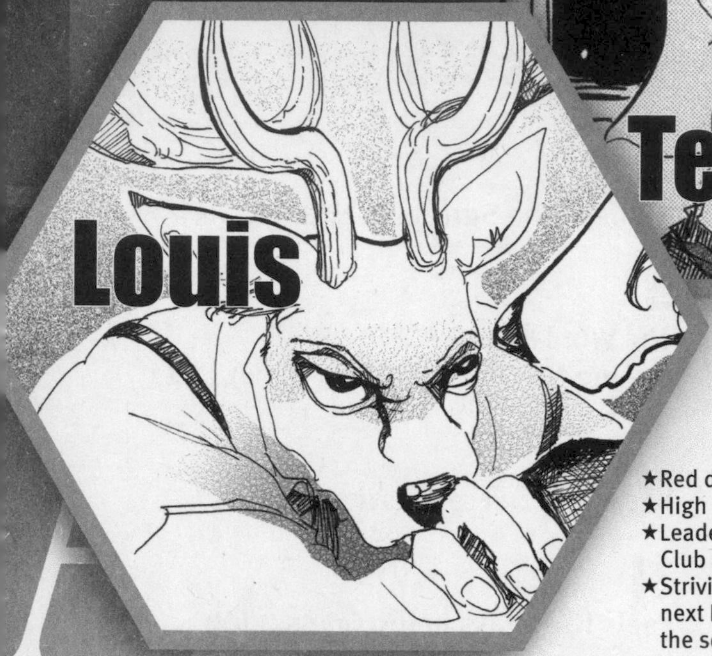
Louis

★Red deer ♂
★High school third-year
★Leader of the Drama Club actors pool
★Striving to become the next Beastar and rule the school

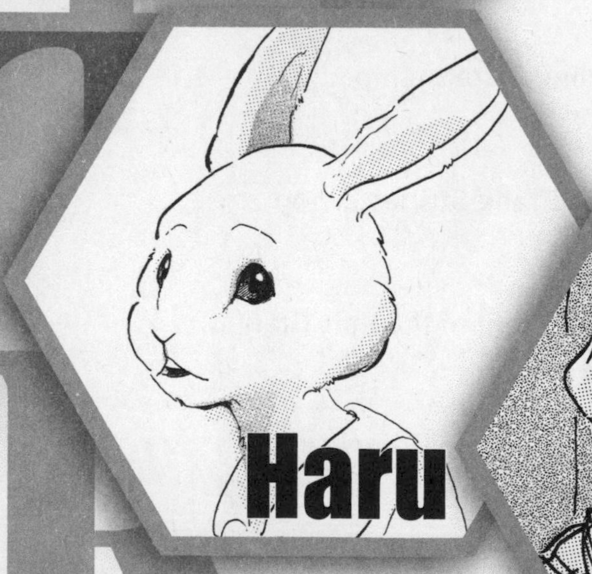
Haru

★Netherland dwarf rabbit ♀
★High school third-year
★Member of the Gardening Club

★Labrador retriever ♂
★High school second-year
★Legoshi's best friend

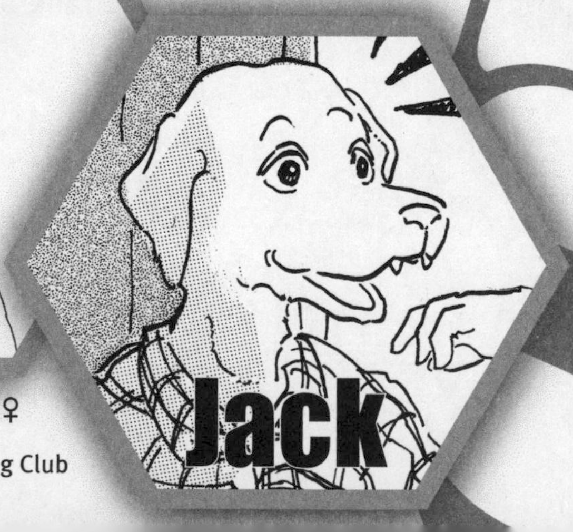
Jack

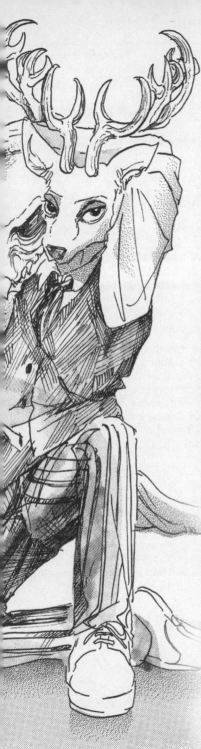

BEASTARS
Volume 2

CONTENTS

Chapter 8: Sighs of the Surrogate Mother

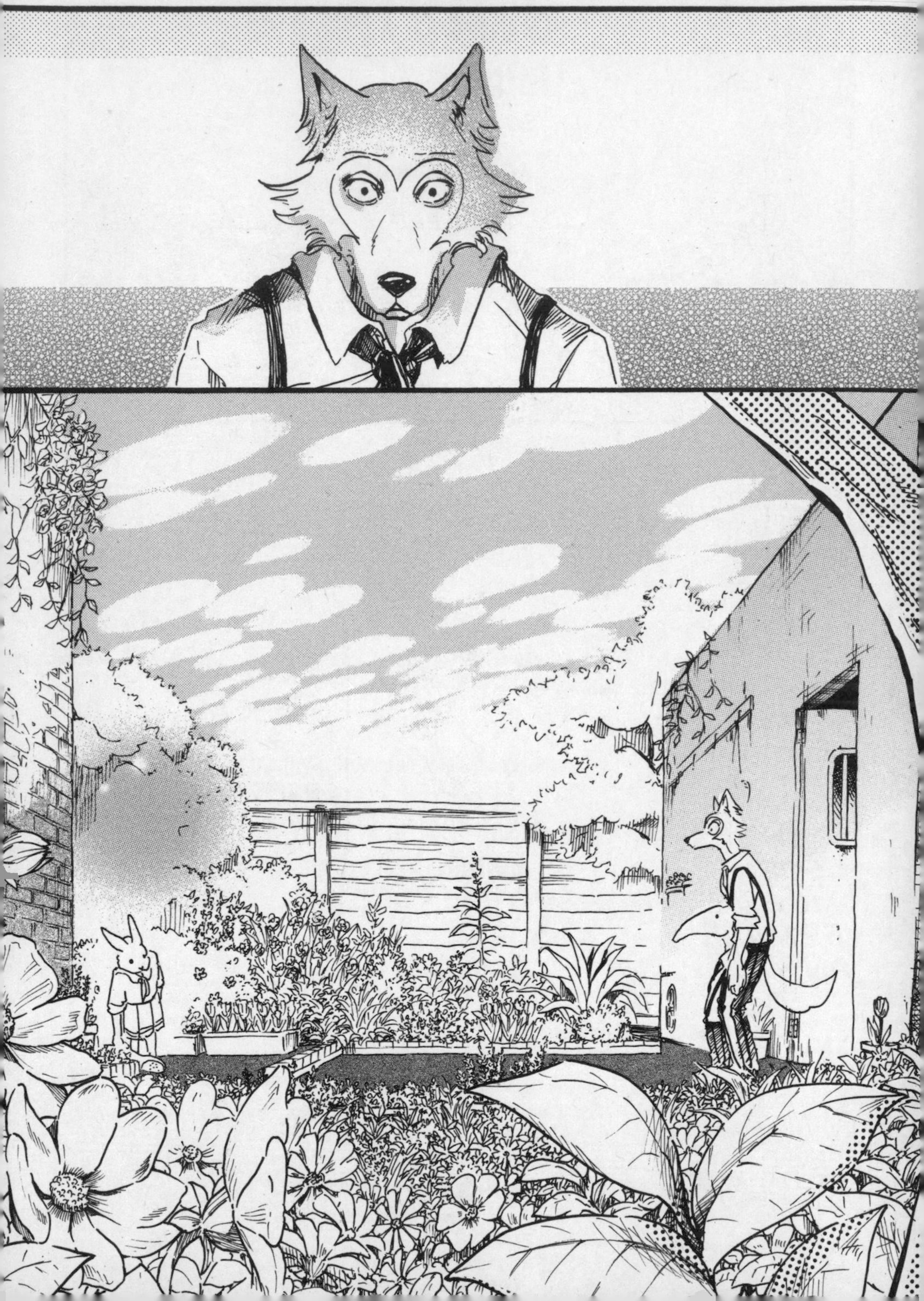

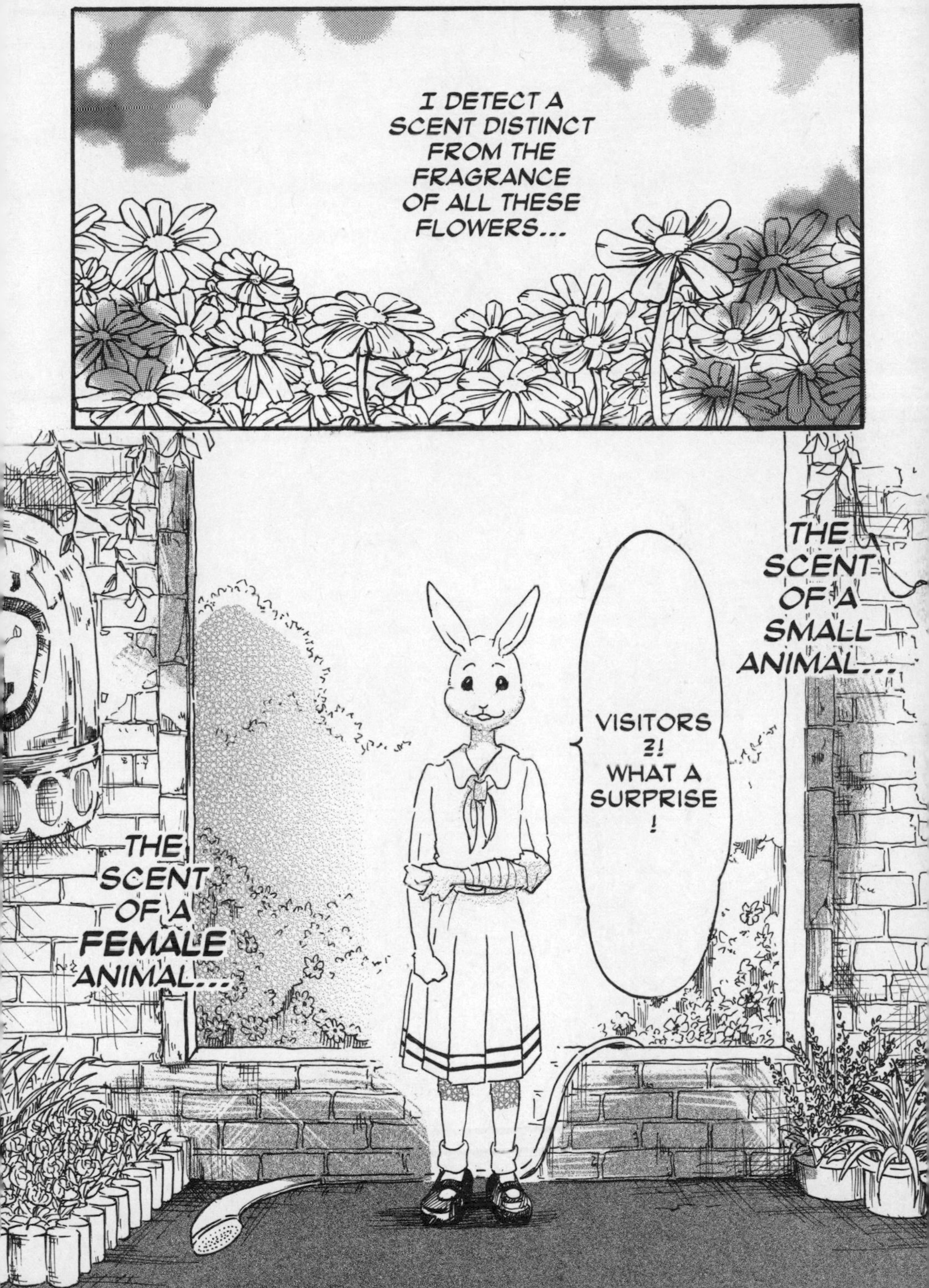
I DETECT A SCENT DISTINCT FROM THE FRAGRANCE OF ALL THESE FLOWERS...
THE SCENT OF A SMALL ANIMAL...
VISITORS ?! WHAT A SURPRISE !
THE SCENT OF A FEMALE ANIMAL...

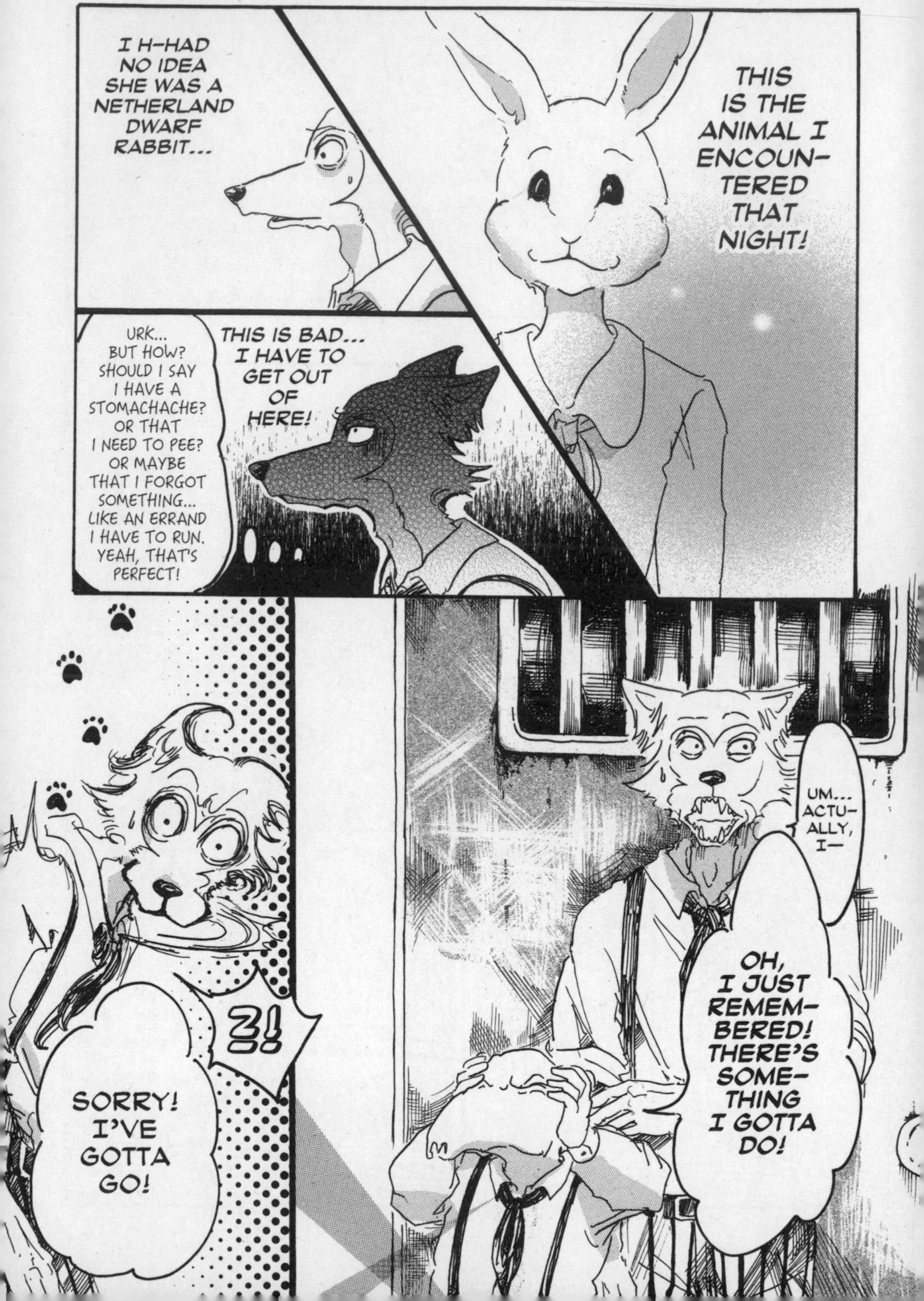
THIS IS THE ANIMAL I ENCOUNTERED THAT NIGHT!
I H-HAD NO IDEA SHE WAS A NETHERLAND DWARF RABBIT...
THIS IS BAD... I HAVE TO GET OUT OF HERE!
URK... BUT HOW? SHOULD I SAY I HAVE A STOMACHACHE? OR THAT I NEED TO PEE? OR MAYBE THAT I FORGOT SOMETHING... LIKE AN ERRAND I HAVE TO RUN. YEAH, THAT'S PERFECT!
UM... ACTUALLY, I—
OH, I JUST REMEMBERED! THERE'S SOMETHING I GOTTA DO!
SORRY! I'VE GOTTA GO!

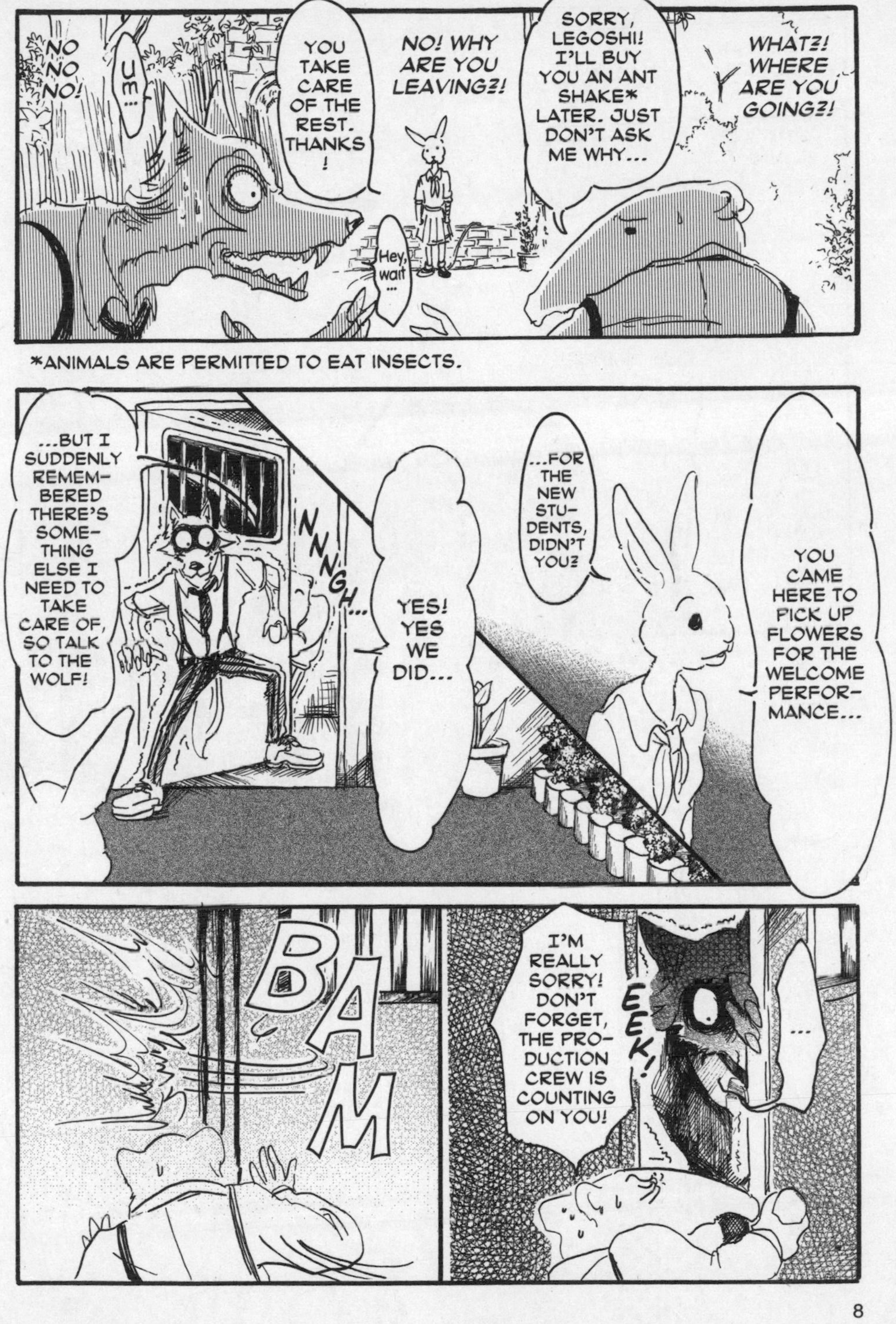
WHAT?! WHERE ARE YOU GOING?!
SORRY, LEGOSHI! I'LL BUY YOU AN ANT SHAKE* LATER. JUST DON'T ASK ME WHY...
NO! WHY ARE YOU LEAVING?!
YOU TAKE CARE OF THE REST. THANKS!
Hey, wait...
Um...
NO NO NO!
*ANIMALS ARE PERMITTED TO EAT INSECTS.
YOU CAME HERE TO PICK UP FLOWERS FOR THE WELCOME PERFORMANCE...
...FOR THE NEW STUDENTS, DIDN'T YOU?
YES! YES WE DID...
NNNGH...
...BUT I SUDDENLY REMEMBERED THERE'S SOMETHING ELSE I NEED TO TAKE CARE OF, SO TALK TO THE WOLF!
...
EEK!
I'M REALLY SORRY! DON'T FORGET, THE PRODUCTION CREW IS COUNTING ON YOU!
BAM

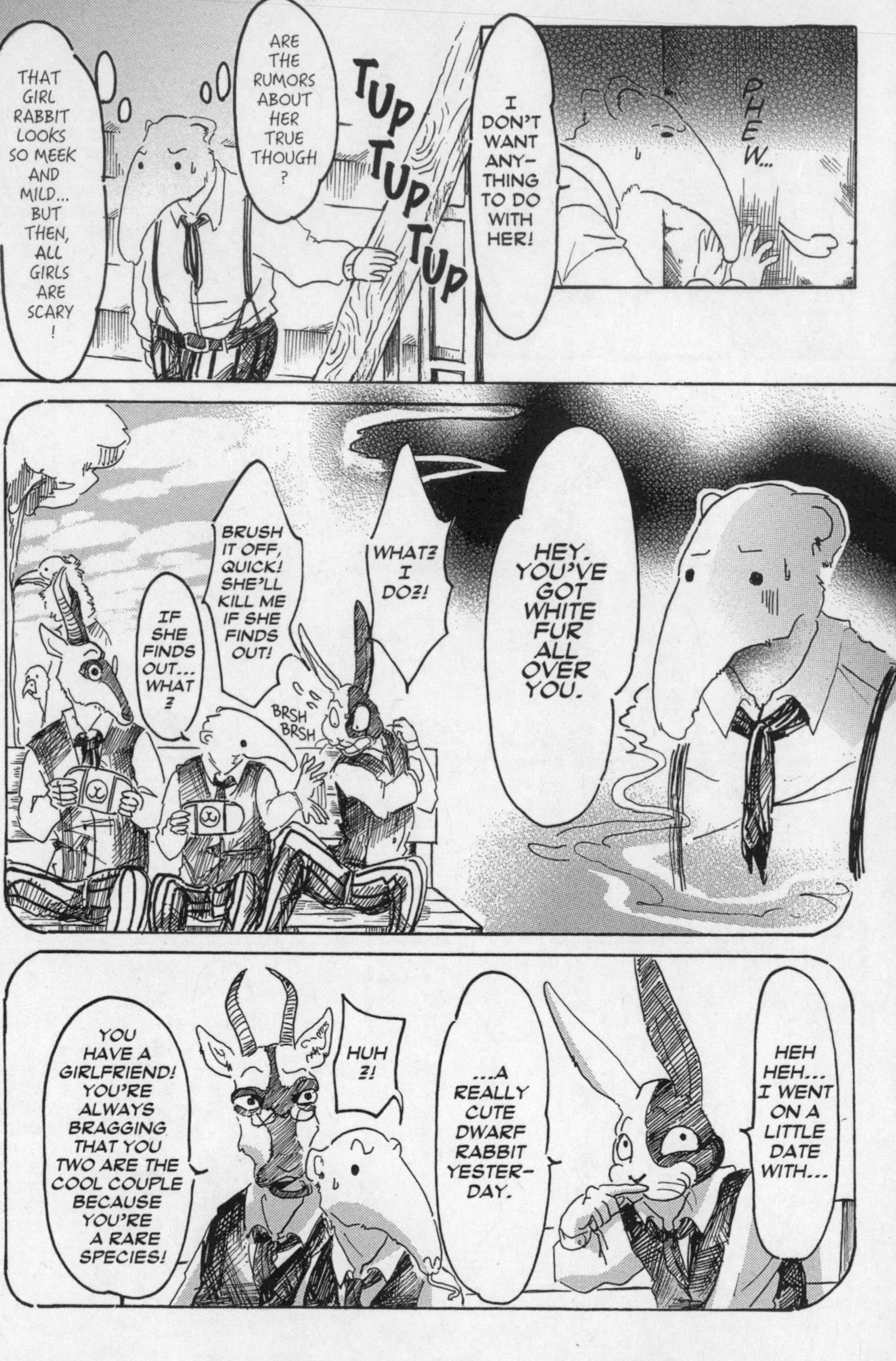
PHEW...
I DON'T WANT ANYTHING TO DO WITH HER!
TUP TUP TUP TUP
ARE THE RUMORS ABOUT HER TRUE THOUGH?
THAT GIRL RABBIT LOOKS SO MEEK AND MILD... BUT THEN, ALL GIRLS ARE SCARY!
HEY. YOU'VE GOT WHITE FUR ALL OVER YOU.
WHAT?! I DO?!
BRUSH IT OFF, QUICK! SHE'LL KILL ME IF SHE FINDS OUT!
BRSH BRSH
IF SHE FINDS OUT... WHAT?
HEH HEH... I WENT ON A LITTLE DATE WITH...
...A REALLY CUTE DWARF RABBIT YESTERDAY.
HUH?!
YOU HAVE A GIRLFRIEND! YOU'RE ALWAYS BRAGGING THAT YOU TWO ARE THE COOL COUPLE BECAUSE YOU'RE A RARE SPECIES!

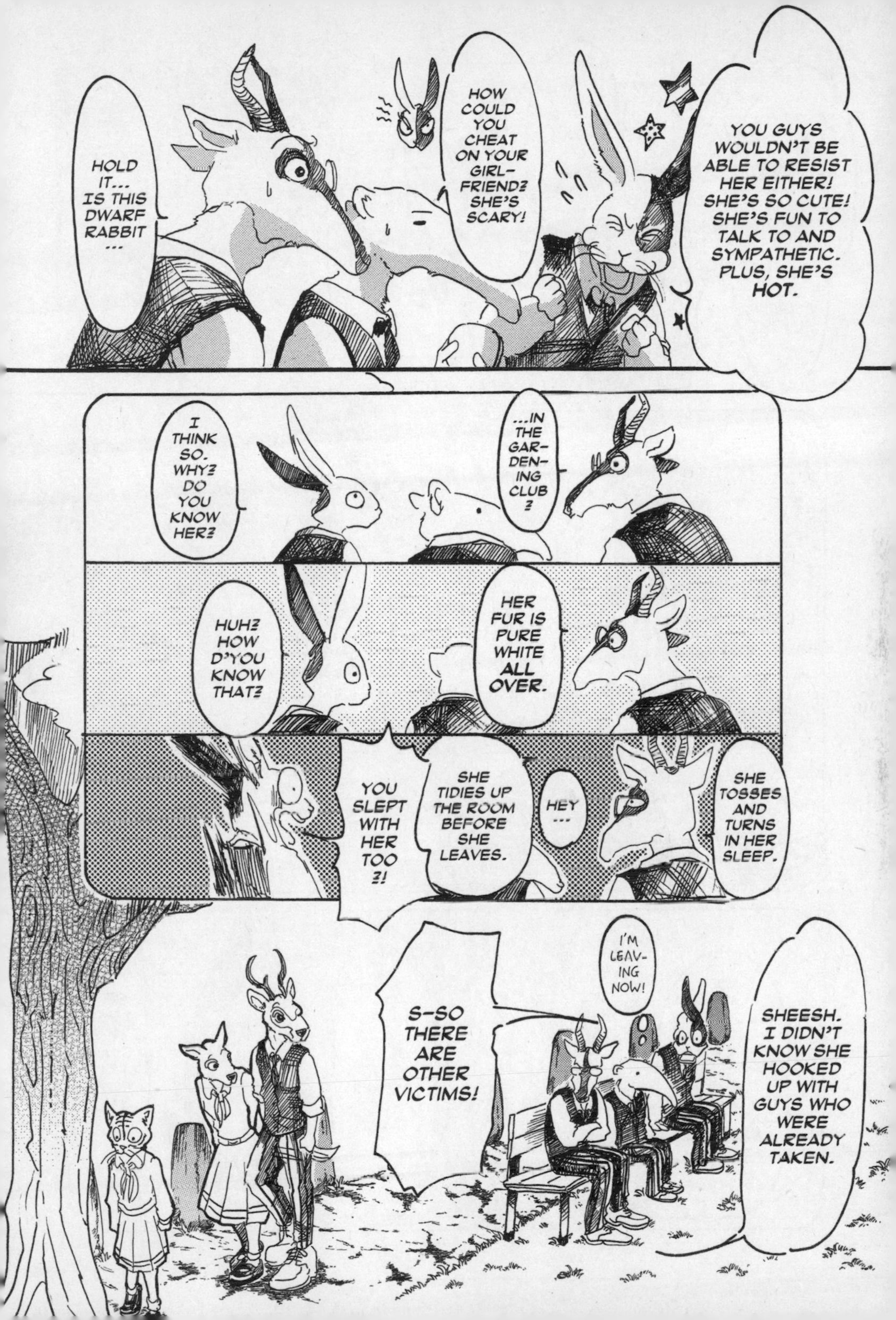
YOU GUYS WOULDN'T BE ABLE TO RESIST HER EITHER! SHE'S SO CUTE! SHE'S FUN TO TALK TO AND SYMPATHETIC. PLUS, SHE'S HOT.
HOW COULD YOU CHEAT ON YOUR GIRLFRIEND? SHE'S SCARY!
HOLD IT... IS THIS DWARF RABBIT...
...IN THE GARDENING CLUB?
I THINK SO. WHY? DO YOU KNOW HER?
HER FUR IS PURE WHITE ALL OVER.
HUH? HOW D'YOU KNOW THAT?
SHE TOSSES AND TURNS IN HER SLEEP.
HEY...
SHE TIDIES UP THE ROOM BEFORE SHE LEAVES.
YOU SLEPT WITH HER TOO?!
SHEESH. I DIDN'T KNOW SHE HOOKED UP WITH GUYS WHO WERE ALREADY TAKEN.
I'M LEAVING NOW!
S-SO THERE ARE OTHER VICTIMS!

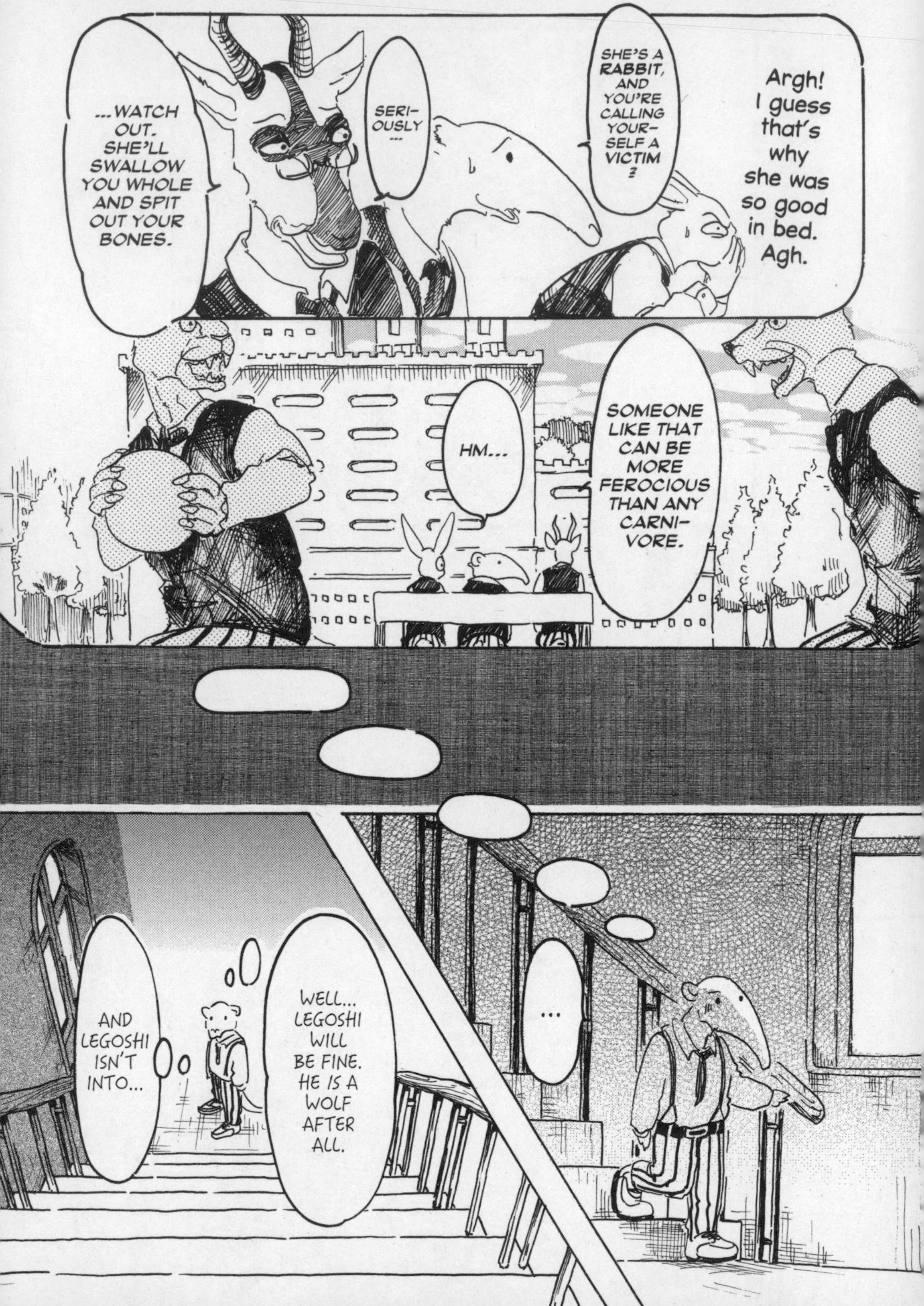
Argh! I guess that's why she was so good in bed. Agh.
SHE'S A RABBIT, AND YOU'RE CALLING YOURSELF A VICTIM?
SERIOUSLY...
...WATCH OUT. SHE'LL SWALLOW YOU WHOLE AND SPIT OUT YOUR BONES.
SOMEONE LIKE THAT CAN BE MORE FEROCIOUS THAN ANY CARNIVORE.
HM...
...
WELL... LEGOSHI WILL BE FINE. HE IS A WOLF AFTER ALL.
AND LEGOSHI ISN'T INTO...

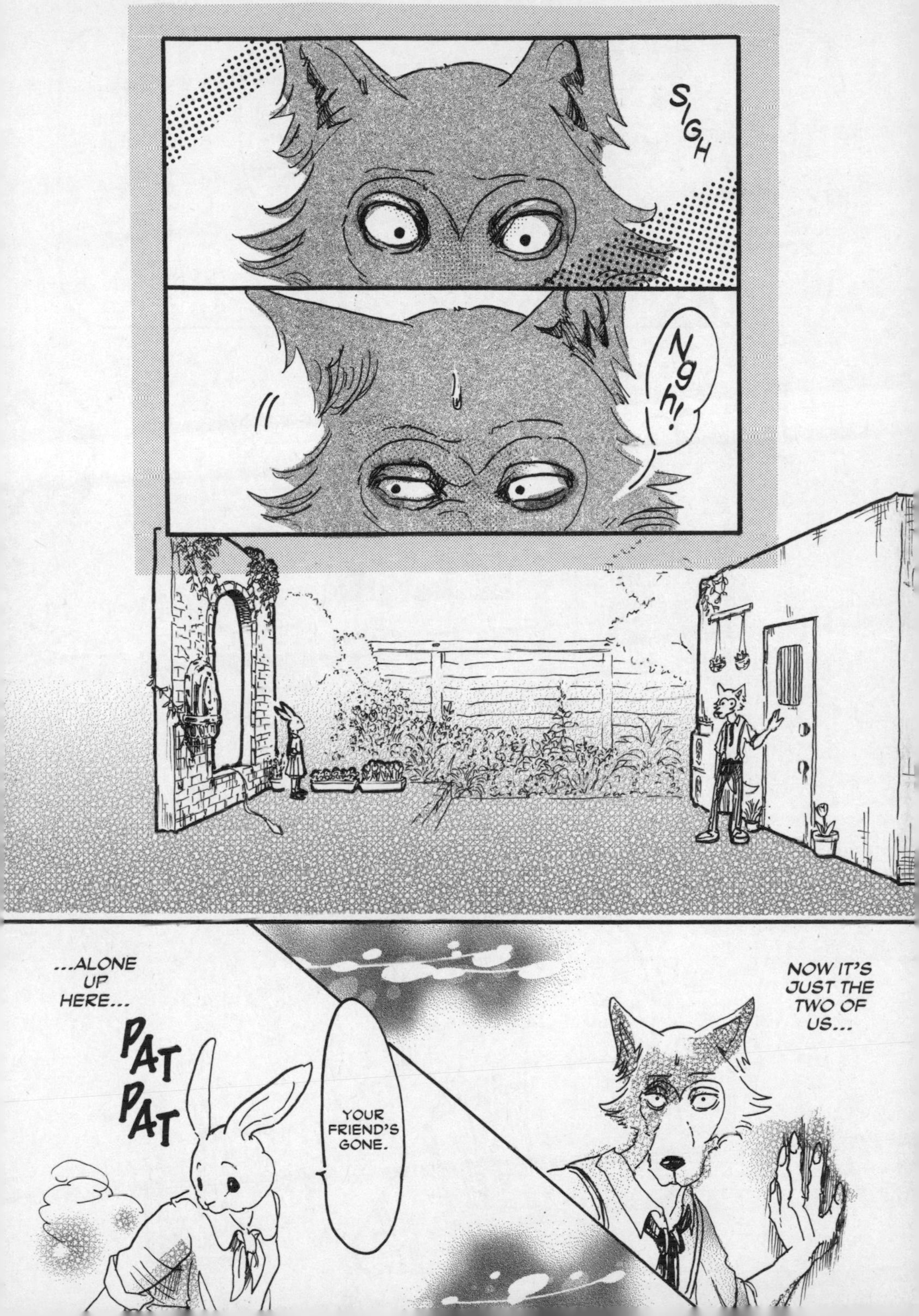
SIGH
Ngh!
NOW IT'S JUST THE TWO OF US...
YOUR FRIEND'S GONE.
...ALONE UP HERE...
PAT PAT

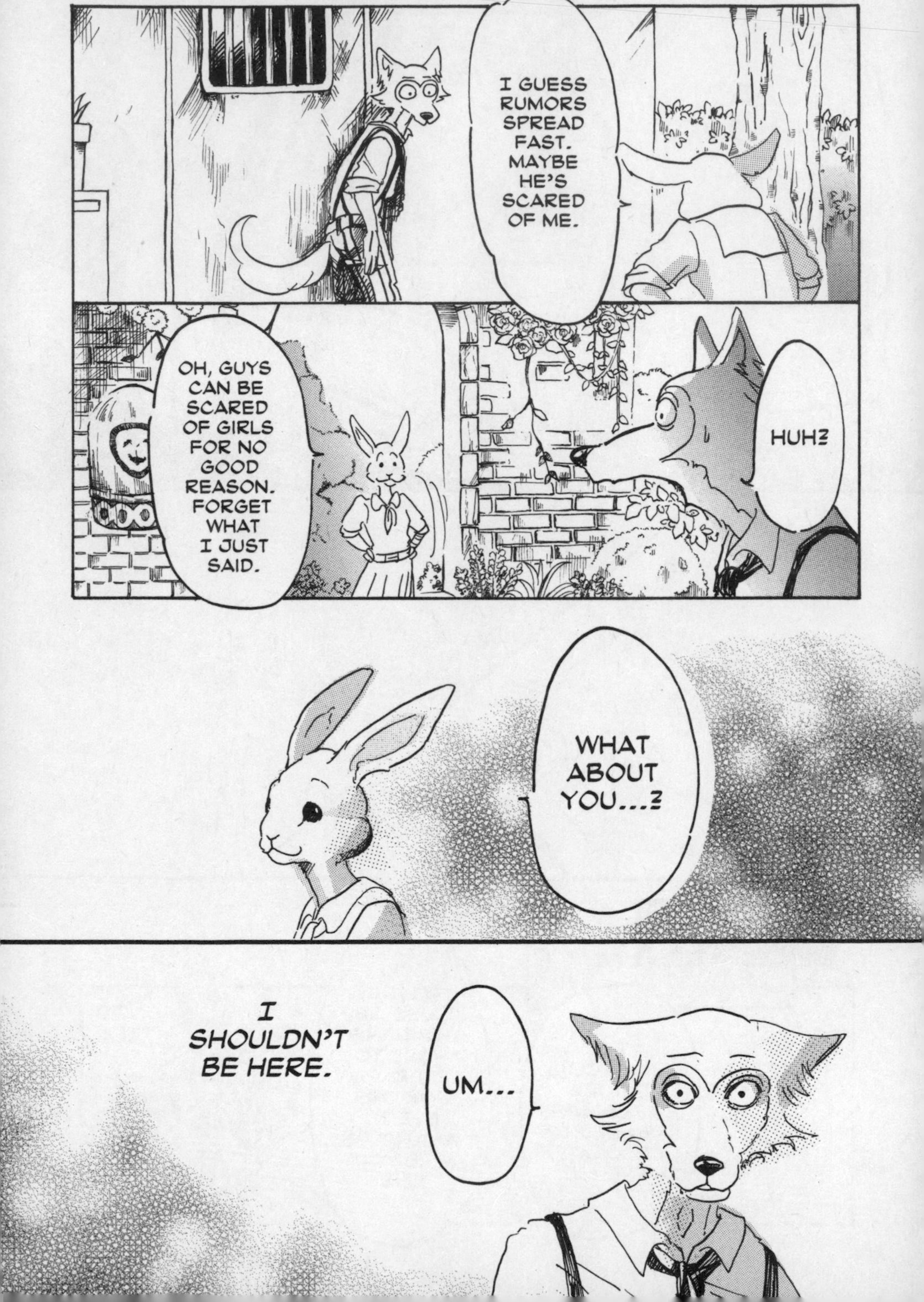
I GUESS RUMORS SPREAD FAST. MAYBE HE'S SCARED OF ME.
HUH?
OH, GUYS CAN BE SCARED OF GIRLS FOR NO GOOD REASON. FORGET WHAT I JUST SAID.
WHAT ABOUT YOU...?
UM...
I SHOULDN'T BE HERE.

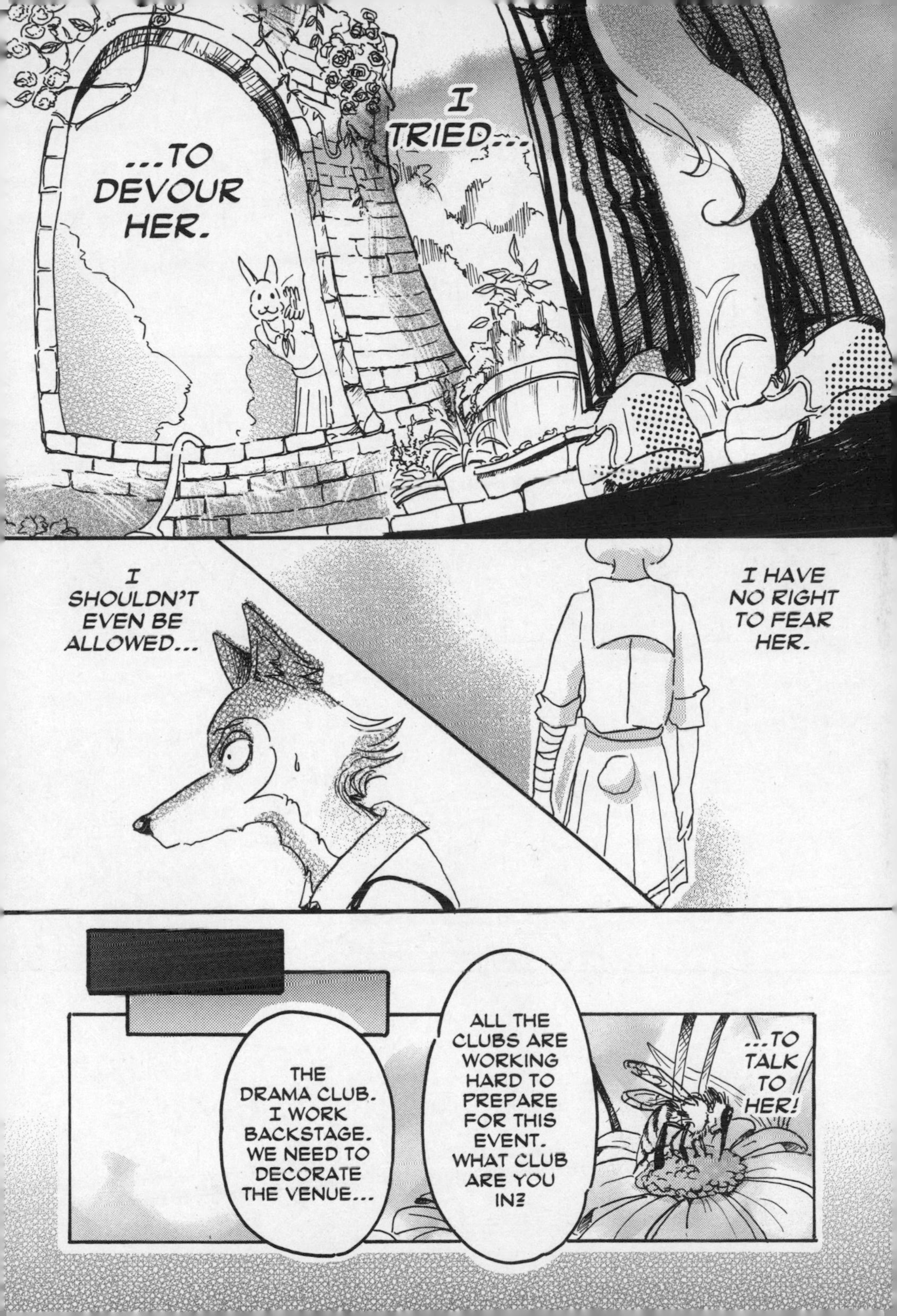
I TRIED...
...TO DEVOUR HER.
I HAVE NO RIGHT TO FEAR HER.
I SHOULDN'T EVEN BE ALLOWED...
...TO TALK TO HER!
ALL THE CLUBS ARE WORKING HARD TO PREPARE FOR THIS EVENT. WHAT CLUB ARE YOU IN?
THE DRAMA CLUB. I WORK BACKSTAGE. WE NEED TO DECORATE THE VENUE...

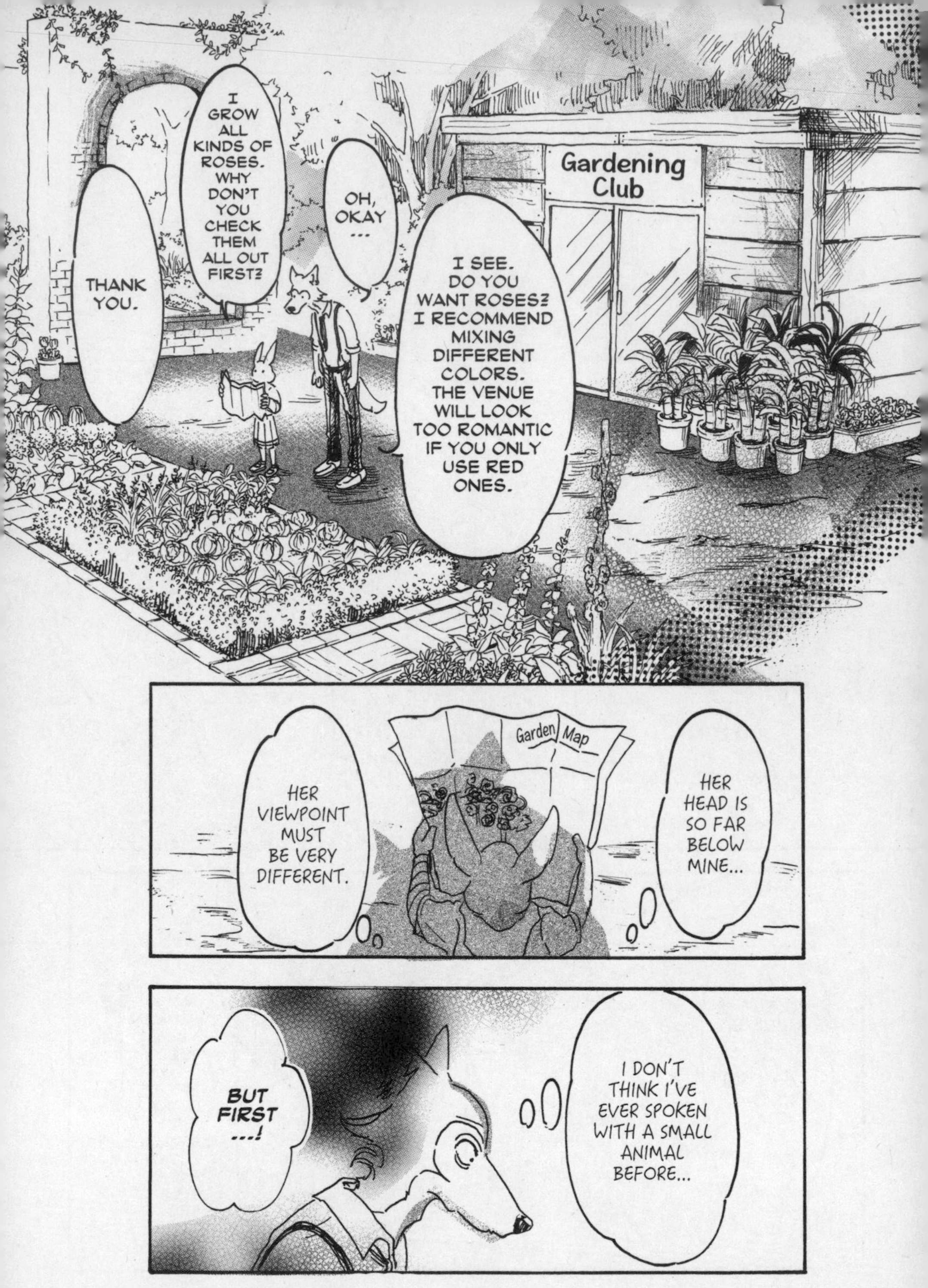
Gardening Club
I SEE. DO YOU WANT ROSES? I RECOMMEND MIXING DIFFERENT COLORS. THE VENUE WILL LOOK TOO ROMANTIC IF YOU ONLY USE RED ONES.
OH, OKAY...
I GROW ALL KINDS OF ROSES. WHY DON'T YOU CHECK THEM ALL OUT FIRST?
THANK YOU.
HER HEAD IS SO FAR BELOW MINE...
Garden Map
HER VIEWPOINT MUST BE VERY DIFFERENT.
I DON'T THINK I'VE EVER SPOKEN WITH A SMALL ANIMAL BEFORE...
BUT FIRST...!

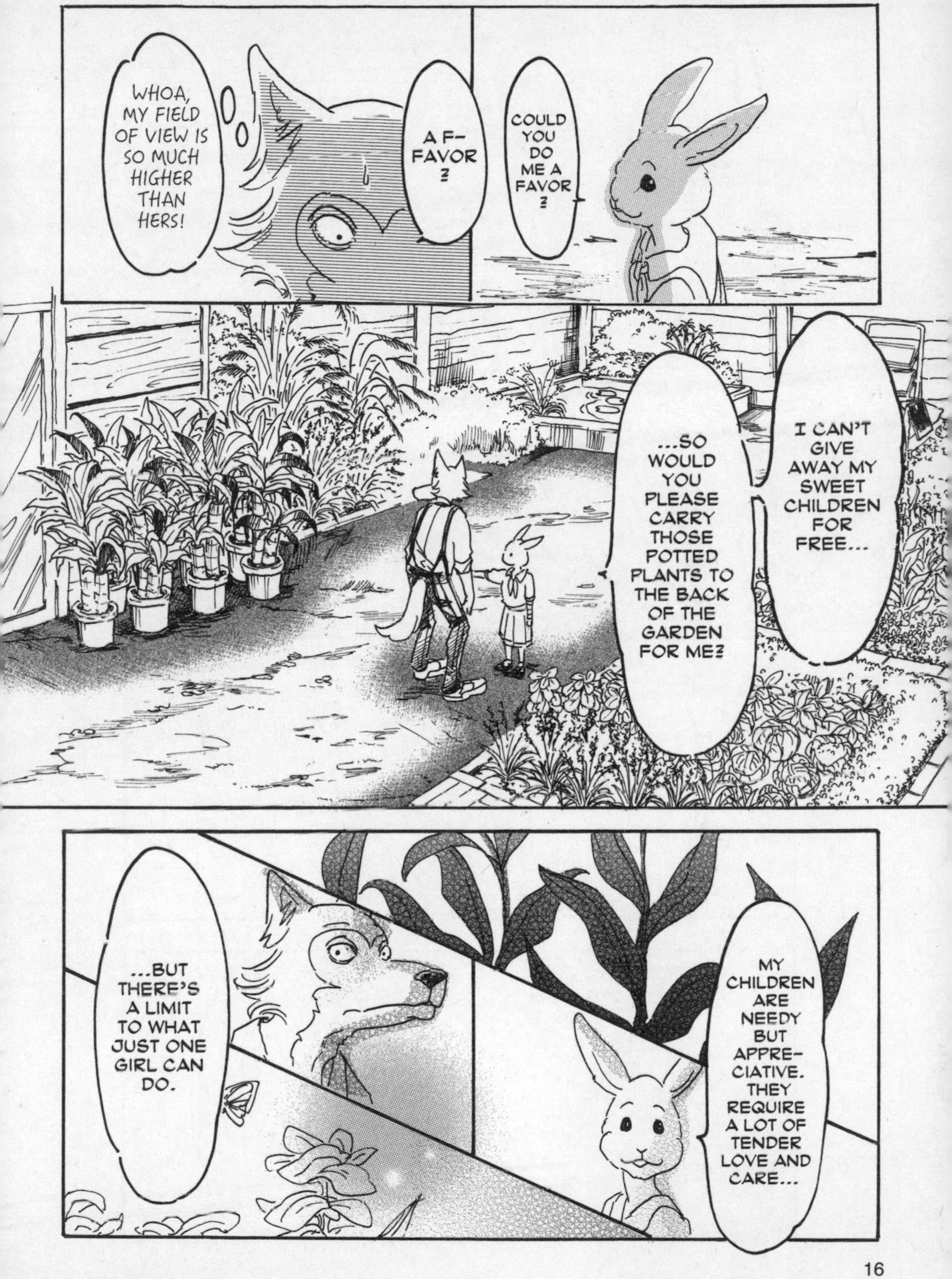
COULD YOU DO ME A FAVOR?
A F-FAVOR?
WHOA, MY FIELD OF VIEW IS SO MUCH HIGHER THAN HERS!
I CAN'T GIVE AWAY MY SWEET CHILDREN FOR FREE...
...SO WOULD YOU PLEASE CARRY THOSE POTTED PLANTS TO THE BACK OF THE GARDEN FOR ME?
MY CHILDREN ARE NEEDY BUT APPRECIATIVE. THEY REQUIRE A LOT OF TENDER LOVE AND CARE...
...BUT THERE'S A LIMIT TO WHAT JUST ONE GIRL CAN DO.

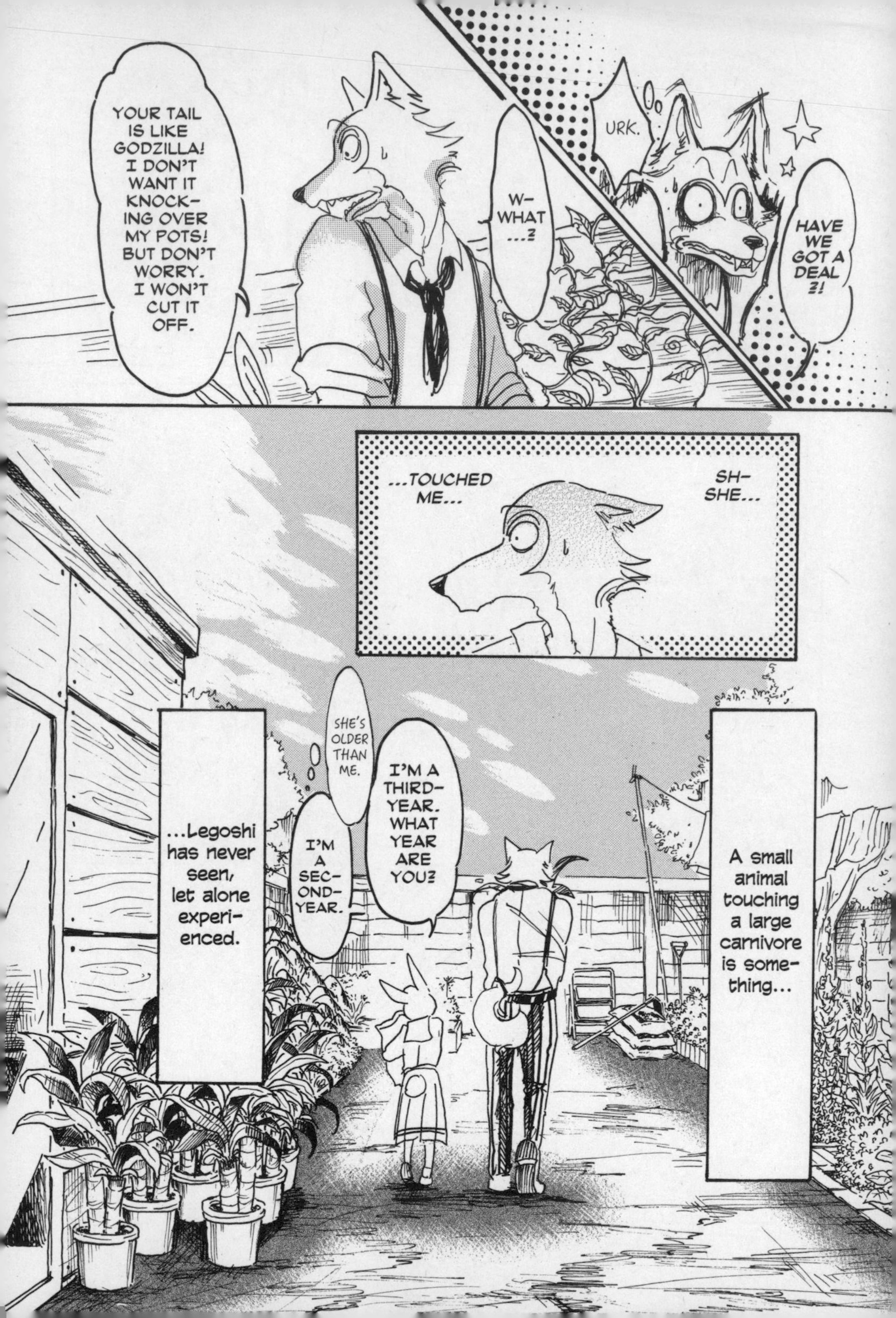
HAVE WE GOT A DEAL?!
URK.
W-WHAT...?
YOUR TAIL IS LIKE GODZILLA! I DON'T WANT IT KNOCKING OVER MY POTS! BUT DON'T WORRY. I WON'T CUT IT OFF.
SH-SHE...
...TOUCHED ME...
A small animal touching a large carnivore is something...
I'M A THIRD-YEAR. WHAT YEAR ARE YOU?
SHE'S OLDER THAN ME.
I'M A SECOND-YEAR.
...Legoshi has never seen, let alone experienced.

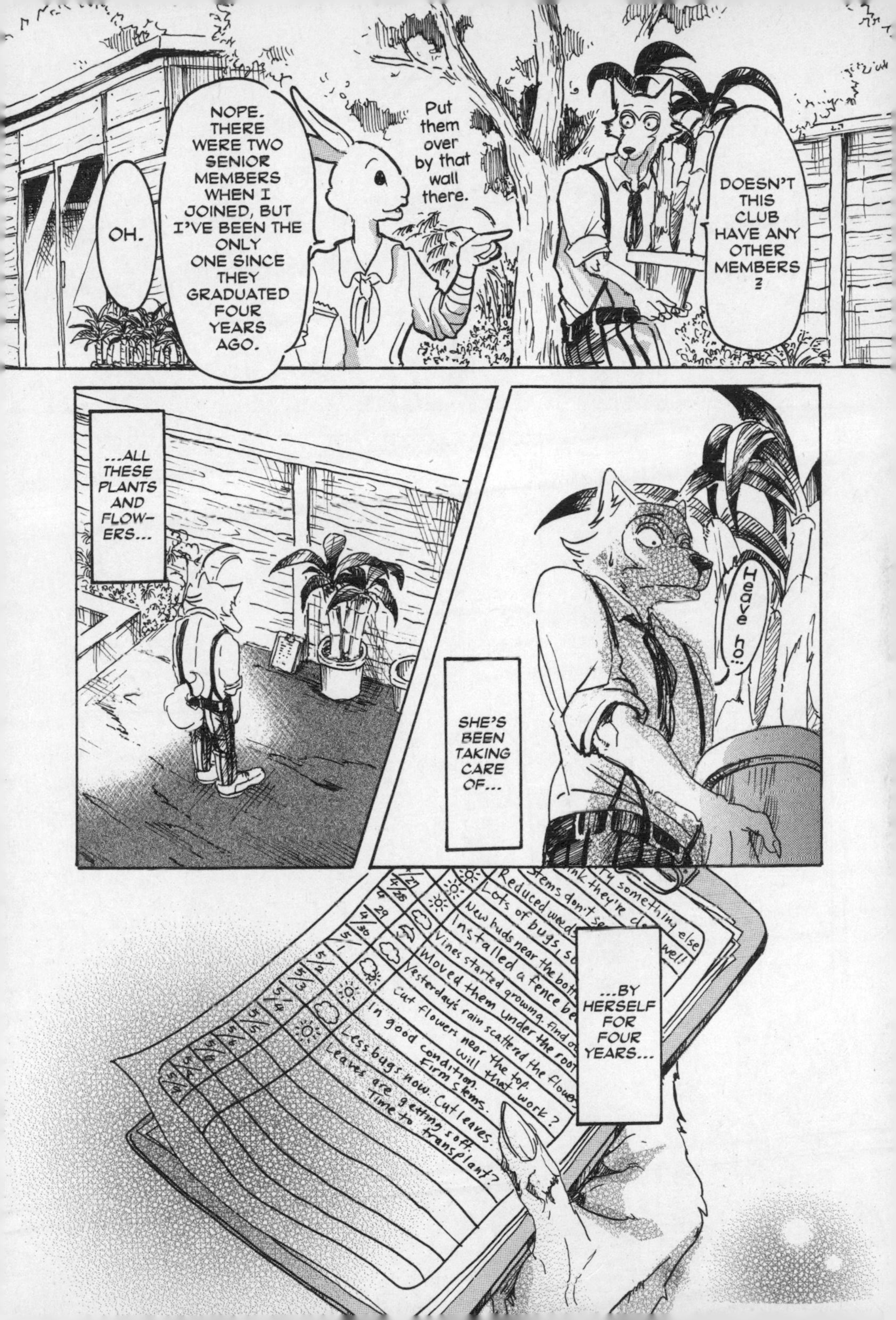
DOESN'T THIS CLUB HAVE ANY OTHER MEMBERS?
Put them over by that wall there.
NOPE. THERE WERE TWO SENIOR MEMBERS WHEN I JOINED, BUT I'VE BEEN THE ONLY ONE SINCE THEY GRADUATED FOUR YEARS AGO.
OH.
Heave ho...
SHE'S BEEN TAKING CARE OF...
...ALL THESE PLANTS AND FLOWERS...
Cut flowers near the top. will that work?
In good condition. Firm stems.
Less bugs now. Cut leaves.
Leaves are getting soft. Time to transplant?
...BY HERSELF FOR FOUR YEARS...

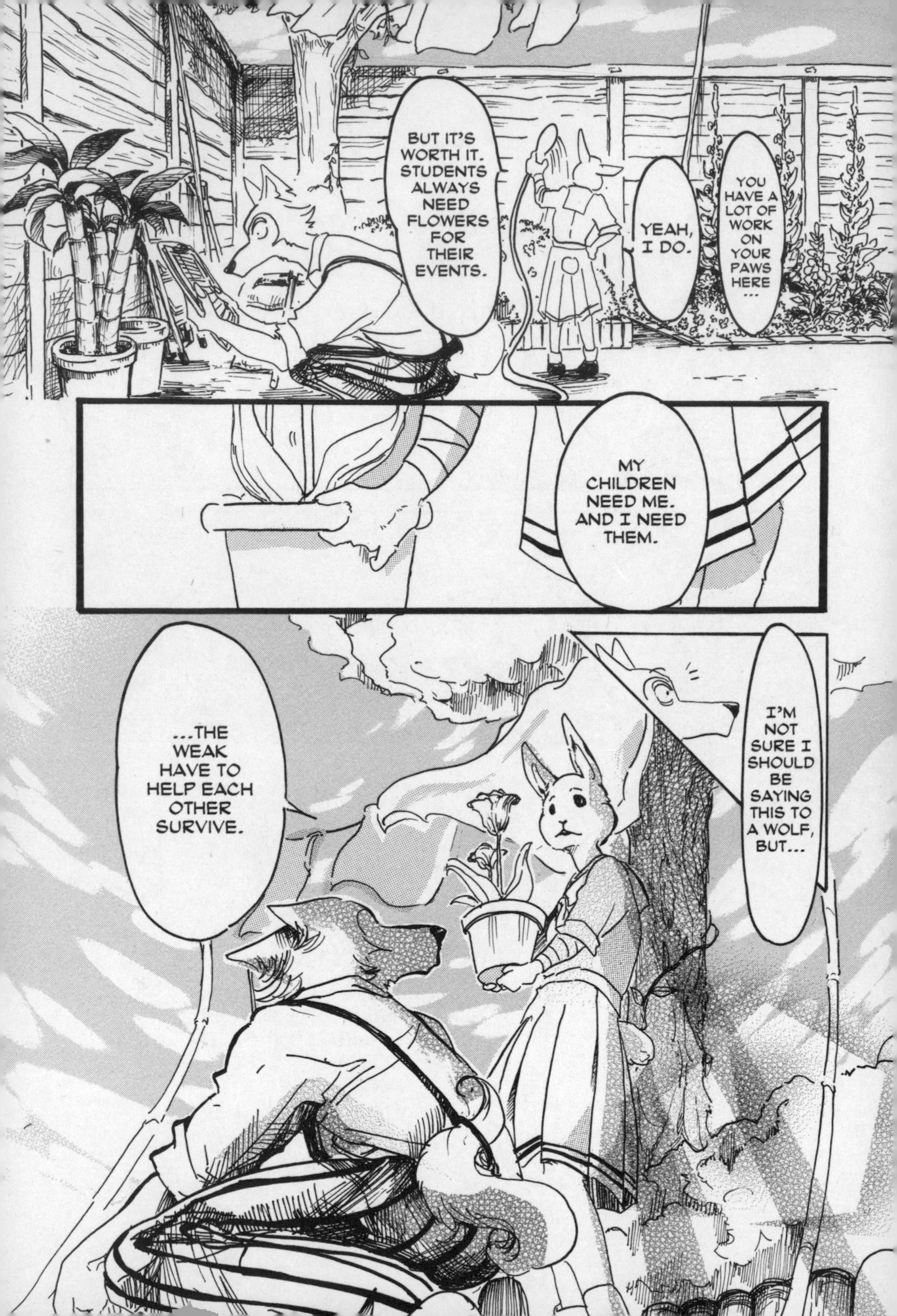
YOU HAVE A LOT OF WORK ON YOUR PAWS HERE...
YEAH, I DO.
BUT IT'S WORTH IT. STUDENTS ALWAYS NEED FLOWERS FOR THEIR EVENTS.
MY CHILDREN NEED ME. AND I NEED THEM.
I'M NOT SURE I SHOULD BE SAYING THIS TO A WOLF, BUT...
...THE WEAK HAVE TO HELP EACH OTHER SURVIVE.

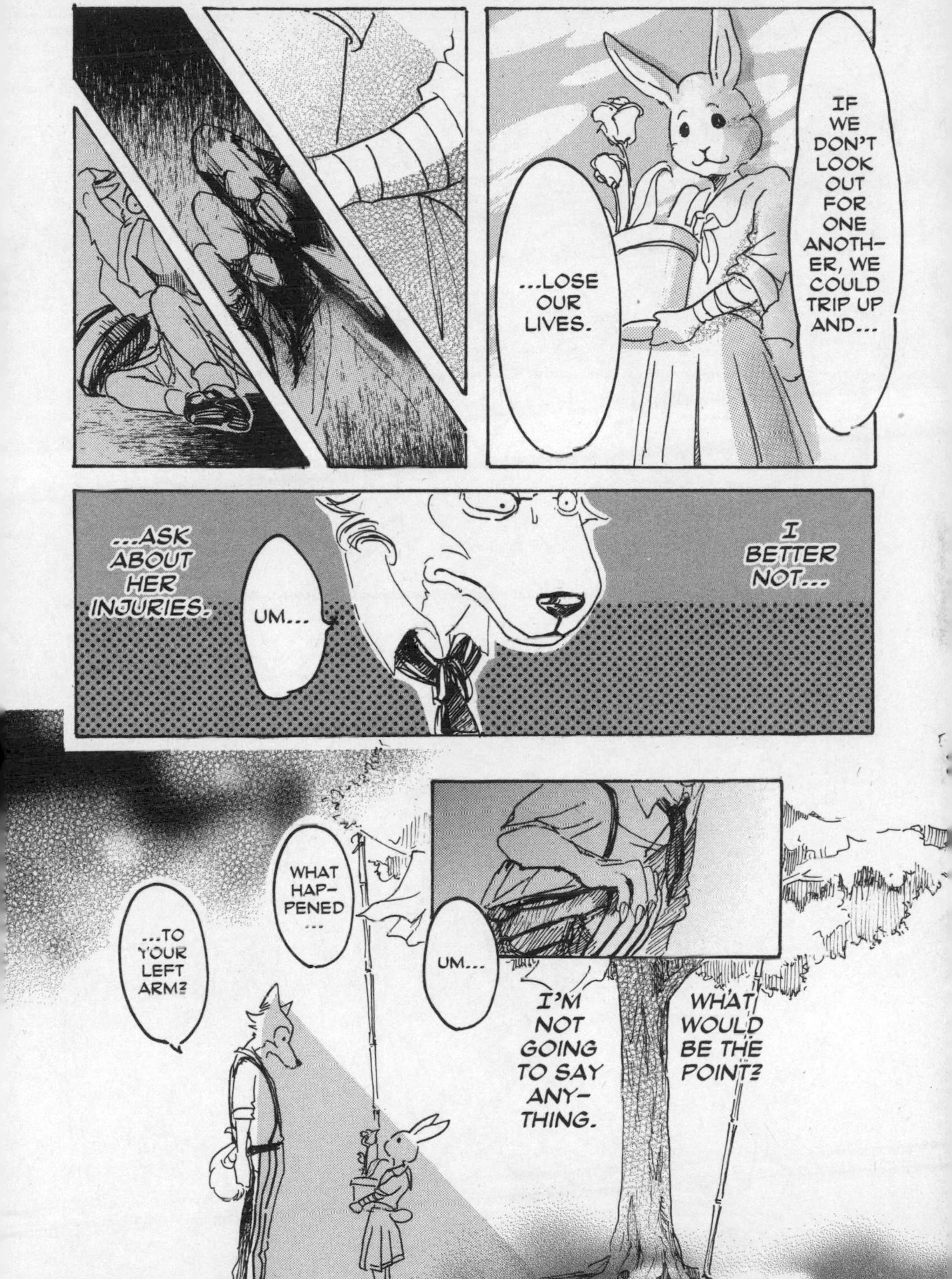
IF WE DON'T LOOK OUT FOR ONE ANOTHER, WE COULD TRIP UP AND...
...LOSE OUR LIVES.
I BETTER NOT...
...ASK ABOUT HER INJURIES.
UM...
WHAT WOULD BE THE POINT?
I'M NOT GOING TO SAY ANY-THING.
UM...
WHAT HAP-PENED...
...TO YOUR LEFT ARM?

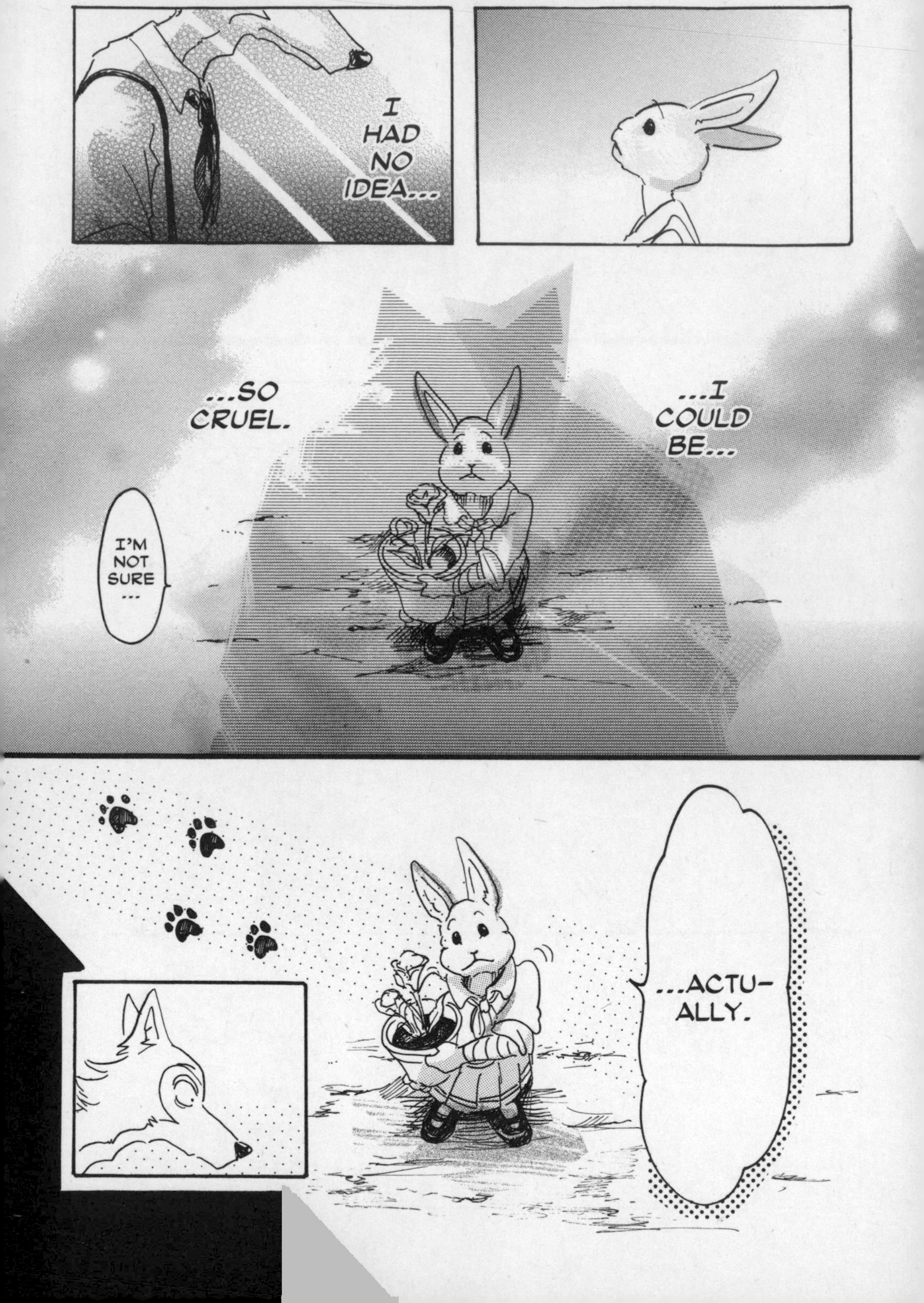
I HAD NO IDEA...
...I COULD BE...
...SO CRUEL.
I'M NOT SURE ...
...ACTU-ALLY.

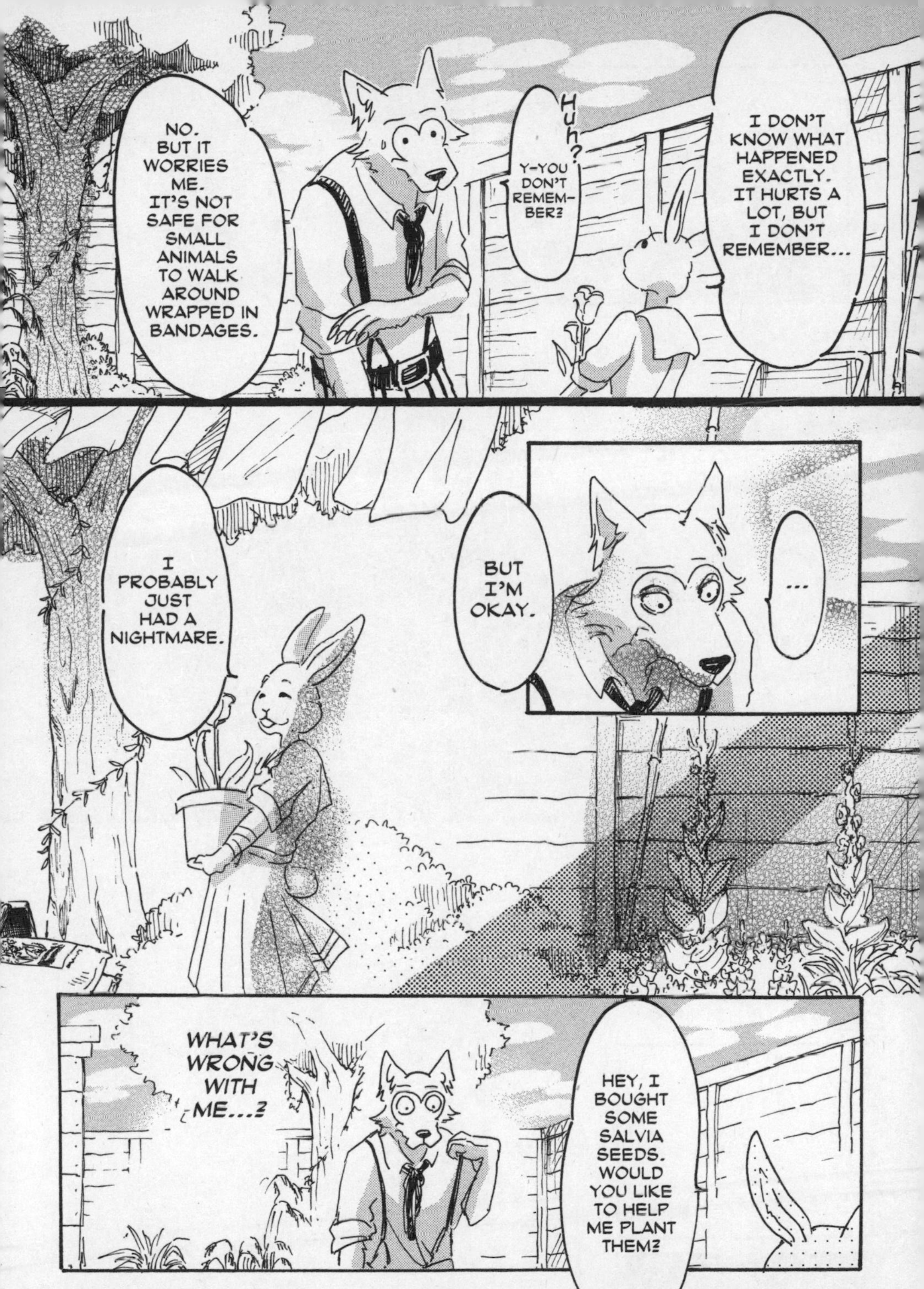
I DON'T KNOW WHAT HAPPENED EXACTLY. IT HURTS A LOT, BUT I DON'T REMEMBER...
Huh?
Y-YOU DON'T REMEMBER?
NO. BUT IT WORRIES ME. IT'S NOT SAFE FOR SMALL ANIMALS TO WALK AROUND WRAPPED IN BANDAGES.
...
BUT I'M OKAY.
I PROBABLY JUST HAD A NIGHTMARE.
HEY, I BOUGHT SOME SALVIA SEEDS. WOULD YOU LIKE TO HELP ME PLANT THEM?
WHAT'S WRONG WITH ME...?

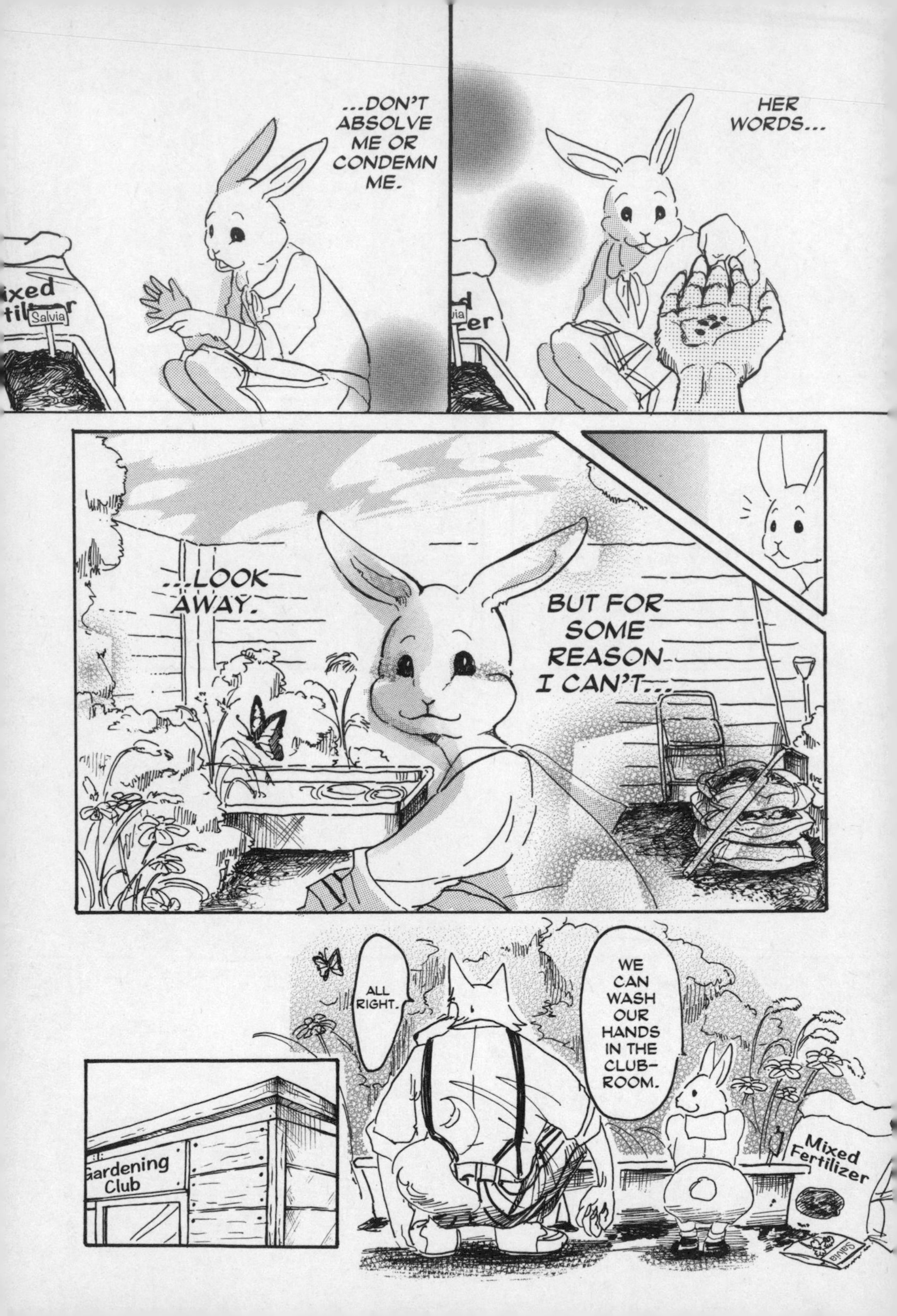
HER WORDS...
...DON'T ABSOLVE ME OR CONDEMN ME.
Salvia
BUT FOR SOME REASON I CAN'T...
...LOOK AWAY.
WE CAN WASH OUR HANDS IN THE CLUB-ROOM.
ALL RIGHT.
Mixed Fertilizer
Salvia
Gardening Club

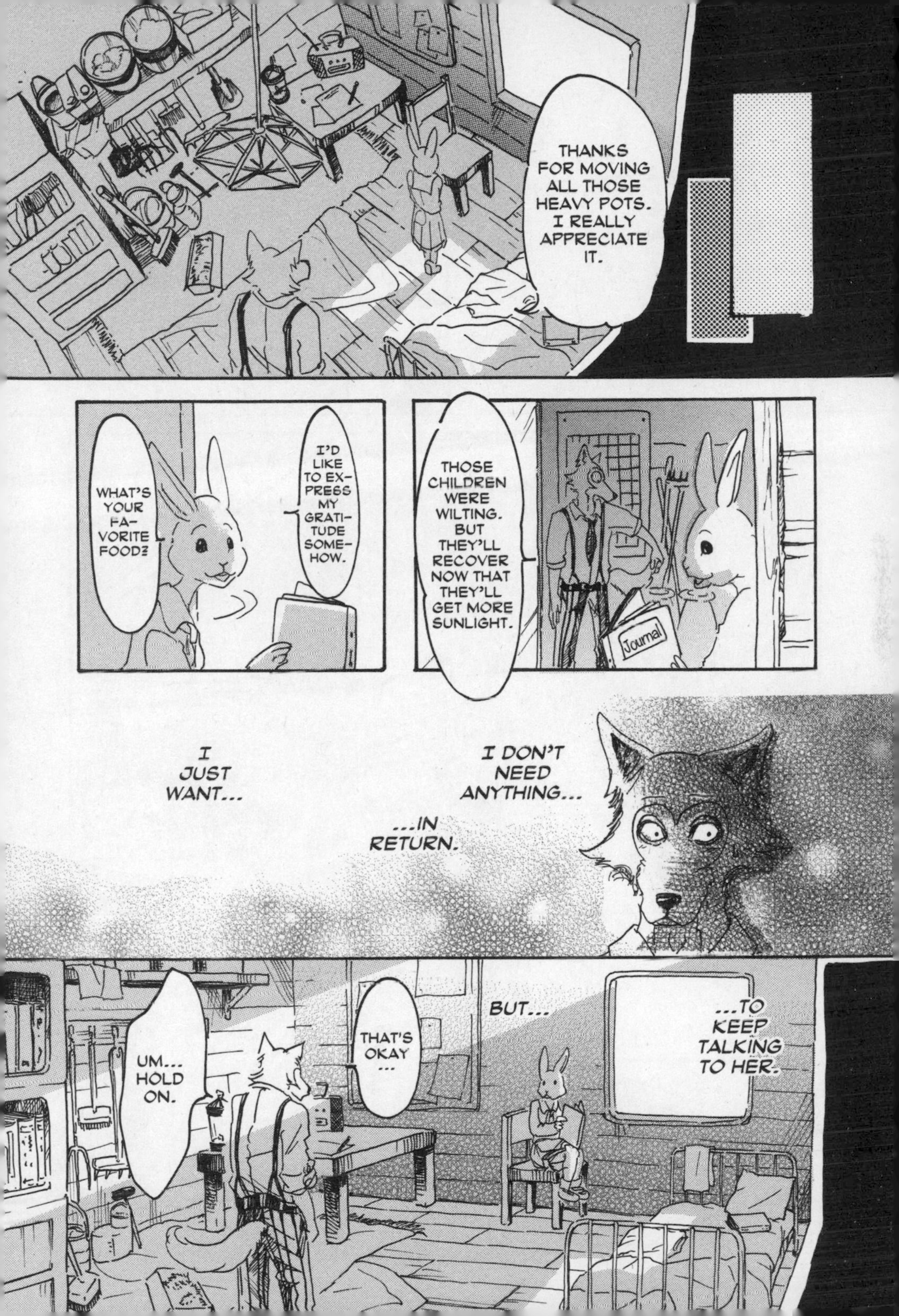
THANKS FOR MOVING ALL THOSE HEAVY POTS. I REALLY APPRECIATE IT.
THOSE CHILDREN WERE WILTING. BUT THEY'LL RECOVER NOW THAT THEY'LL GET MORE SUNLIGHT.
Journal
I'D LIKE TO EXPRESS MY GRATITUDE SOMEHOW.
WHAT'S YOUR FAVORITE FOOD?
I DON'T NEED ANYTHING...
...IN RETURN.
I JUST WANT...
...TO KEEP TALKING TO HER.
BUT...
THAT'S OKAY...
UM... HOLD ON.

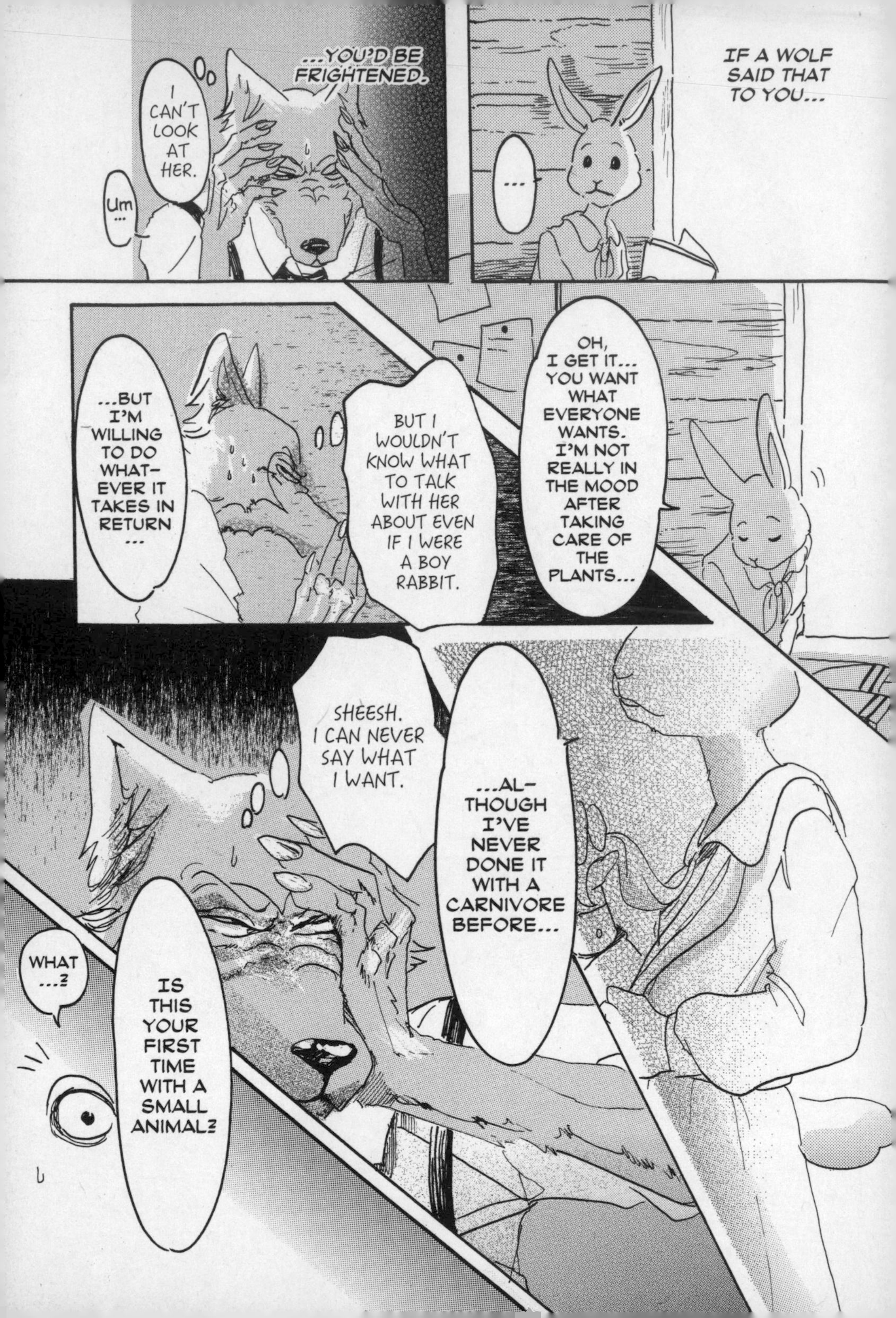
IF A WOLF SAID THAT TO YOU...
...
...YOU'D BE FRIGHTENED.
I CAN'T LOOK AT HER.
Um...
OH, I GET IT... YOU WANT WHAT EVERYONE WANTS. I'M NOT REALLY IN THE MOOD AFTER TAKING CARE OF THE PLANTS...
BUT I WOULDN'T KNOW WHAT TO TALK WITH HER ABOUT EVEN IF I WERE A BOY RABBIT.
...BUT I'M WILLING TO DO WHAT-EVER IT TAKES IN RETURN...
...AL-THOUGH I'VE NEVER DONE IT WITH A CARNIVORE BEFORE...
SHEESH. I CAN NEVER SAY WHAT I WANT.
IS THIS YOUR FIRST TIME WITH A SMALL ANIMAL?
WHAT...?

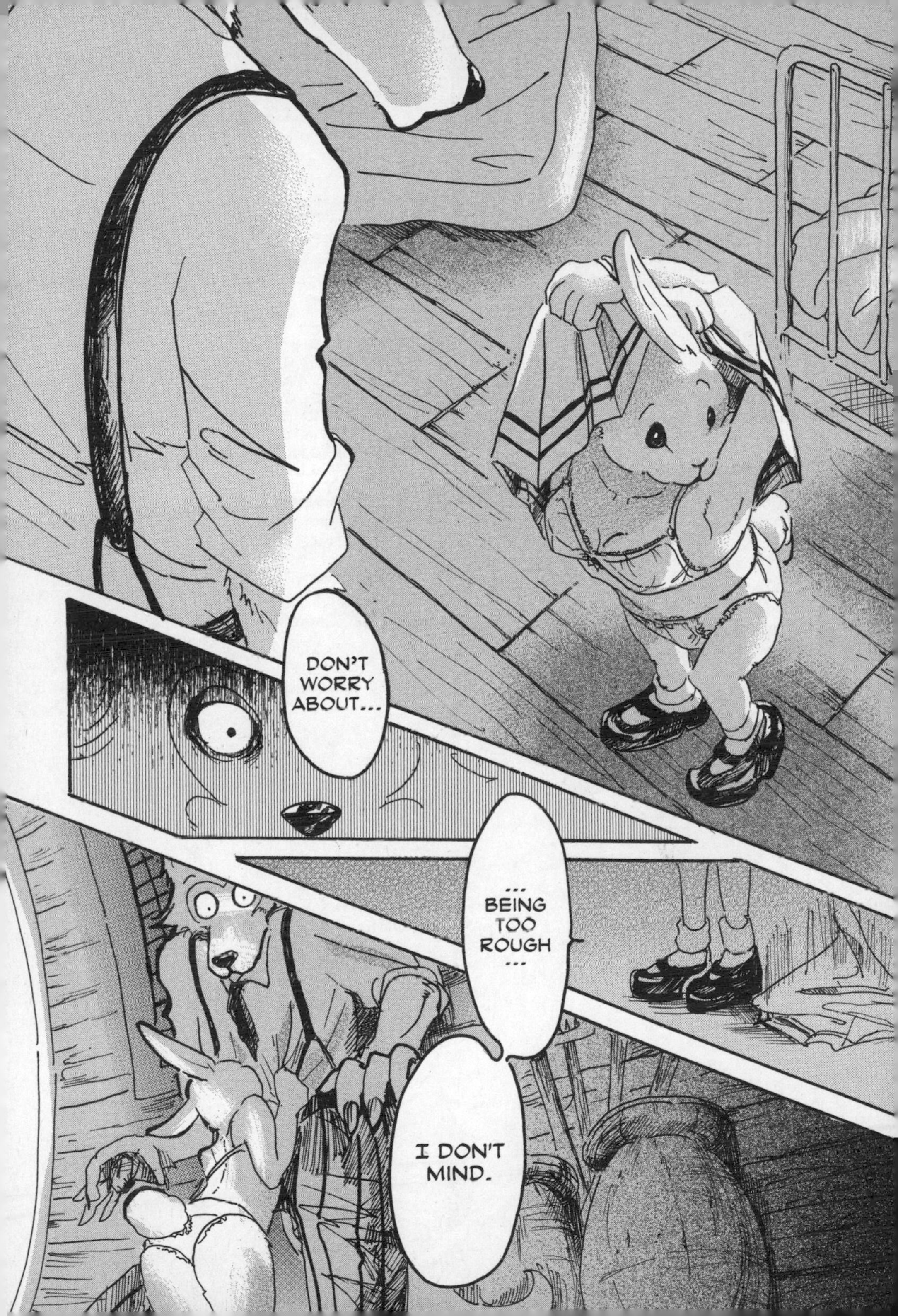
DON'T WORRY ABOUT...
... BEING TOO ROUGH ...
I DON'T MIND.

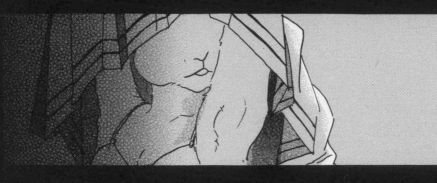

A WHITE RABBIT IS...

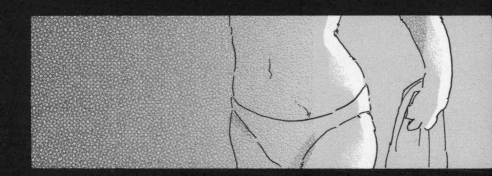

...TAKING OFF HER WHITE UNIFORM IN FRONT OF ME.

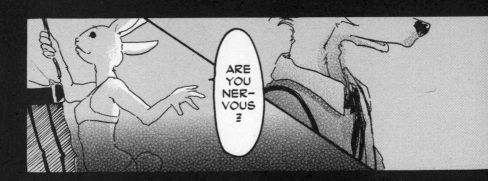

Chapter 9: The Wind Rises (Where No One Can Feel It Blow)

Chapter 9: The Wind Rises (Where No One Can Feel It Blow)

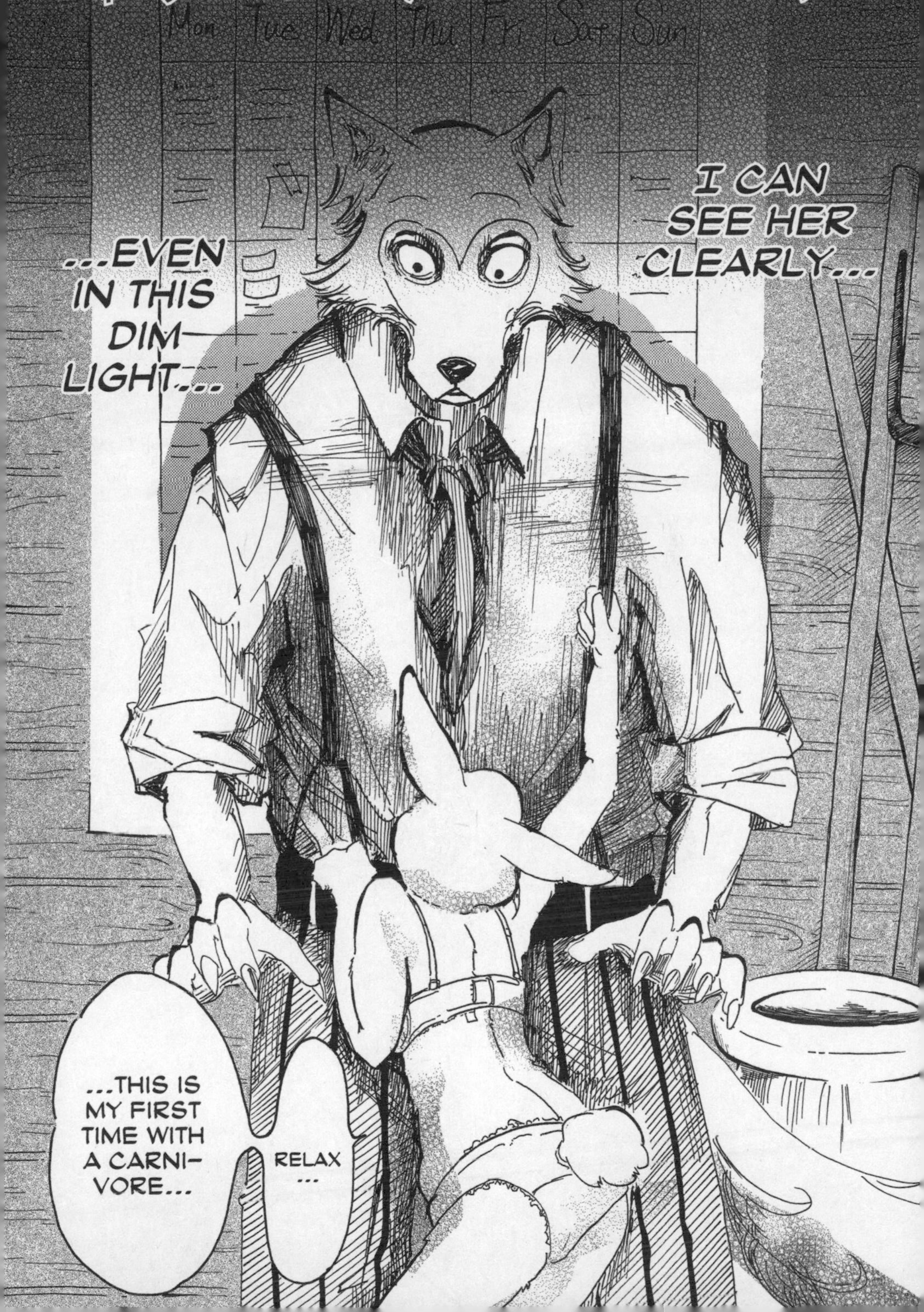
Mon Tue Wed Thu Fri Sat Sun
I CAN SEE HER CLEARLY...
...EVEN IN THIS DIM LIGHT...
...THIS IS MY FIRST TIME WITH A CARNIVORE...
RELAX ...

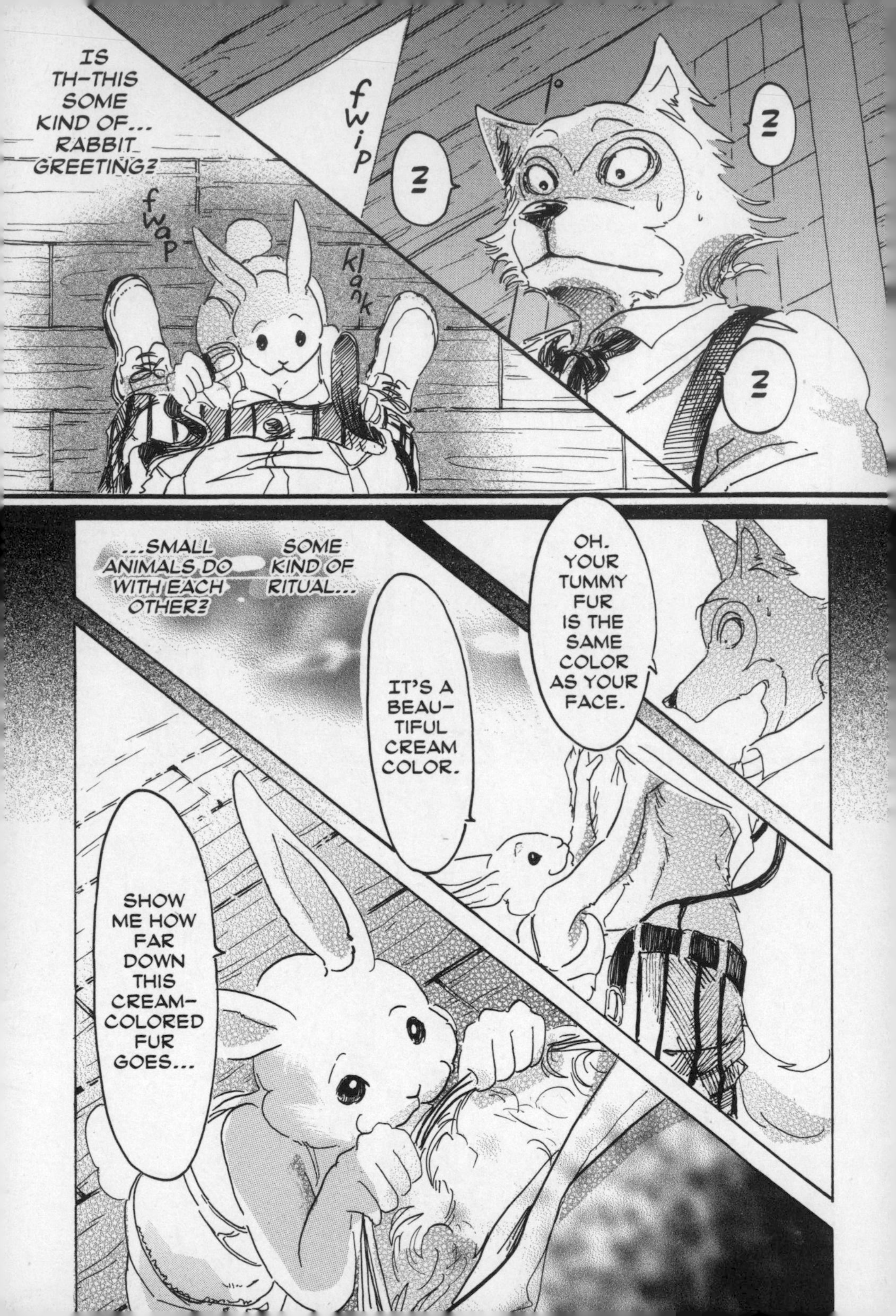
fwip
IS TH-THIS SOME KIND OF... RABBIT GREETING?
fwap
klank
OH. YOUR TUMMY FUR IS THE SAME COLOR AS YOUR FACE.
SOME KIND OF RITUAL...
...SMALL ANIMALS DO WITH EACH OTHER?
IT'S A BEAU-TIFUL CREAM COLOR.
SHOW ME HOW FAR DOWN THIS CREAM-COLORED FUR GOES...

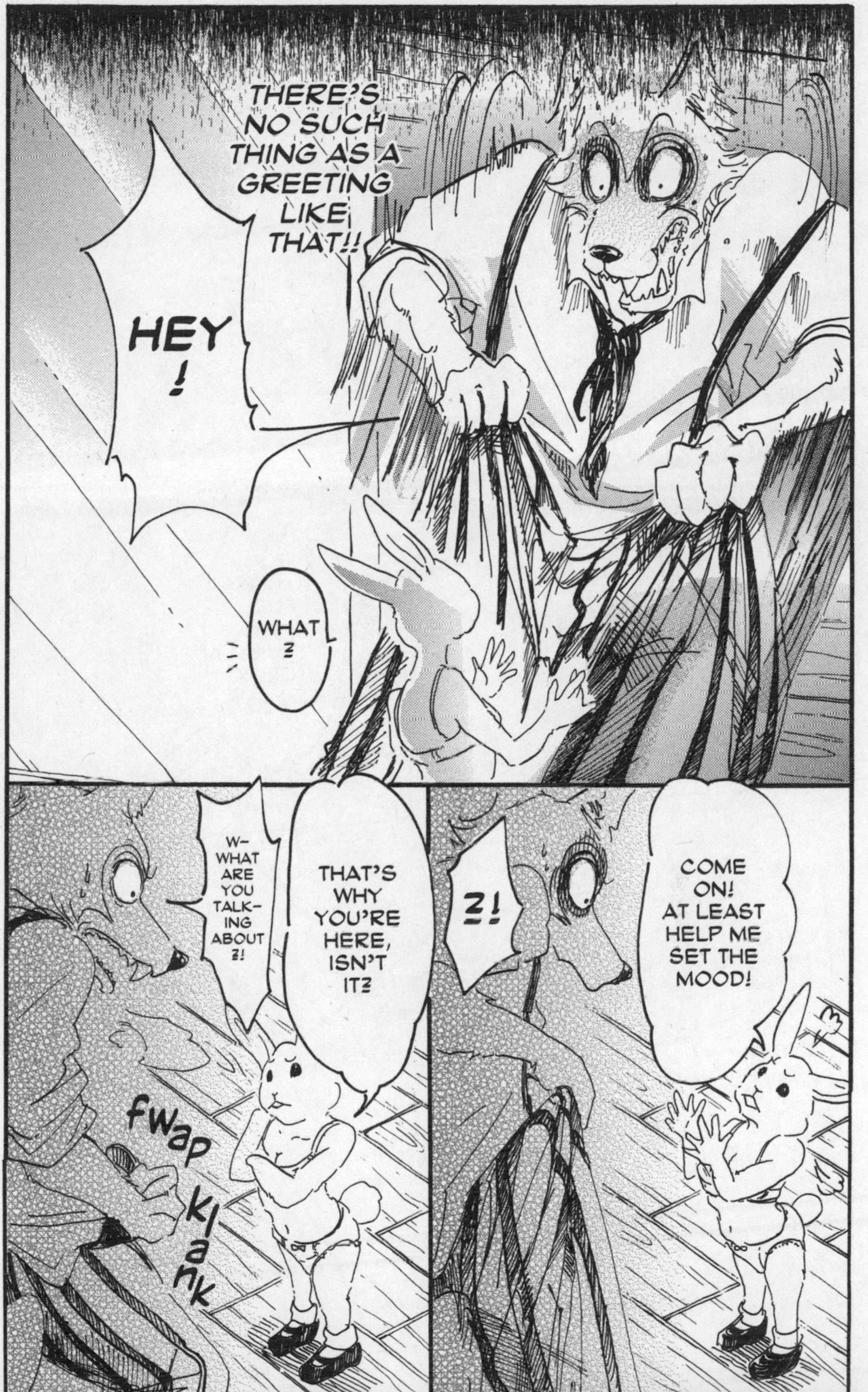
THERE'S NO SUCH THING AS A GREETING LIKE THAT!!
HEY!
WHAT?
COME ON! AT LEAST HELP ME SET THE MOOD!
?!
THAT'S WHY YOU'RE HERE, ISN'T IT?
W-WHAT ARE YOU TALKING ABOUT?!
fwap
klank

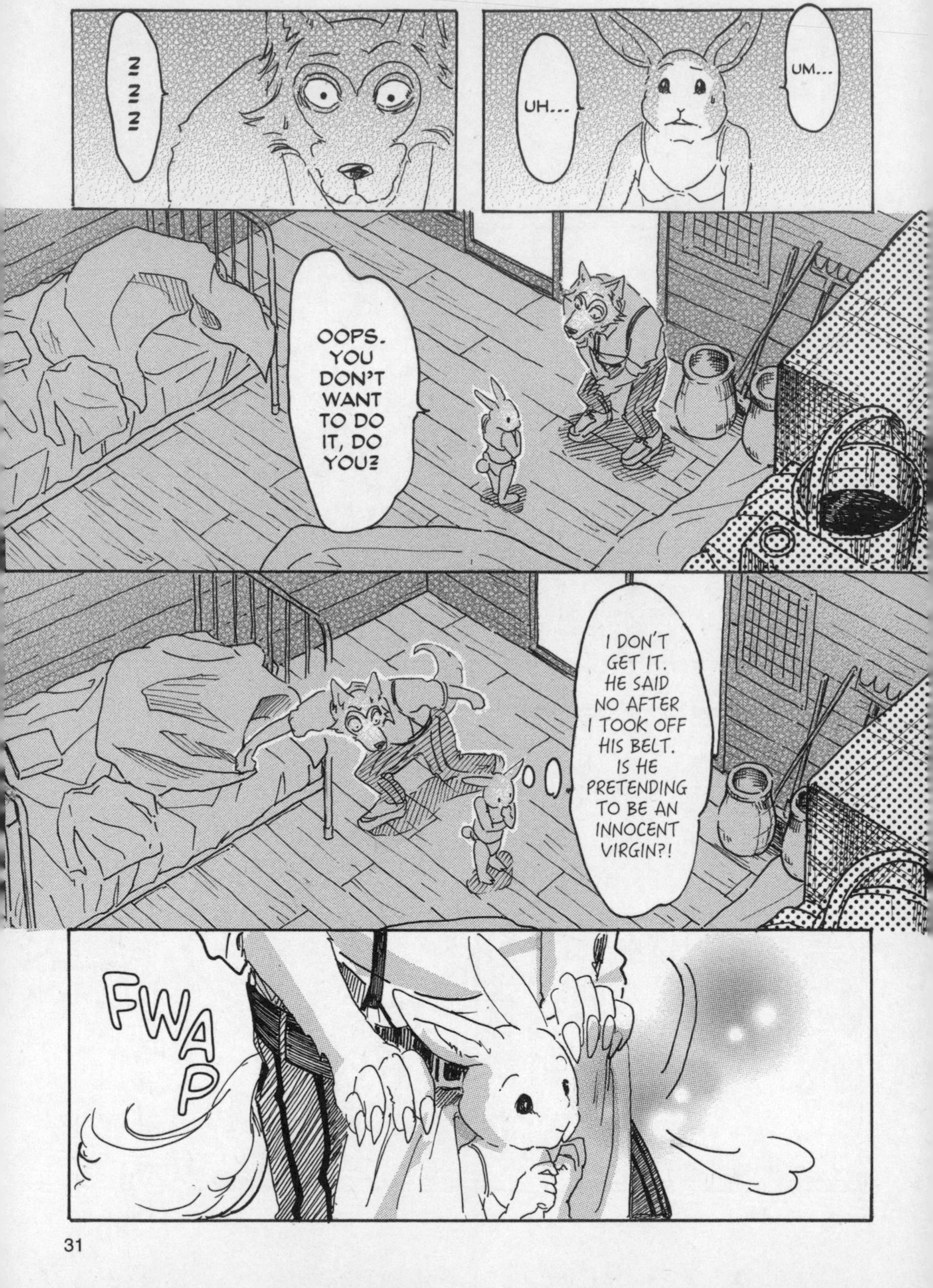
UM...
UH...
?!?!?!
OOPS. YOU DON'T WANT TO DO IT, DO YOU?
I DON'T GET IT. HE SAID NO AFTER I TOOK OFF HIS BELT. IS HE PRETENDING TO BE AN INNOCENT VIRGIN?!
FWAP

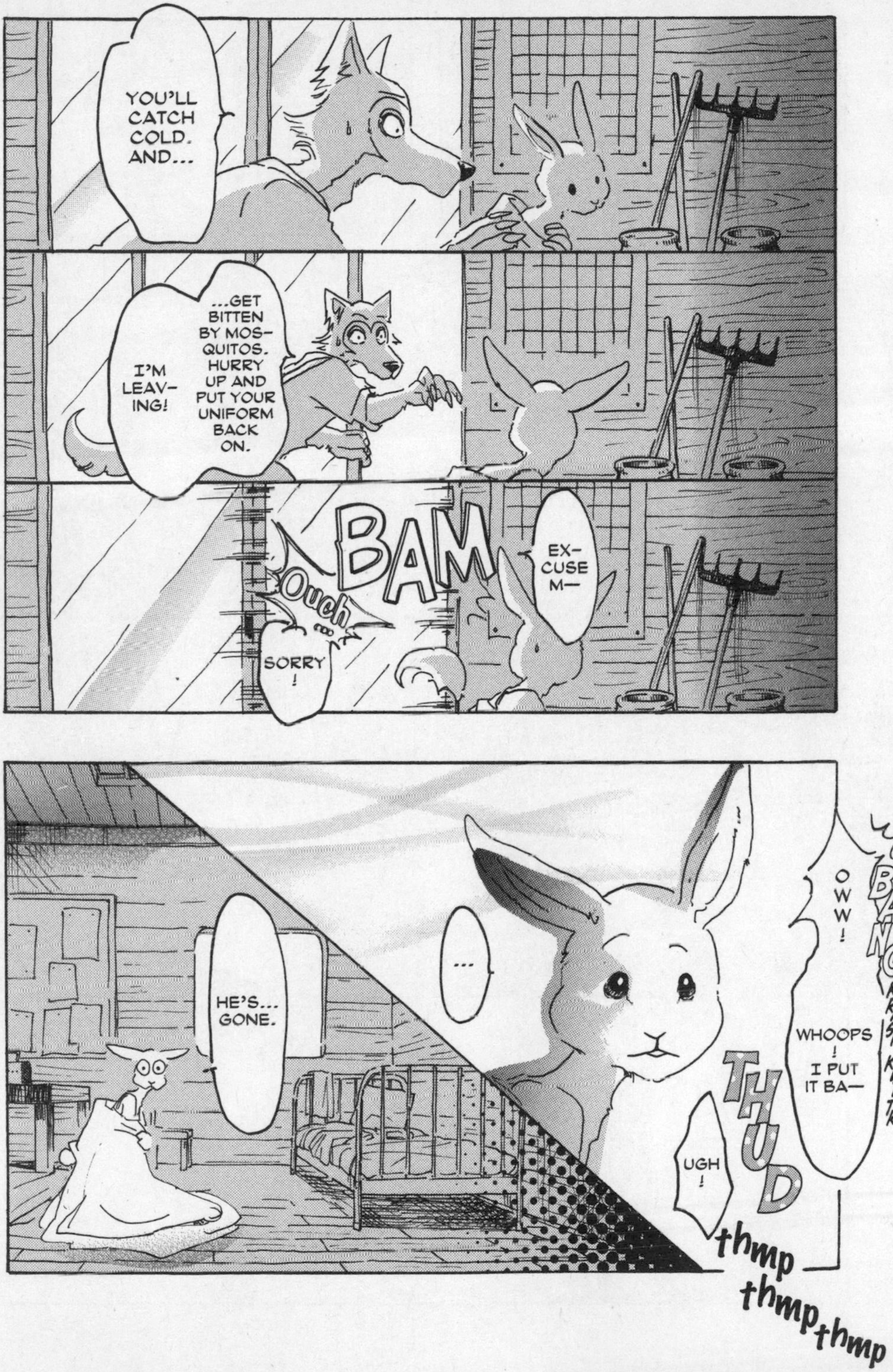
YOU'LL CATCH COLD. AND...
...GET BITTEN BY MOSQUITOS. HURRY UP AND PUT YOUR UNIFORM BACK ON.
I'M LEAVING!
EXCUSE M—
BAM
Ouch
SORRY!
OWW!
BANG
KRASH KLTTR
WHOOPS! I PUT IT BA—
THUD
UGH!
thmp thmp thmp
...
HE'S... GONE.

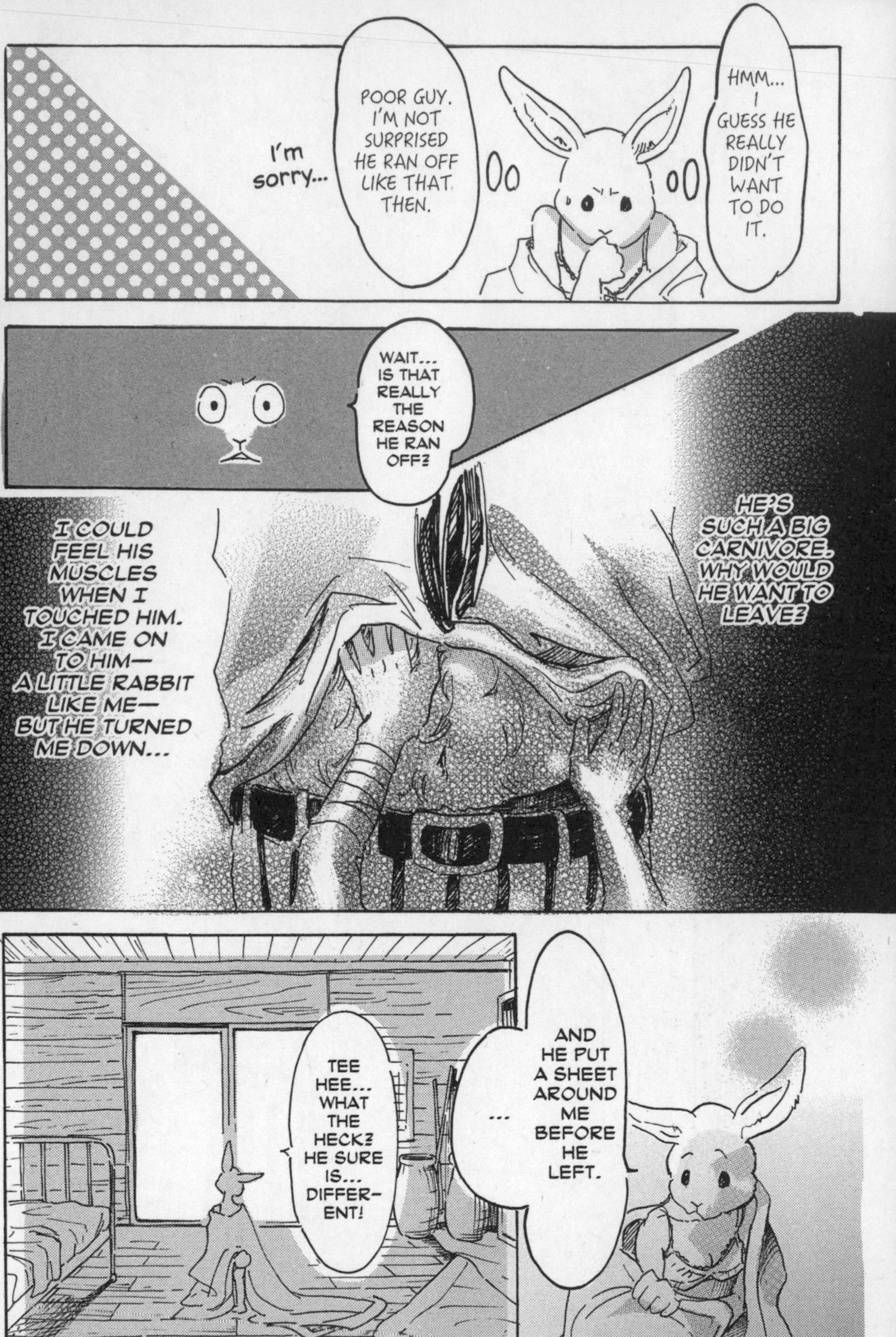
HMM... I GUESS HE REALLY DIDN'T WANT TO DO IT.
POOR GUY. I'M NOT SURPRISED HE RAN OFF LIKE THAT THEN.
I'm sorry...
WAIT... IS THAT REALLY THE REASON HE RAN OFF?
HE'S SUCH A BIG CARNIVORE. WHY WOULD HE WANT TO LEAVE?
I COULD FEEL HIS MUSCLES WHEN I TOUCHED HIM. I CAME ON TO HIM—A LITTLE RABBIT LIKE ME—BUT HE TURNED ME DOWN...
AND HE PUT A SHEET AROUND ME BEFORE HE LEFT.
...
TEE HEE... WHAT THE HECK? HE SURE IS... DIFFER-ENT!

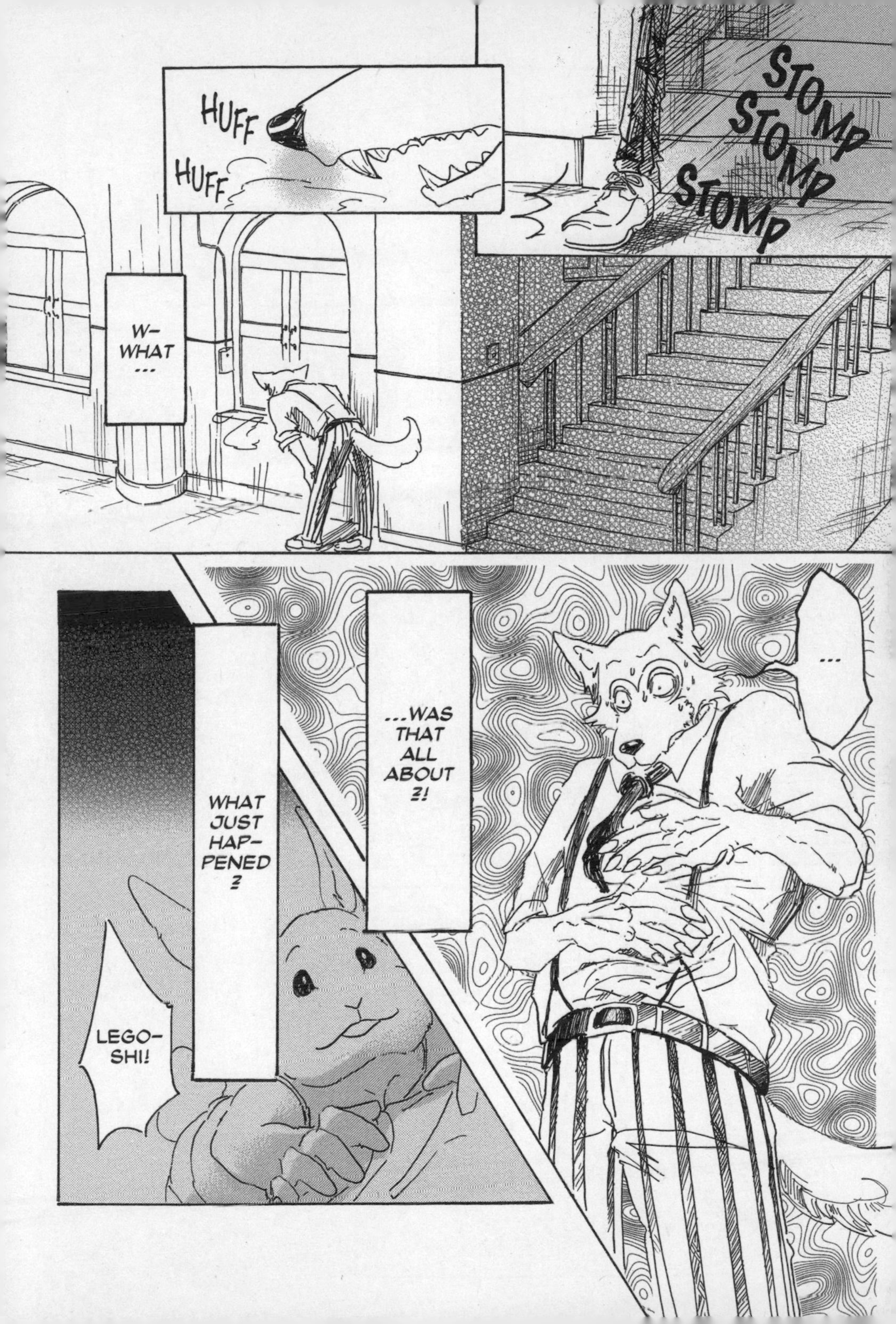
STOMP STOMP STOMP
HUFF HUFF
W-WHAT...
...
...WAS THAT ALL ABOUT?!
WHAT JUST HAP-PENED?
LEGO-SHI!

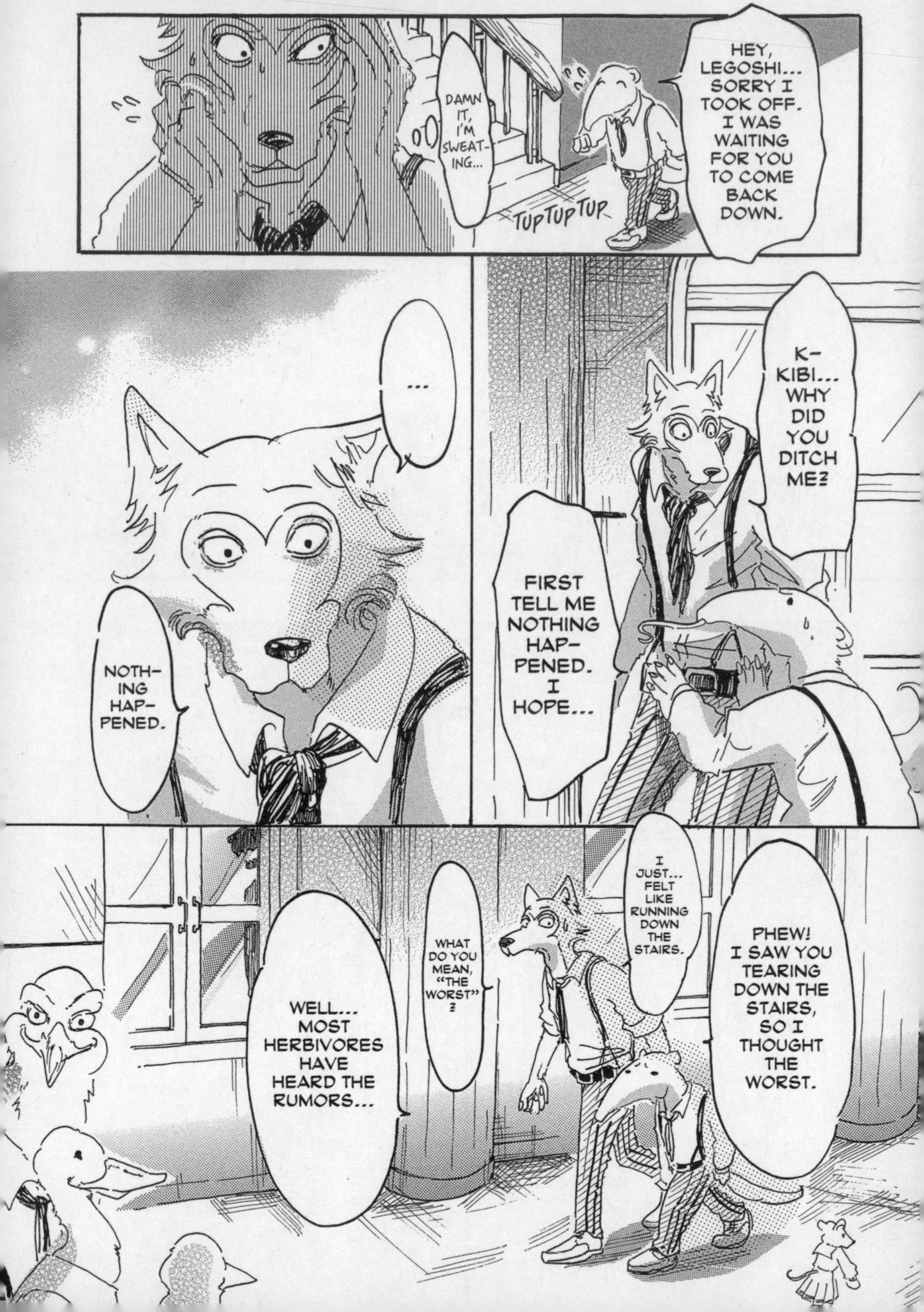
HEY, LEGOSHI... SORRY I TOOK OFF. I WAS WAITING FOR YOU TO COME BACK DOWN.
TUP TUP TUP
DAMN IT, I'M SWEATING...
K-KIBI... WHY DID YOU DITCH ME?
FIRST TELL ME NOTHING HAPPENED. I HOPE...
...
NOTHING HAPPENED.
PHEW! I SAW YOU TEARING DOWN THE STAIRS, SO I THOUGHT THE WORST.
I JUST... FELT LIKE RUNNING DOWN THE STAIRS.
WHAT DO YOU MEAN, "THE WORST"?
WELL... MOST HERBIVORES HAVE HEARD THE RUMORS...

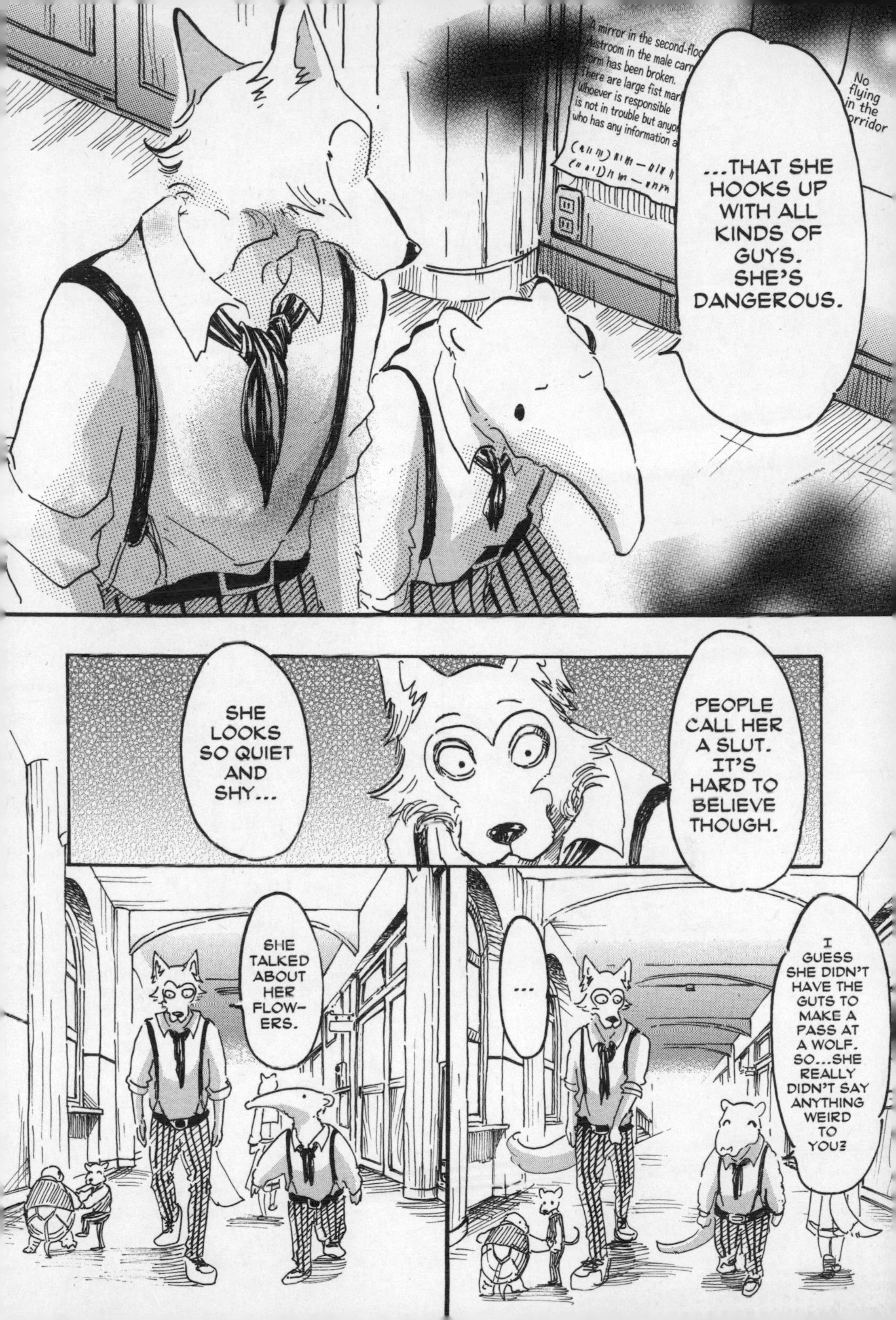

A mirror in the
restroom in the male
has been broken.
There are large fist
Whoever is responsible
is not in trouble but
who has any information
No flying in the
...THAT SHE HOOKS UP WITH ALL KINDS OF GUYS. SHE'S DANGEROUS.
PEOPLE CALL HER A SLUT. IT'S HARD TO BELIEVE THOUGH.
SHE LOOKS SO QUIET AND SHY...
I GUESS SHE DIDN'T HAVE THE GUTS TO MAKE A PASS AT A WOLF. SO...SHE REALLY DIDN'T SAY ANYTHING WEIRD TO YOU?
...
SHE TALKED ABOUT HER FLOWERS.

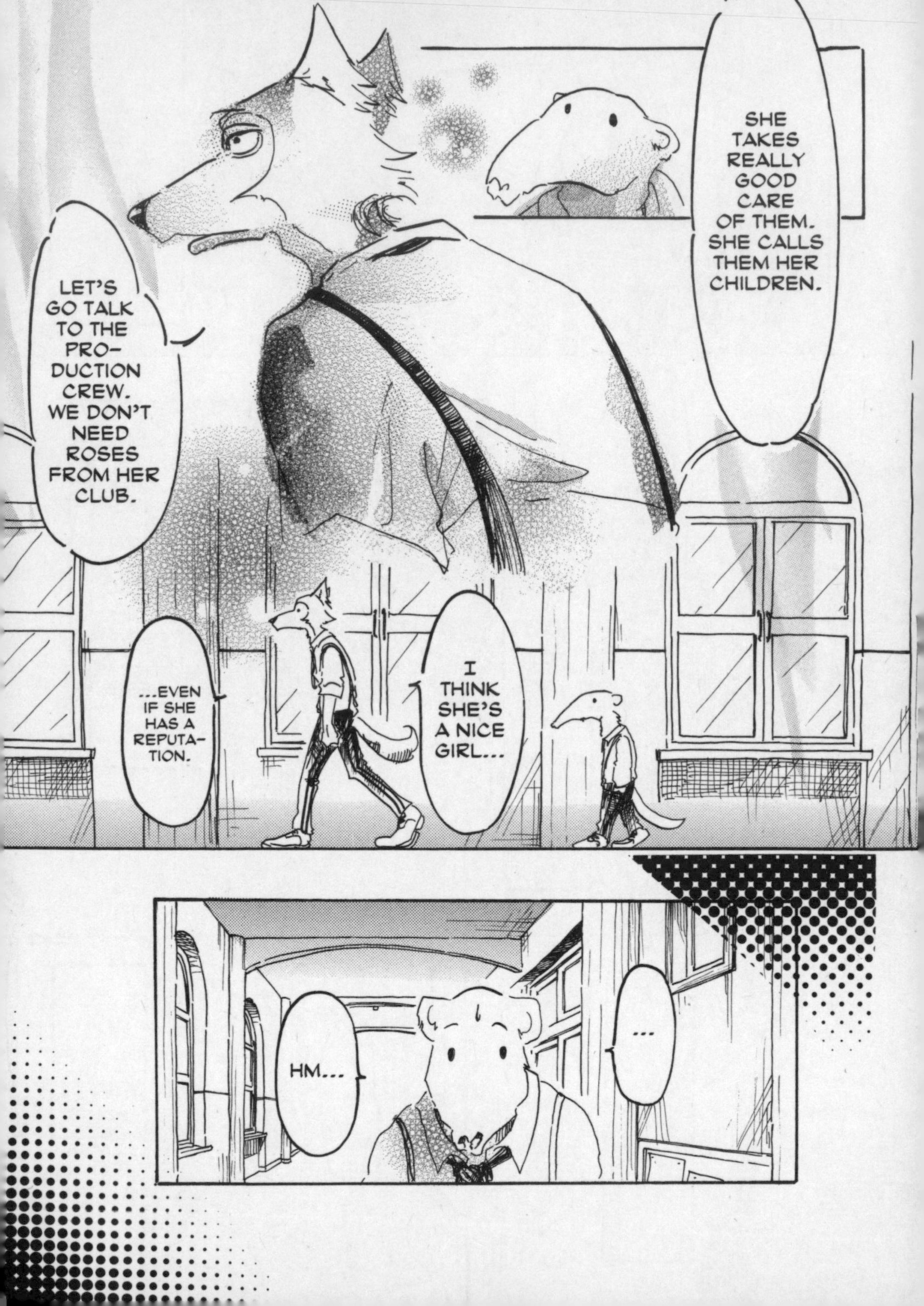
SHE TAKES REALLY GOOD CARE OF THEM. SHE CALLS THEM HER CHILDREN.
LET'S GO TALK TO THE PRO-DUCTION CREW. WE DON'T NEED ROSES FROM HER CLUB.
I THINK SHE'S A NICE GIRL...
...EVEN IF SHE HAS A REPUTA-TION.
...
HM...

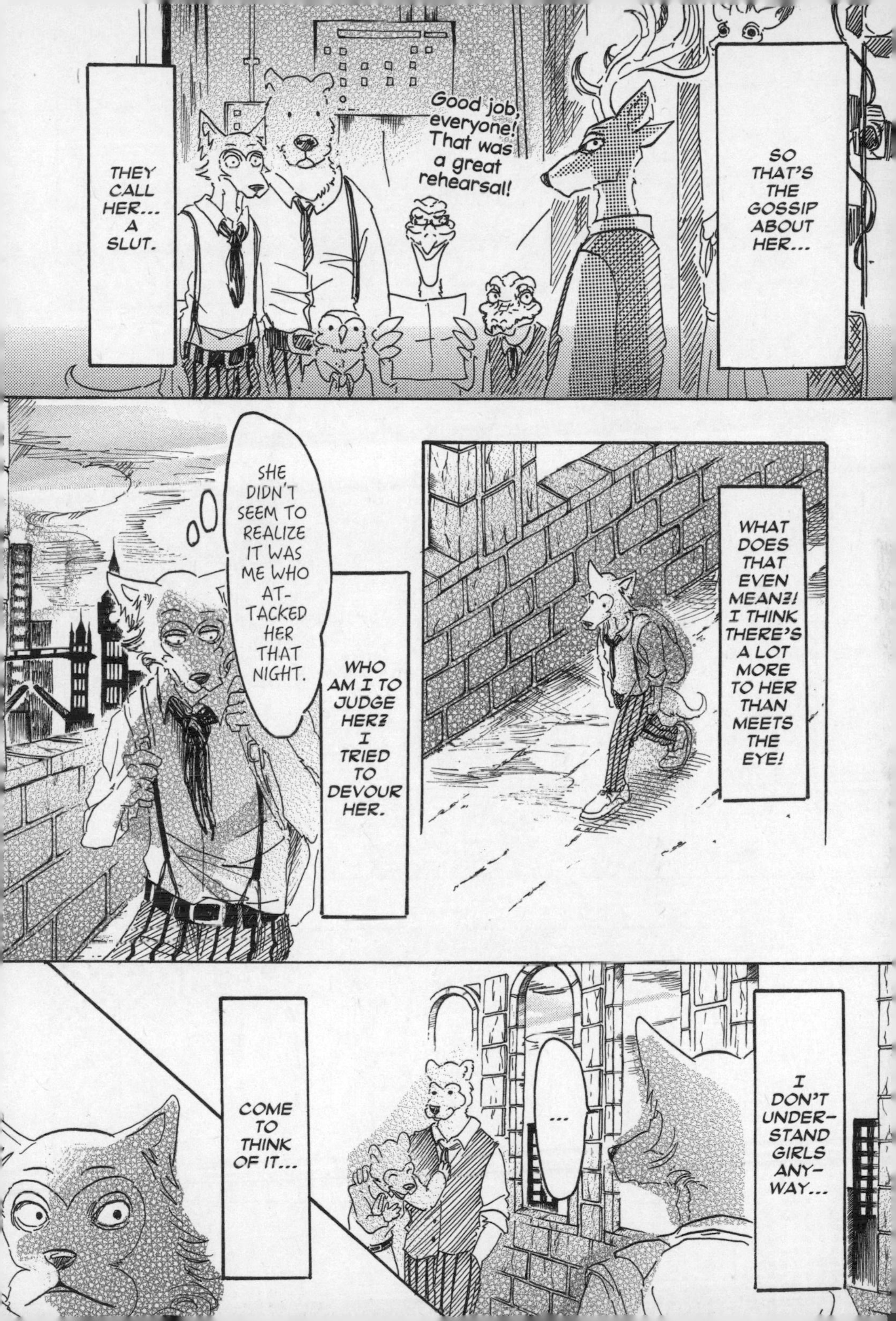
SO THAT'S THE GOSSIP ABOUT HER...
Good job, everyone! That was a great rehearsal!
THEY CALL HER... A SLUT.
WHAT DOES THAT EVEN MEAN?! I THINK THERE'S A LOT MORE TO HER THAN MEETS THE EYE!
SHE DIDN'T SEEM TO REALIZE IT WAS ME WHO ATTACKED HER THAT NIGHT.
WHO AM I TO JUDGE HER? I TRIED TO DEVOUR HER.
I DON'T UNDERSTAND GIRLS ANYWAY...
...
COME TO THINK OF IT...

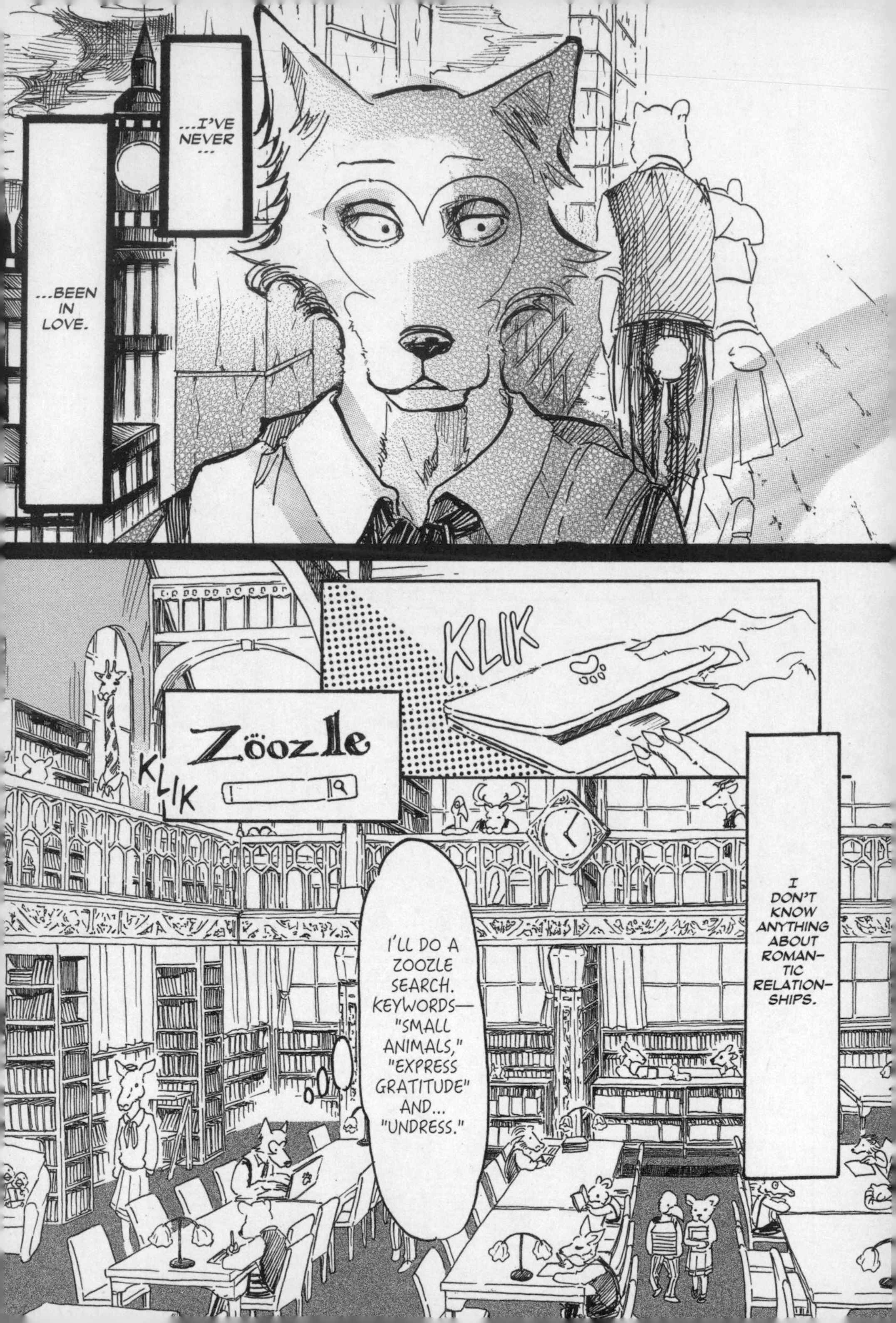
...I'VE NEVER ---
...BEEN IN LOVE.
I DON'T KNOW ANYTHING ABOUT ROMANTIC RELATIONSHIPS.
KLIK
Zöozle
KLIK
I'LL DO A ZOOZLE SEARCH. KEYWORDS—"SMALL ANIMALS," "EXPRESS GRATITUDE" AND... "UNDRESS."

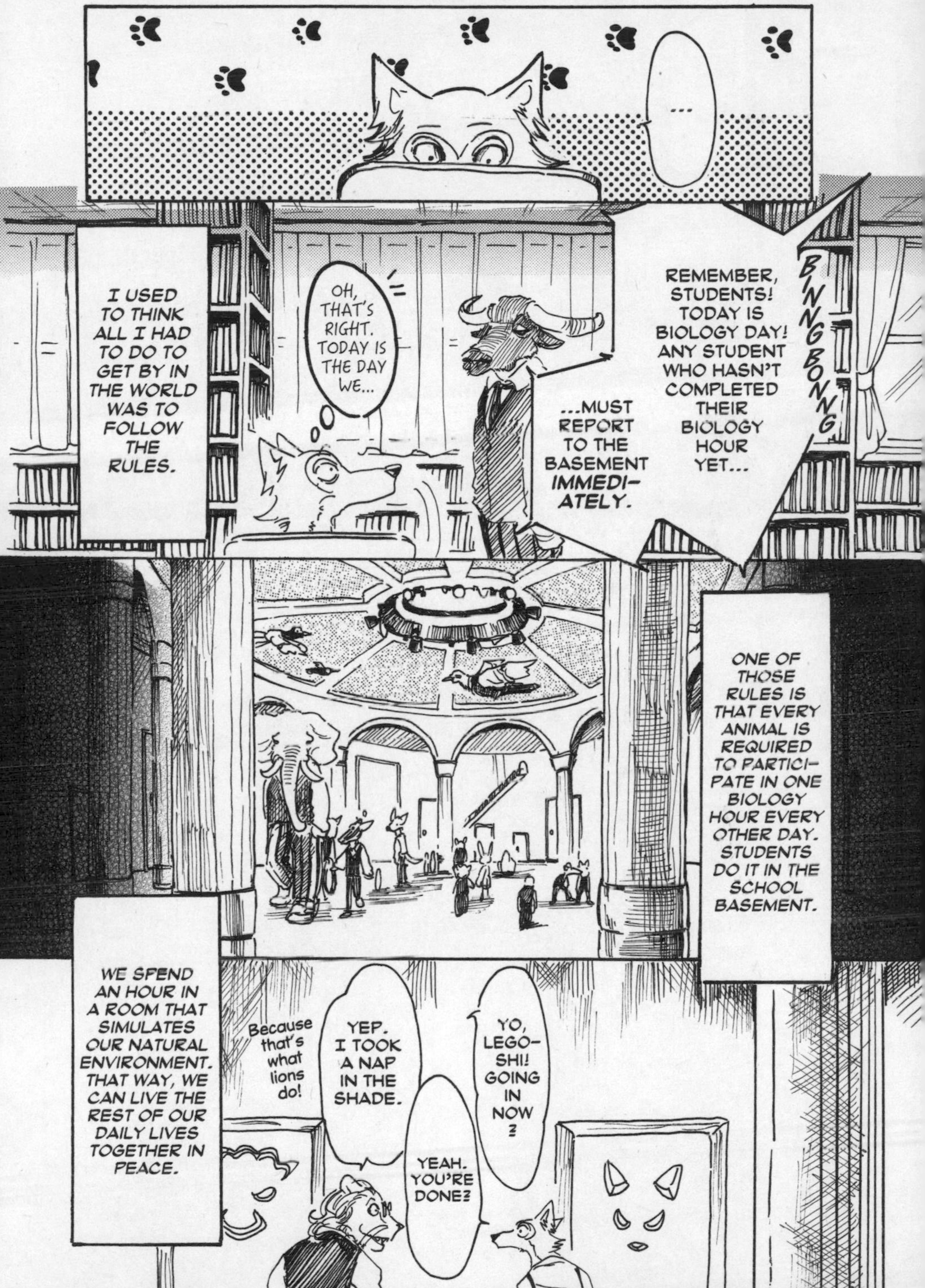
...
BINGBONG
REMEMBER, STUDENTS! TODAY IS BIOLOGY DAY! ANY STUDENT WHO HASN'T COMPLETED THEIR BIOLOGY HOUR YET...
...MUST REPORT TO THE BASEMENT *IMMEDIATELY*.
OH, THAT'S RIGHT. TODAY IS THE DAY WE...
I USED TO THINK ALL I HAD TO DO TO GET BY IN THE WORLD WAS TO FOLLOW THE RULES.
ONE OF THOSE RULES IS THAT EVERY ANIMAL IS REQUIRED TO PARTICIPATE IN ONE BIOLOGY HOUR EVERY OTHER DAY. STUDENTS DO IT IN THE SCHOOL BASEMENT.
YO, LEGOSHI! GOING IN NOW?
YEAH. YOU'RE DONE?
YEP. I TOOK A NAP IN THE SHADE.
Because that's what lions do!
WE SPEND AN HOUR IN A ROOM THAT SIMULATES OUR NATURAL ENVIRONMENT. THAT WAY, WE CAN LIVE THE REST OF OUR DAILY LIVES TOGETHER IN PEACE.

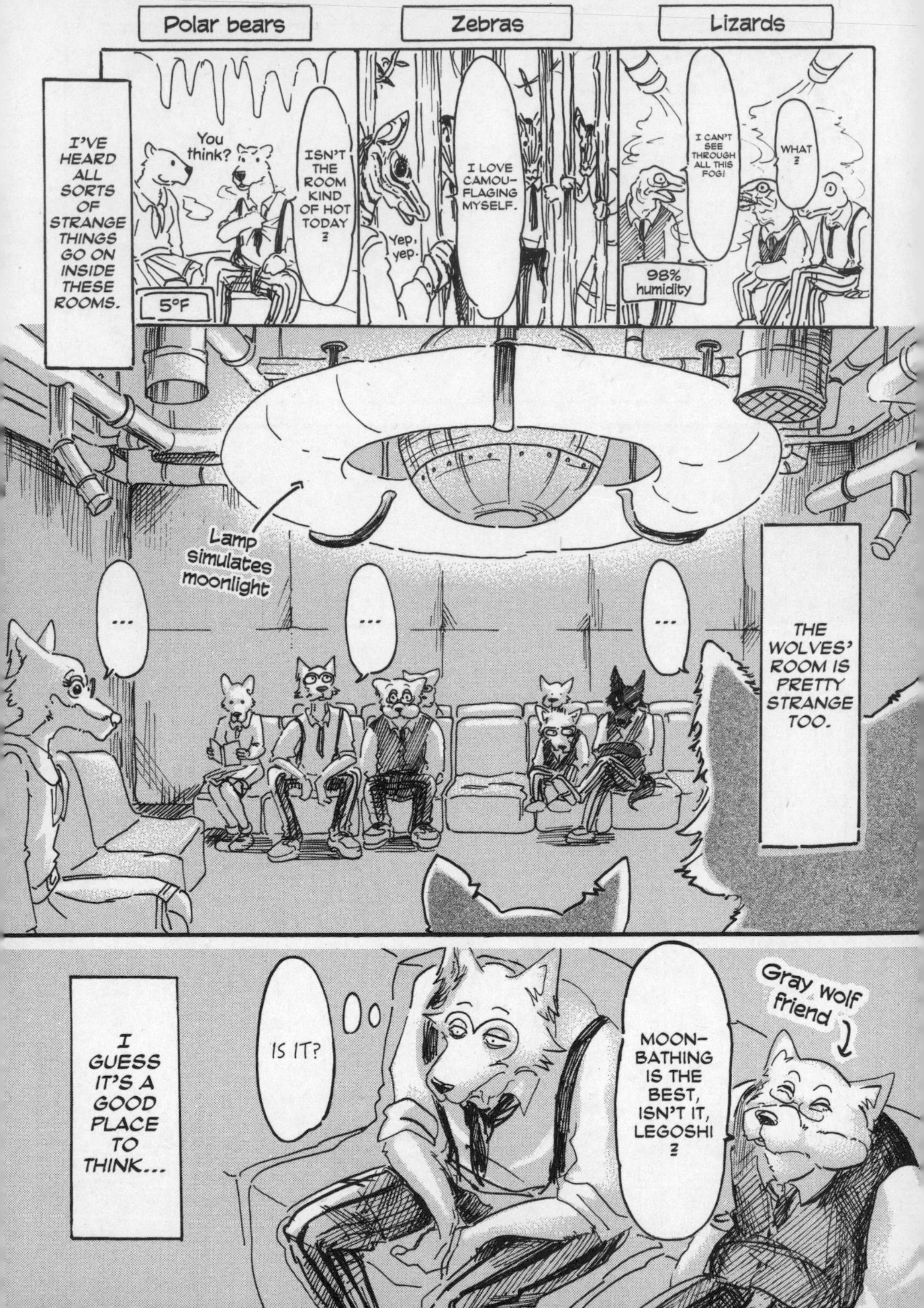
Lizards
WHAT?
I CAN'T SEE THROUGH ALL THIS FOG!
98% humidity
Zebras
I LOVE CAMOUFLAGING MYSELF.
Yep, yep.
Polar bears
ISN'T THE ROOM KIND OF HOT TODAY?
You think?
5°F
I'VE HEARD ALL SORTS OF STRANGE THINGS GO ON INSIDE THESE ROOMS.
THE WOLVES' ROOM IS PRETTY STRANGE TOO.
...
...
Lamp simulates moonlight
...
Gray wolf friend
MOON-BATHING IS THE BEST, ISN'T IT, LEGOSHI?
IS IT?
I GUESS IT'S A GOOD PLACE TO THINK...

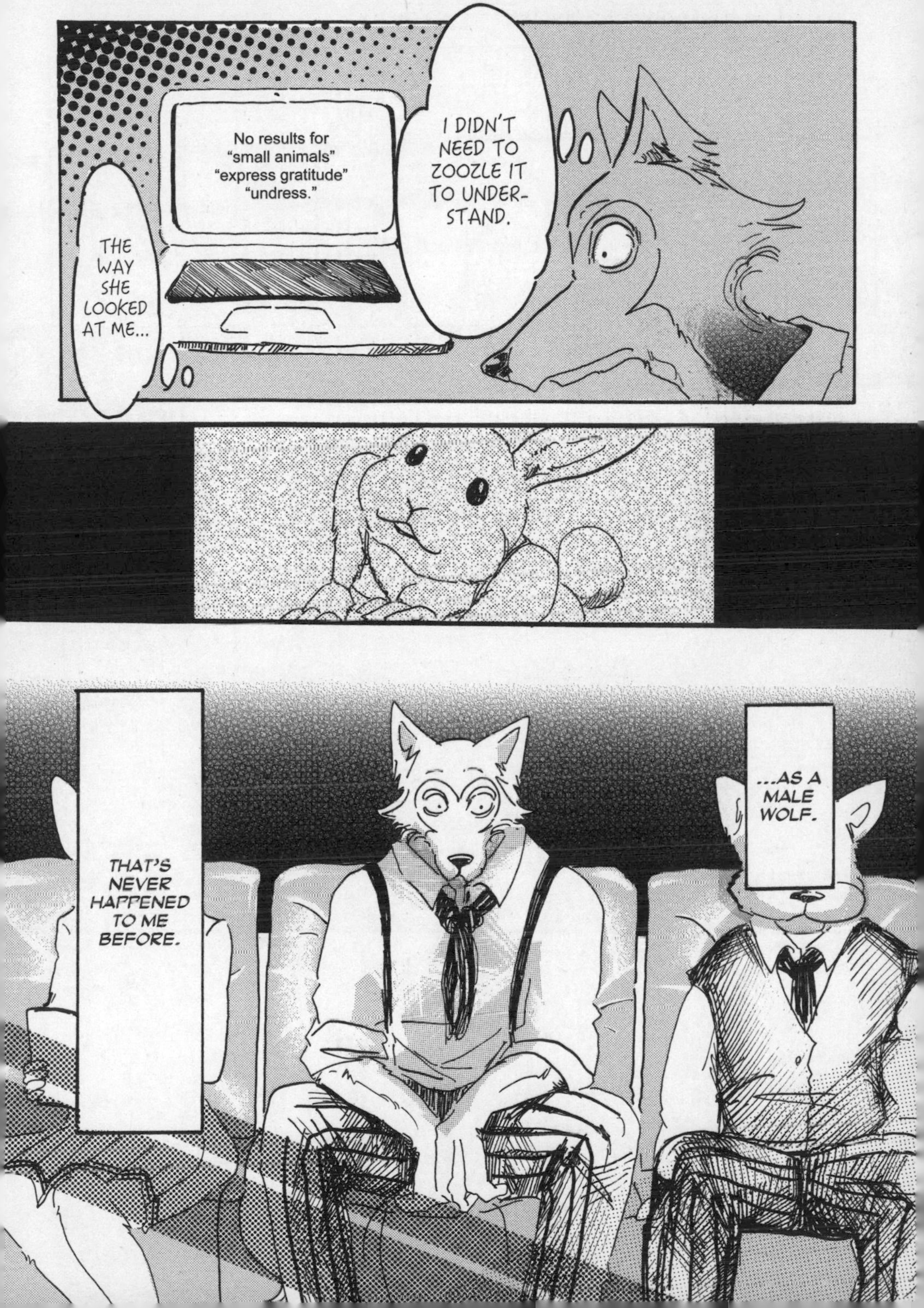
I DIDN'T NEED TO ZOOZLE IT TO UNDER-STAND.
No results for "small animals" "express gratitude" "undress."
THE WAY SHE LOOKED AT ME...
...AS A MALE WOLF.
THAT'S NEVER HAPPENED TO ME BEFORE.

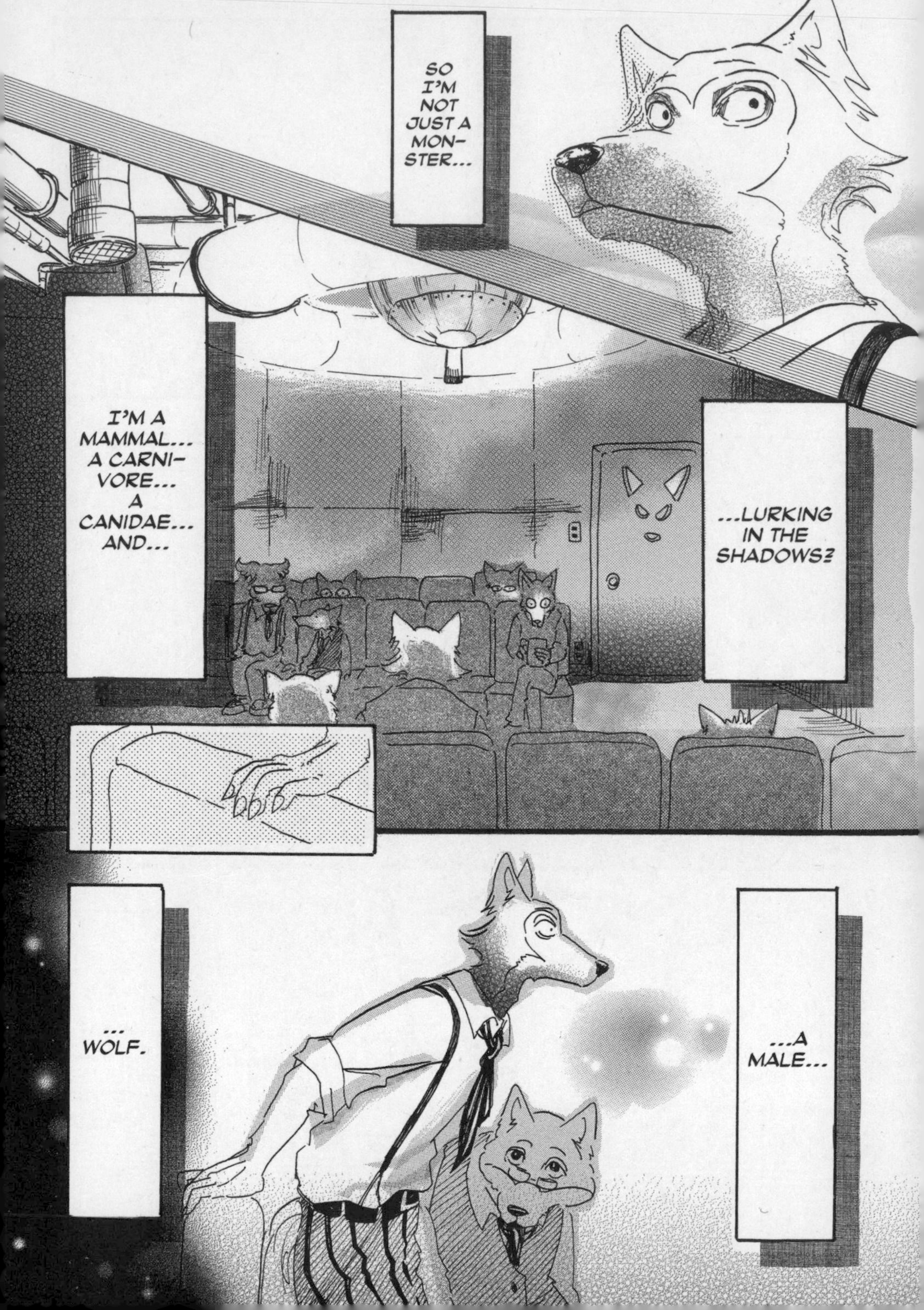
SO I'M NOT JUST A MON-STER...
I'M A MAMMAL... A CARNI-VORE... A CANIDAE... AND...
...LURKING IN THE SHADOWS?
...A MALE...
... WOLF.

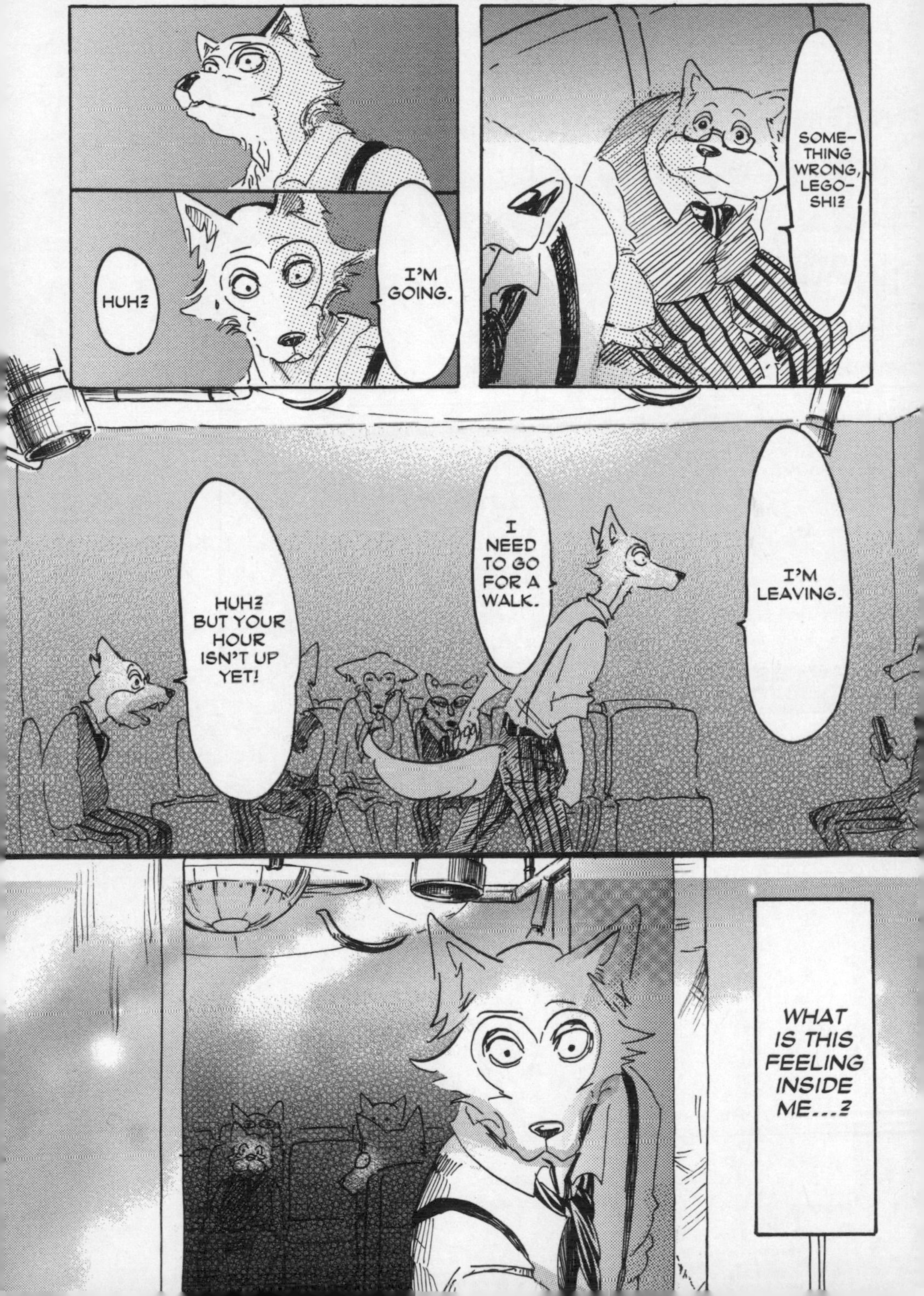
SOMETHING WRONG, LEGOSHI?
I'M GOING.
HUH?
I'M LEAVING.
I NEED TO GO FOR A WALK.
HUH? BUT YOUR HOUR ISN'T UP YET!
WHAT IS THIS FEELING INSIDE ME...?

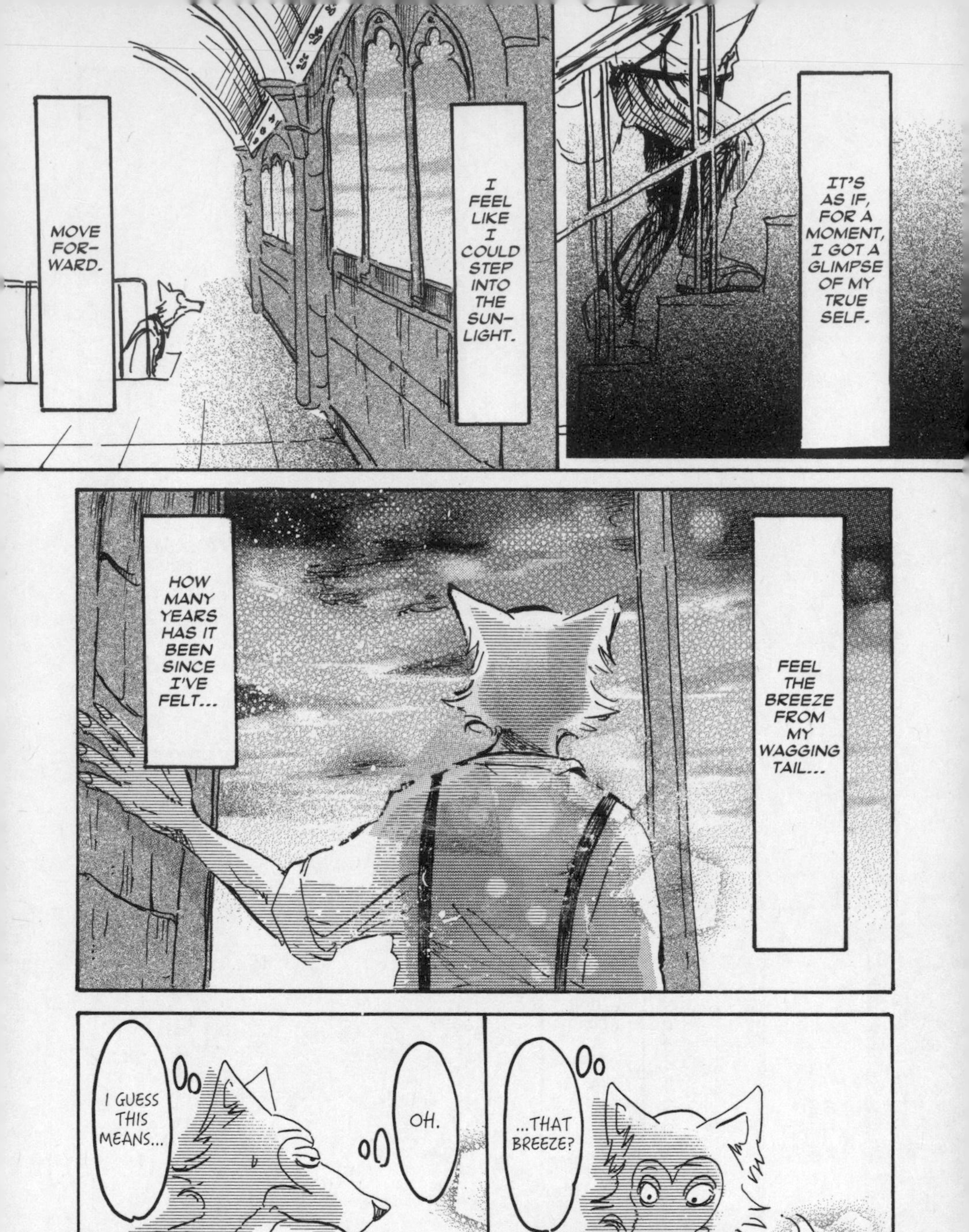
IT'S AS IF, FOR A MOMENT, I GOT A GLIMPSE OF MY TRUE SELF.
I FEEL LIKE I COULD STEP INTO THE SUN-LIGHT.
MOVE FOR-WARD.
FEEL THE BREEZE FROM MY WAGGING TAIL...
HOW MANY YEARS HAS IT BEEN SINCE I'VE FELT...
...THAT BREEZE?
OH.
I GUESS THIS MEANS...

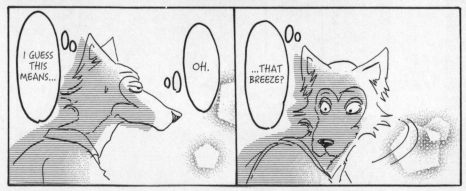

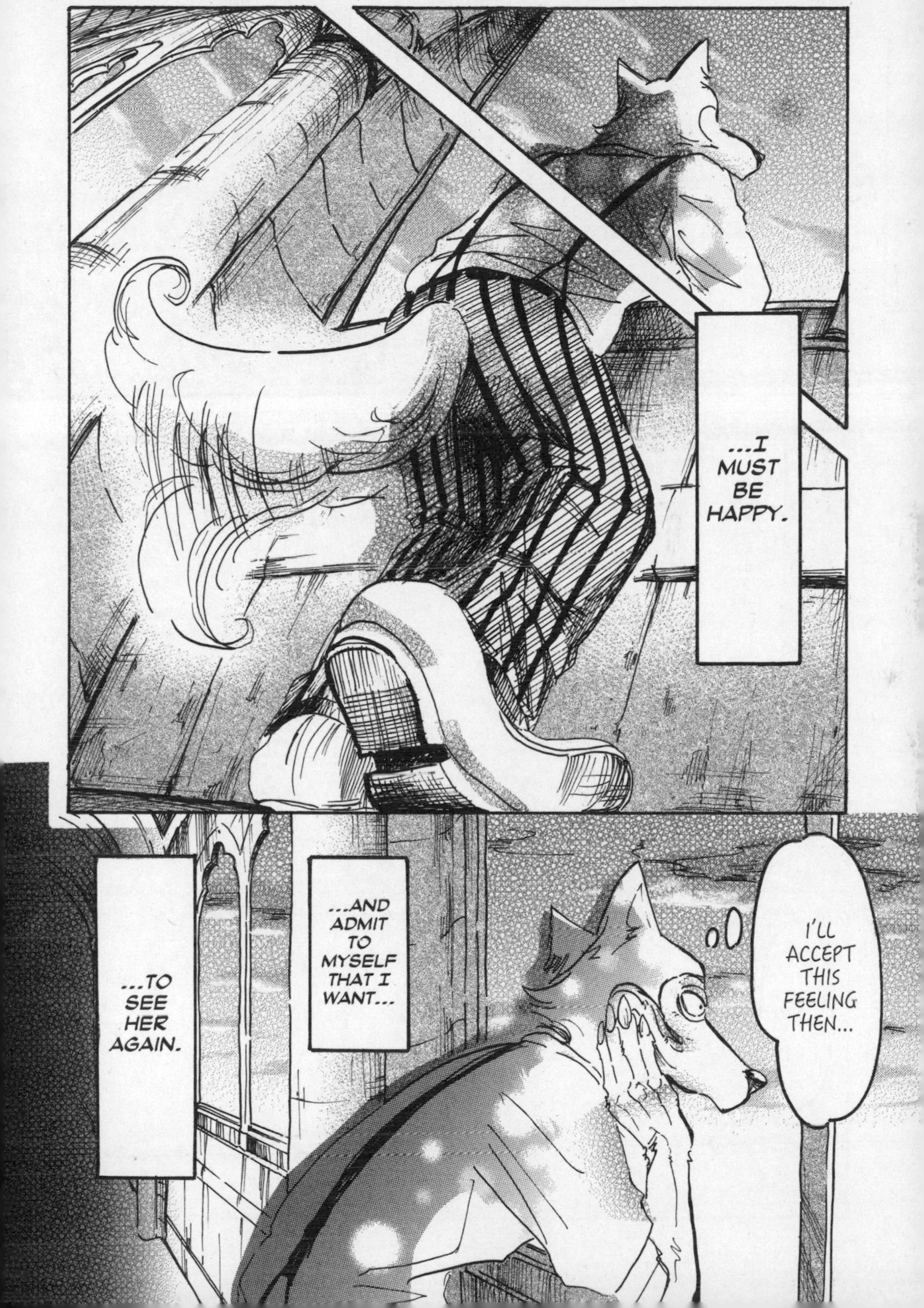
...I MUST BE HAPPY.
I'LL ACCEPT THIS FEELING THEN...
...AND ADMIT TO MYSELF THAT I WANT...
...TO SEE HER AGAIN.

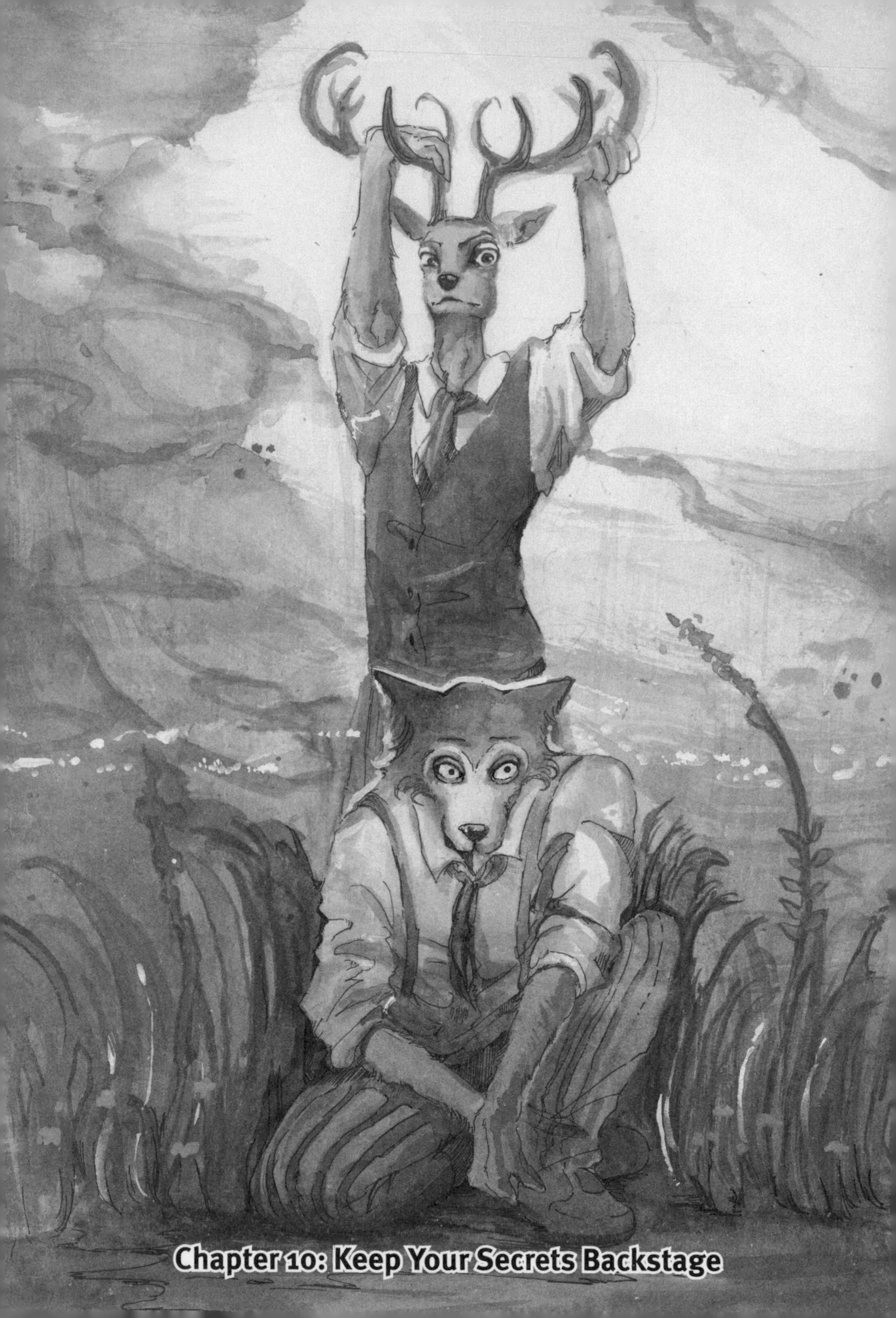

Chapter 10: Keep Your Secrets Backstage

BEASTARS
Vol. 2

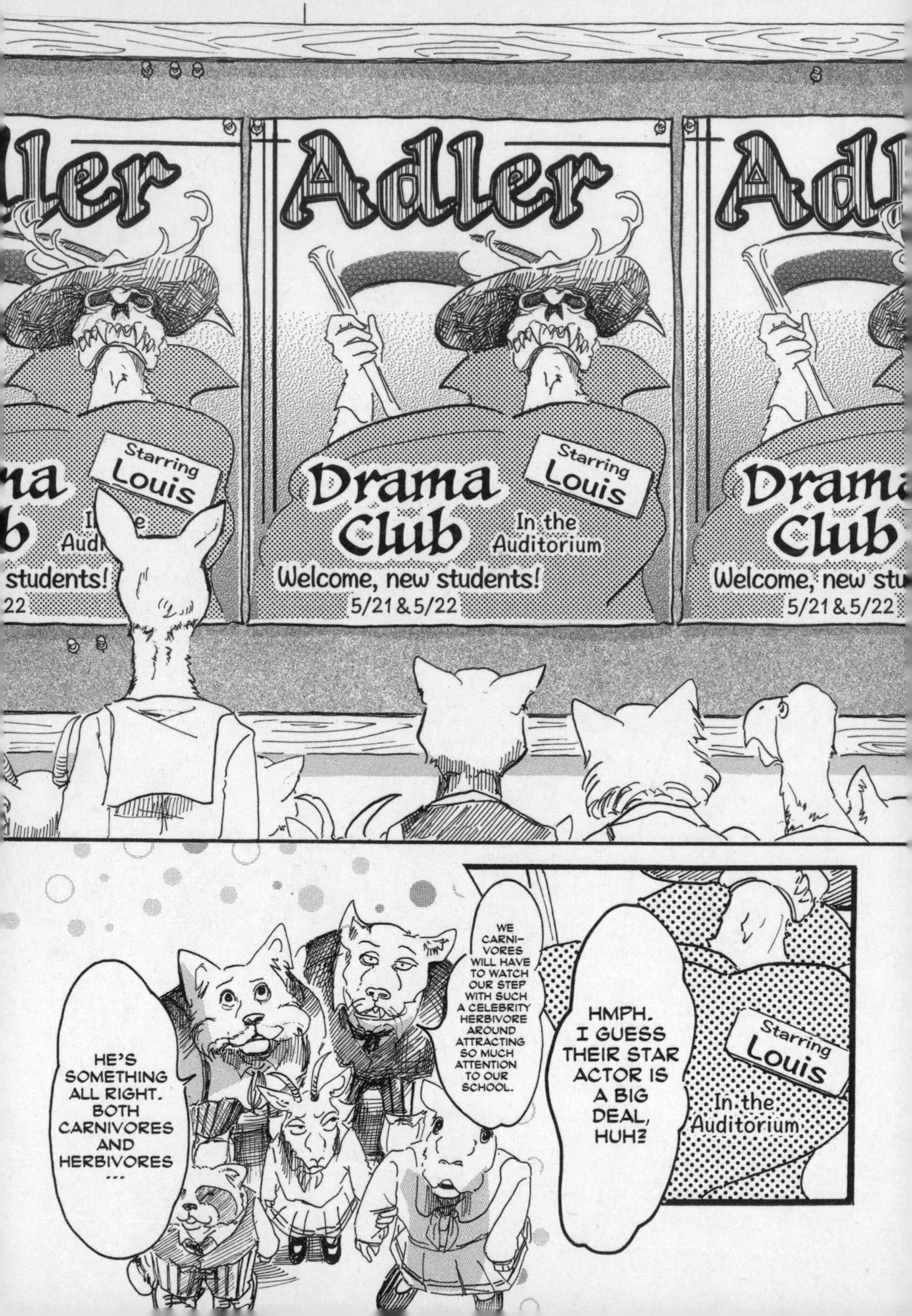
Adler
Starring Louis
Drama Club
In the Auditorium
Welcome, new students!
5/21&5/22
Starring Louis
In the Auditorium
HMPH. I GUESS THEIR STAR ACTOR IS A BIG DEAL, HUH?
WE CARNIVORES WILL HAVE TO WATCH OUR STEP WITH SUCH A CELEBRITY HERBIVORE AROUND ATTRACTING SO MUCH ATTENTION TO OUR SCHOOL.
HE'S SOMETHING ALL RIGHT. BOTH CARNIVORES AND HERBIVORES...

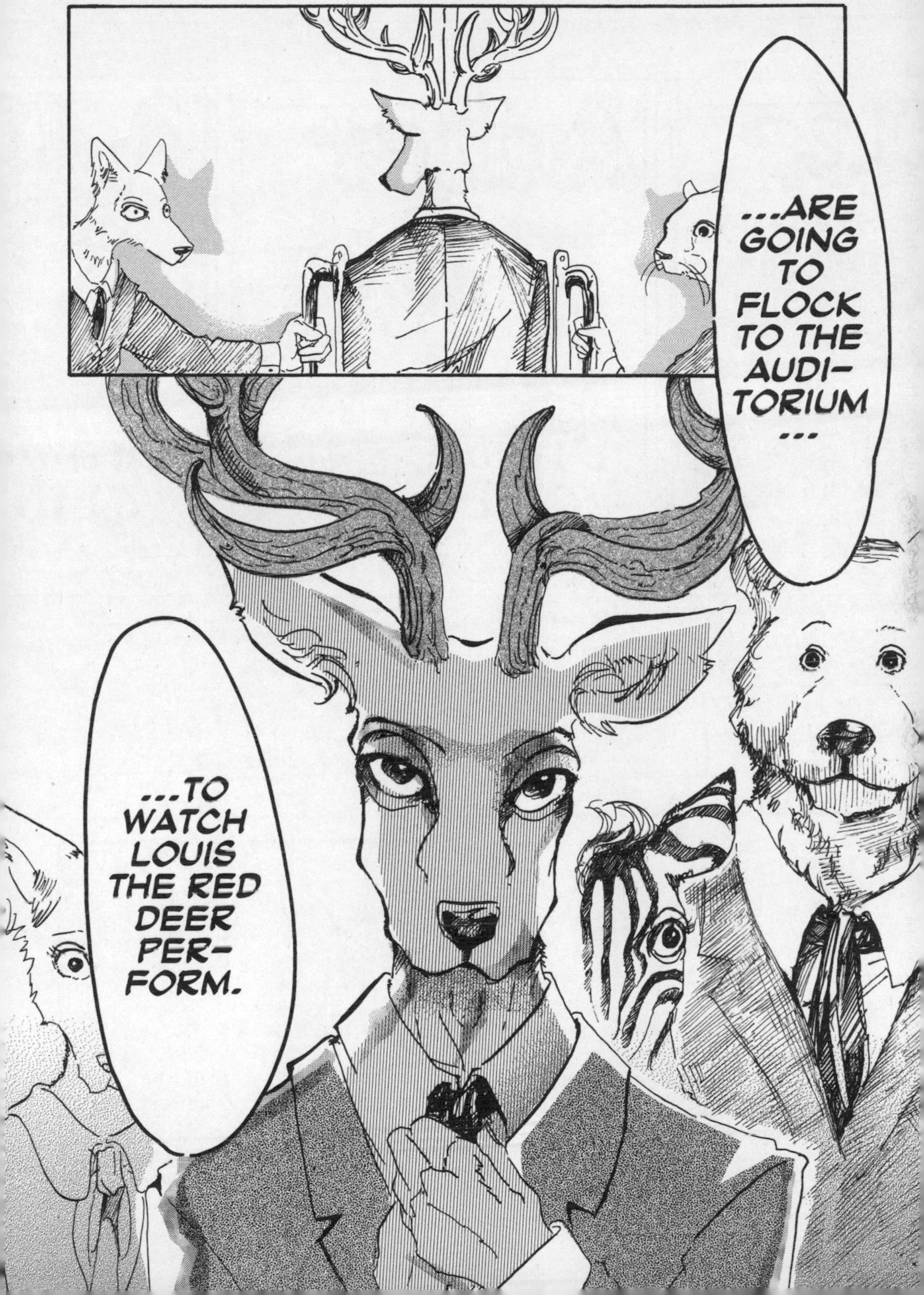
...ARE GOING TO FLOCK TO THE AUDI-TORIUM ...
...TO WATCH LOUIS THE RED DEER PER-FORM.

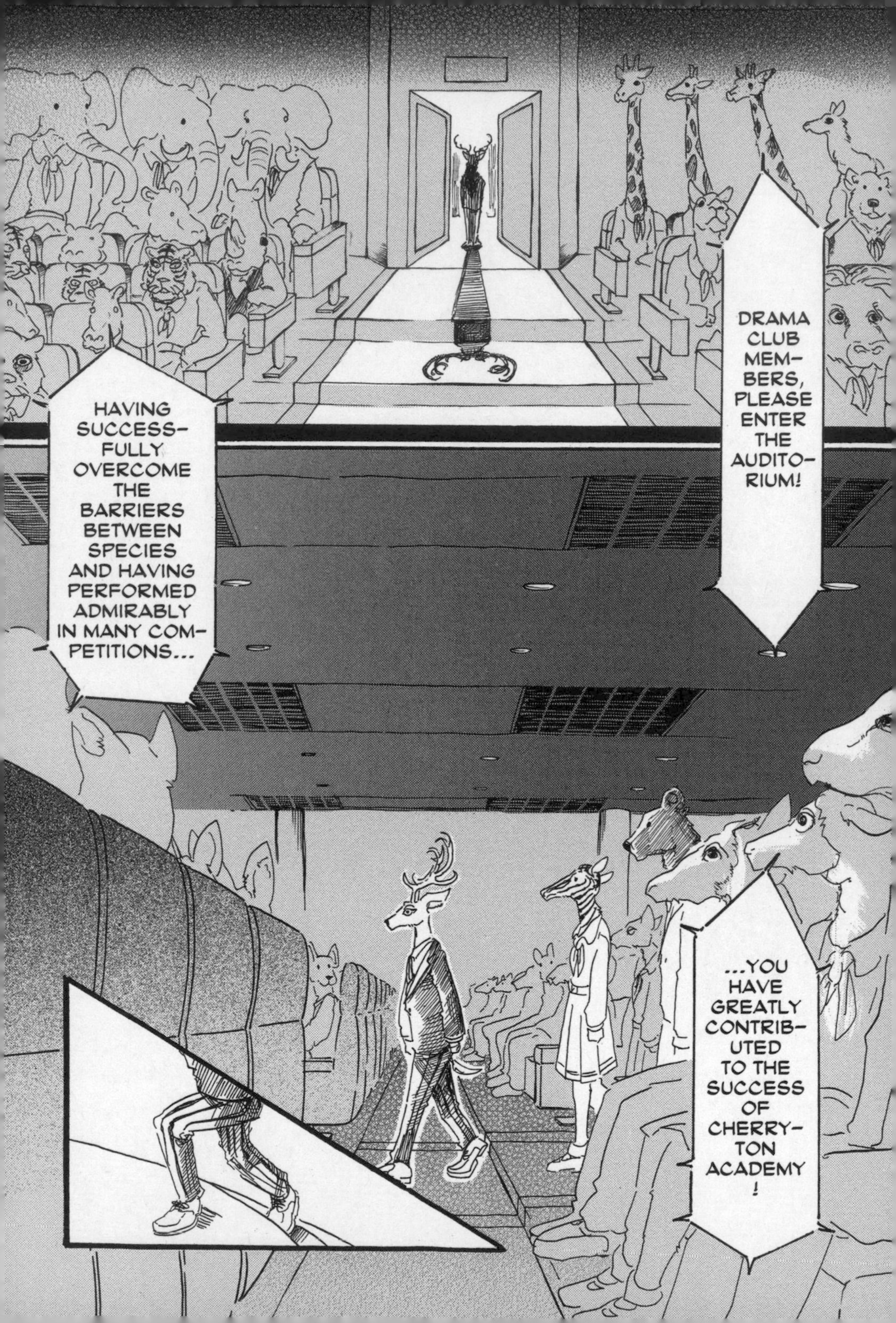
DRAMA CLUB MEMBERS, PLEASE ENTER THE AUDITORIUM!
HAVING SUCCESSFULLY OVERCOME THE BARRIERS BETWEEN SPECIES AND HAVING PERFORMED ADMIRABLY IN MANY COMPETITIONS...
...YOU HAVE GREATLY CONTRIBUTED TO THE SUCCESS OF CHERRYTON ACADEMY!

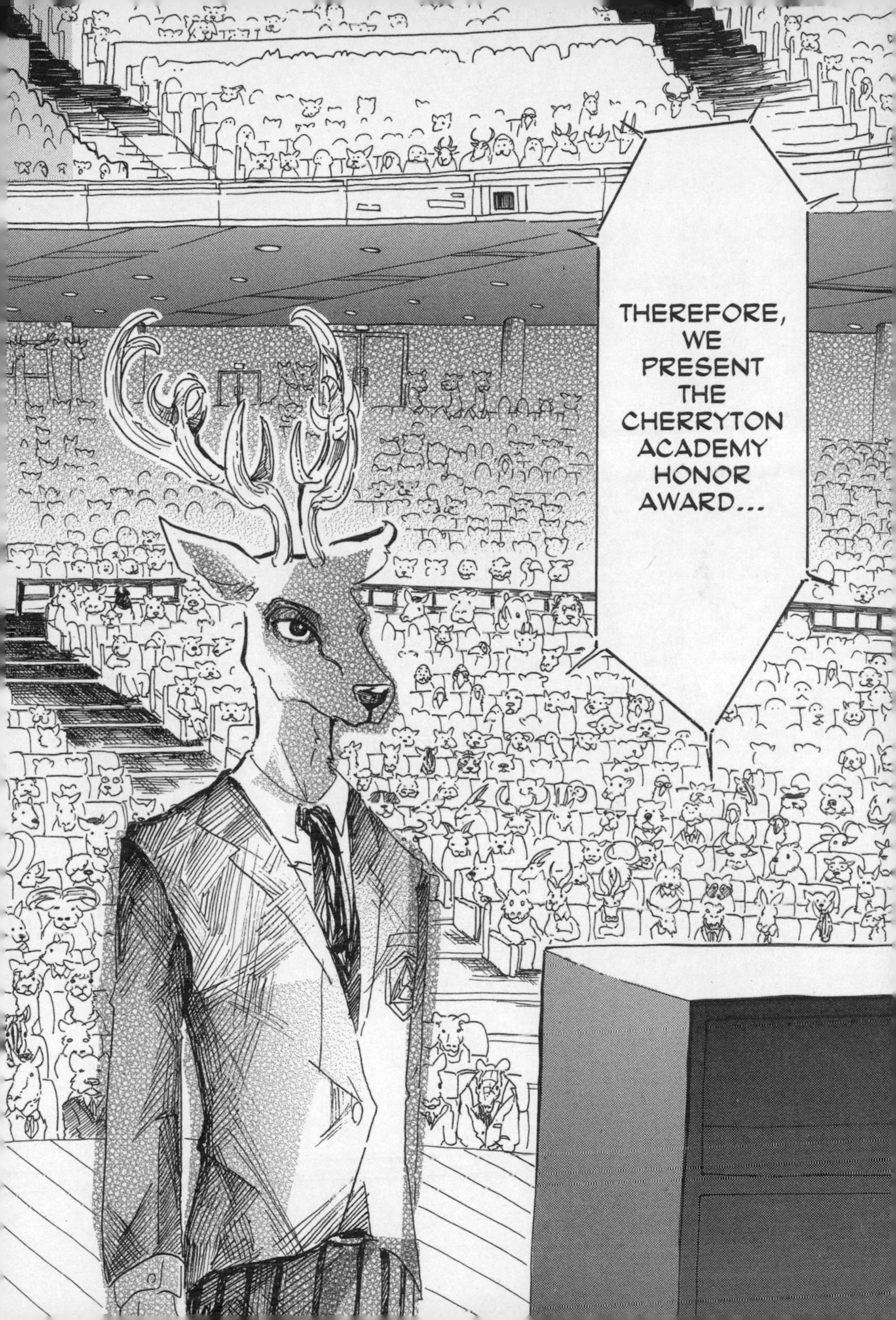
THEREFORE, WE PRESENT THE CHERRYTON ACADEMY HONOR AWARD...

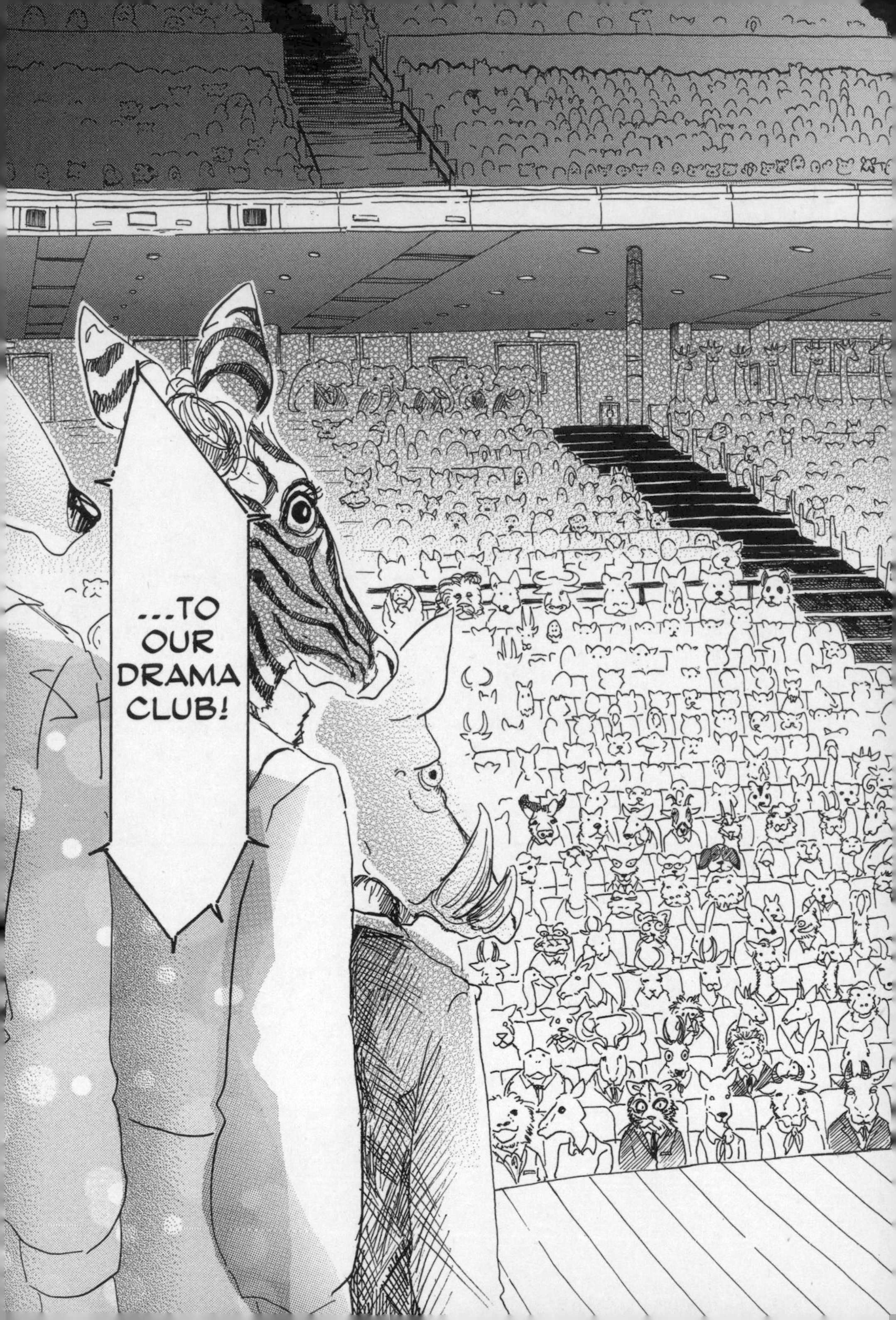
...TO OUR DRAMA CLUB!

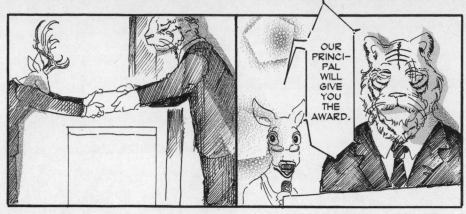

OUR PRINCIPAL WILL GIVE YOU THE AWARD.

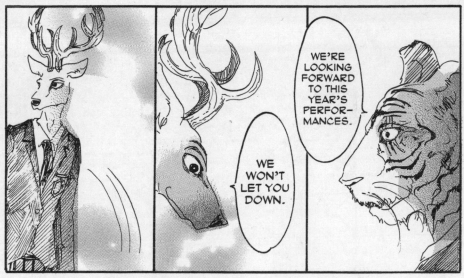

WE'RE LOOKING FORWARD TO THIS YEAR'S PERFORMANCES.

WE WON'T LET YOU DOWN.

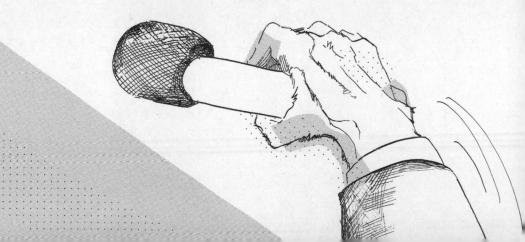

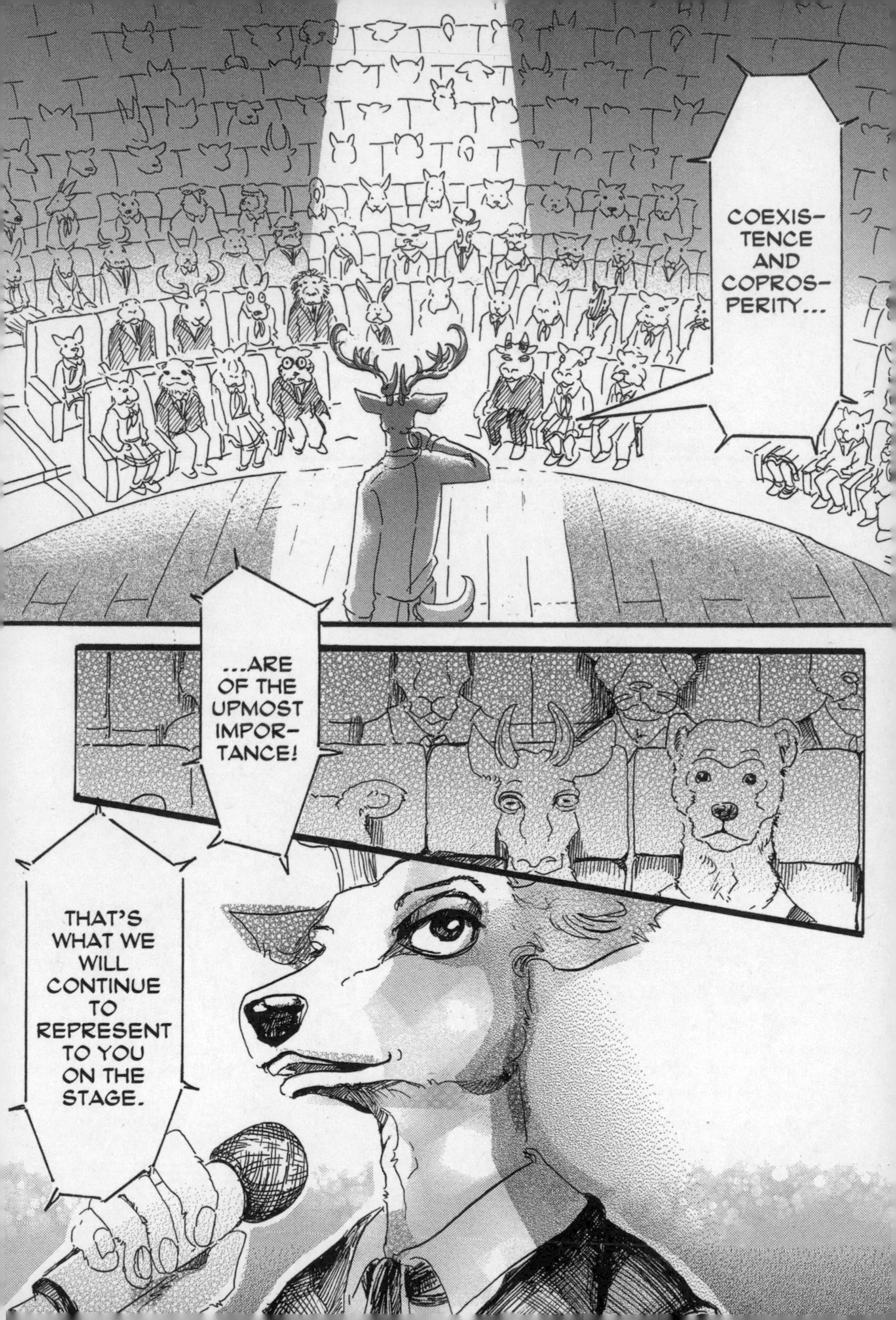
COEXISTENCE AND COPROSPERITY...
...ARE OF THE UPMOST IMPORTANCE!
THAT'S WHAT WE WILL CONTINUE TO REPRESENT TO YOU ON THE STAGE.

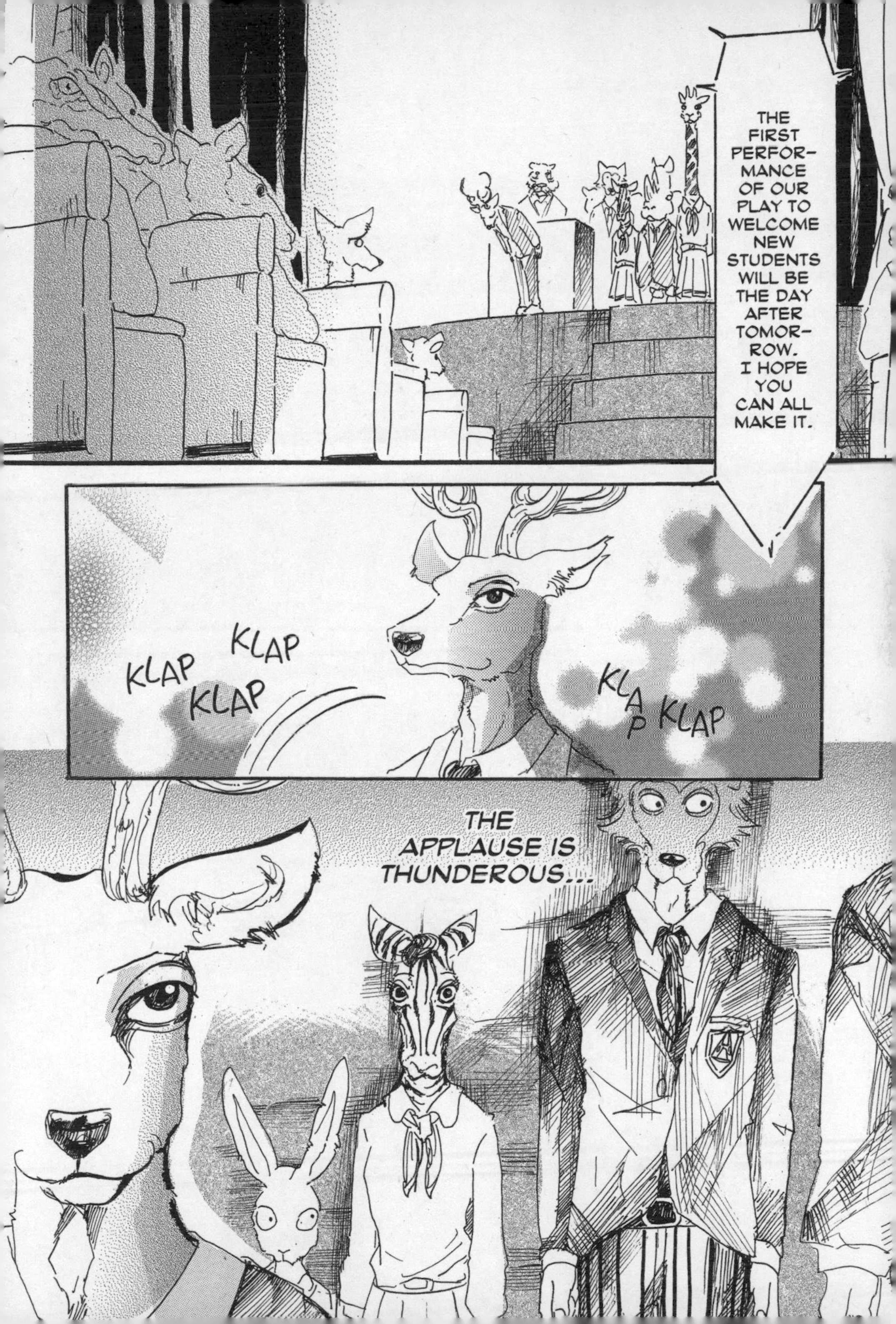
THE FIRST PERFORMANCE OF OUR PLAY TO WELCOME NEW STUDENTS WILL BE THE DAY AFTER TOMORROW. I HOPE YOU CAN ALL MAKE IT.
KLAP KLAP
KLAP
KLAP
KLAP
THE APPLAUSE IS THUNDEROUS...

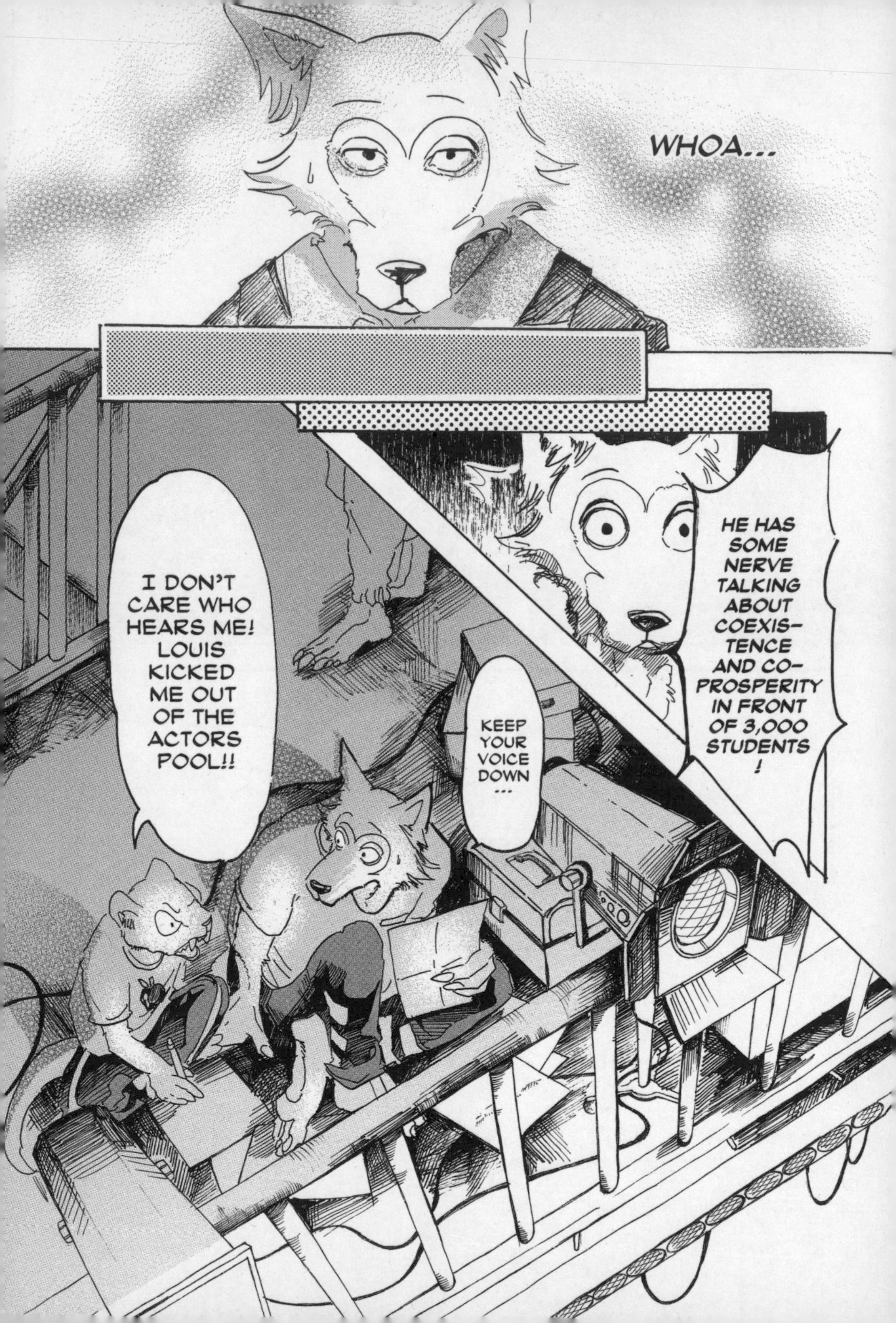
WHOA...
HE HAS SOME NERVE TALKING ABOUT COEXISTENCE AND CO-PROSPERITY IN FRONT OF 3,000 STUDENTS!
KEEP YOUR VOICE DOWN...
I DON'T CARE WHO HEARS ME! LOUIS KICKED ME OUT OF THE ACTORS POOL!!

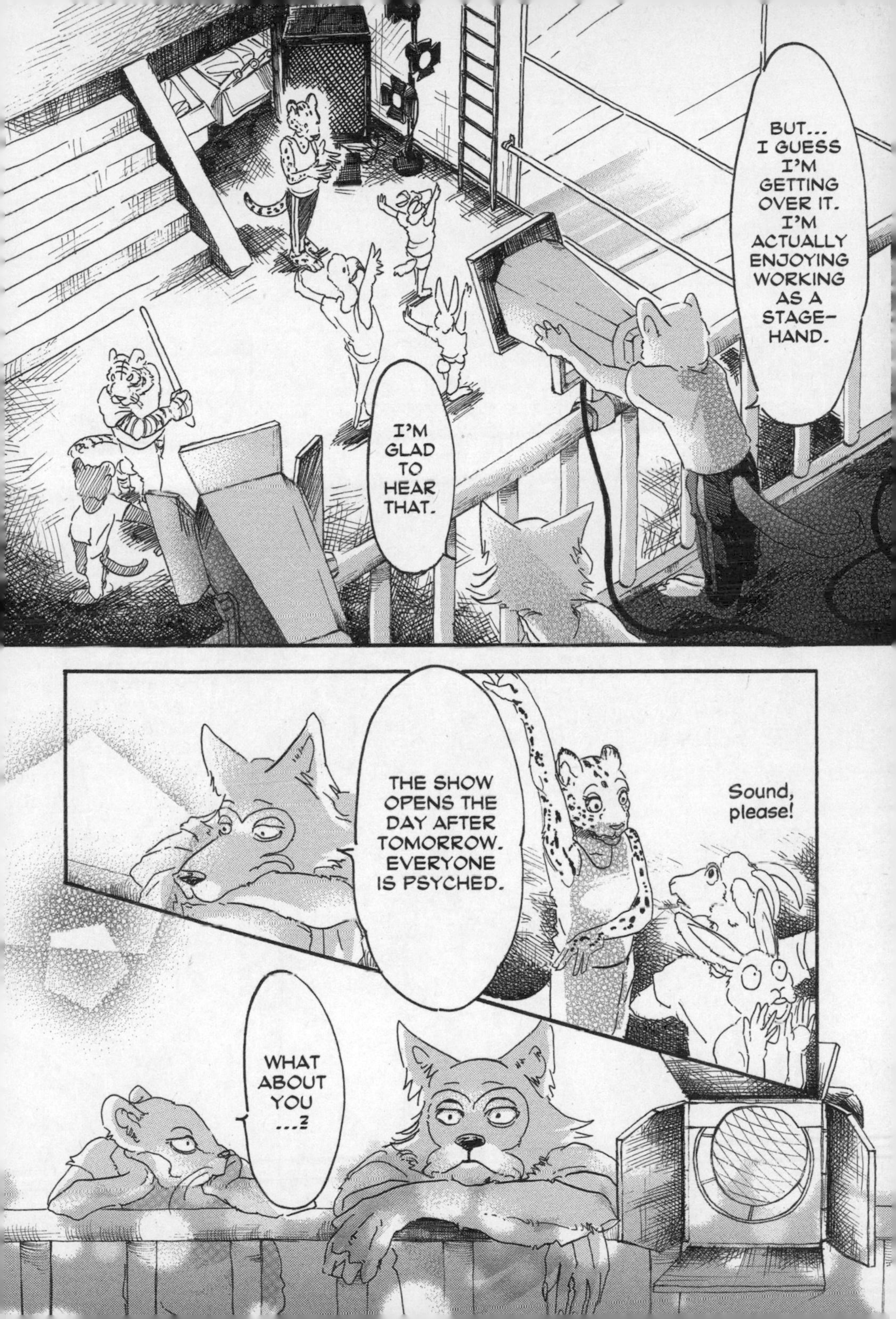
BUT... I GUESS I'M GETTING OVER IT. I'M ACTUALLY ENJOYING WORKING AS A STAGE-HAND.
I'M GLAD TO HEAR THAT.
Sound, please!
THE SHOW OPENS THE DAY AFTER TOMORROW. EVERYONE IS PSYCHED.
WHAT ABOUT YOU ...?

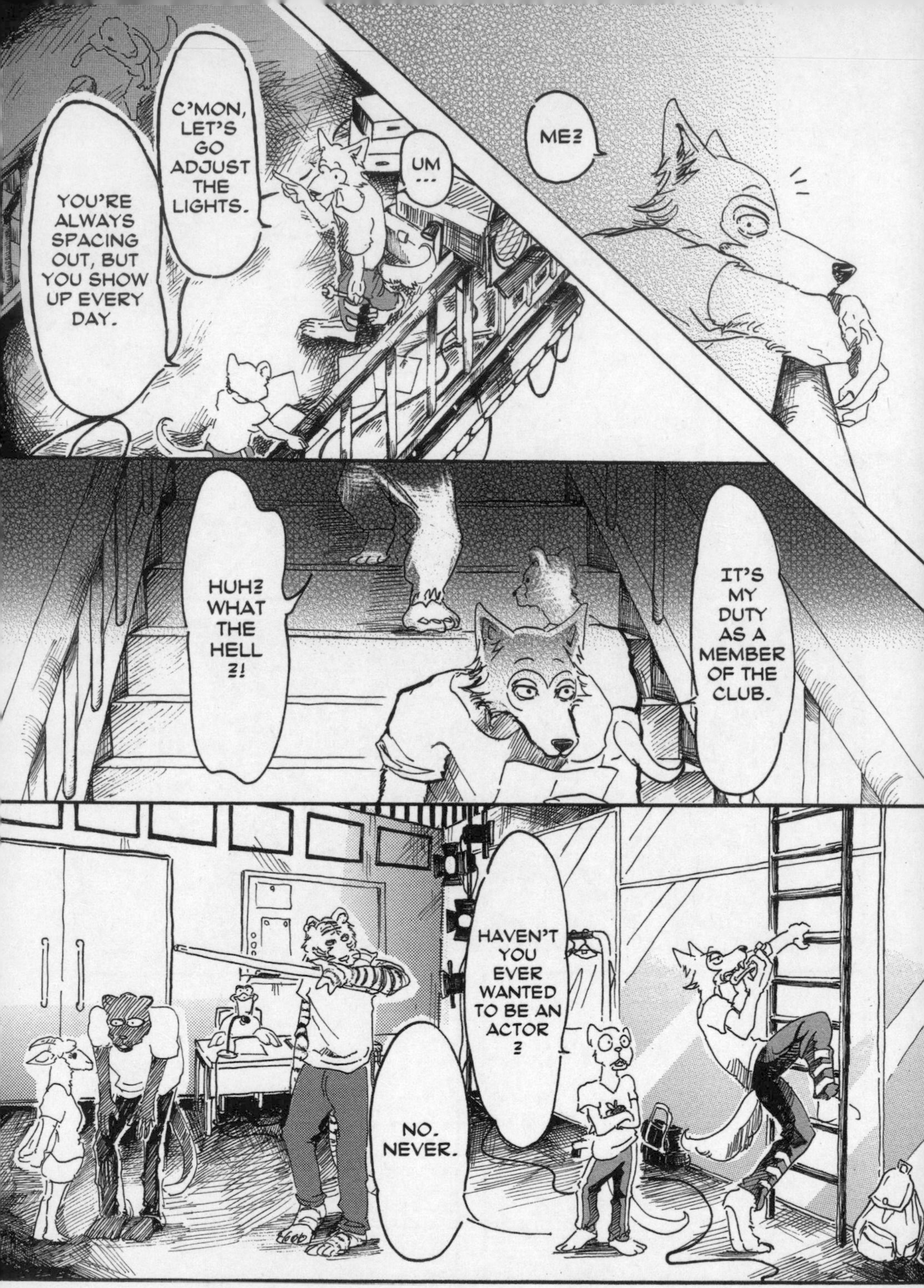
ME?
UM...
C'MON, LET'S GO ADJUST THE LIGHTS.
YOU'RE ALWAYS SPACING OUT, BUT YOU SHOW UP EVERY DAY.
IT'S MY DUTY AS A MEMBER OF THE CLUB.
HUH? WHAT THE HELL?!
HAVEN'T YOU EVER WANTED TO BE AN ACTOR?
NO. NEVER.

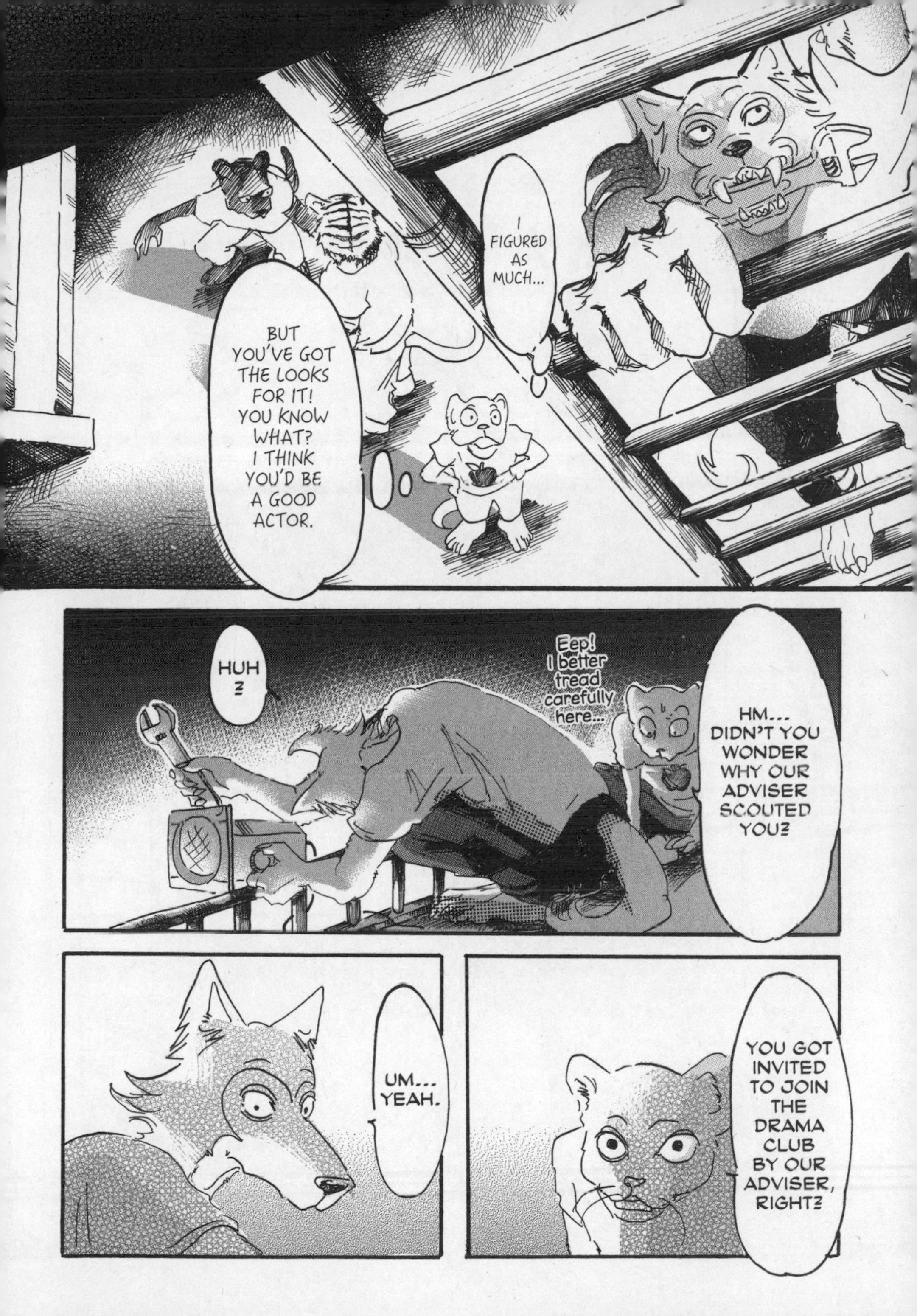
I FIGURED AS MUCH...
BUT YOU'VE GOT THE LOOKS FOR IT! YOU KNOW WHAT? I THINK YOU'D BE A GOOD ACTOR.
HM... DIDN'T YOU WONDER WHY OUR ADVISER SCOUTED YOU?
Eep! I better tread carefully here...
HUH?
YOU GOT INVITED TO JOIN THE DRAMA CLUB BY OUR ADVISER, RIGHT?
UM... YEAH.

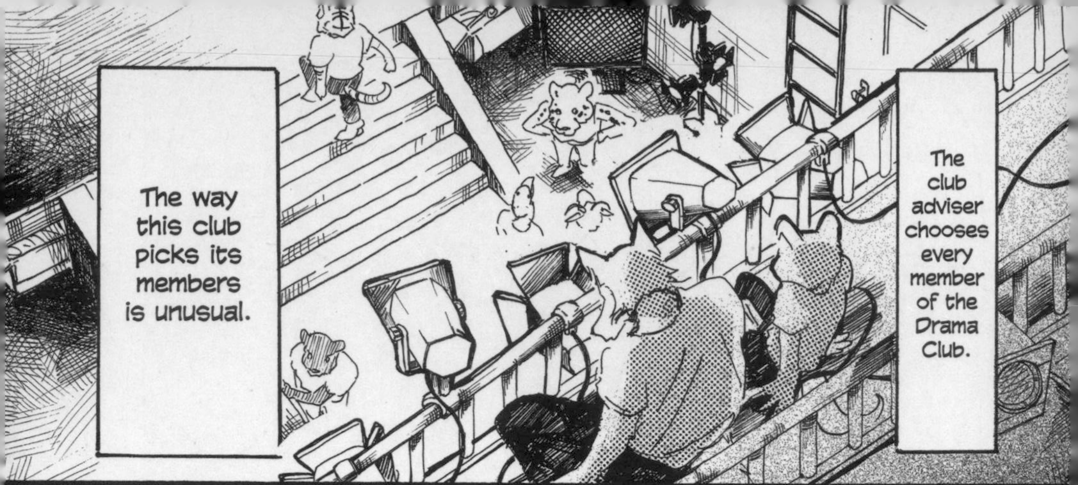
The club adviser chooses every member of the Drama Club.
The way this club picks its members is unusual.

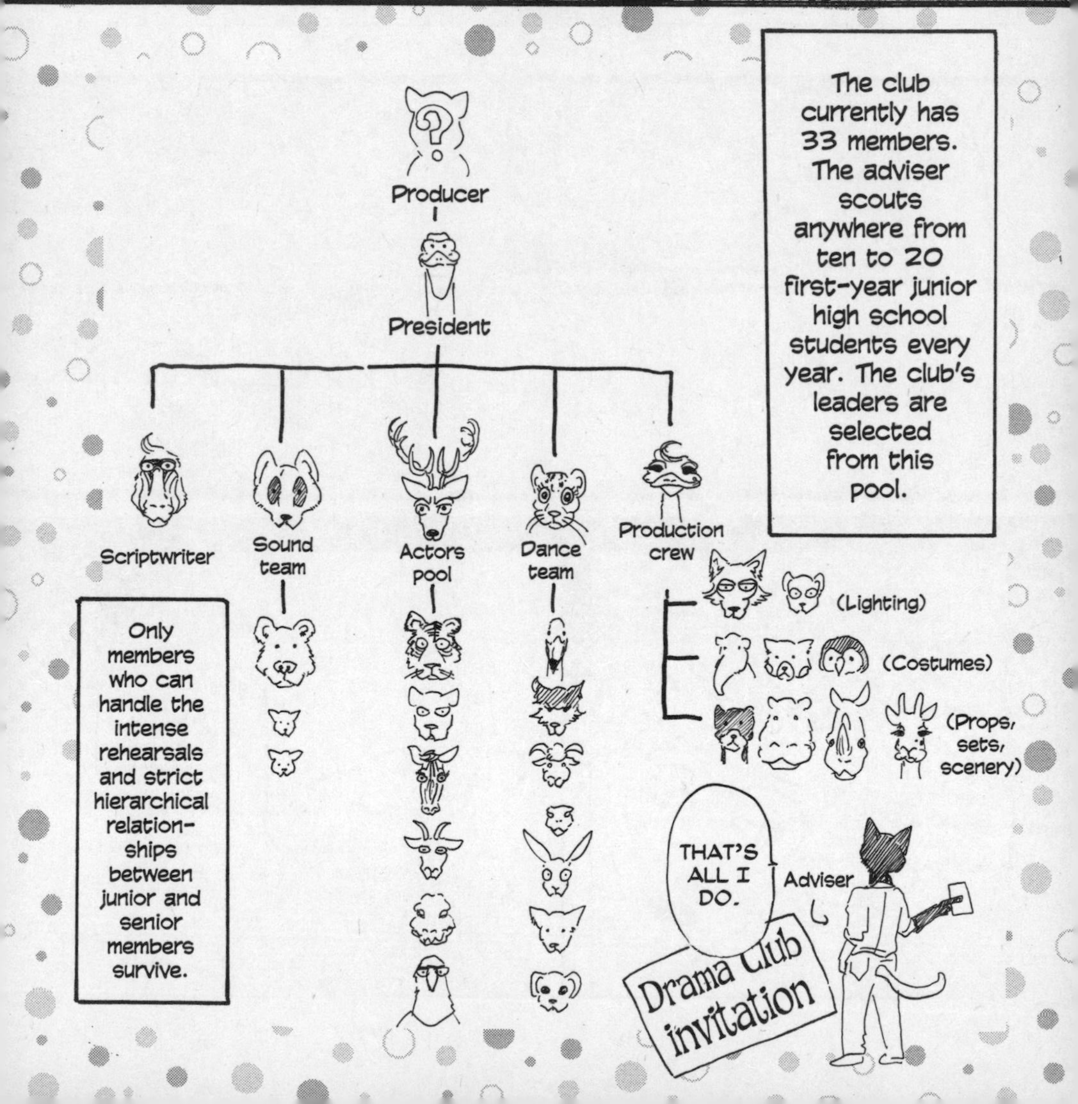
The club currently has 33 members. The adviser scouts anywhere from ten to 20 first-year junior high school students every year. The club's leaders are selected from this pool.
Producer
President
Production crew
(Lighting)
(Costumes)
(Props, sets, scenery)
Dance team
Actors pool
Sound team
Scriptwriter
Only members who can handle the intense rehearsals and strict hierarchical relation-ships between junior and senior members survive.
THAT'S ALL I DO.
Adviser
Drama Club invitation

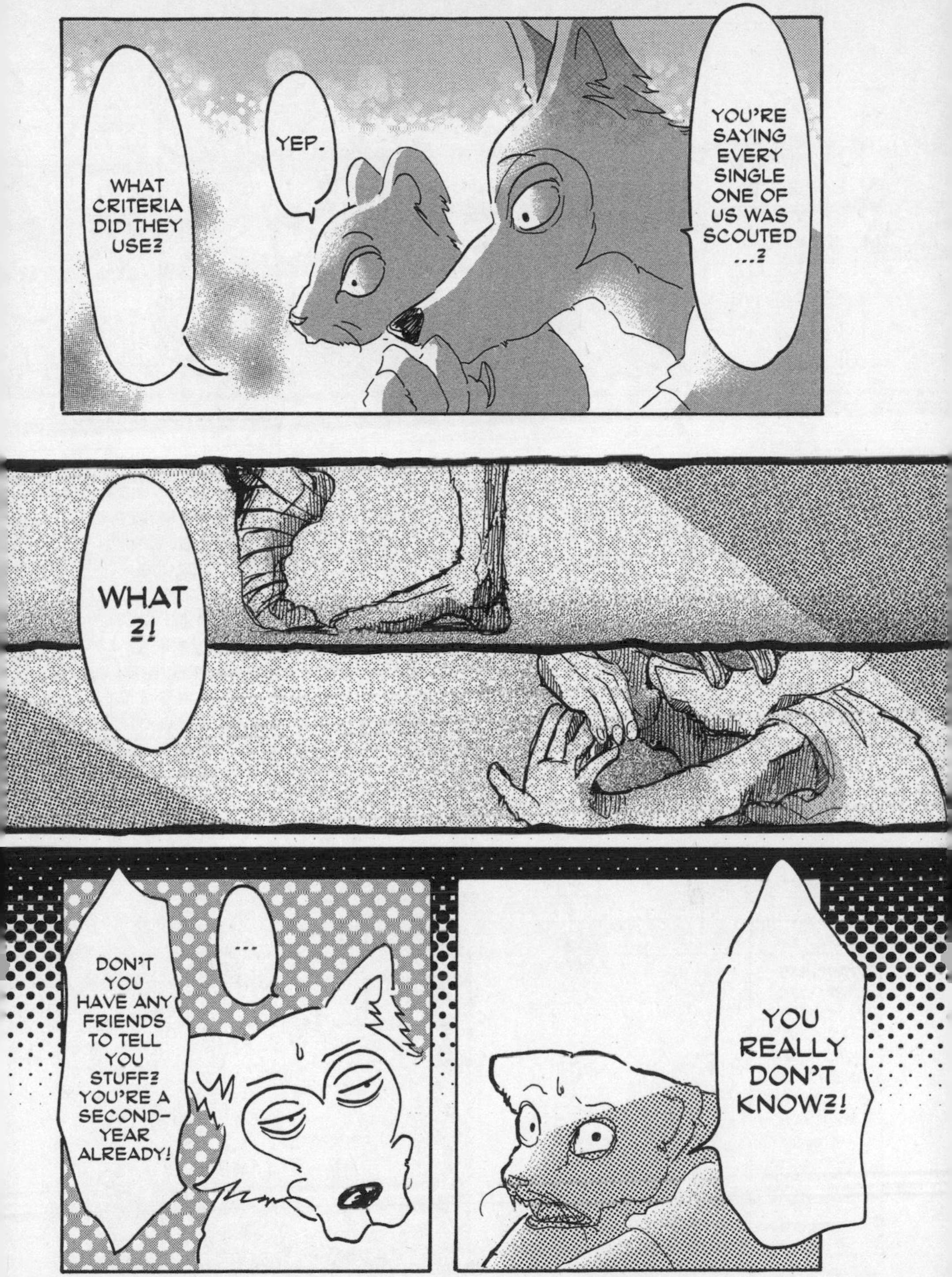
YOU'RE SAYING EVERY SINGLE ONE OF US WAS SCOUTED ...?
YEP.
WHAT CRITERIA DID THEY USE?
WHAT?!
YOU REALLY DON'T KNOW?!
...
DON'T YOU HAVE ANY FRIENDS TO TELL YOU STUFF? YOU'RE A SECOND-YEAR ALREADY!

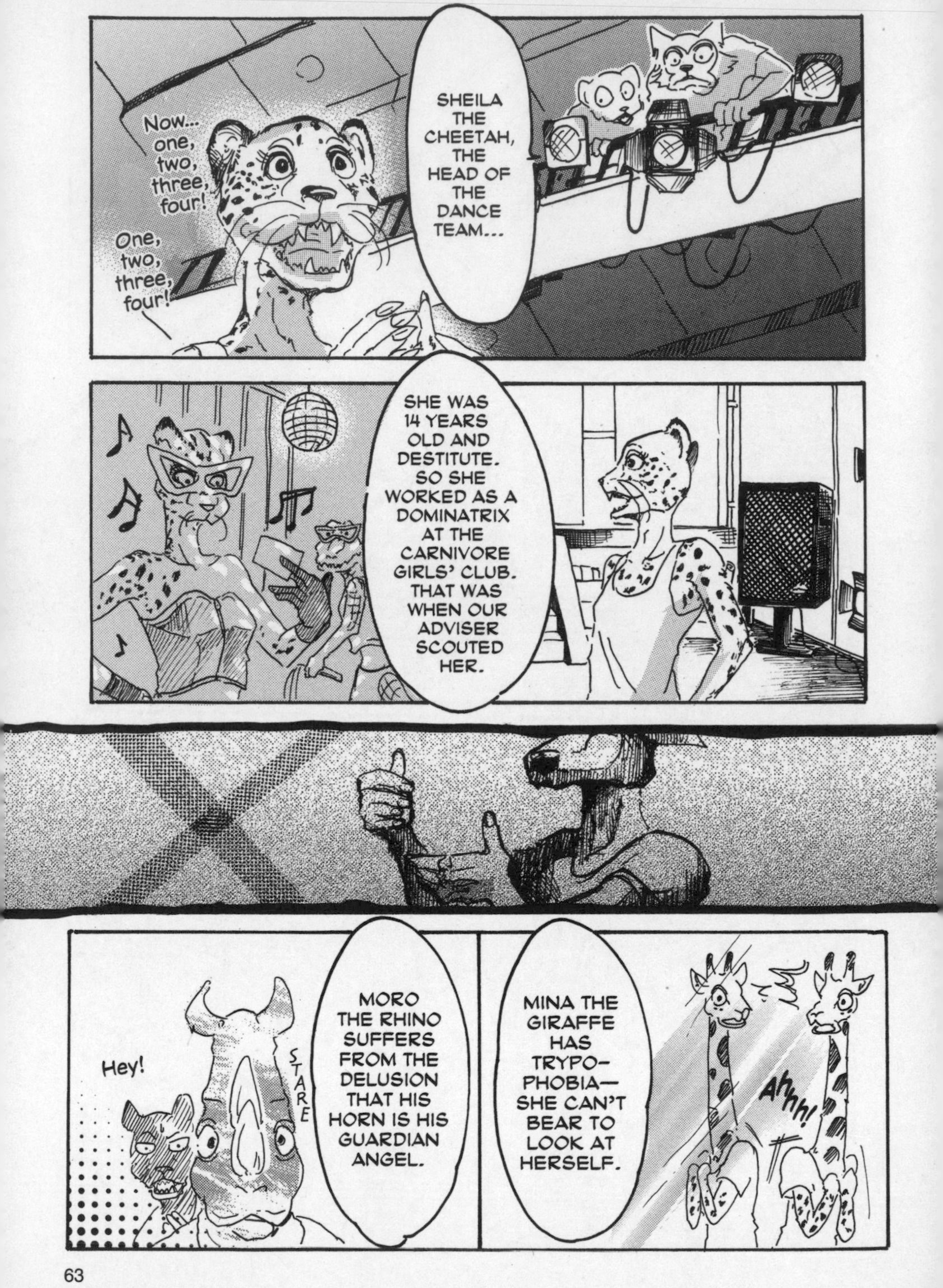
SHEILA THE CHEETAH, THE HEAD OF THE DANCE TEAM...
Now... one, two, three, four!
One, two, three, four!
SHE WAS 14 YEARS OLD AND DESTITUTE. SO SHE WORKED AS A DOMINATRIX AT THE CARNIVORE GIRLS' CLUB. THAT WAS WHEN OUR ADVISER SCOUTED HER.
MINA THE GIRAFFE HAS TRYPO-PHOBIA—SHE CAN'T BEAR TO LOOK AT HERSELF.
Ahhh!
MORO THE RHINO SUFFERS FROM THE DELUSION THAT HIS HORN IS HIS GUARDIAN ANGEL.
STARE
Hey!

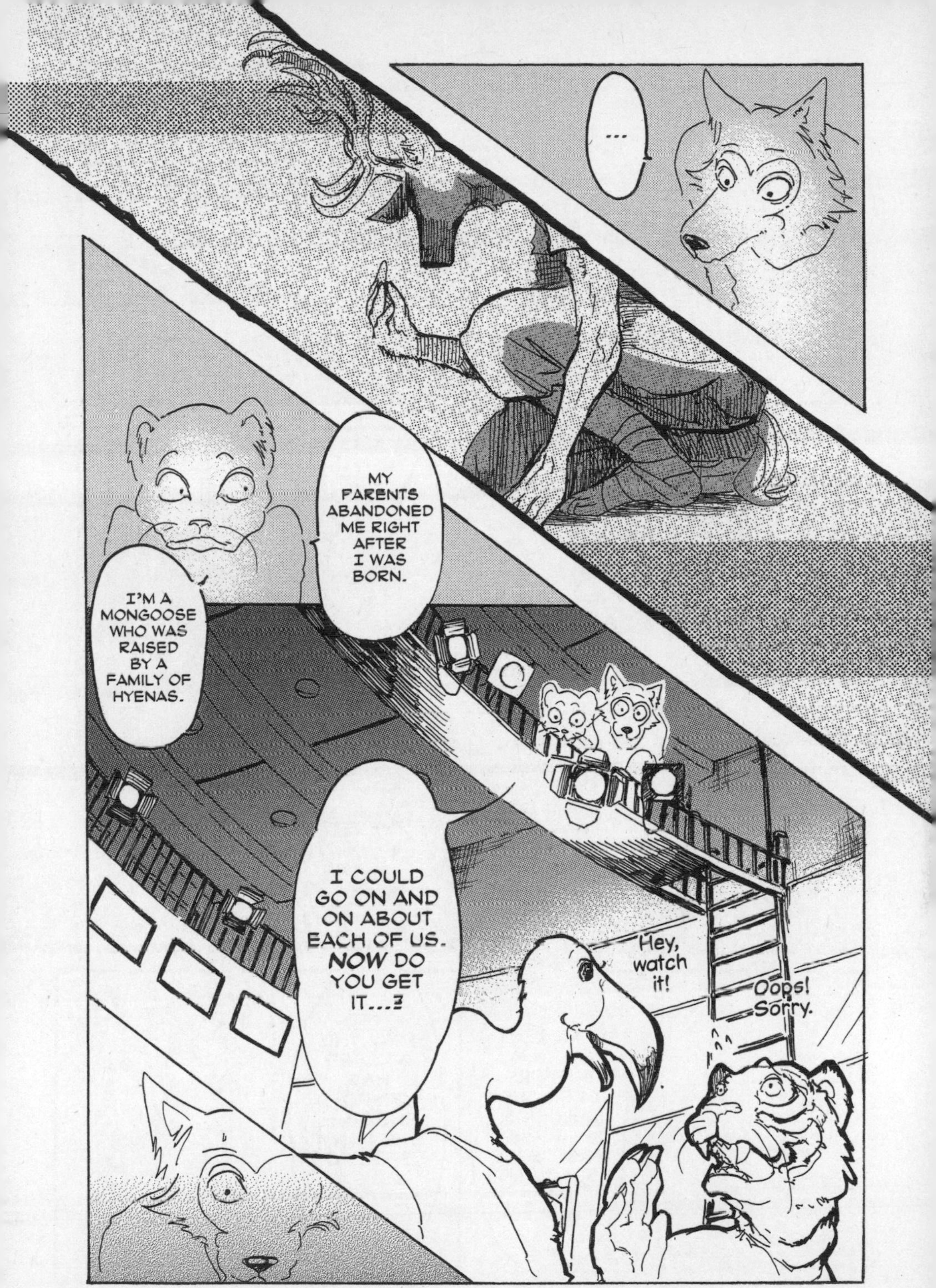
...
MY PARENTS ABANDONED ME RIGHT AFTER I WAS BORN.
I'M A MONGOOSE WHO WAS RAISED BY A FAMILY OF HYENAS.
Hey, watch it!
Oops! Sorry.
I COULD GO ON AND ON ABOUT EACH OF US. **NOW** DO YOU GET IT...?

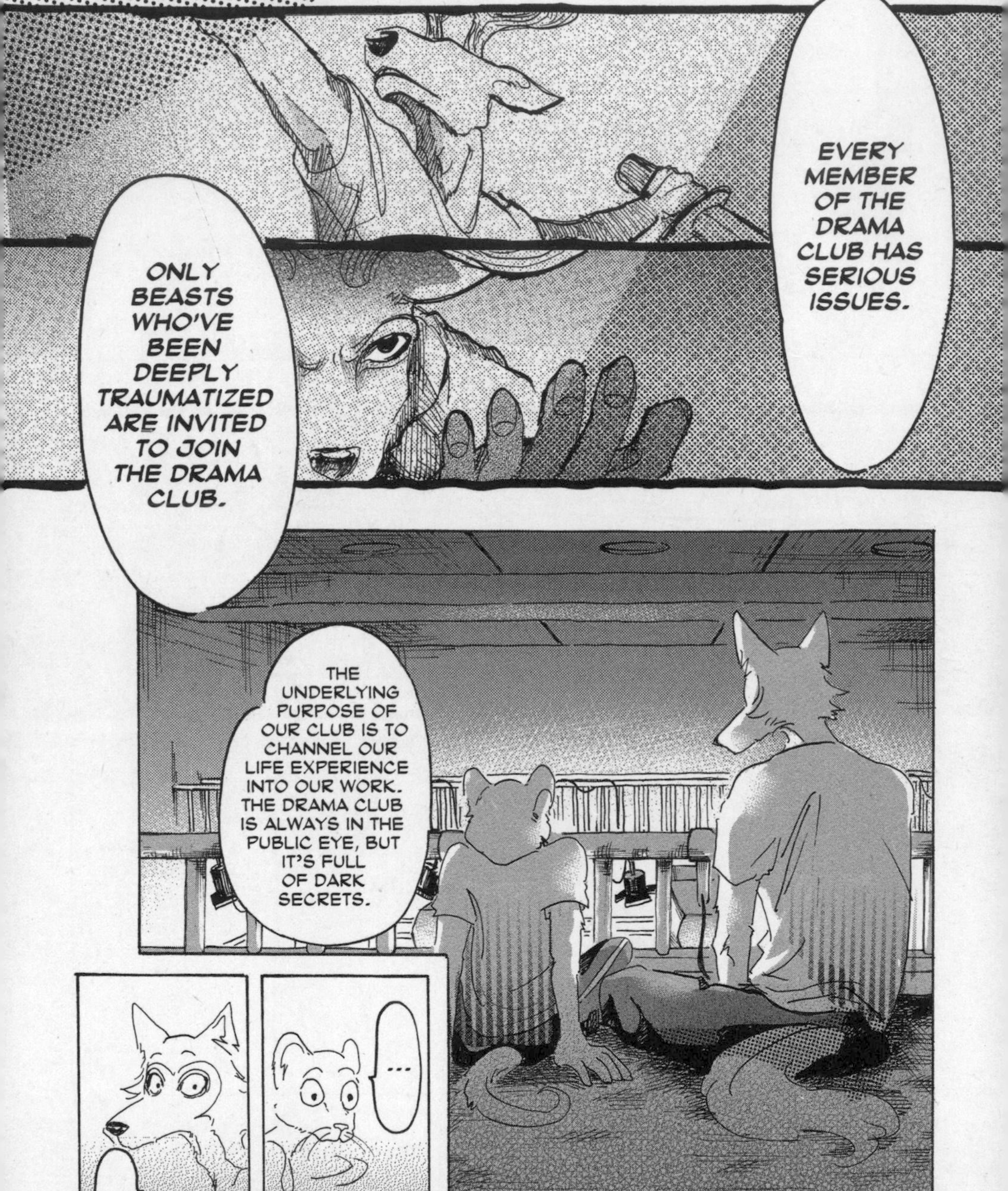
EVERY MEMBER OF THE DRAMA CLUB HAS SERIOUS ISSUES.
ONLY BEASTS WHO'VE BEEN DEEPLY TRAUMATIZED ARE INVITED TO JOIN THE DRAMA CLUB.
THE UNDERLYING PURPOSE OF OUR CLUB IS TO CHANNEL OUR LIFE EXPERIENCE INTO OUR WORK. THE DRAMA CLUB IS ALWAYS IN THE PUBLIC EYE, BUT IT'S FULL OF DARK SECRETS.
...
...

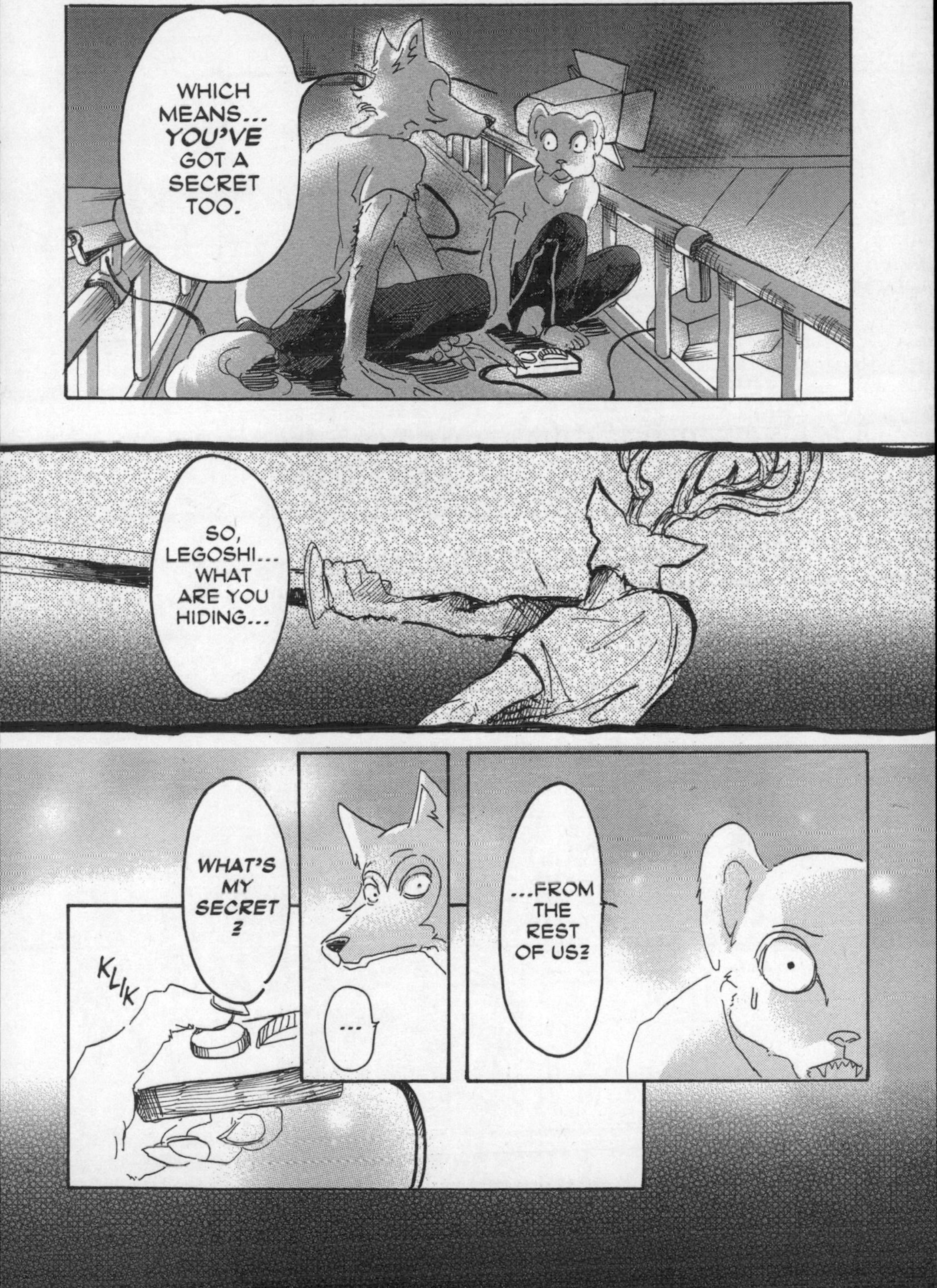
WHICH MEANS... YOU'VE GOT A SECRET TOO.
SO, LEGOSHI... WHAT ARE YOU HIDING...
...FROM THE REST OF US?
...
WHAT'S MY SECRET?
KLIK

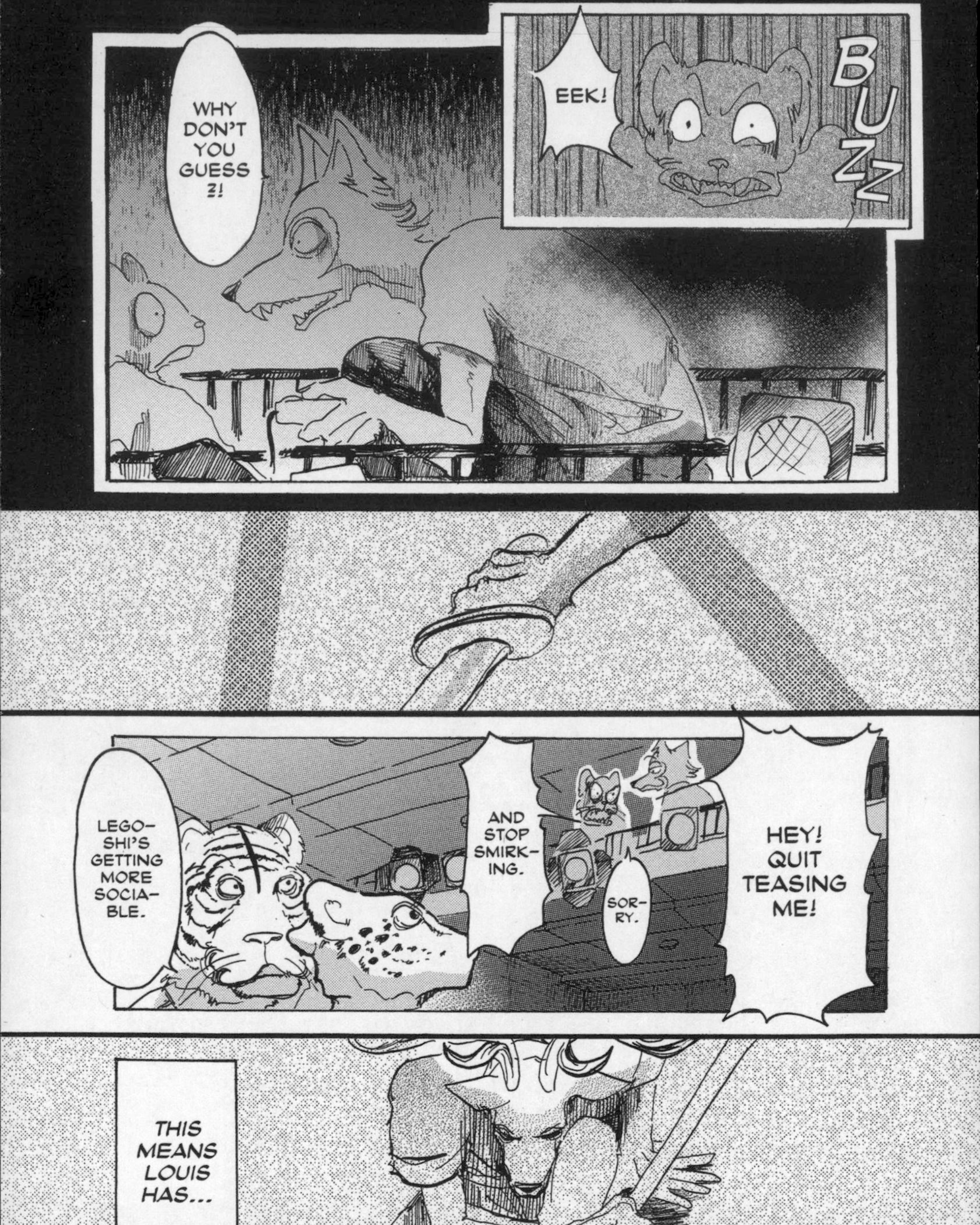
EEK!
BUZZ
WHY DON'T YOU GUESS?!
HEY! QUIT TEASING ME!
AND STOP SMIRKING.
SORRY.
LEGOSHI'S GETTING MORE SOCIABLE.
THIS MEANS LOUIS HAS...

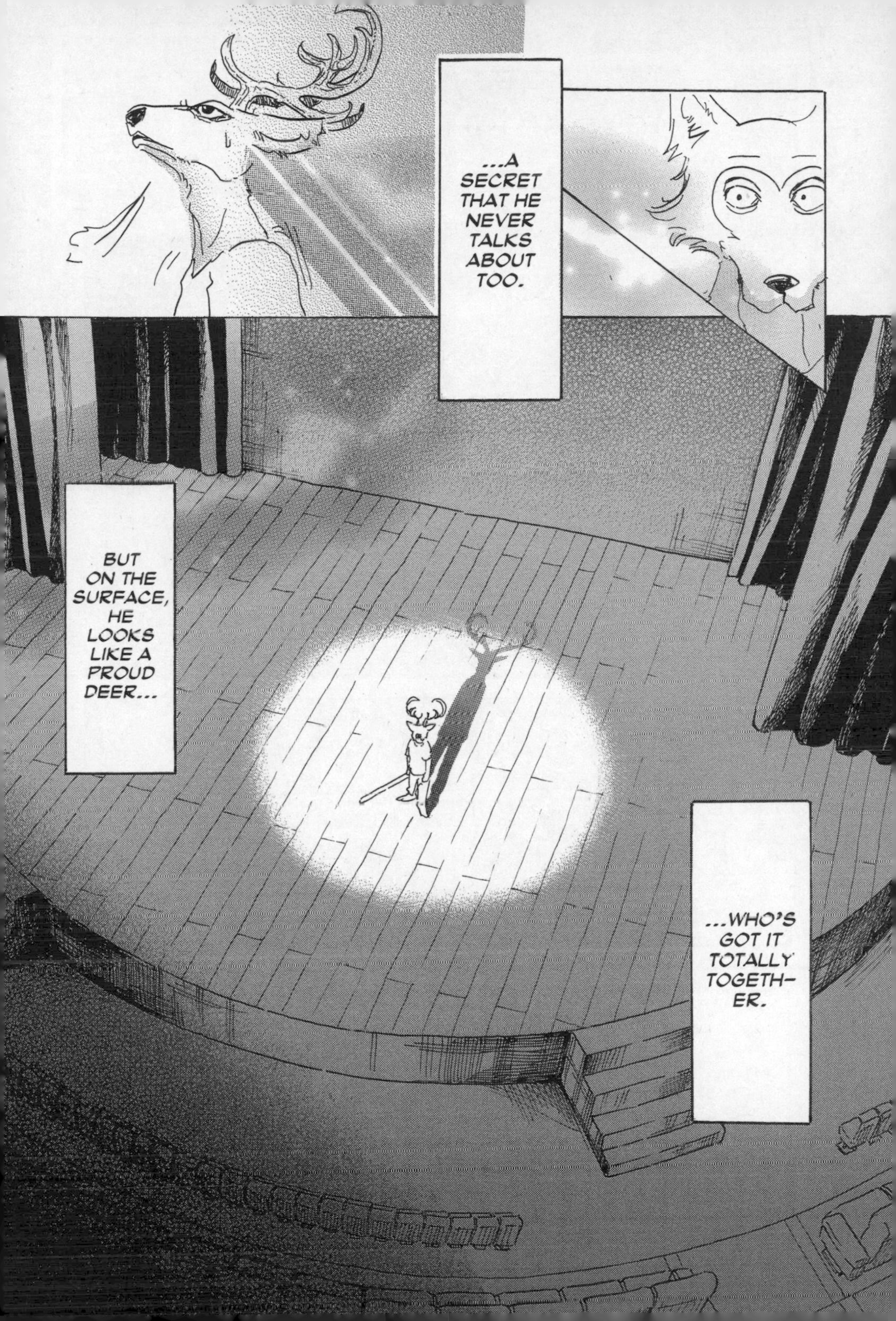
...A SECRET THAT HE NEVER TALKS ABOUT TOO.
BUT ON THE SURFACE, HE LOOKS LIKE A PROUD DEER...
...WHO'S GOT IT TOTALLY TOGETH-ER.

Chapter 11: Feels like Glass in the Gums

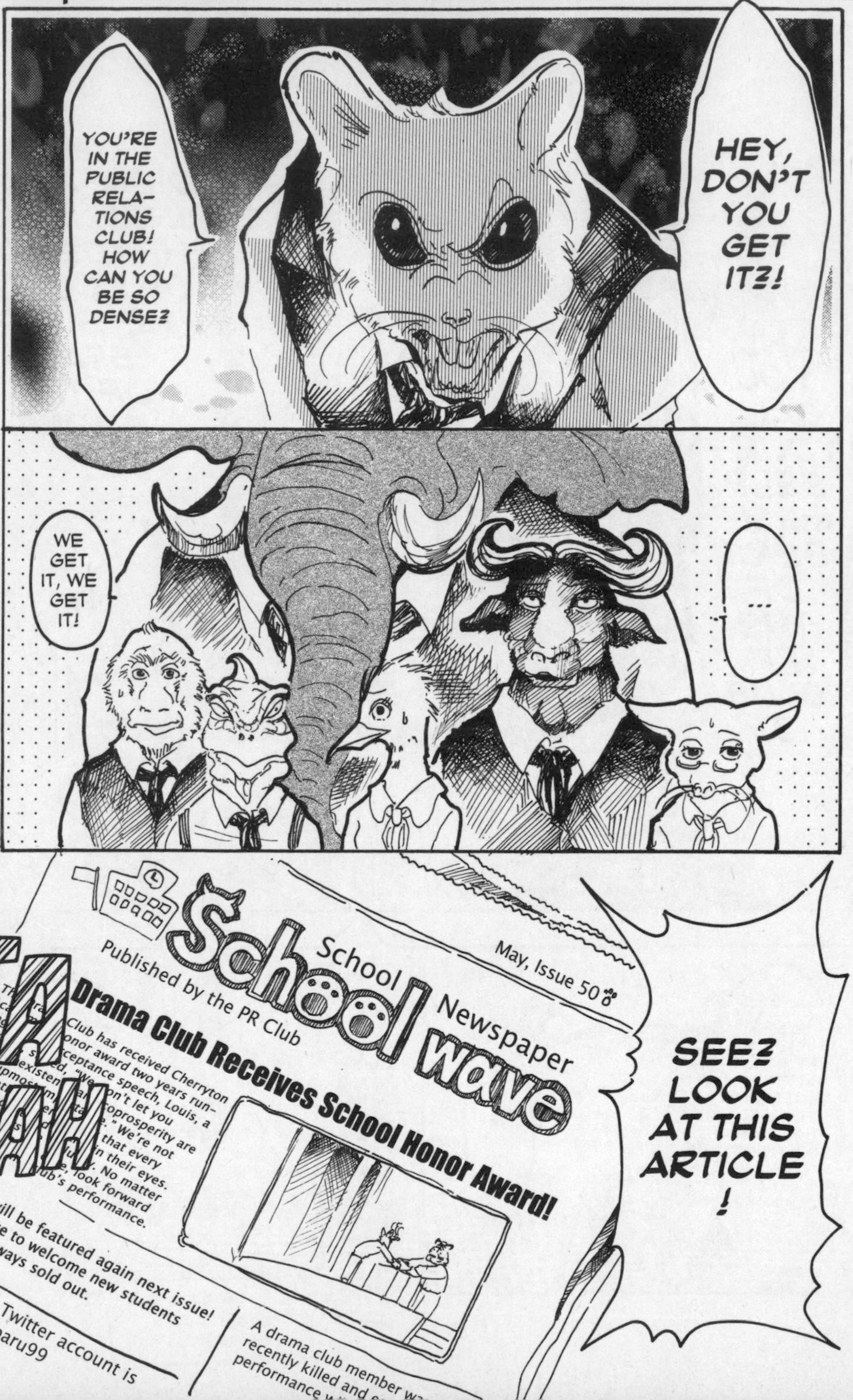
HEY, DON'T YOU GET IT?!
YOU'RE IN THE PUBLIC RELA-TIONS CLUB! HOW CAN YOU BE SO DENSE?
...
WE GET IT, WE GET IT!
SEE? LOOK AT THIS ARTICLE!
School Newspaper
School wave
May, Issue 50
Published by the PR Club
Drama Club Receives School Honor Award!
Club has received Cherryton
onor award two years run-
ceptance speech, Louis, a
rosperity are
that every
in their eyes.
No matter
look forward
b's performance.
rama club will be featured again next issue!
performance to welcome new students
is always sold out.
u Itagaki's Twitter account is
@itaparu99
A drama club member wa
recently killed and
performance
TA DAH

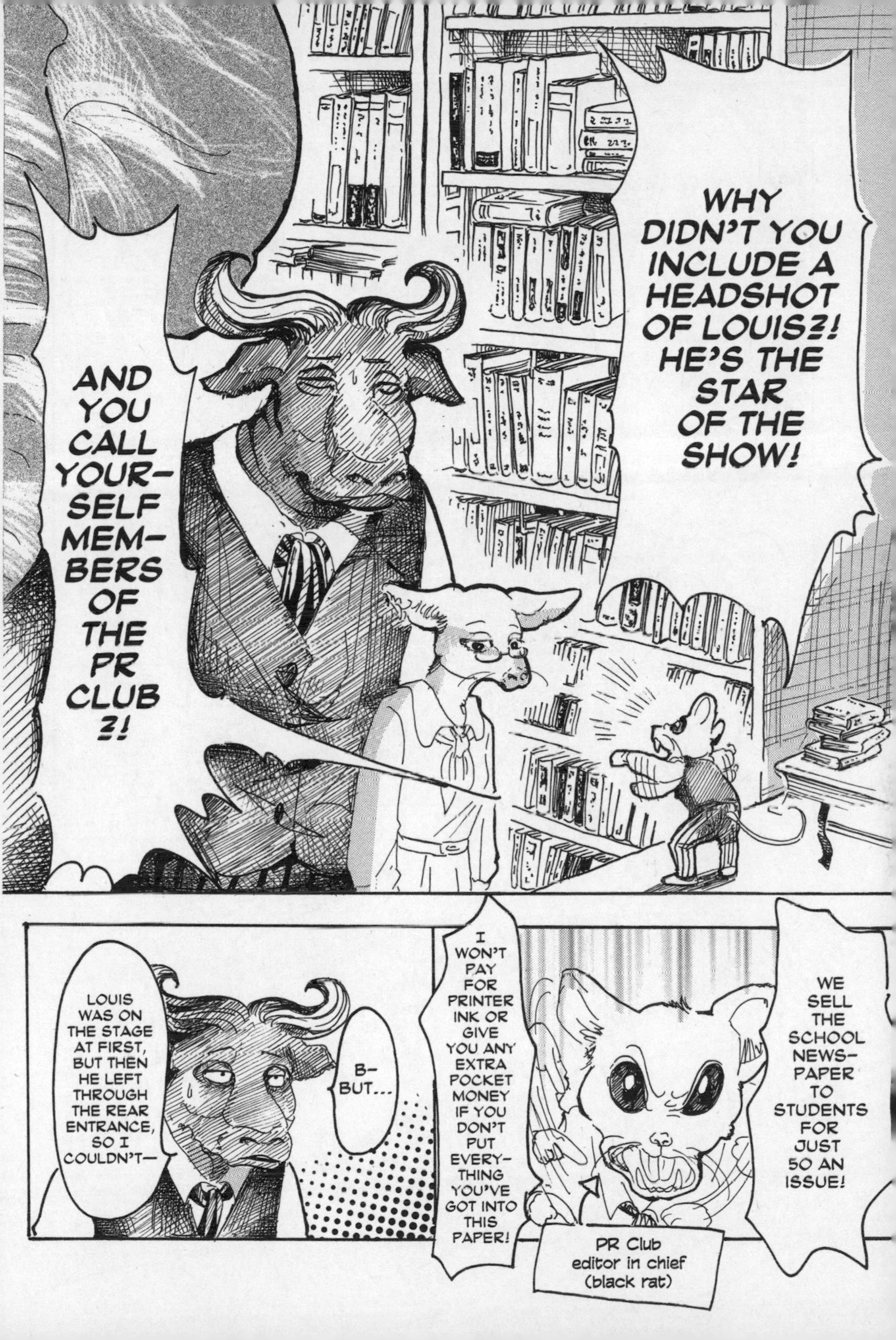
WHY DIDN'T YOU INCLUDE A HEADSHOT OF LOUIS?! HE'S THE STAR OF THE SHOW!
AND YOU CALL YOUR-SELF MEM-BERS OF THE PR CLUB?!
WE SELL THE SCHOOL NEWS-PAPER TO STUDENTS FOR JUST 50 AN ISSUE!
I WON'T PAY FOR PRINTER INK OR GIVE YOU ANY EXTRA POCKET MONEY IF YOU DON'T PUT EVERY-THING YOU'VE GOT INTO THIS PAPER!
PR Club editor in chief (black rat)
B-BUT...
LOUIS WAS ON THE STAGE AT FIRST, BUT THEN HE LEFT THROUGH THE REAR ENTRANCE, SO I COULDN'T—

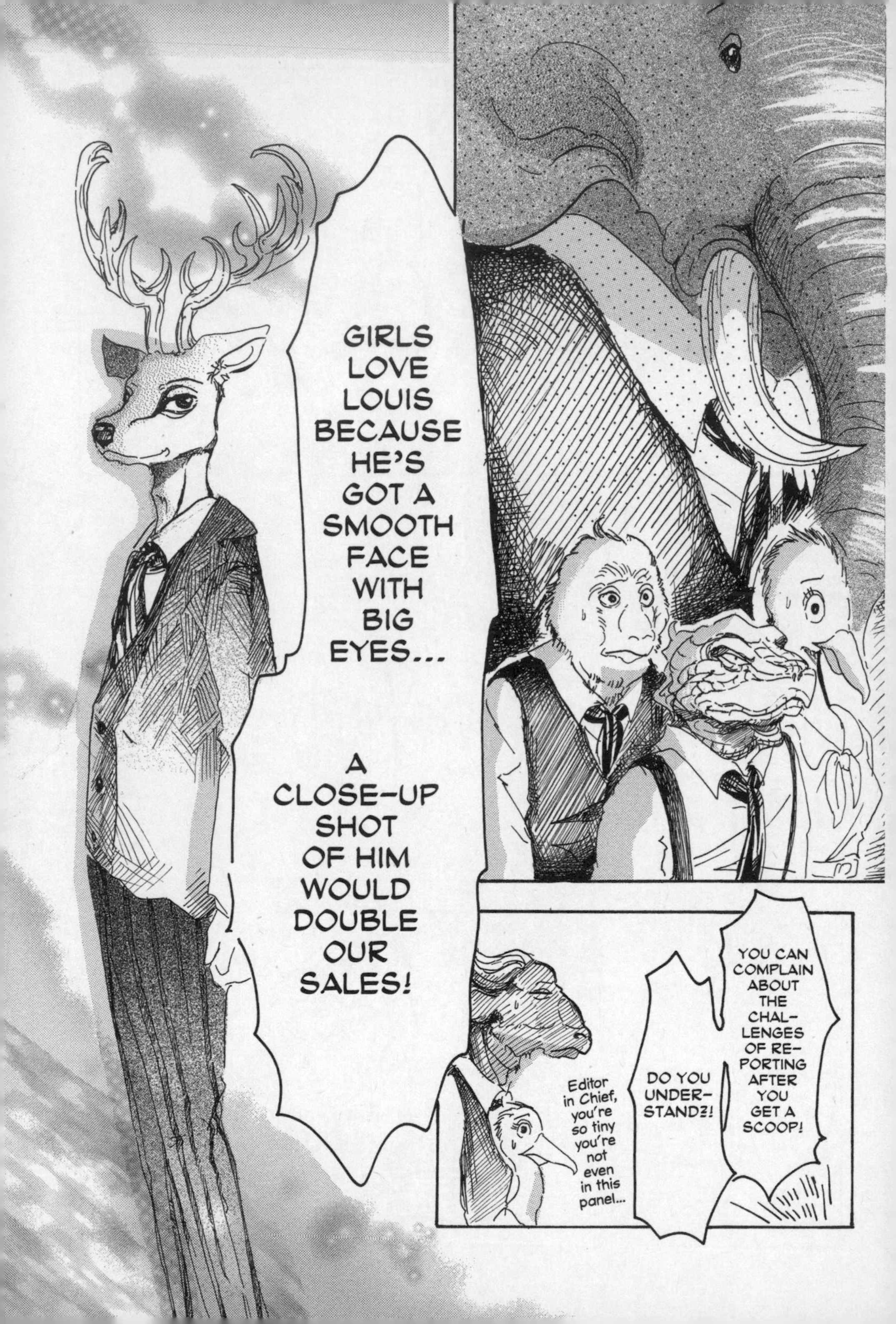
GIRLS LOVE LOUIS BECAUSE HE'S GOT A SMOOTH FACE WITH BIG EYES...
A CLOSE-UP SHOT OF HIM WOULD DOUBLE OUR SALES!
YOU CAN COMPLAIN ABOUT THE CHALLENGES OF REPORTING AFTER YOU GET A SCOOP!
DO YOU UNDERSTAND?!
Editor in Chief, you're so tiny you're not even in this panel...

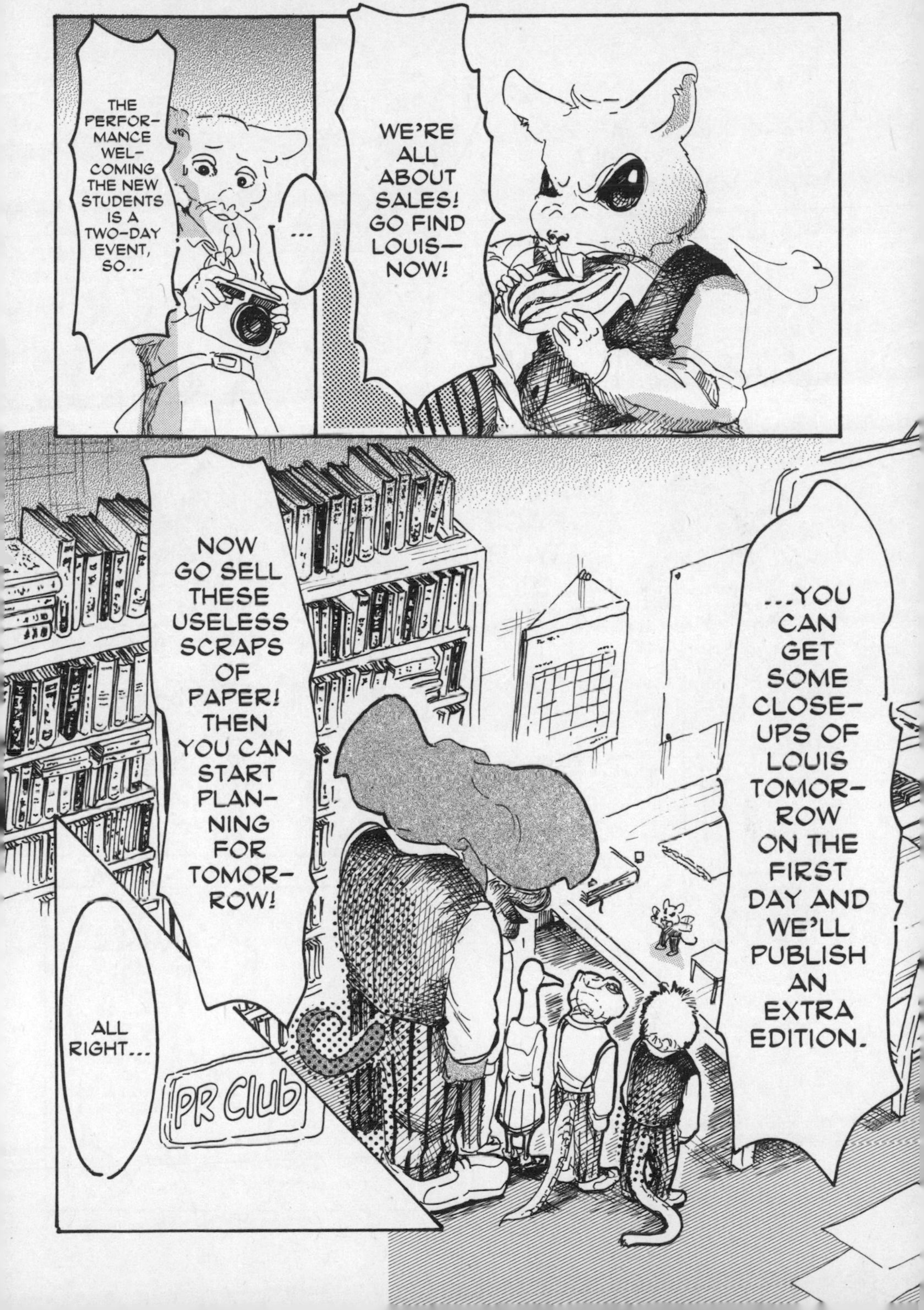
WE'RE ALL ABOUT SALES! GO FIND LOUIS—NOW!
...
THE PERFORMANCE WELCOMING THE NEW STUDENTS IS A TWO-DAY EVENT, SO...
...YOU CAN GET SOME CLOSE-UPS OF LOUIS TOMORROW ON THE FIRST DAY AND WE'LL PUBLISH AN EXTRA EDITION.
NOW GO SELL THESE USELESS SCRAPS OF PAPER! THEN YOU CAN START PLANNING FOR TOMORROW!
ALL RIGHT...
PR Club

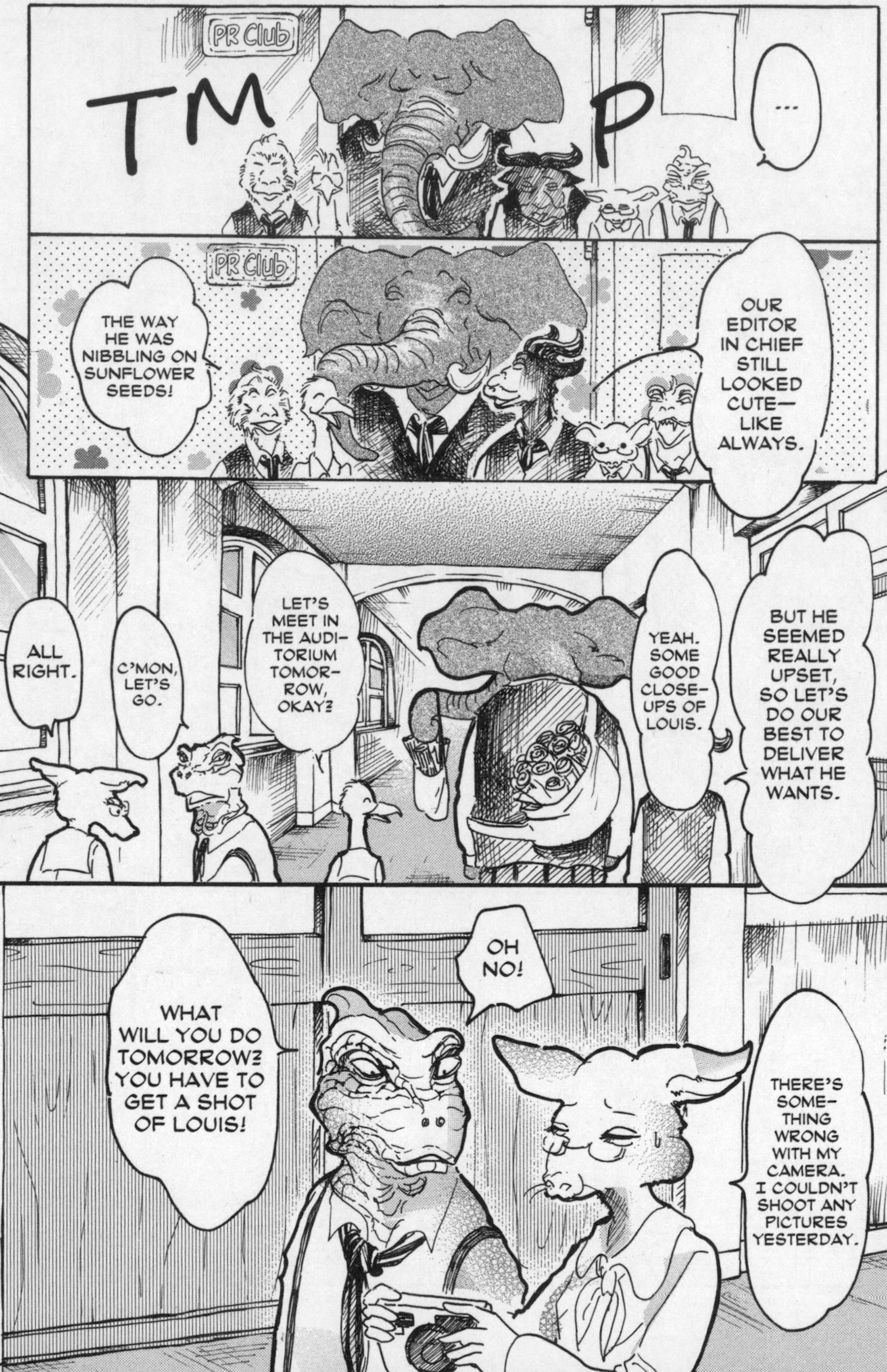
PR Club
...
TMP
PR Club
OUR EDITOR IN CHIEF STILL LOOKED CUTE— LIKE ALWAYS.
THE WAY HE WAS NIBBLING ON SUNFLOWER SEEDS!
BUT HE SEEMED REALLY UPSET, SO LET'S DO OUR BEST TO DELIVER WHAT HE WANTS.
YEAH. SOME GOOD CLOSE-UPS OF LOUIS.
LET'S MEET IN THE AUDITORIUM TOMORROW, OKAY?
C'MON, LET'S GO.
ALL RIGHT.
THERE'S SOMETHING WRONG WITH MY CAMERA. I COULDN'T SHOOT ANY PICTURES YESTERDAY.
OH NO!
WHAT WILL YOU DO TOMORROW? YOU HAVE TO GET A SHOT OF LOUIS!

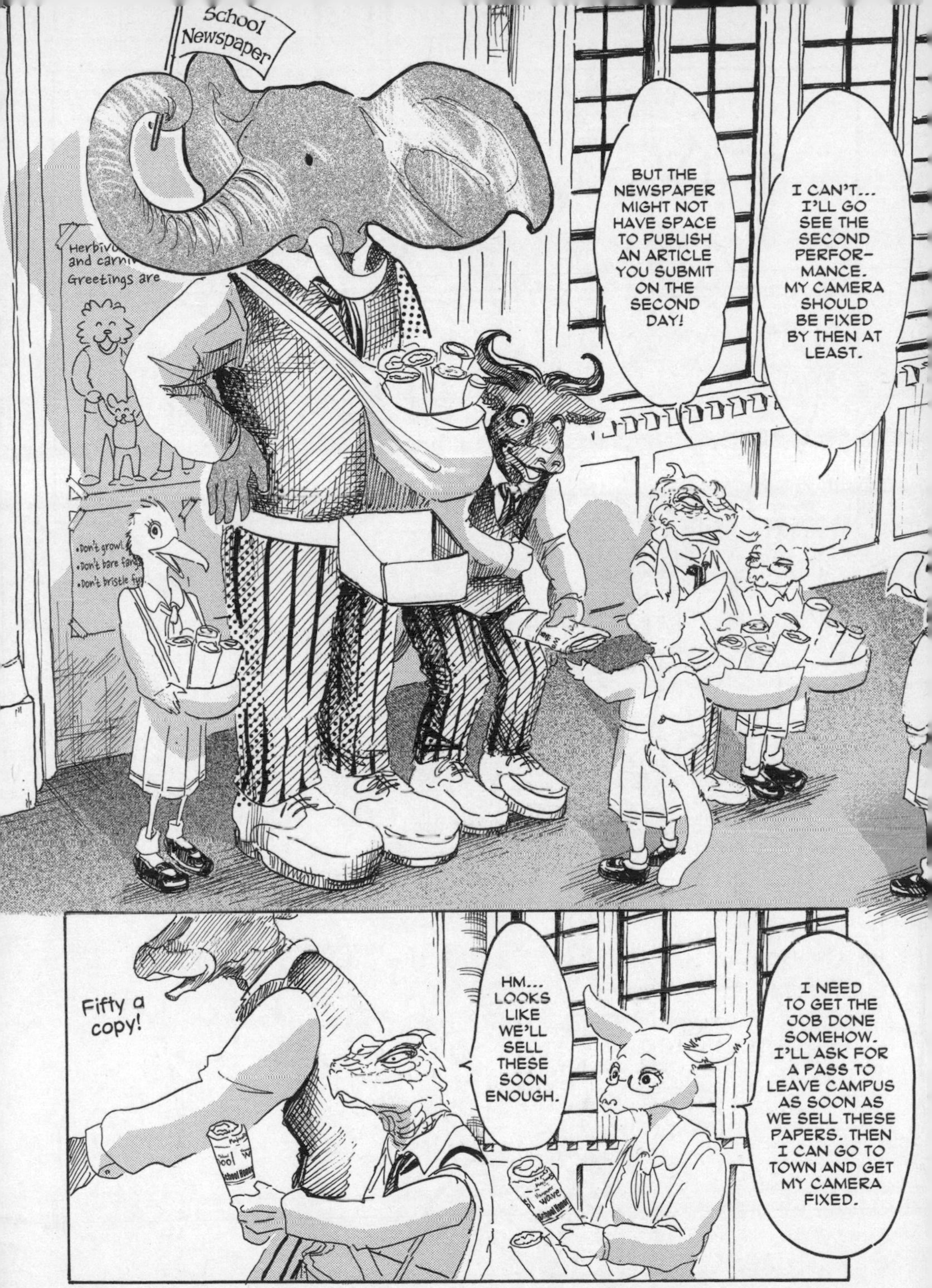
School Newspaper
I CAN'T... I'LL GO SEE THE SECOND PERFOR-MANCE. MY CAMERA SHOULD BE FIXED BY THEN AT LEAST.
BUT THE NEWSPAPER MIGHT NOT HAVE SPACE TO PUBLISH AN ARTICLE YOU SUBMIT ON THE SECOND DAY!
I NEED TO GET THE JOB DONE SOMEHOW. I'LL ASK FOR A PASS TO LEAVE CAMPUS AS SOON AS WE SELL THESE PAPERS. THEN I CAN GO TO TOWN AND GET MY CAMERA FIXED.
HM... LOOKS LIKE WE'LL SELL THESE SOON ENOUGH.
Fifty a copy!

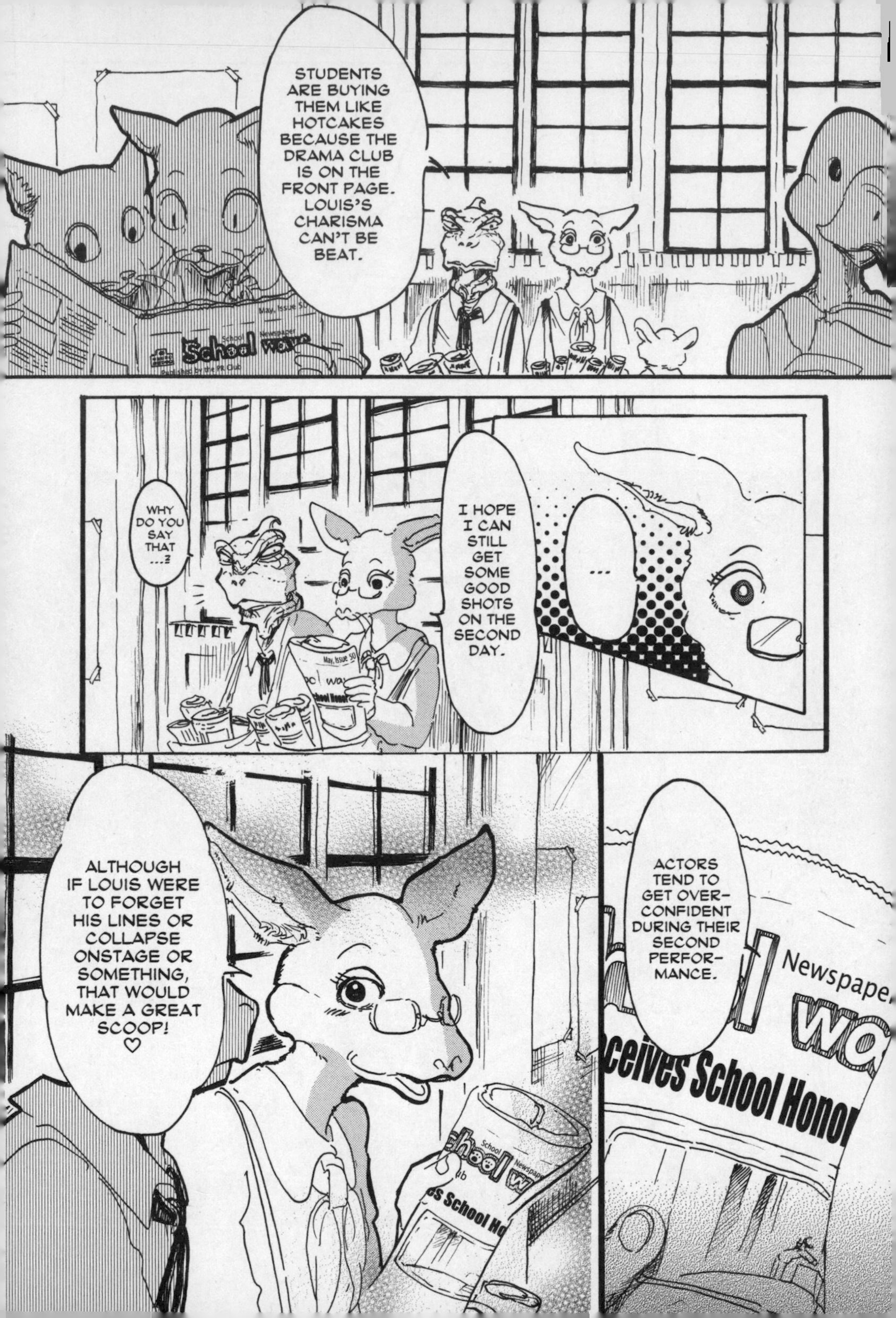
STUDENTS ARE BUYING THEM LIKE HOTCAKES BECAUSE THE DRAMA CLUB IS ON THE FRONT PAGE. LOUIS'S CHARISMA CAN'T BE BEAT.
...
I HOPE I CAN STILL GET SOME GOOD SHOTS ON THE SECOND DAY.
WHY DO YOU SAY THAT ...?
ACTORS TEND TO GET OVER-CONFIDENT DURING THEIR SECOND PERFOR-MANCE.
ALTHOUGH IF LOUIS WERE TO FORGET HIS LINES OR COLLAPSE ONSTAGE OR SOMETHING, THAT WOULD MAKE A GREAT SCOOP! ♡

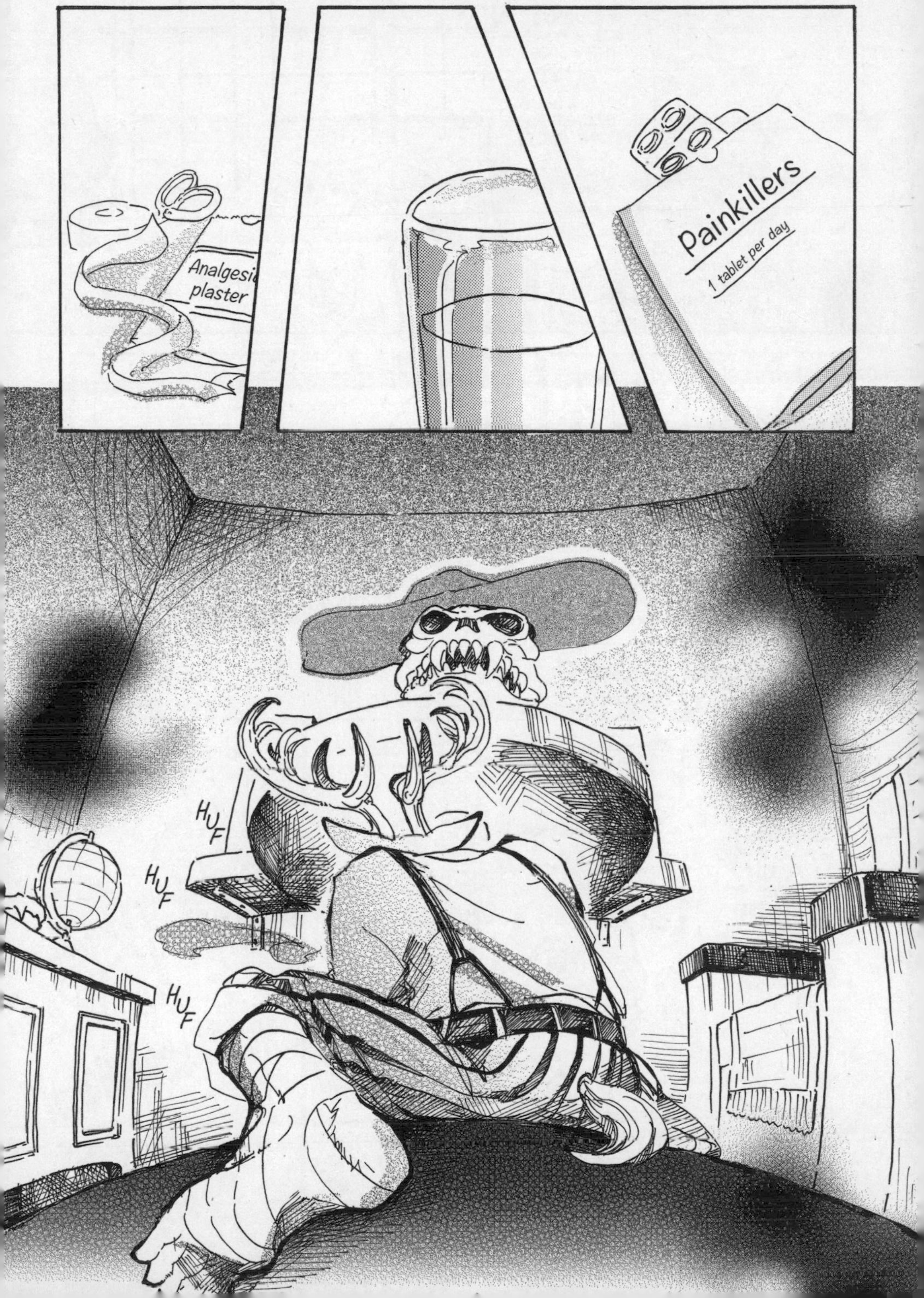
Painkillers
1 tablet per day
Analgesi
plaster
HUF
HUF
HUF

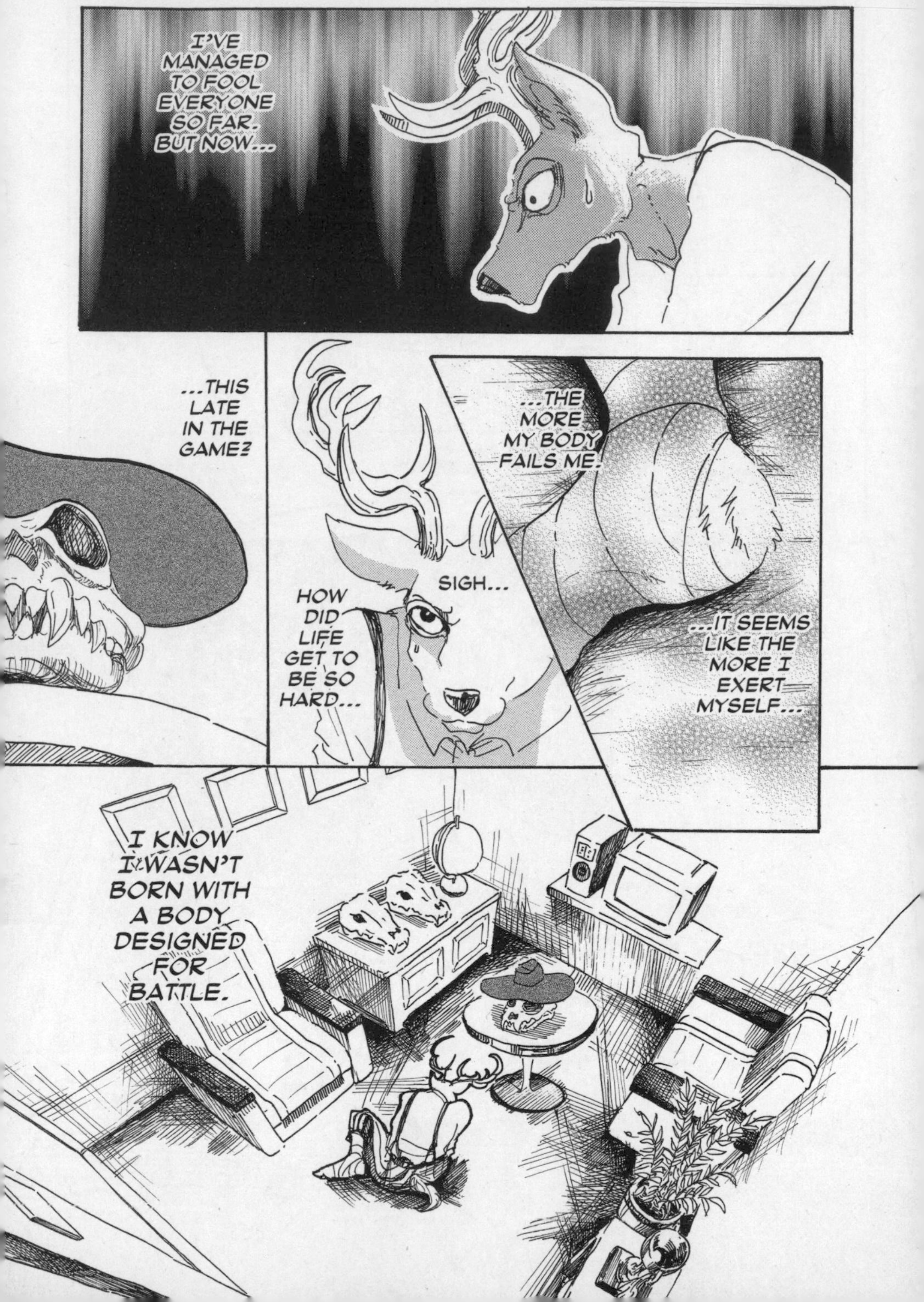
I'VE MANAGED TO FOOL EVERYONE SO FAR. BUT NOW...
...IT SEEMS LIKE THE MORE I EXERT MYSELF...
...THE MORE MY BODY FAILS ME.
SIGH...
HOW DID LIFE GET TO BE SO HARD...
...THIS LATE IN THE GAME?
I KNOW I WASN'T BORN WITH A BODY DESIGNED FOR BATTLE.

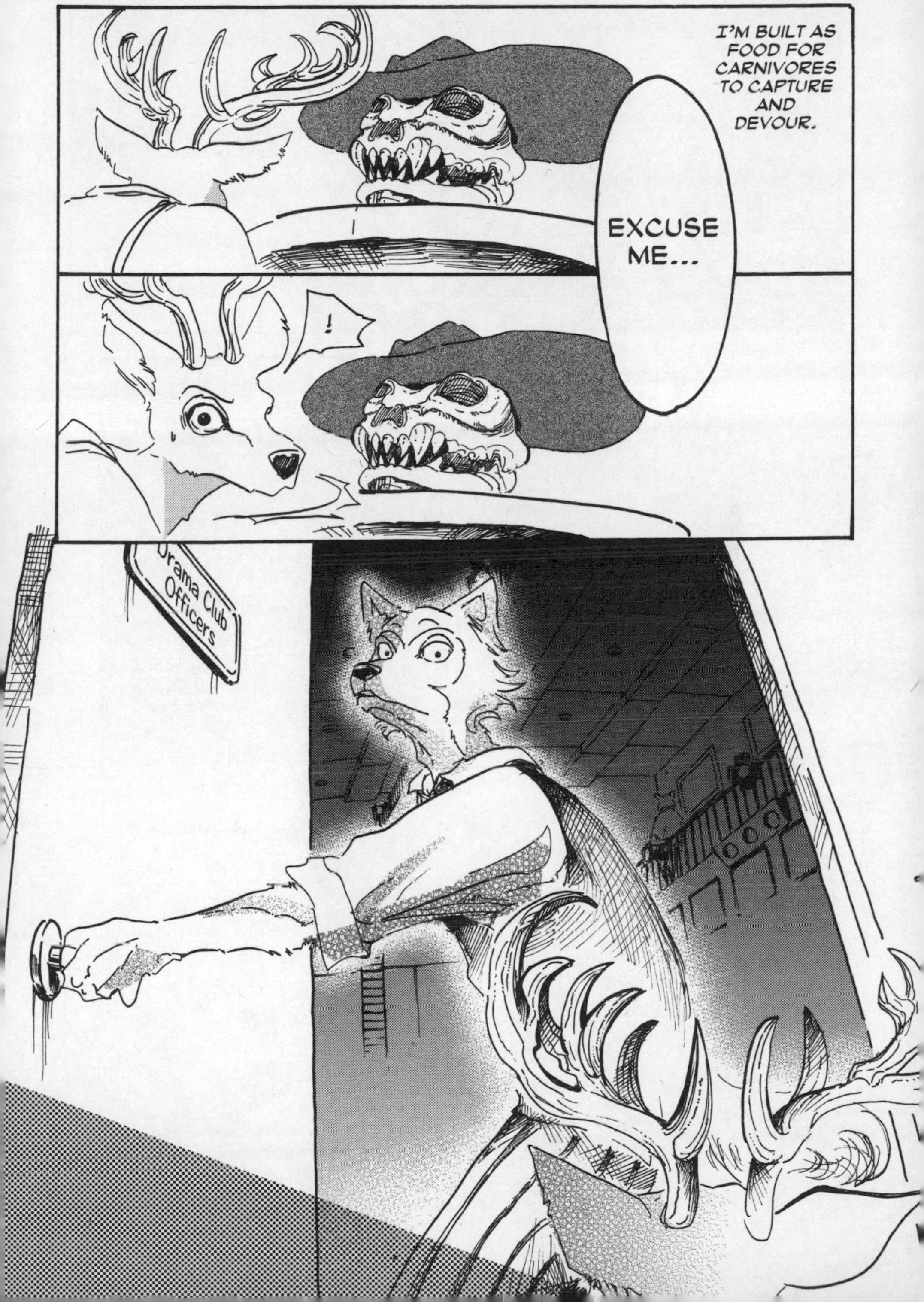
I'M BUILT AS FOOD FOR CARNIVORES TO CAPTURE AND DEVOUR.
EXCUSE ME...
!
Drama Club Officers

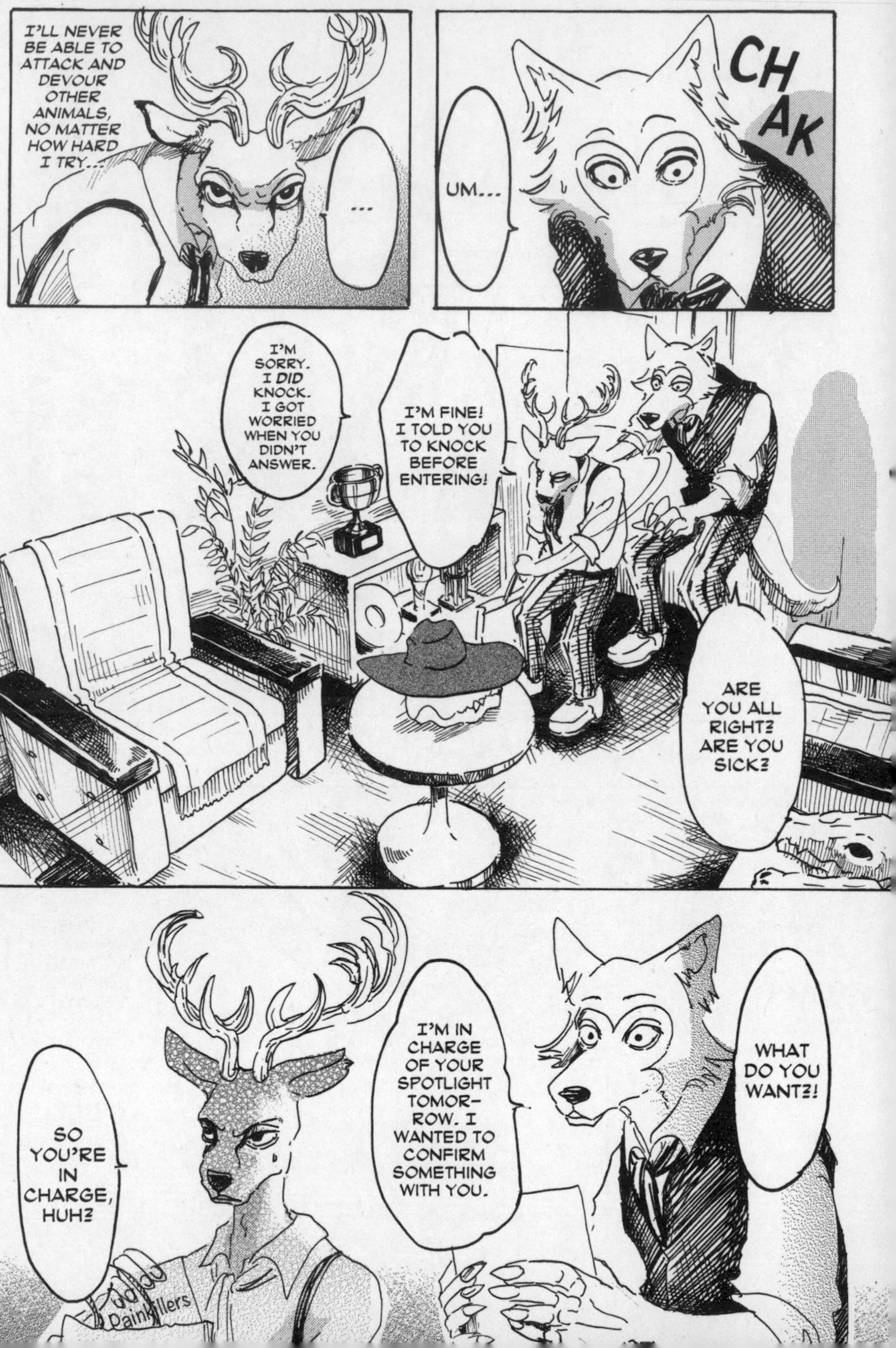
CHAK
UM...
I'LL NEVER BE ABLE TO ATTACK AND DEVOUR OTHER ANIMALS, NO MATTER HOW HARD I TRY...
...
ARE YOU ALL RIGHT? ARE YOU SICK?
I'M FINE! I TOLD YOU TO KNOCK BEFORE ENTERING!
I'M SORRY. I *DID* KNOCK. I GOT WORRIED WHEN YOU DIDN'T ANSWER.
WHAT DO YOU WANT?!
I'M IN CHARGE OF YOUR SPOTLIGHT TOMOR-ROW. I WANTED TO CONFIRM SOMETHING WITH YOU.
SO YOU'RE IN CHARGE, HUH?
Painkillers

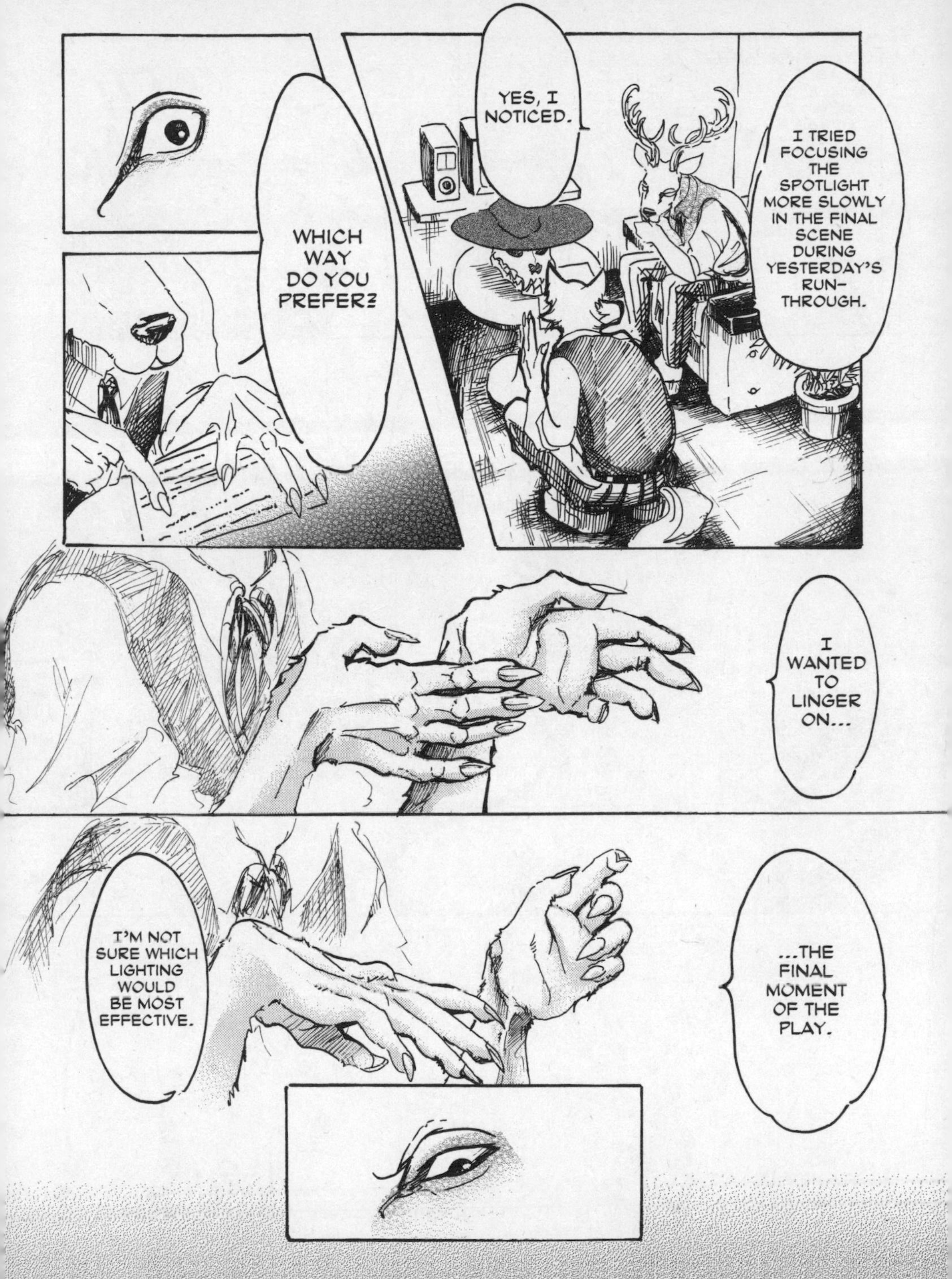
I TRIED FOCUSING THE SPOTLIGHT MORE SLOWLY IN THE FINAL SCENE DURING YESTERDAY'S RUN-THROUGH.
YES, I NOTICED.
WHICH WAY DO YOU PREFER?
I WANTED TO LINGER ON...
...THE FINAL MOMENT OF THE PLAY.
I'M NOT SURE WHICH LIGHTING WOULD BE MOST EFFECTIVE.

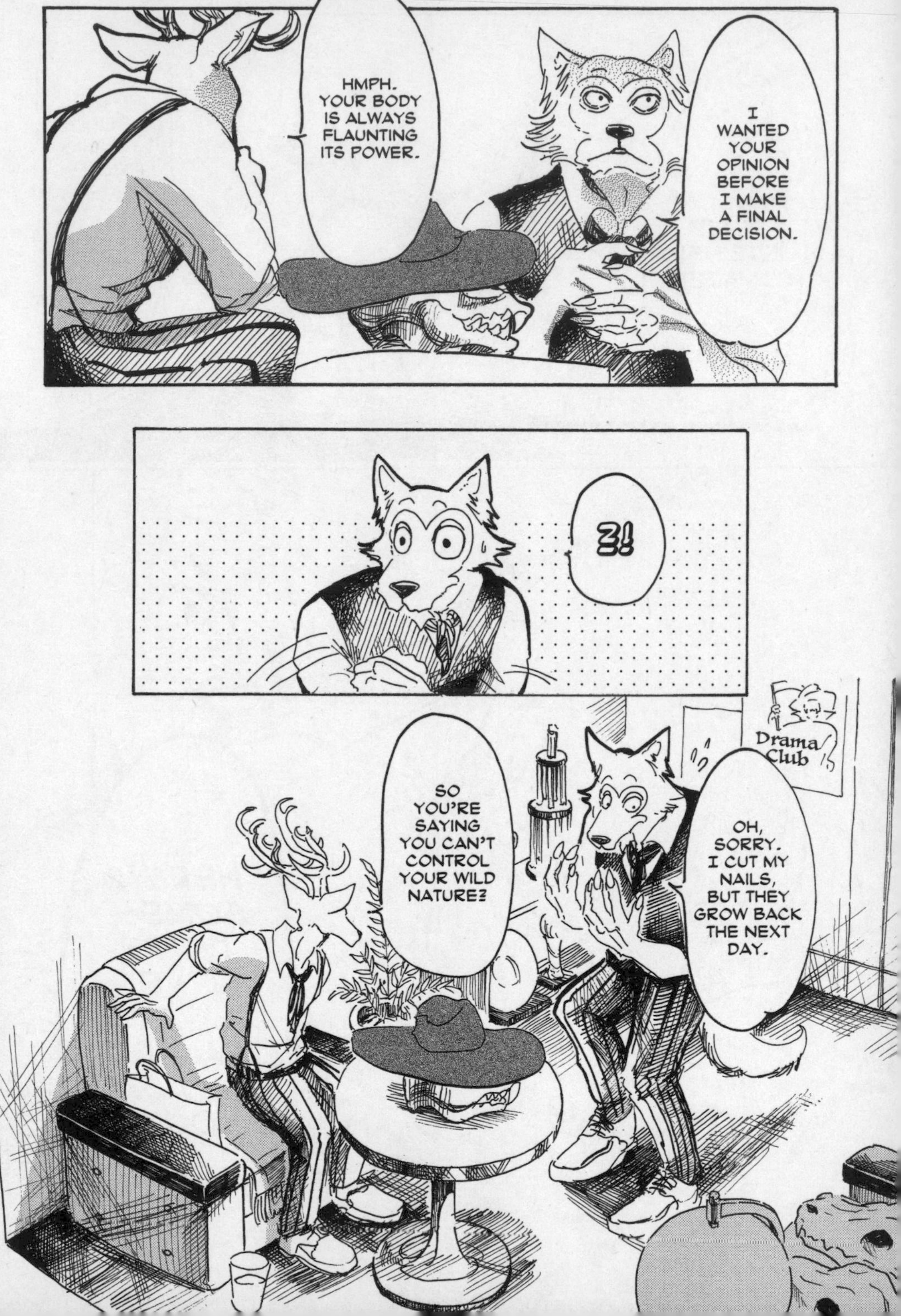
I WANTED YOUR OPINION BEFORE I MAKE A FINAL DECISION.
HMPH. YOUR BODY IS ALWAYS FLAUNTING ITS POWER.
?!
Drama Club
OH, SORRY. I CUT MY NAILS, BUT THEY GROW BACK THE NEXT DAY.
SO YOU'RE SAYING YOU CAN'T CONTROL YOUR WILD NATURE?

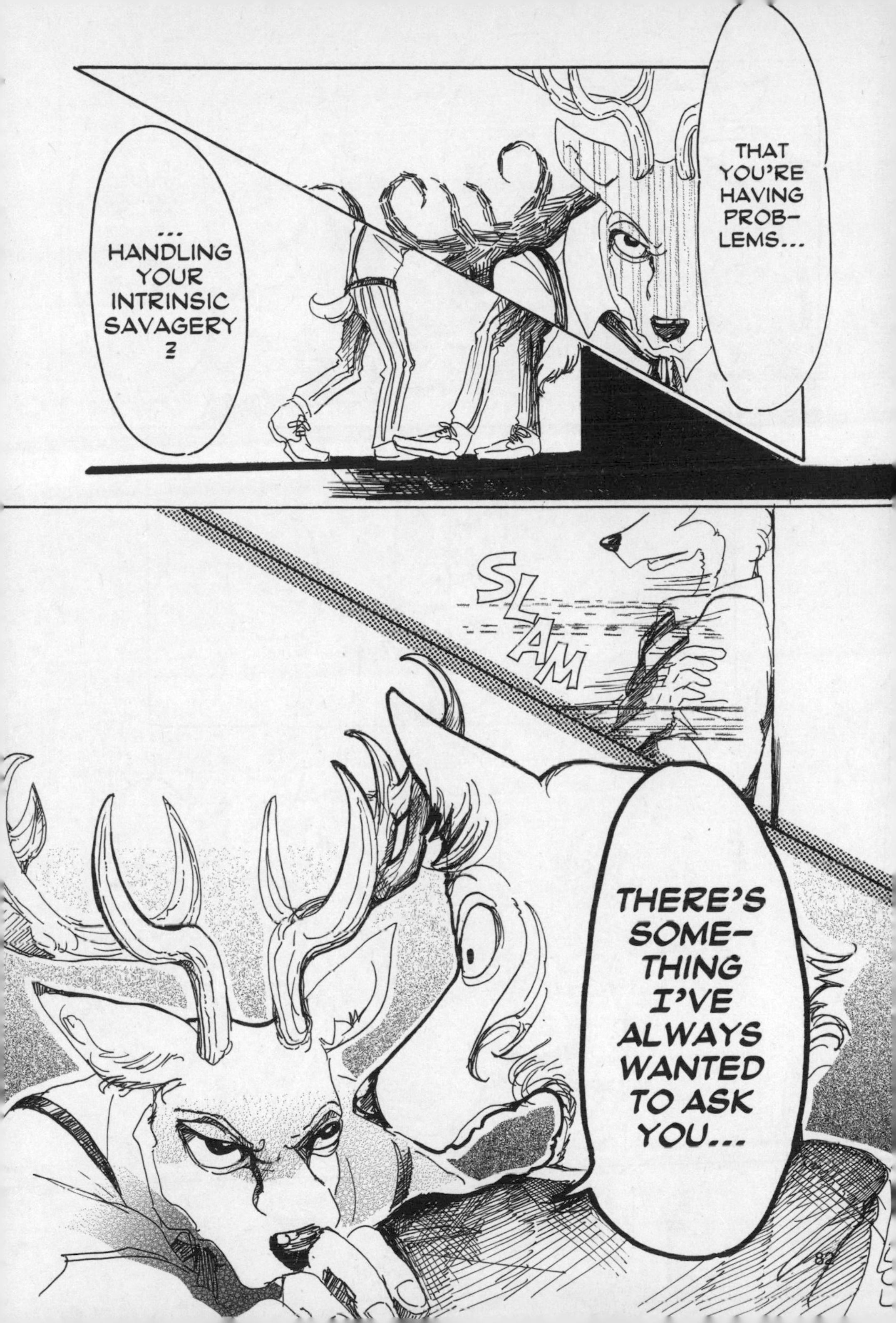
THAT YOU'RE HAVING PROB-LEMS...
...HANDLING YOUR INTRINSIC SAVAGERY?
SLAM
THERE'S SOME-THING I'VE ALWAYS WANTED TO ASK YOU...

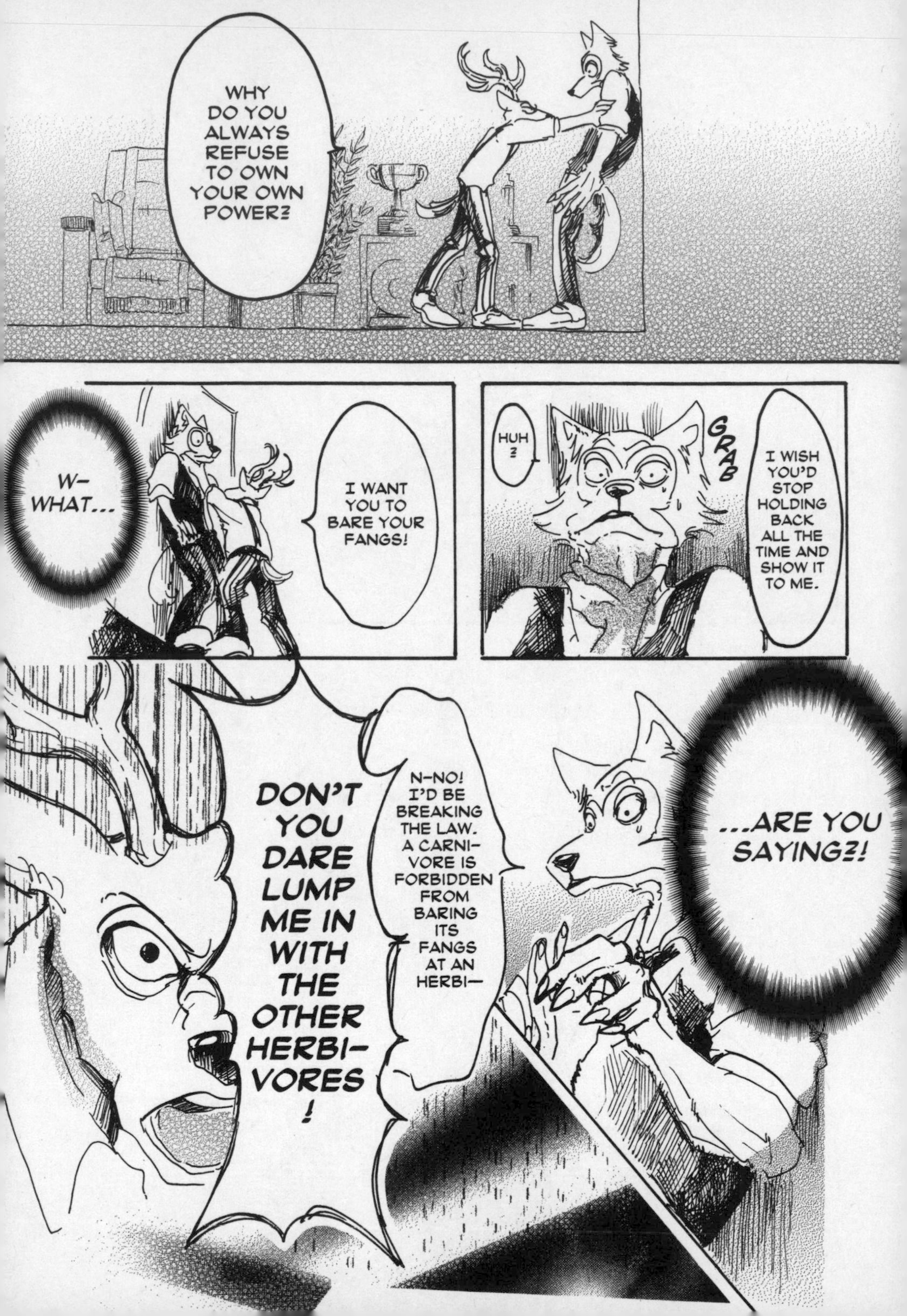
WHY DO YOU ALWAYS REFUSE TO OWN YOUR OWN POWER?
I WISH YOU'D STOP HOLDING BACK ALL THE TIME AND SHOW IT TO ME.
GRAB
HUH?
I WANT YOU TO BARE YOUR FANGS!
W-WHAT...
...ARE YOU SAYING?!
N-NO! I'D BE BREAKING THE LAW. A CARNIVORE IS FORBIDDEN FROM BARING ITS FANGS AT AN HERBI—
DON'T YOU DARE LUMP ME IN WITH THE OTHER HERBIVORES!

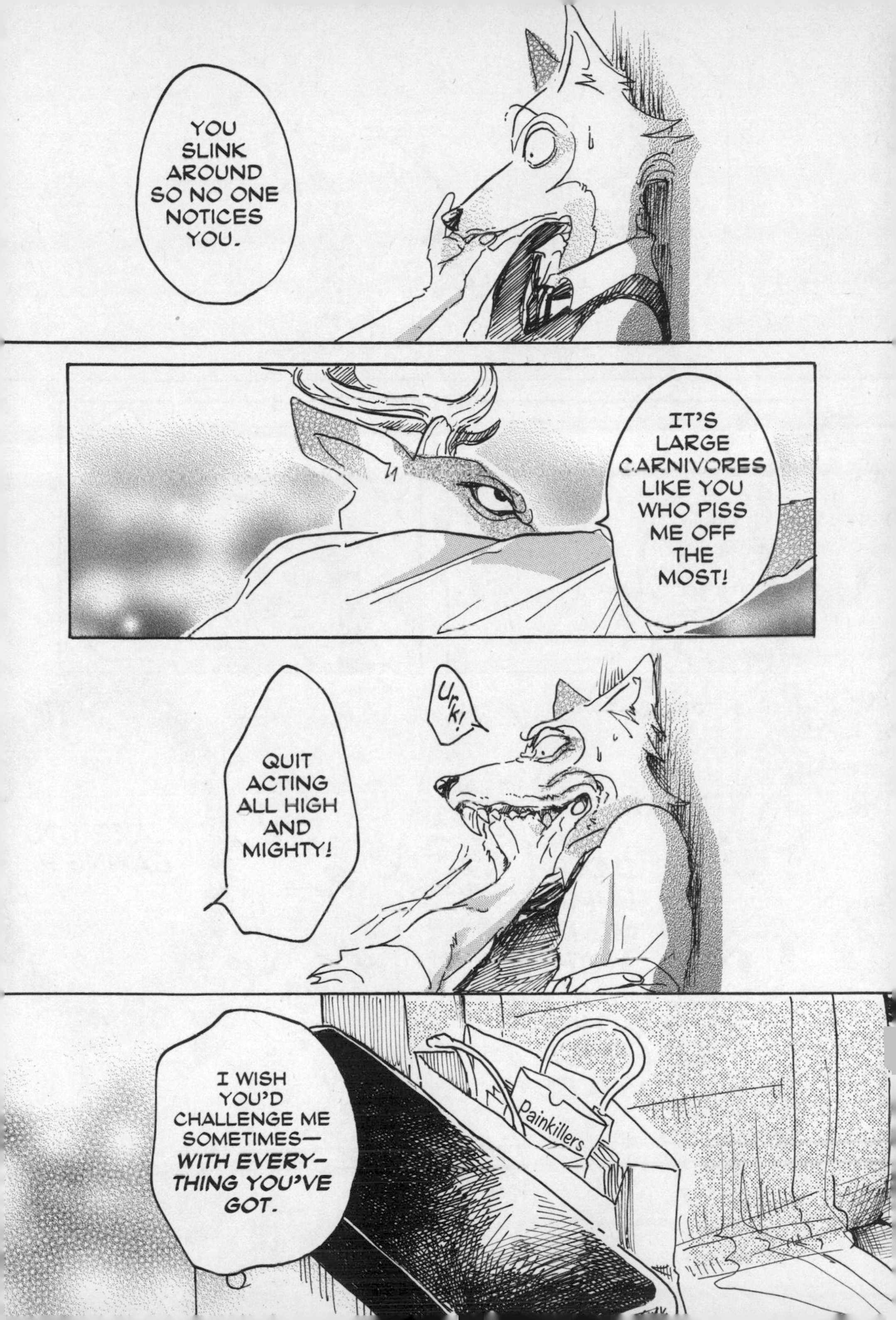
YOU SLINK AROUND SO NO ONE NOTICES YOU.
IT'S LARGE CARNIVORES LIKE YOU WHO PISS ME OFF THE MOST!
Urk!
QUIT ACTING ALL HIGH AND MIGHTY!
I WISH YOU'D CHALLENGE ME SOMETIMES— *WITH EVERY-THING YOU'VE GOT.*
Painkillers

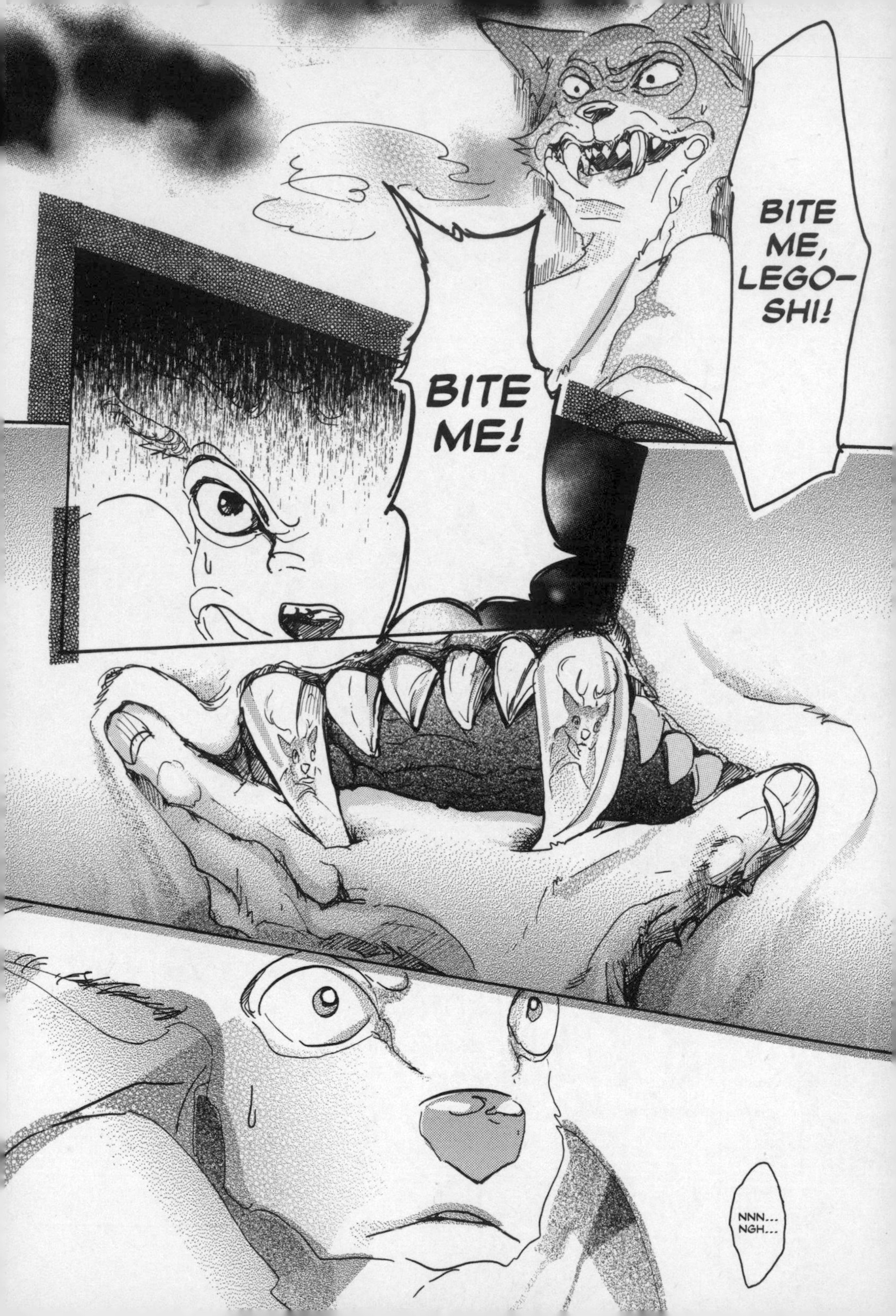
BITE ME, LEGO-SHI!
BITE ME!
NNN... NGH...

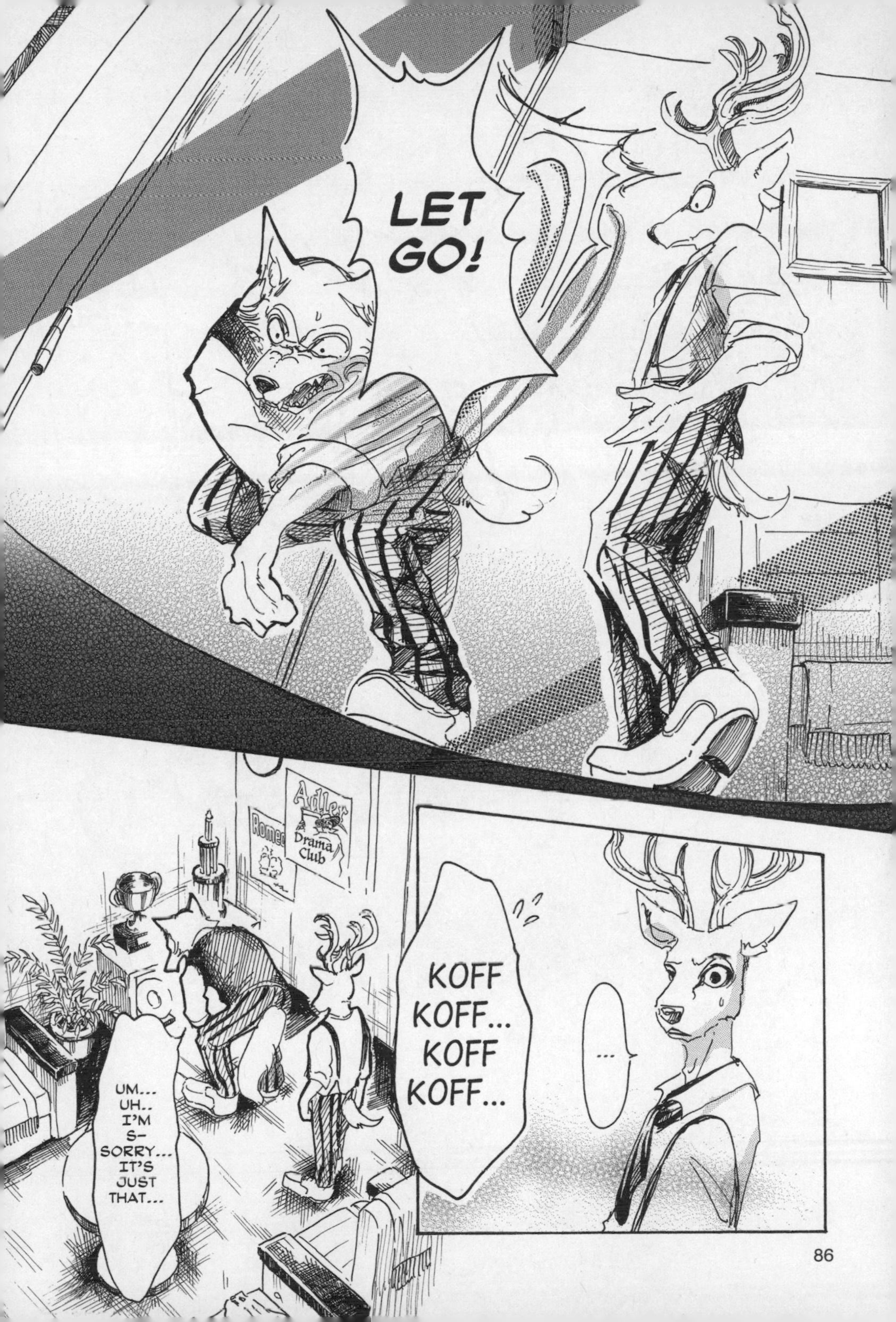
LET GO!
...
KOFF KOFF... KOFF KOFF...
Adler Drama Club
Romeo
UM... UH.. I'M S-SORRY... IT'S JUST THAT...

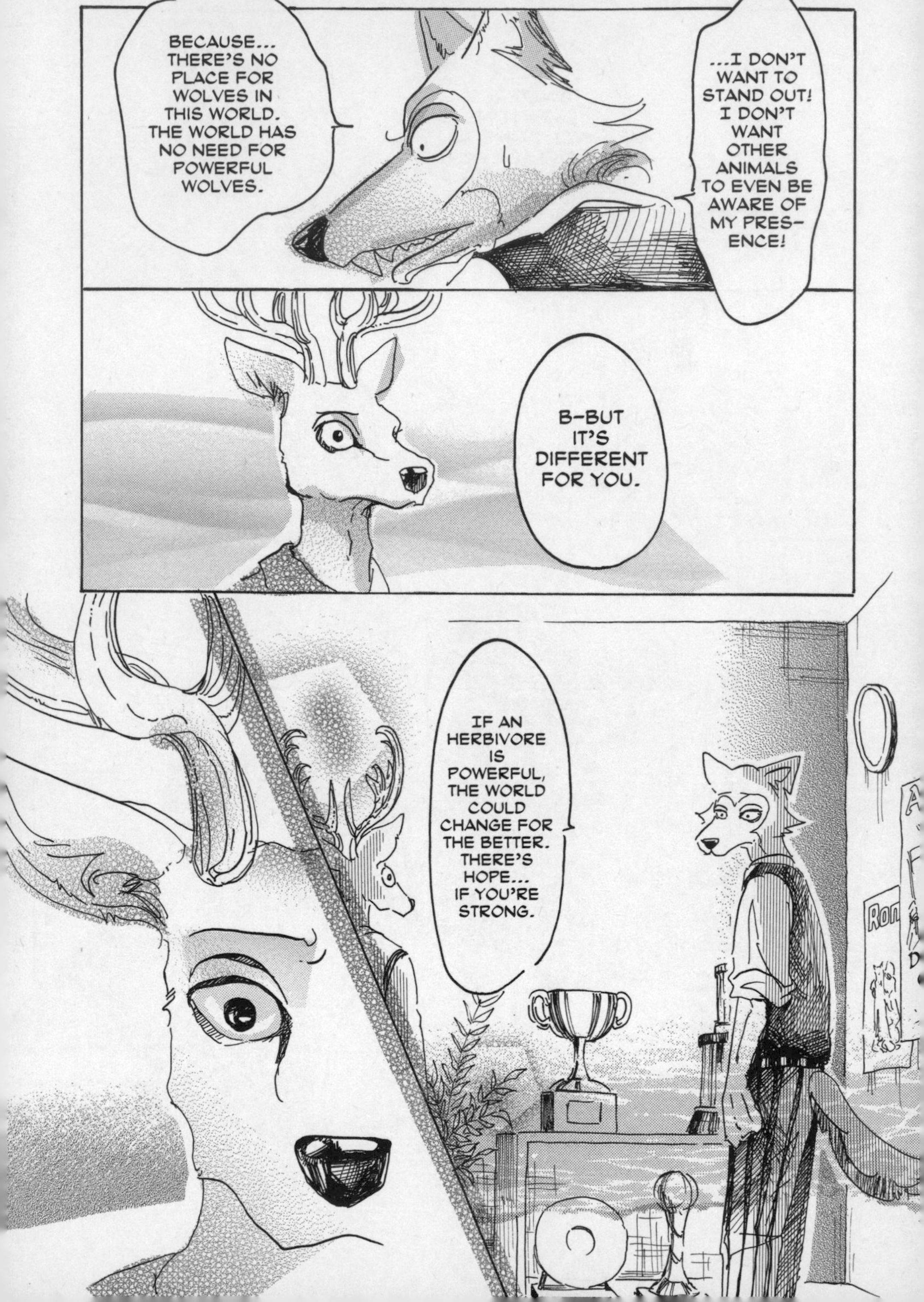
...I DON'T WANT TO STAND OUT! I DON'T WANT OTHER ANIMALS TO EVEN BE AWARE OF MY PRES-ENCE!
BECAUSE... THERE'S NO PLACE FOR WOLVES IN THIS WORLD. THE WORLD HAS NO NEED FOR POWERFUL WOLVES.
B-BUT IT'S DIFFERENT FOR YOU.
IF AN HERBIVORE IS POWERFUL, THE WORLD COULD CHANGE FOR THE BETTER. THERE'S HOPE... IF YOU'RE STRONG.

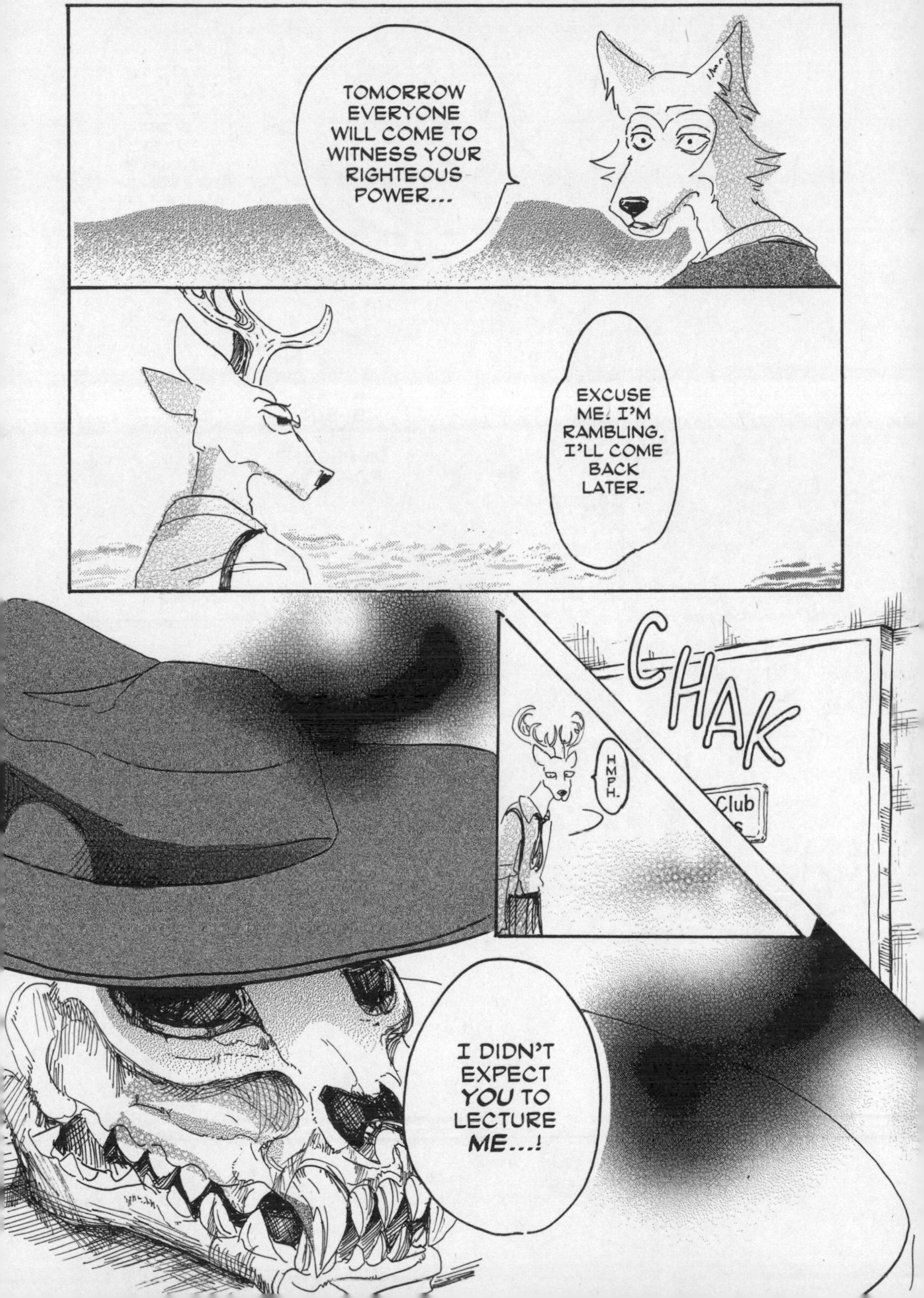
TOMORROW EVERYONE WILL COME TO WITNESS YOUR RIGHTEOUS POWER...
EXCUSE ME. I'M RAMBLING. I'LL COME BACK LATER.
CHAK
HMPH.
Club
I DIDN'T EXPECT *YOU* TO LECTURE *ME*...!

Chapter 12: Dazzling Dictatorship

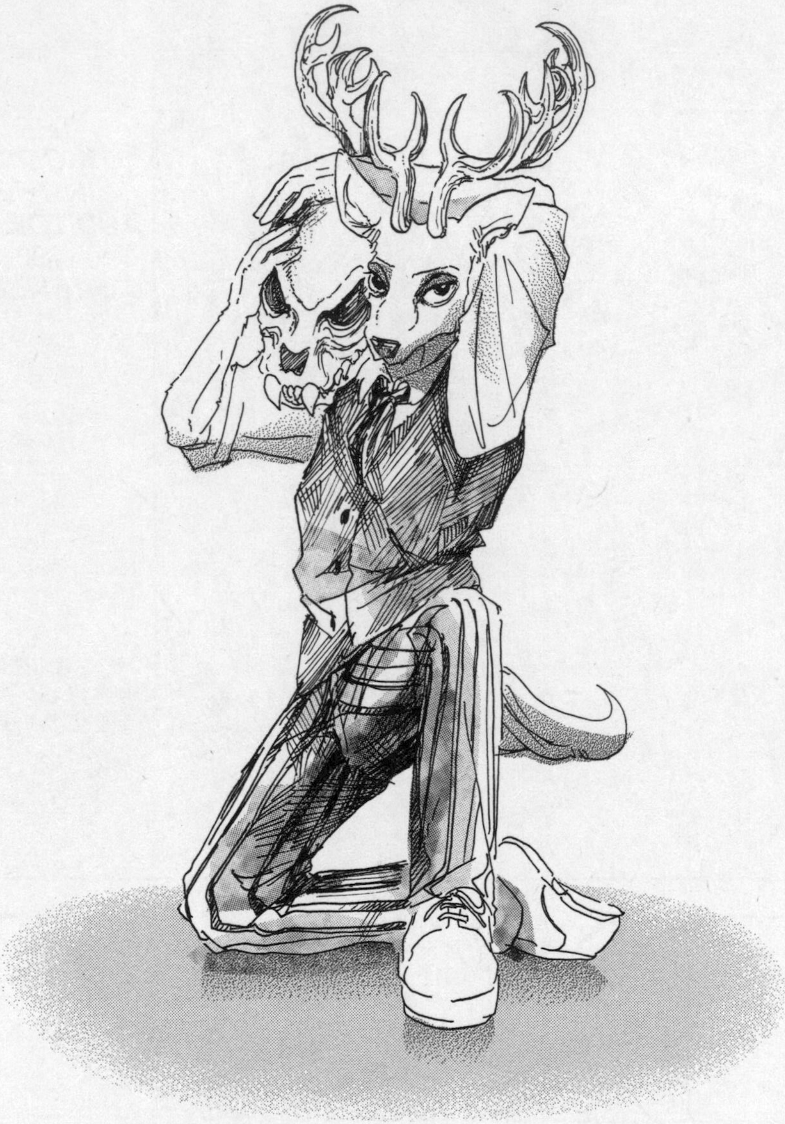

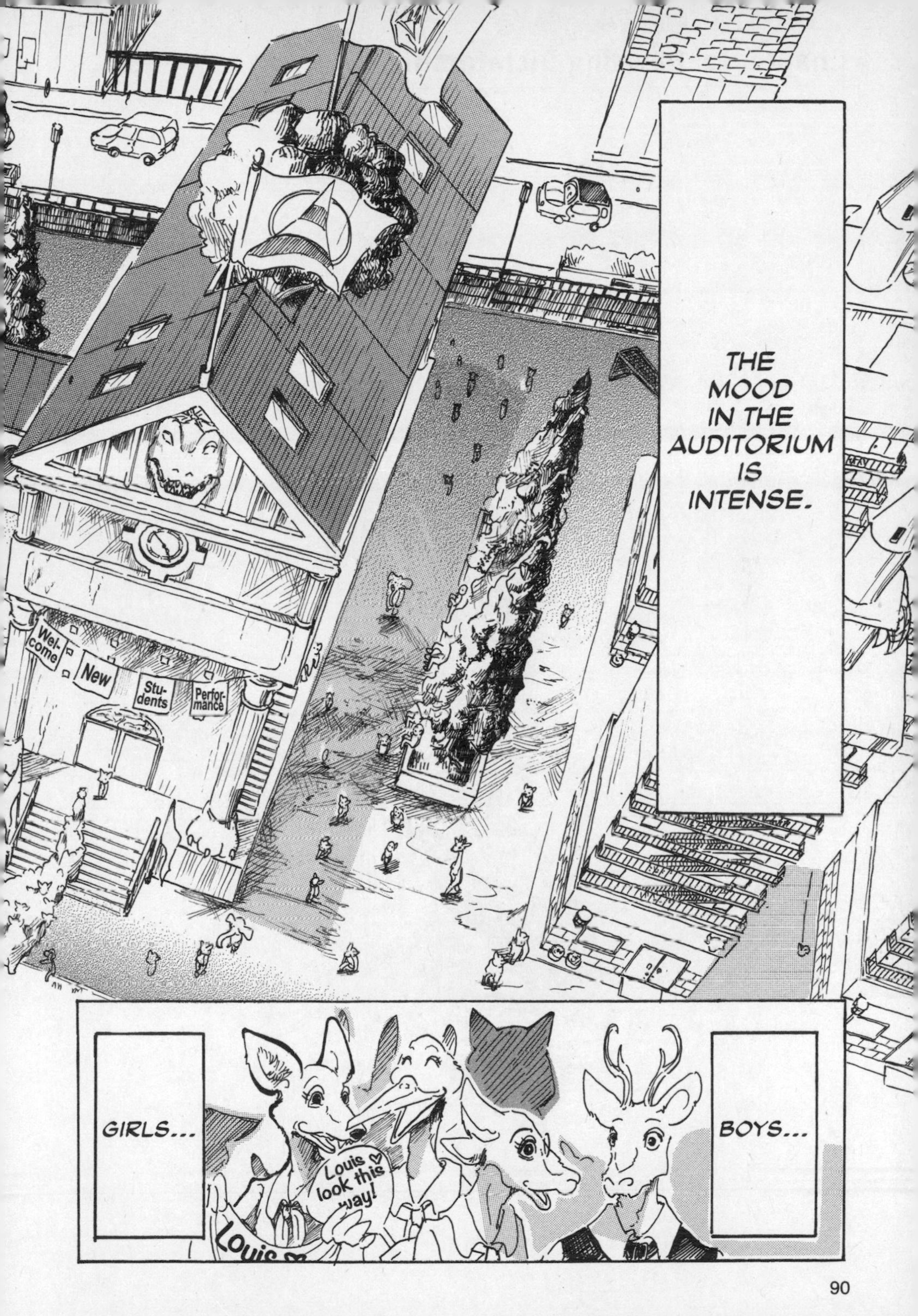
THE MOOD IN THE AUDITORIUM IS INTENSE.
Wel-come
New
Stu-dents
Perfor-mance
BOYS...
GIRLS...
Louis ♡ look this way!
Louis ♡

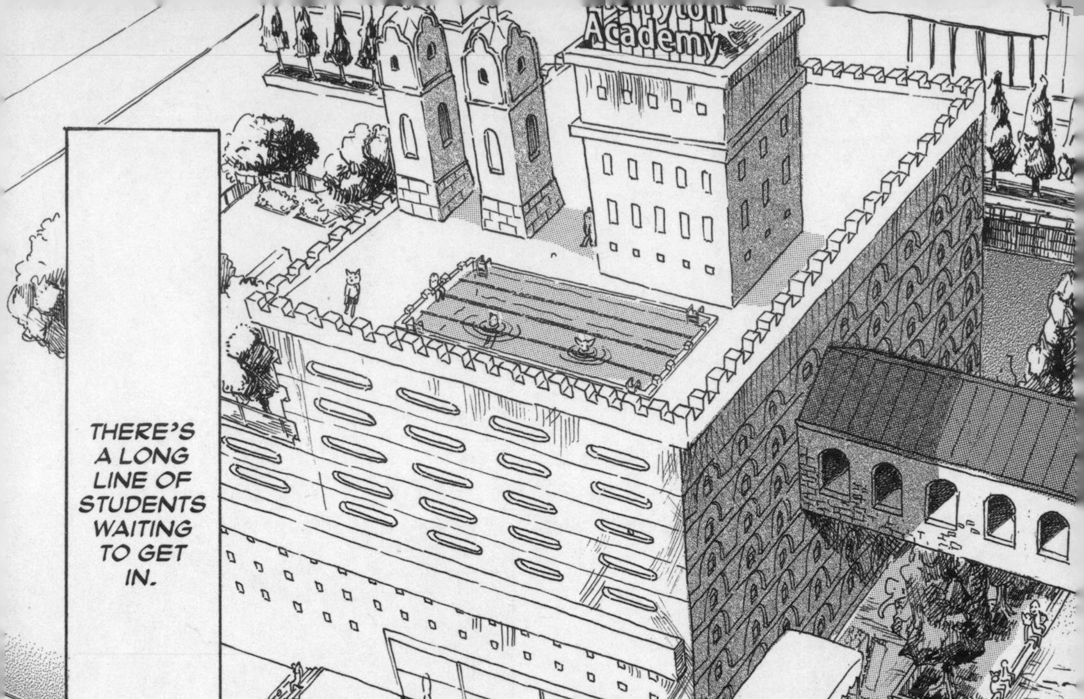
Academy
THERE'S A LONG LINE OF STUDENTS WAITING TO GET IN.

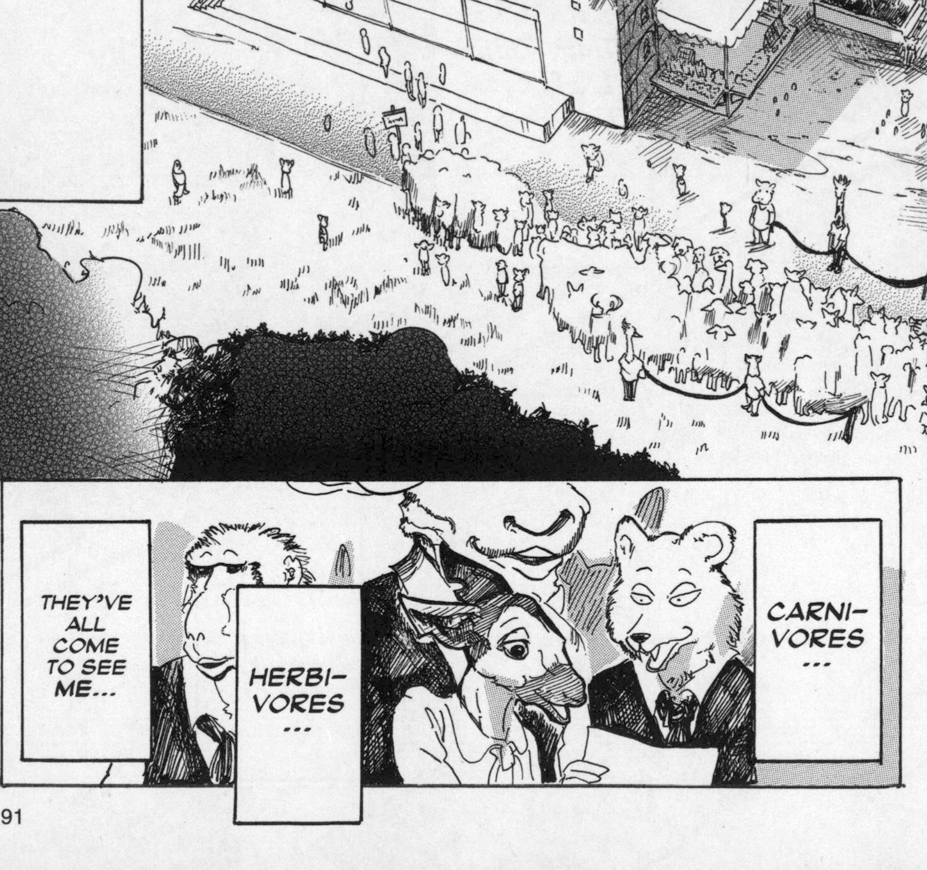
CARNI-VORES...
HERBI-VORES...
THEY'VE ALL COME TO SEE ME...

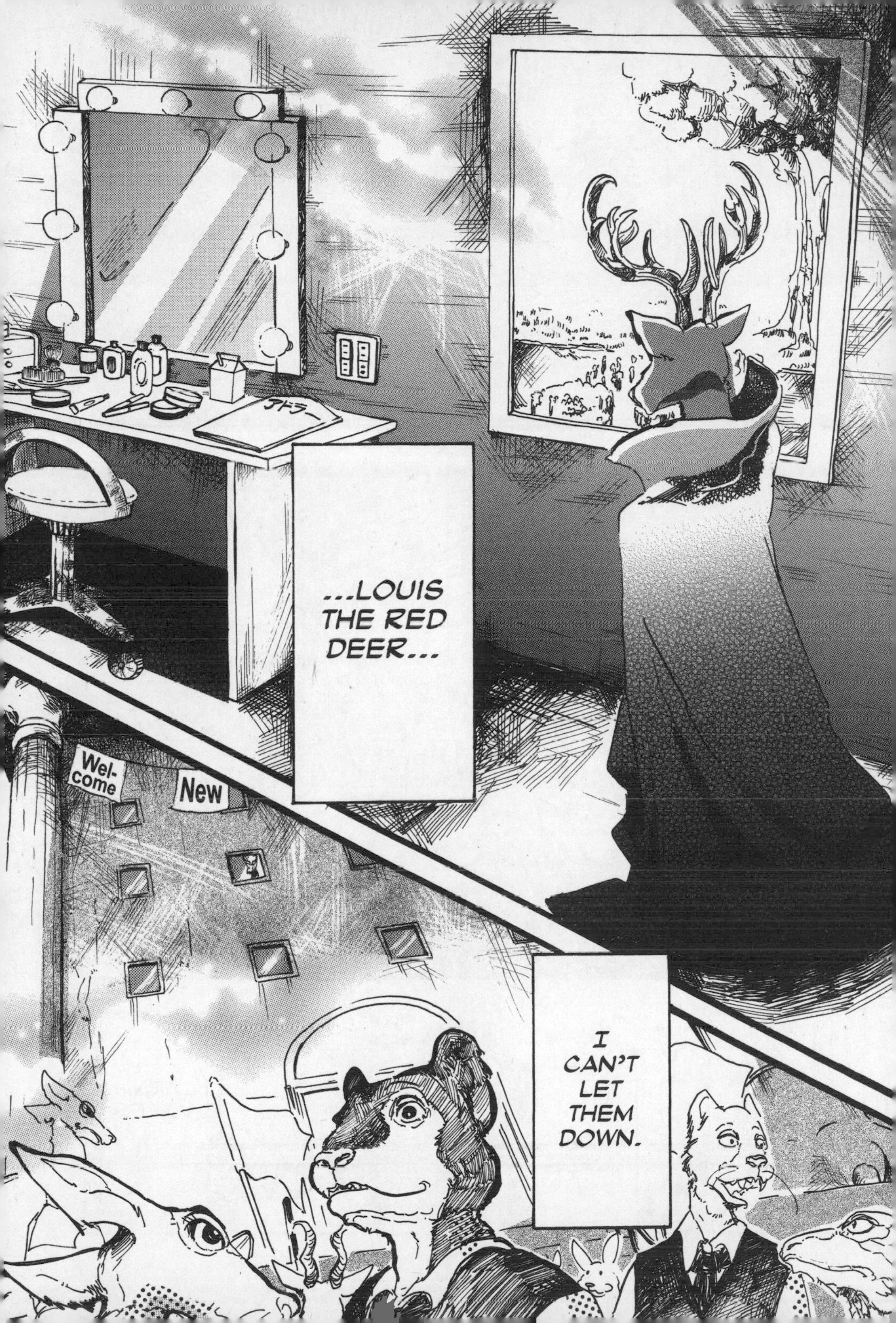
アドラー
...LOUIS THE RED DEER...
Wel-come
New
I CAN'T LET THEM DOWN.

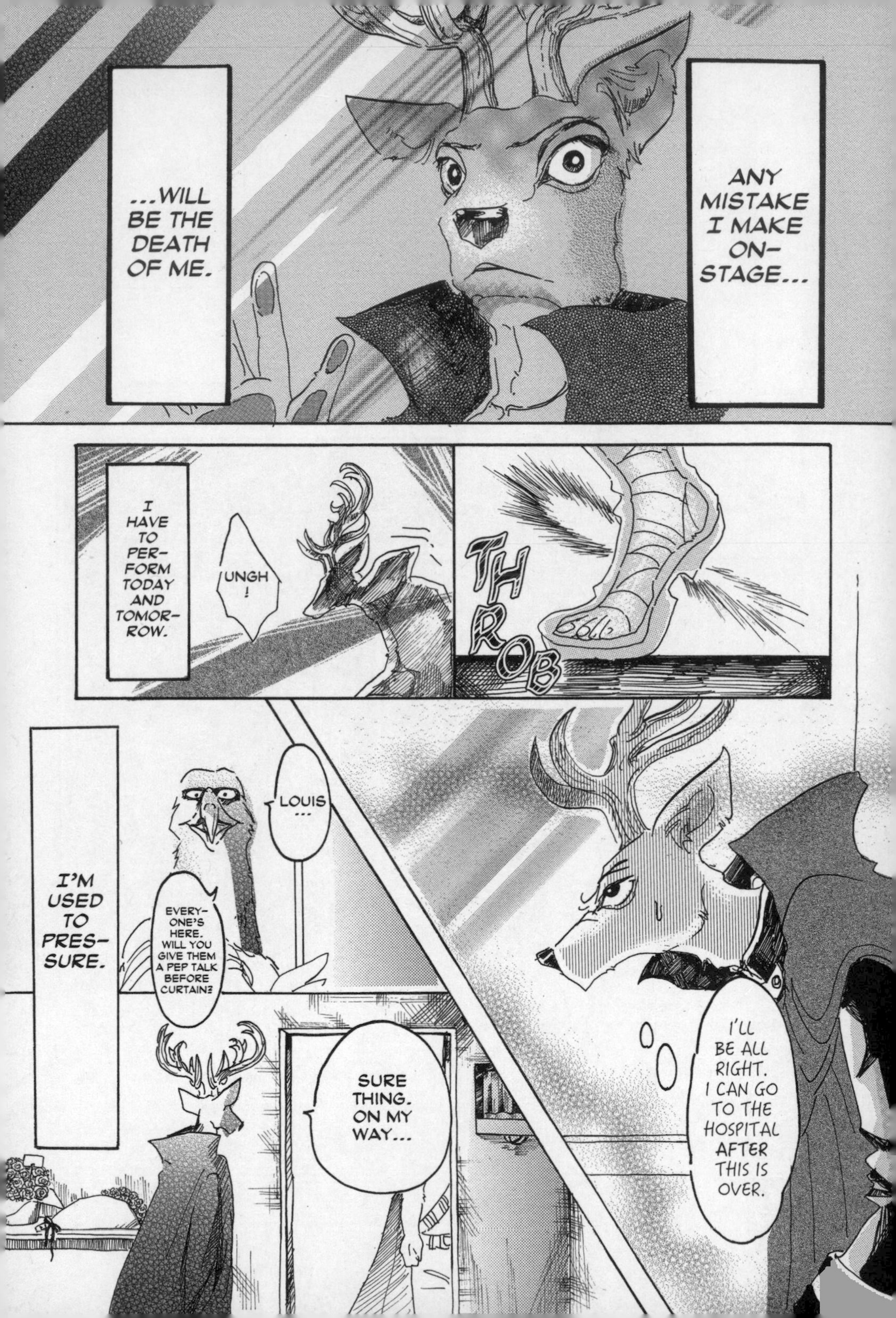
ANY MISTAKE I MAKE ON-STAGE...
...WILL BE THE DEATH OF ME.
THROB
I HAVE TO PER-FORM TODAY AND TOMOR-ROW.
UNGH!
I'LL BE ALL RIGHT. I CAN GO TO THE HOSPITAL AFTER THIS IS OVER.
LOUIS...
EVERY-ONE'S HERE. WILL YOU GIVE THEM A PEP TALK BEFORE CURTAIN?
I'M USED TO PRES-SURE.
SURE THING. ON MY WAY...

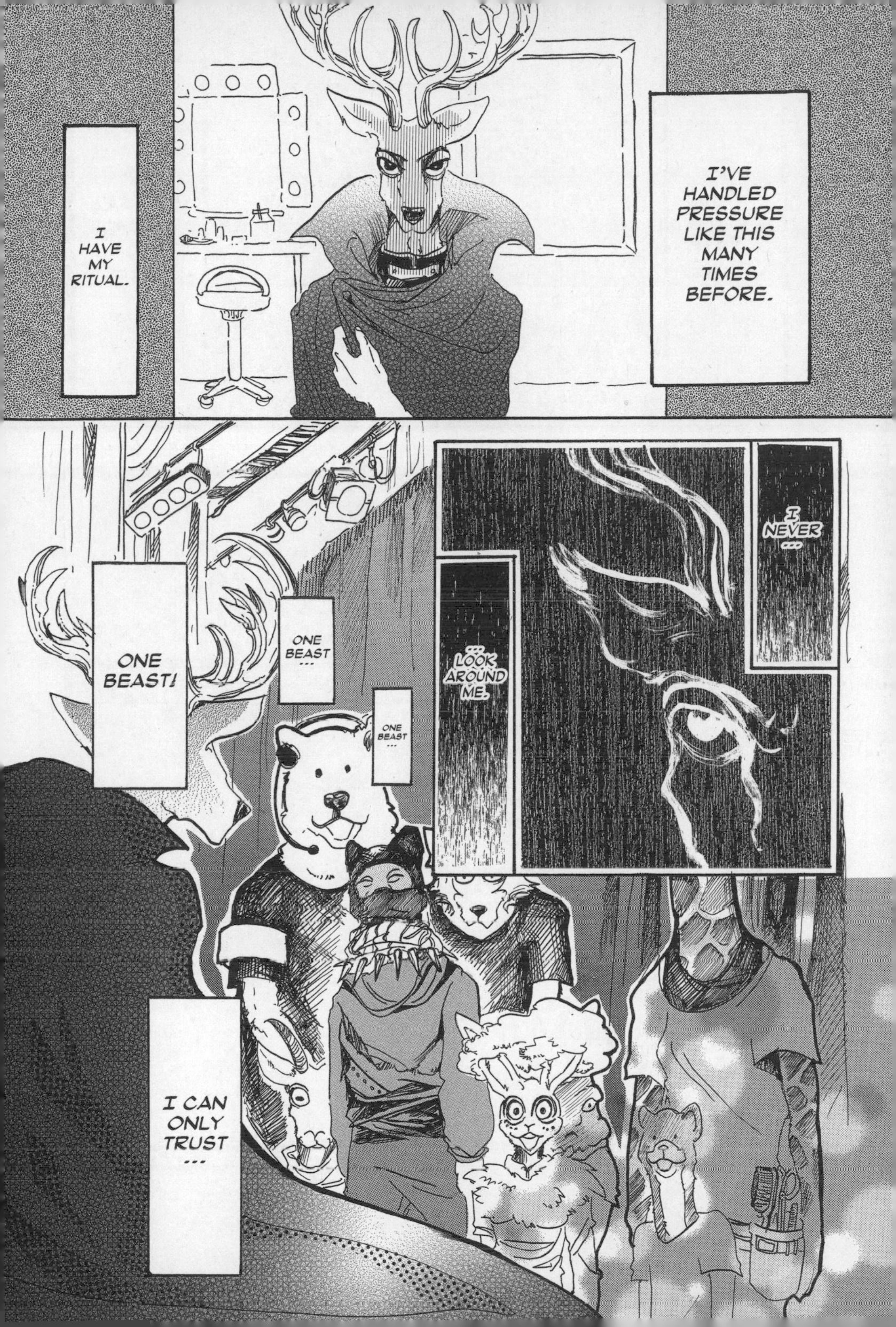
I'VE HANDLED PRESSURE LIKE THIS MANY TIMES BEFORE.
I HAVE MY RITUAL.
I NEVER...
...LOOK AROUND ME.
ONE BEAST!
ONE BEAST...
ONE BEAST...
I CAN ONLY TRUST...

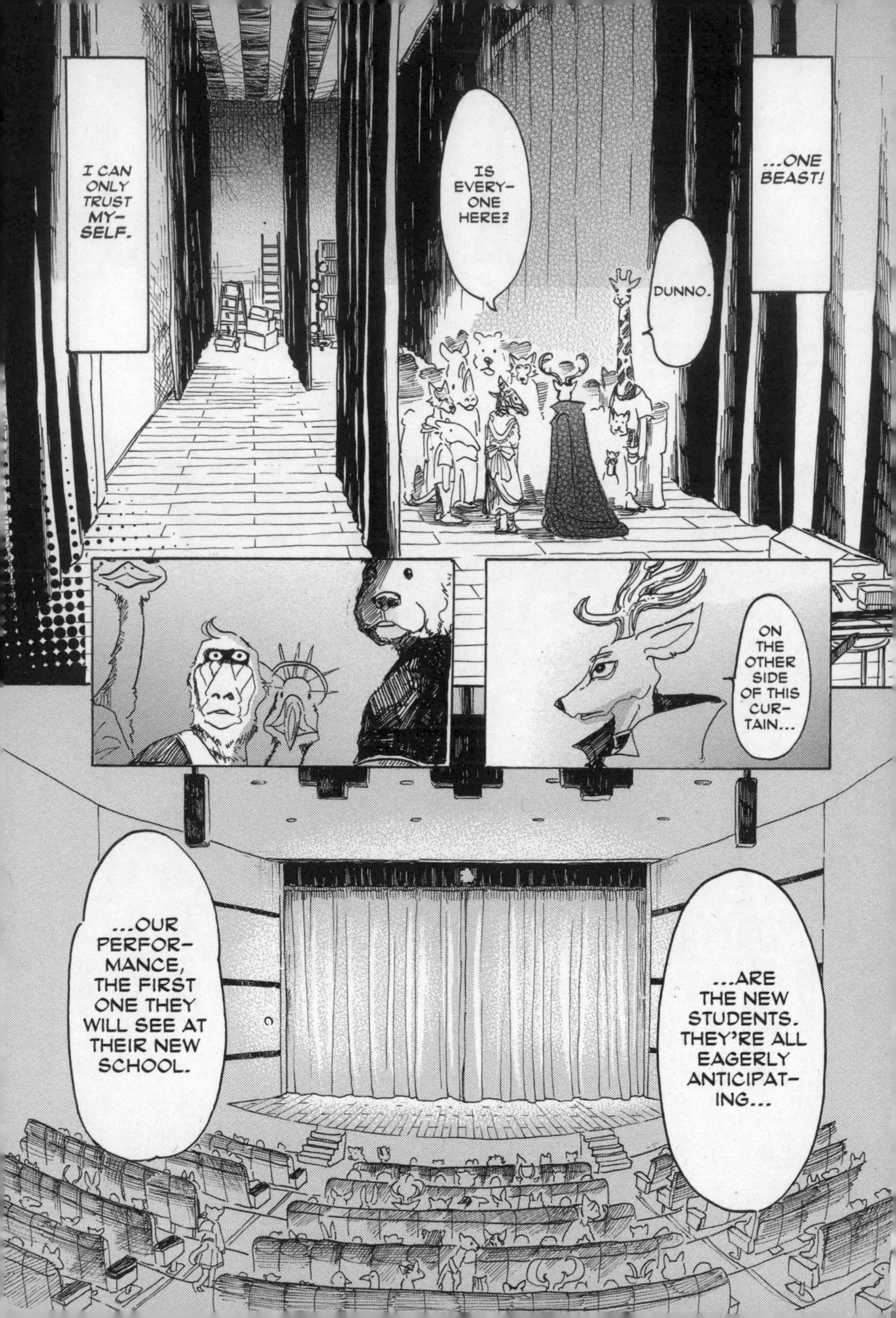
...ONE BEAST!
IS EVERY-ONE HERE?
DUNNO.
I CAN ONLY TRUST MY-SELF.
ON THE OTHER SIDE OF THIS CUR-TAIN...
...ARE THE NEW STUDENTS. THEY'RE ALL EAGERLY ANTICIPAT-ING...
...OUR PERFOR-MANCE, THE FIRST ONE THEY WILL SEE AT THEIR NEW SCHOOL.

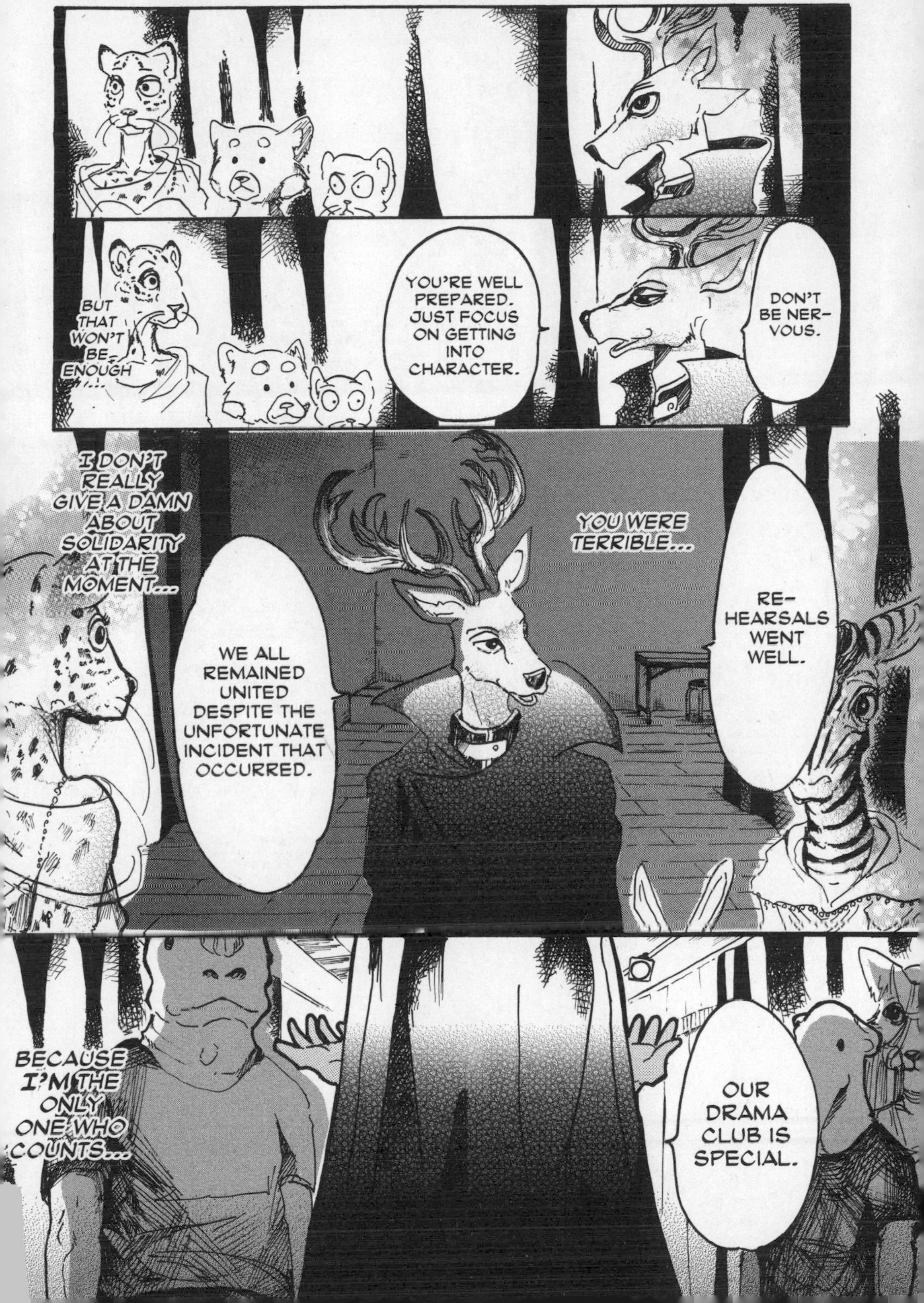
DON'T BE NERVOUS.
YOU'RE WELL PREPARED. JUST FOCUS ON GETTING INTO CHARACTER.
BUT THAT WON'T BE ENOUGH...
REHEARSALS WENT WELL.
YOU WERE TERRIBLE...
WE ALL REMAINED UNITED DESPITE THE UNFORTUNATE INCIDENT THAT OCCURRED.
I DON'T REALLY GIVE A DAMN ABOUT SOLIDARITY AT THE MOMENT...
OUR DRAMA CLUB IS SPECIAL.
BECAUSE I'M THE ONLY ONE WHO COUNTS...

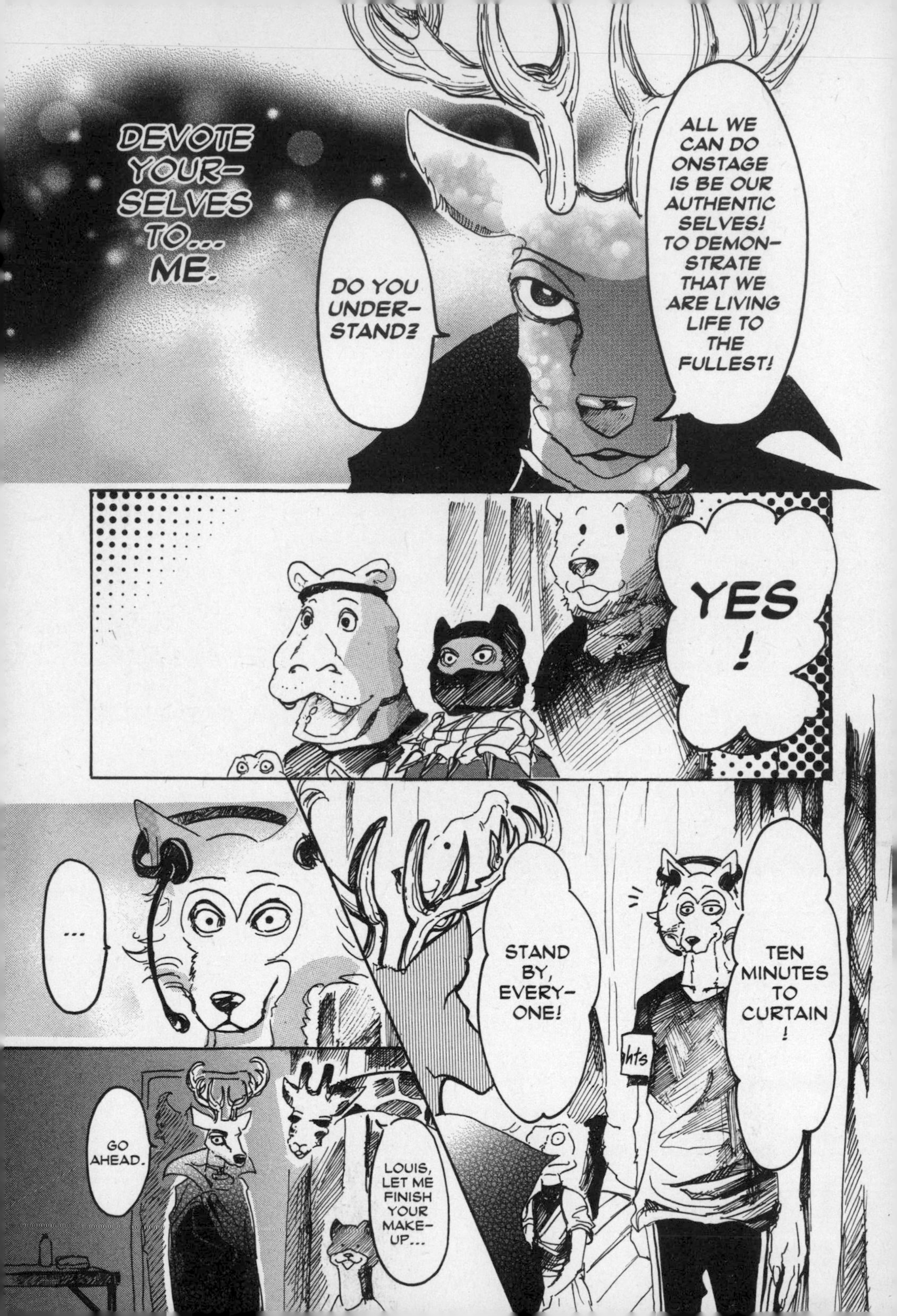
ALL WE CAN DO ONSTAGE IS BE OUR AUTHENTIC SELVES! TO DEMONSTRATE THAT WE ARE LIVING LIFE TO THE FULLEST!
DO YOU UNDERSTAND?
DEVOTE YOURSELVES TO... ME.
YES!
TEN MINUTES TO CURTAIN!
STAND BY, EVERYONE!
...
LOUIS, LET ME FINISH YOUR MAKE-UP...
GO AHEAD.

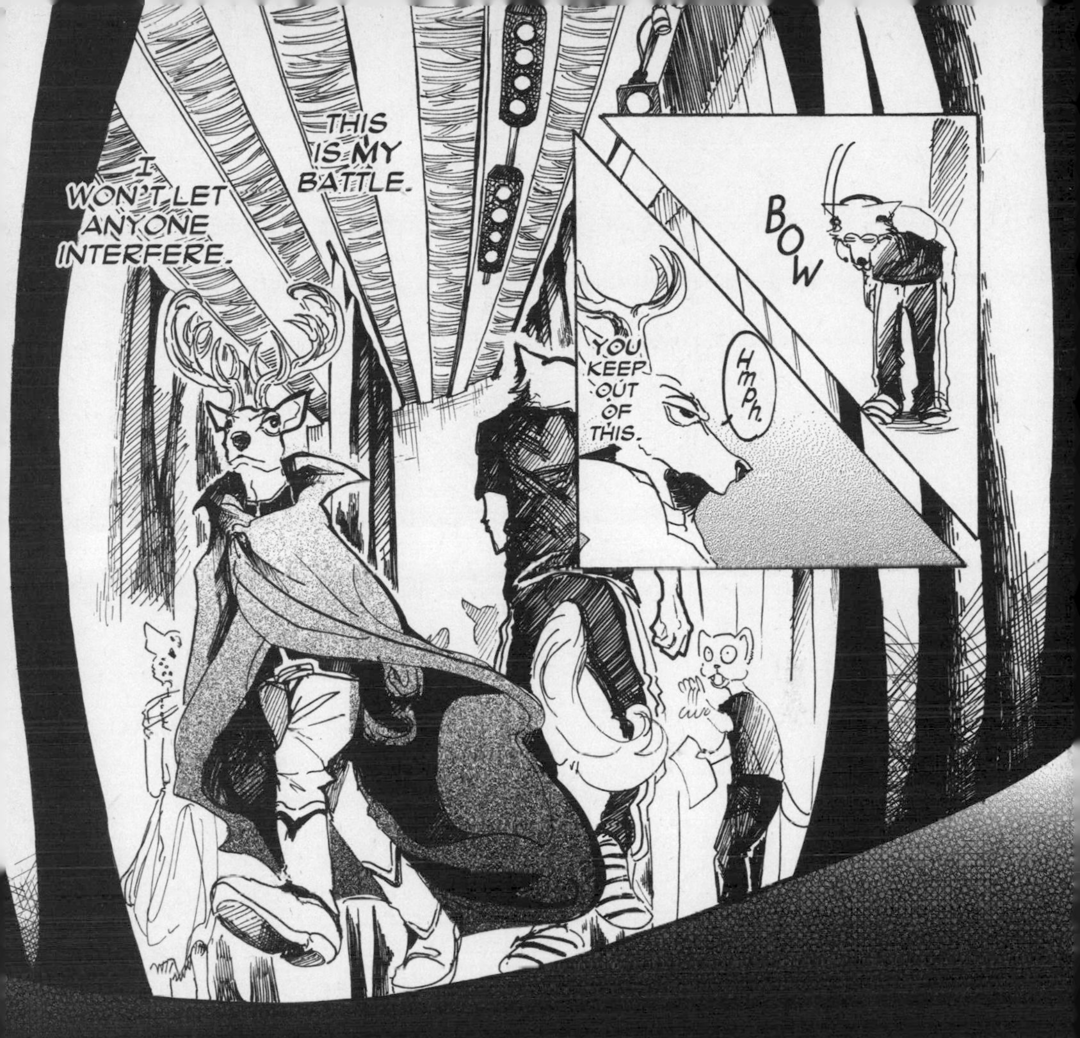
BOW
Hmph
YOU KEEP OUT OF THIS.
THIS IS MY BATTLE.
I WON'T LET ANYONE INTERFERE.

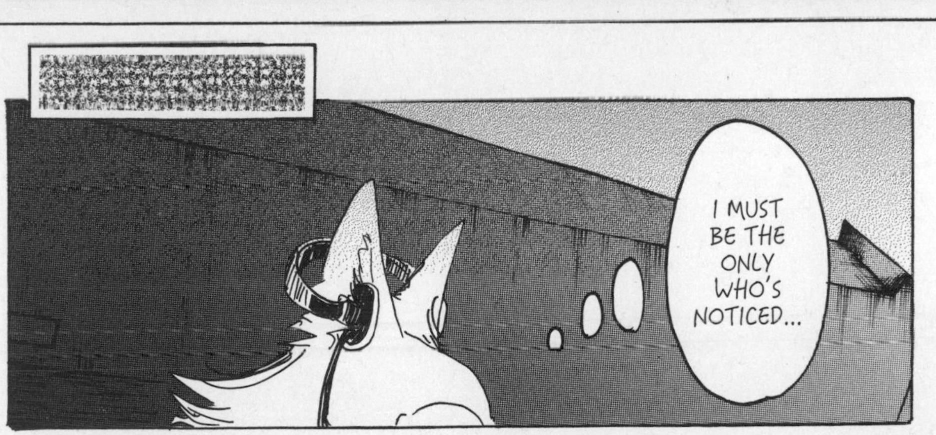
I MUST BE THE ONLY WHO'S NOTICED...

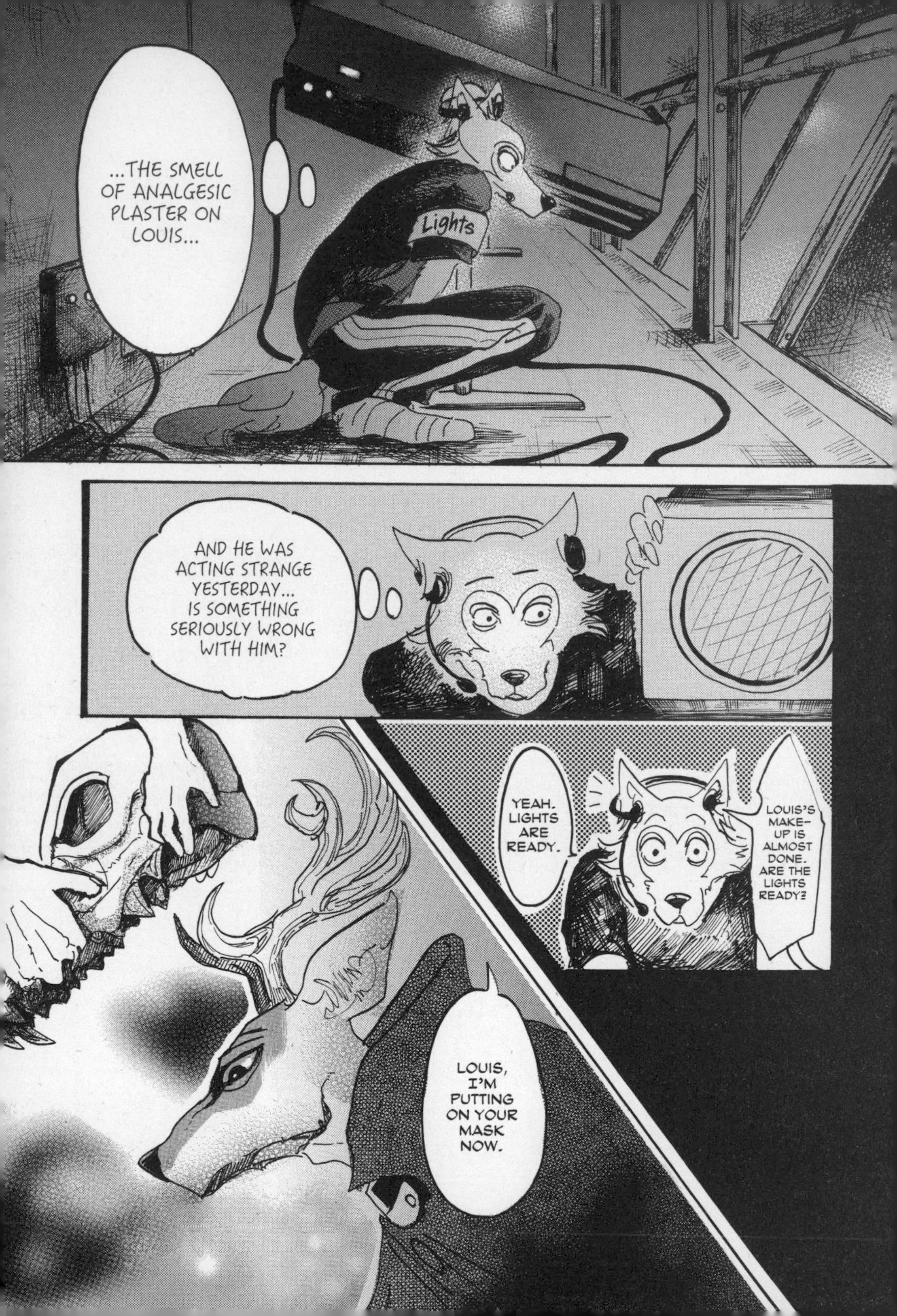
...THE SMELL OF ANALGESIC PLASTER ON LOUIS...
Lights
AND HE WAS ACTING STRANGE YESTERDAY... IS SOMETHING SERIOUSLY WRONG WITH HIM?
LOUIS'S MAKE-UP IS ALMOST DONE. ARE THE LIGHTS READY?
YEAH. LIGHTS ARE READY.
LOUIS, I'M PUTTING ON YOUR MASK NOW.

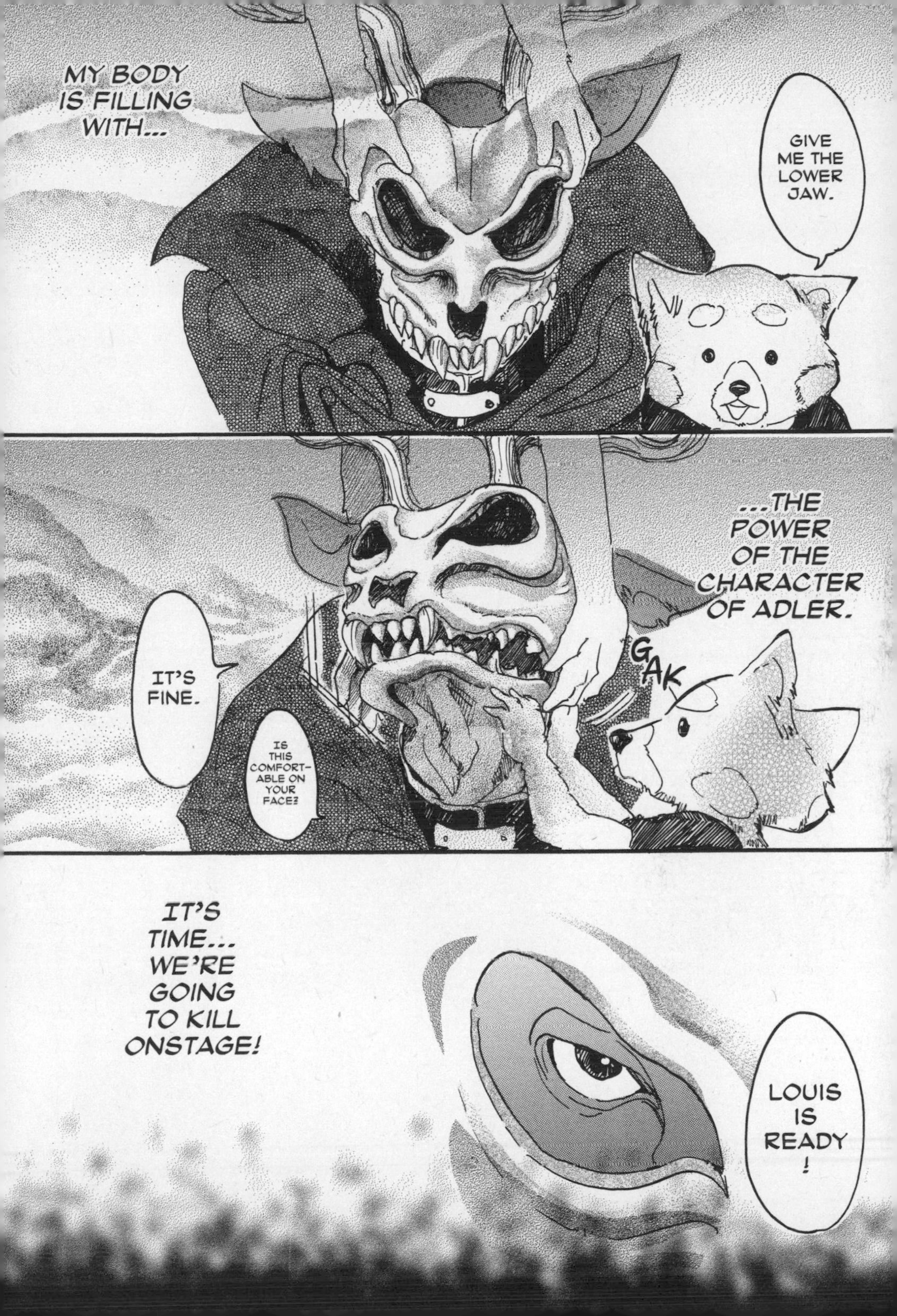
GIVE ME THE LOWER JAW.
MY BODY IS FILLING WITH...
...THE POWER OF THE CHARACTER OF ADLER.
GAK
IT'S FINE.
IS THIS COMFORTABLE ON YOUR FACE?
LOUIS IS READY!
IT'S TIME... WE'RE GOING TO KILL ONSTAGE!

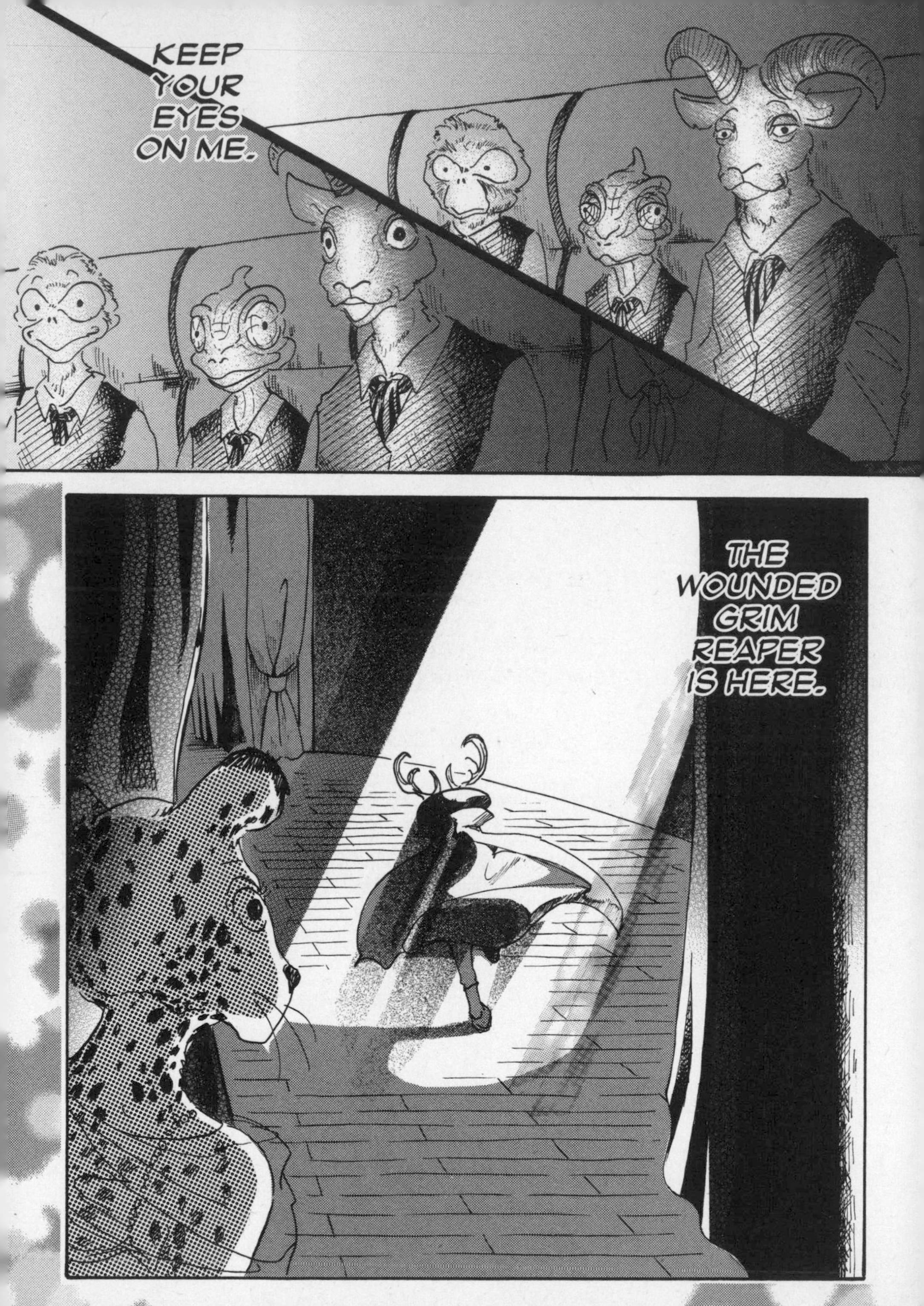
KEEP YOUR EYES ON ME.
THE WOUNDED GRIM REAPER IS HERE.

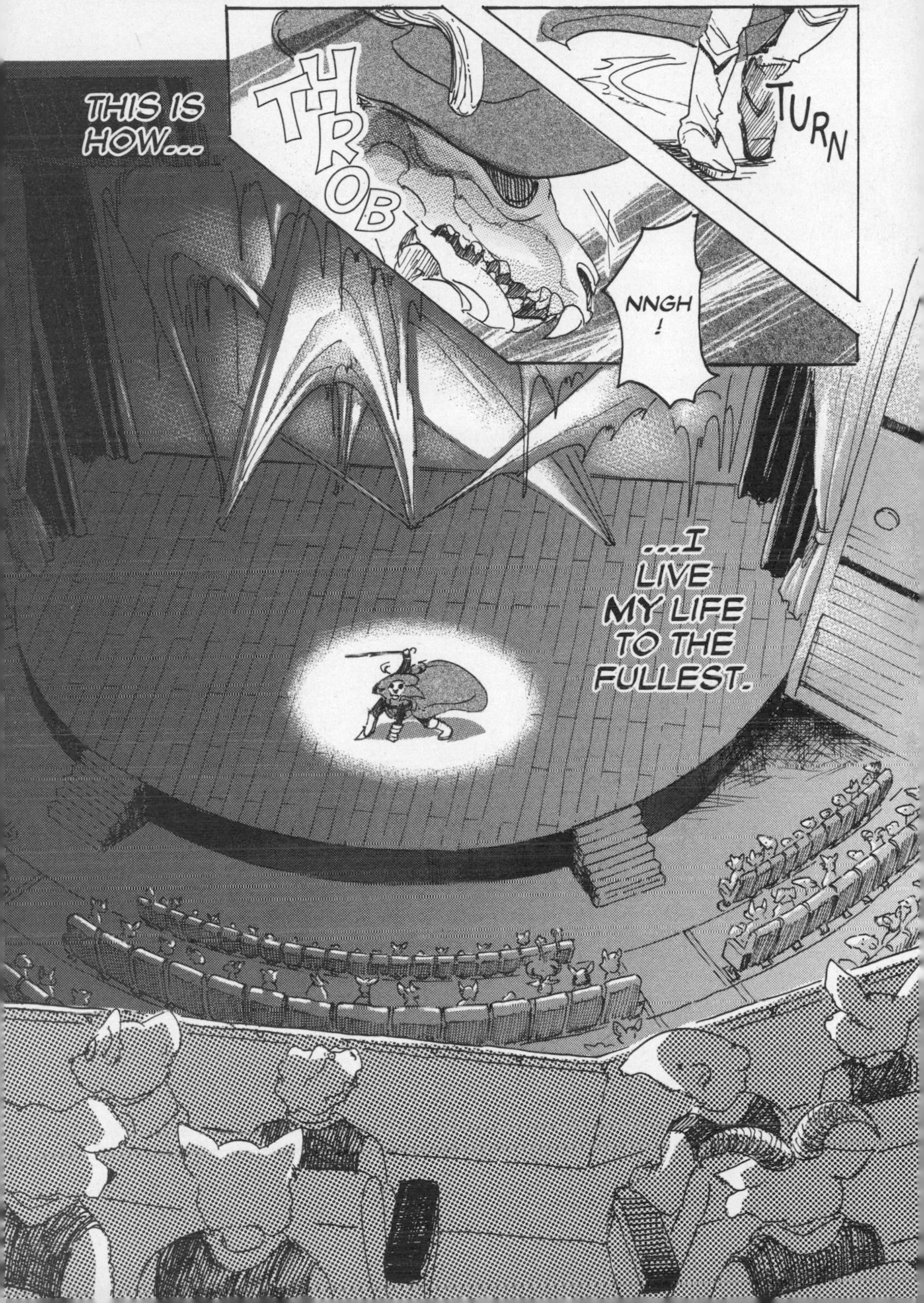
TURN
THROB
NNGH!
THIS IS HOW...
...I LIVE MY LIFE TO THE FULLEST.

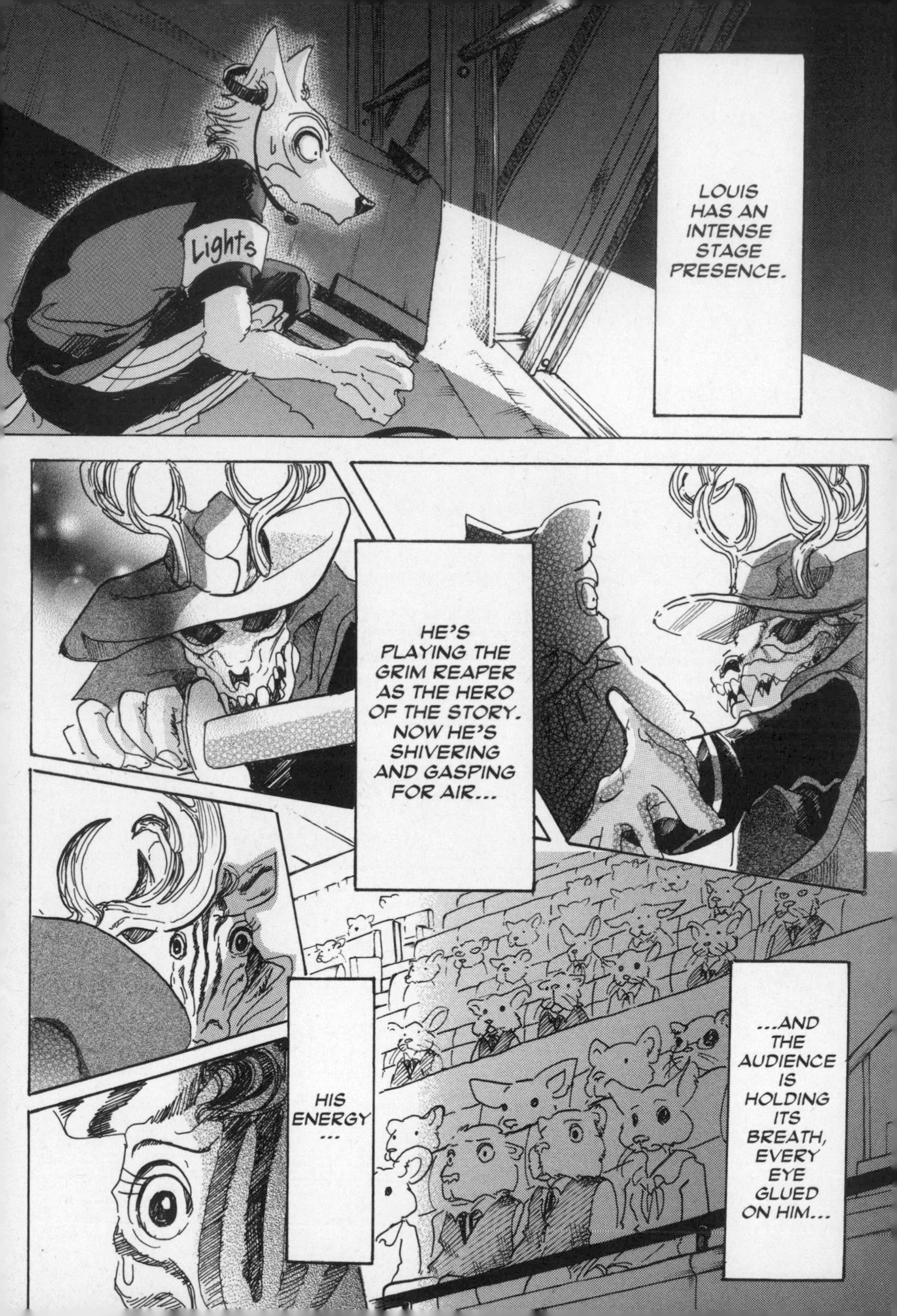
LOUIS HAS AN INTENSE STAGE PRESENCE.
Lights
HE'S PLAYING THE GRIM REAPER AS THE HERO OF THE STORY. NOW HE'S SHIVERING AND GASPING FOR AIR...
...AND THE AUDIENCE IS HOLDING ITS BREATH, EVERY EYE GLUED ON HIM...
HIS ENERGY ...

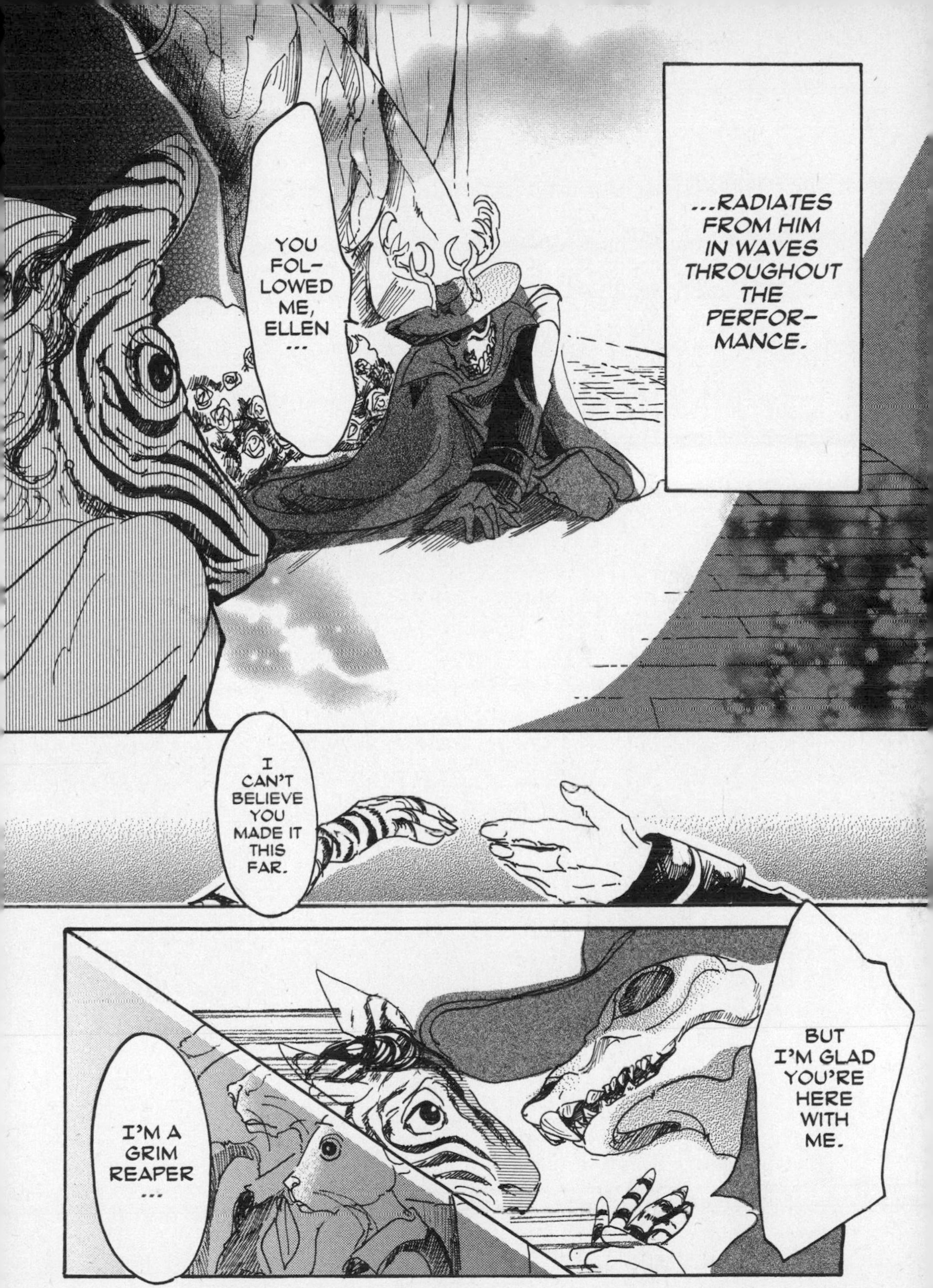
...RADIATES FROM HIM IN WAVES THROUGHOUT THE PERFORMANCE.
YOU FOL-LOWED ME, ELLEN...
I CAN'T BELIEVE YOU MADE IT THIS FAR.
BUT I'M GLAD YOU'RE HERE WITH ME.
I'M A GRIM REAPER...

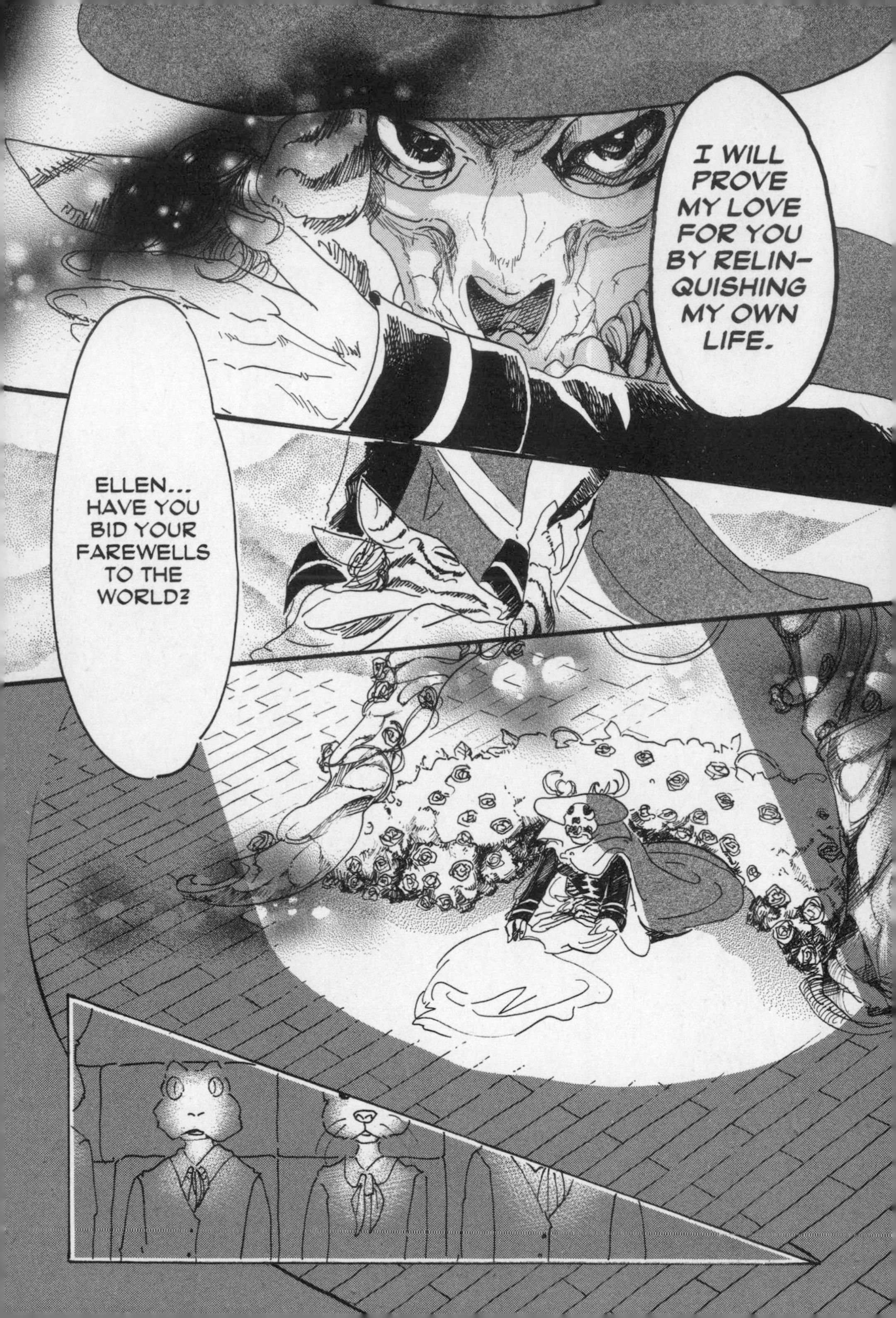
I WILL PROVE MY LOVE FOR YOU BY RELIN-QUISHING MY OWN LIFE.
ELLEN... HAVE YOU BID YOUR FAREWELLS TO THE WORLD?

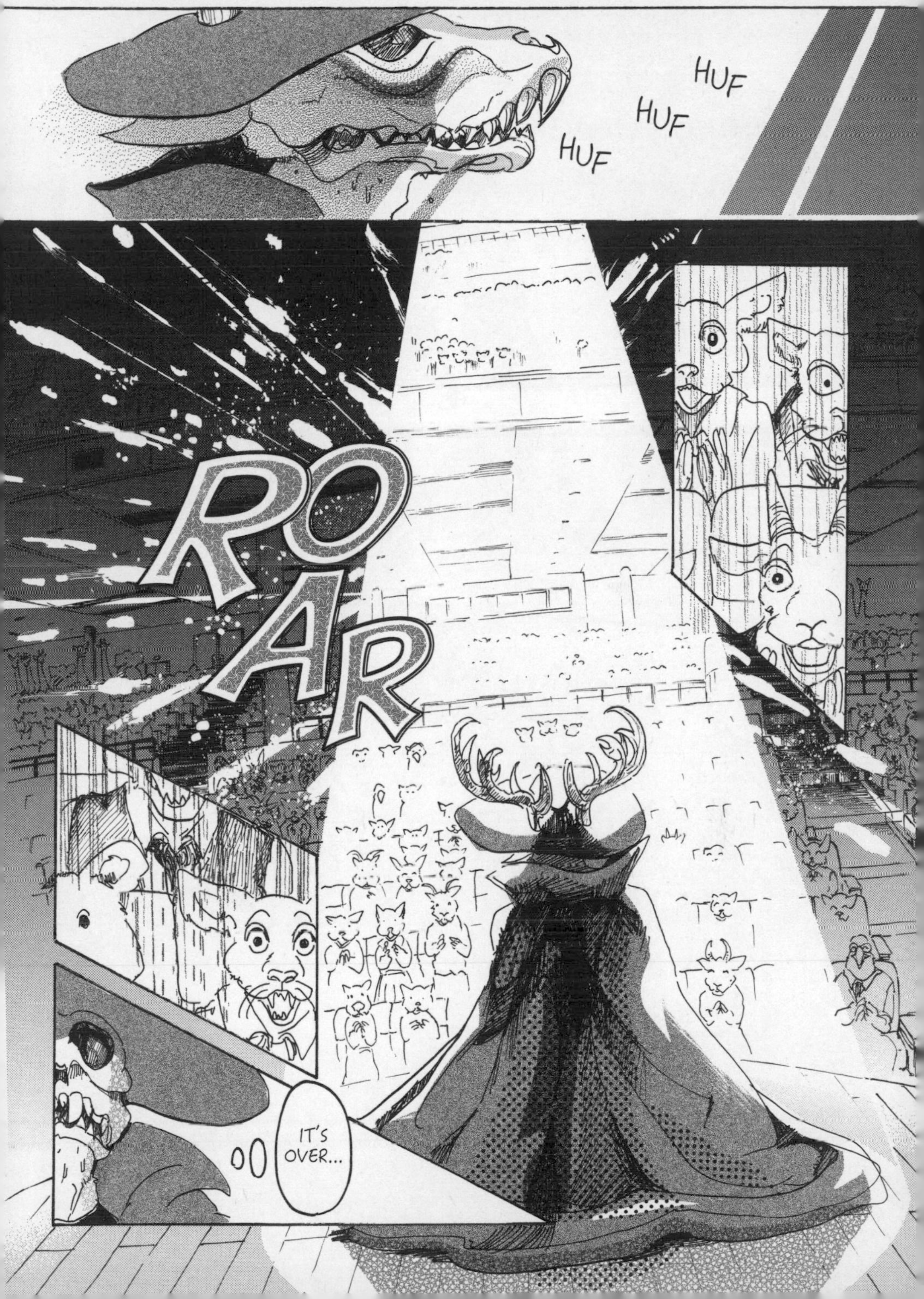
HUF
HUF
HUF
ROAR
IT'S OVER...

THE CURTAIN IS FALLING...
THE AUDIENCE IS APPLAUDING...
THE ENDING OF THE PLAY WENT PERFECTLY.
I STAYED ONSTAGE THE WHOLE TIME. BUT NOW MY LEGS HAVE GONE COMPLETELY NUMB.
MY LEGS ARE...
HOW AM I STILL STANDING?!
MY LEFT FOOT IS SERIOUSLY INJURED, BUT I STILL DID IT. DID YOU SEE ME?!
I DID IT! I PERFORMED UNTIL THE VERY END!

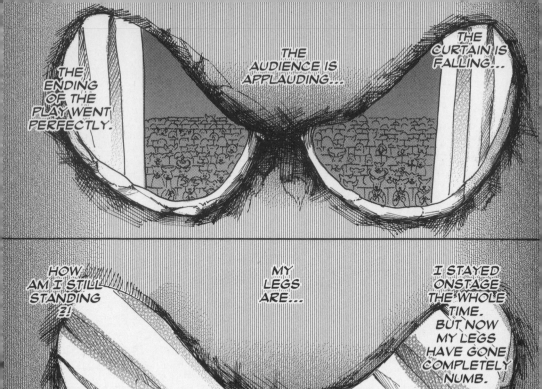

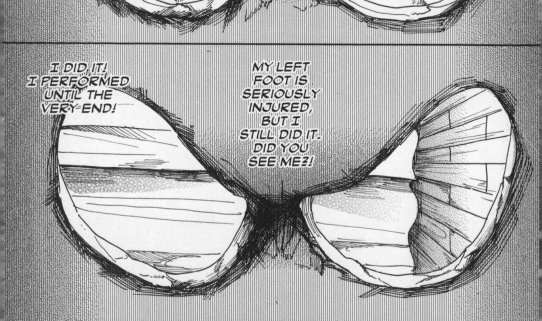

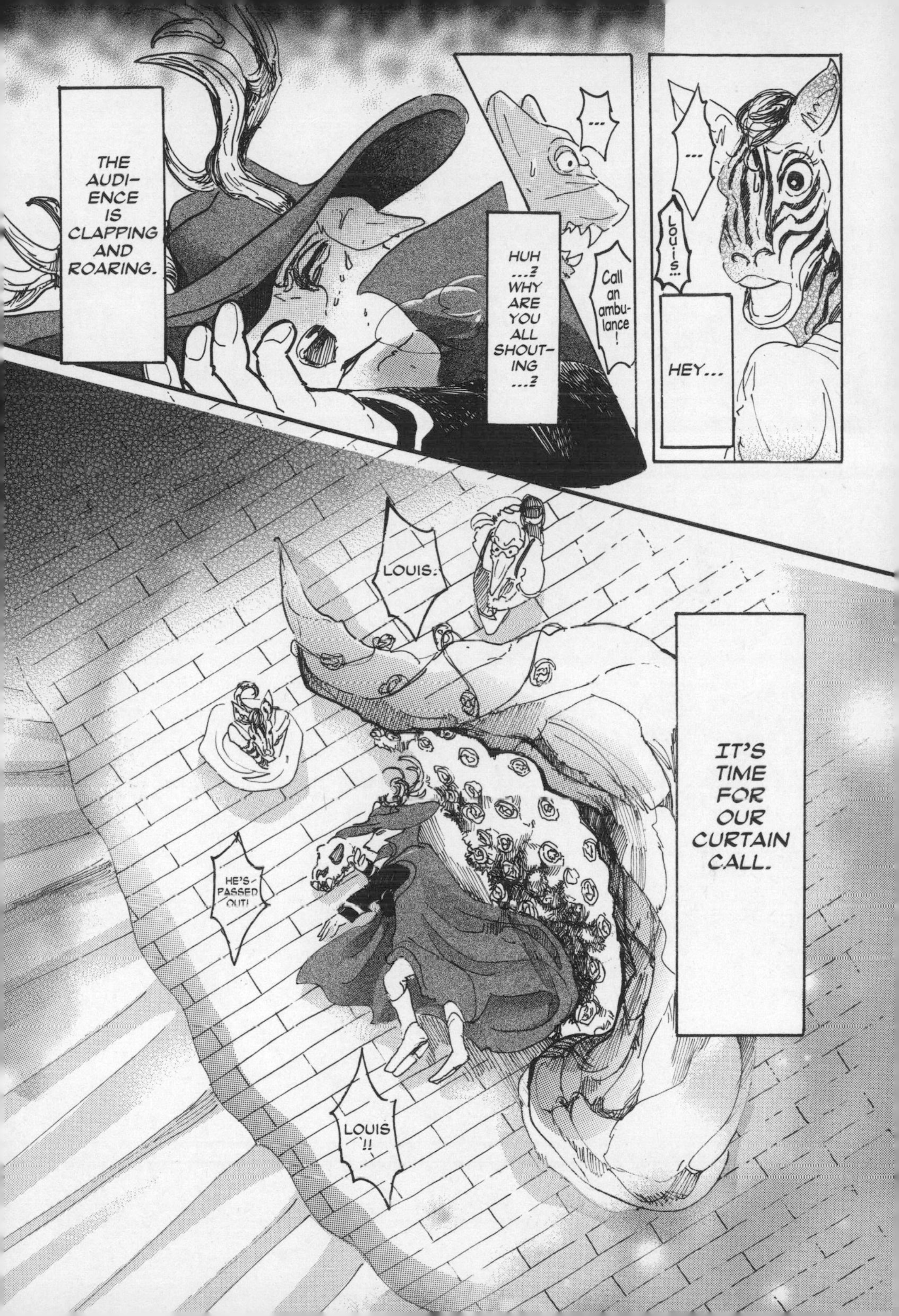
...
LOUIS...
HEY...
...
Call an ambulance!
HUH...? WHY ARE YOU ALL SHOUTING...?
THE AUDIENCE IS CLAPPING AND ROARING.
IT'S TIME FOR OUR CURTAIN CALL.
LOUIS!
HE'S PASSED OUT!
LOUIS!!

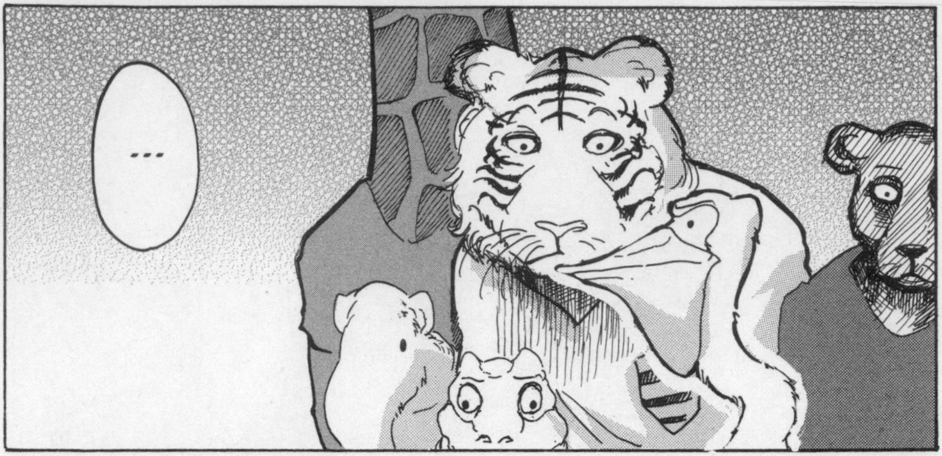
...

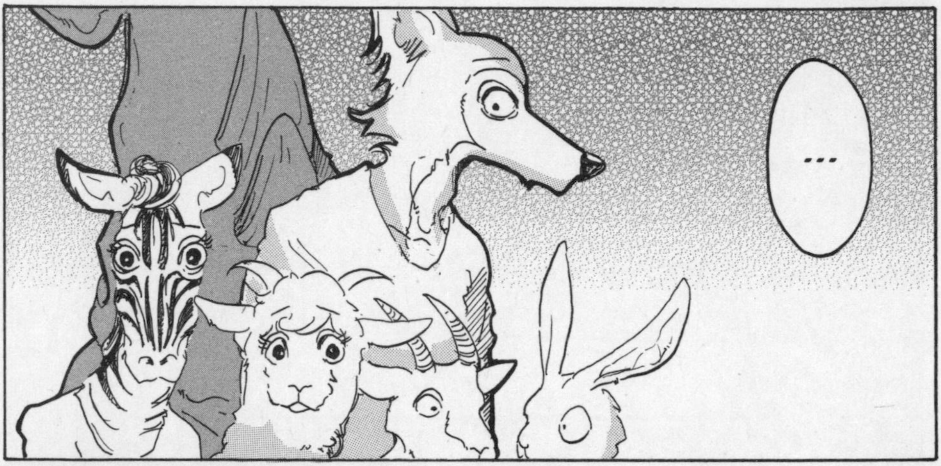
...

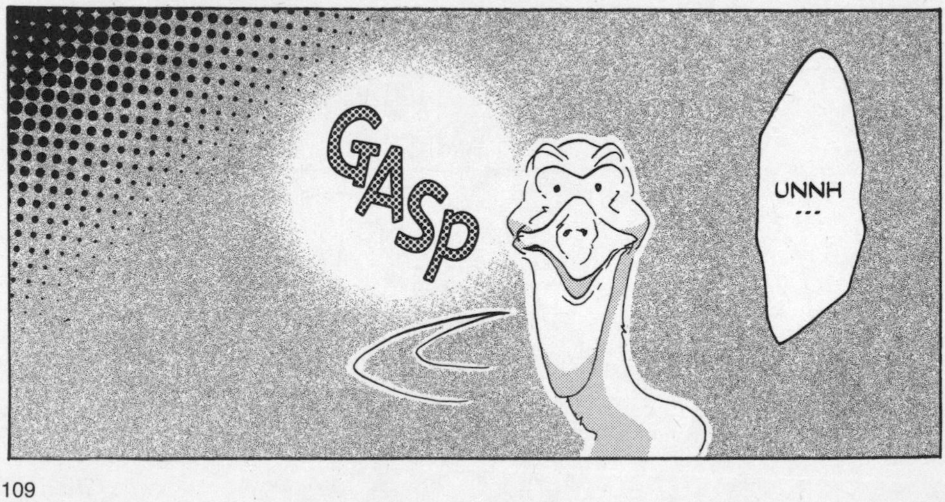
UNNH
...
GASP

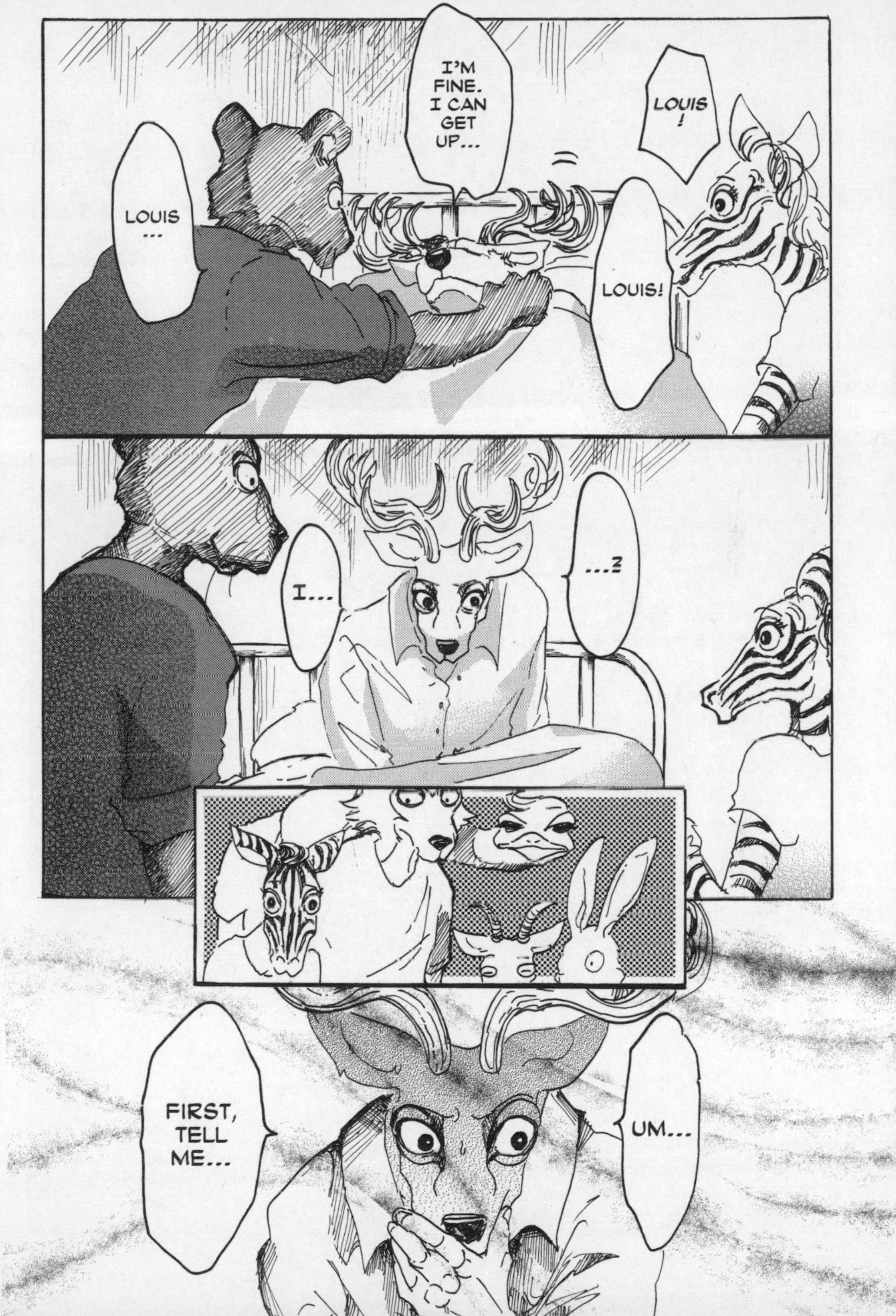
LOUIS !
LOUIS!
I'M FINE. I CAN GET UP...
LOUIS ...
...?
I...
UM...
FIRST, TELL ME...

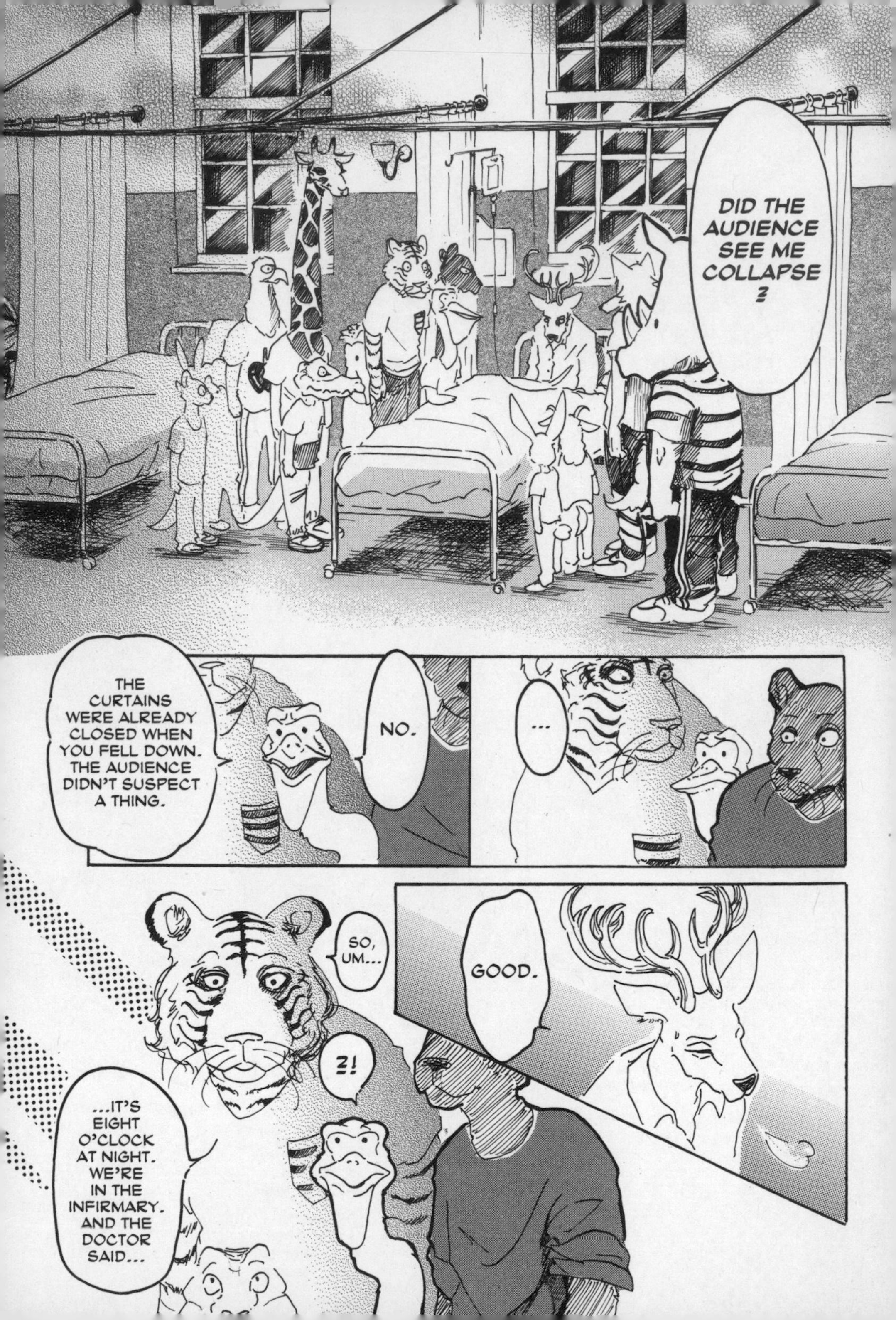
DID THE AUDIENCE SEE ME COLLAPSE?
...
NO.
THE CURTAINS WERE ALREADY CLOSED WHEN YOU FELL DOWN. THE AUDIENCE DIDN'T SUSPECT A THING.
GOOD.
SO, UM...
?!
...IT'S EIGHT O'CLOCK AT NIGHT. WE'RE IN THE INFIRMARY. AND THE DOCTOR SAID...

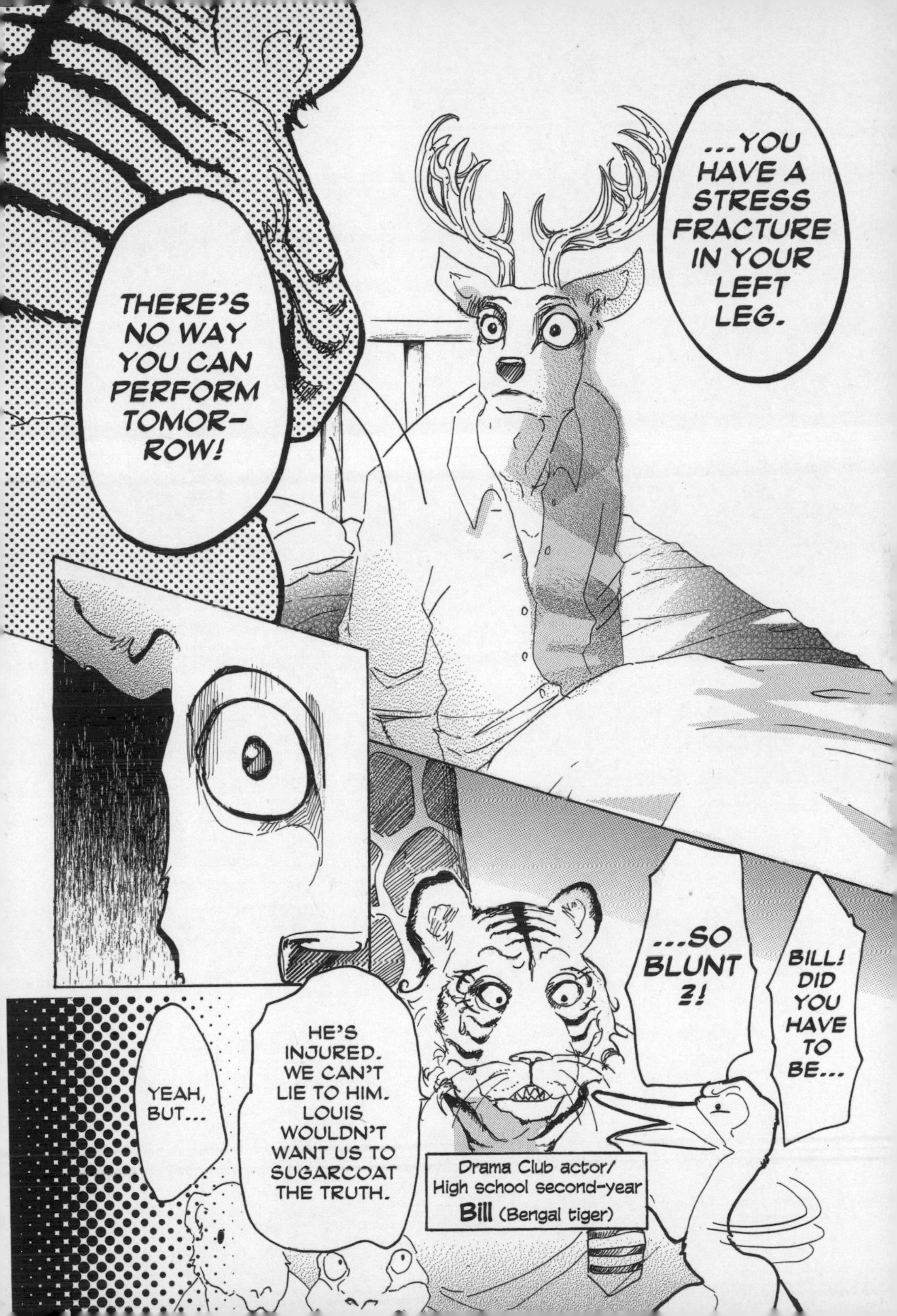
...YOU HAVE A STRESS FRACTURE IN YOUR LEFT LEG.
THERE'S NO WAY YOU CAN PERFORM TOMOR-ROW!
BILL! DID YOU HAVE TO BE...
...SO BLUNT?!
Drama Club actor/ High school second-year Bill (Bengal tiger)
HE'S INJURED. WE CAN'T LIE TO HIM. LOUIS WOULDN'T WANT US TO SUGARCOAT THE TRUTH.
YEAH, BUT...

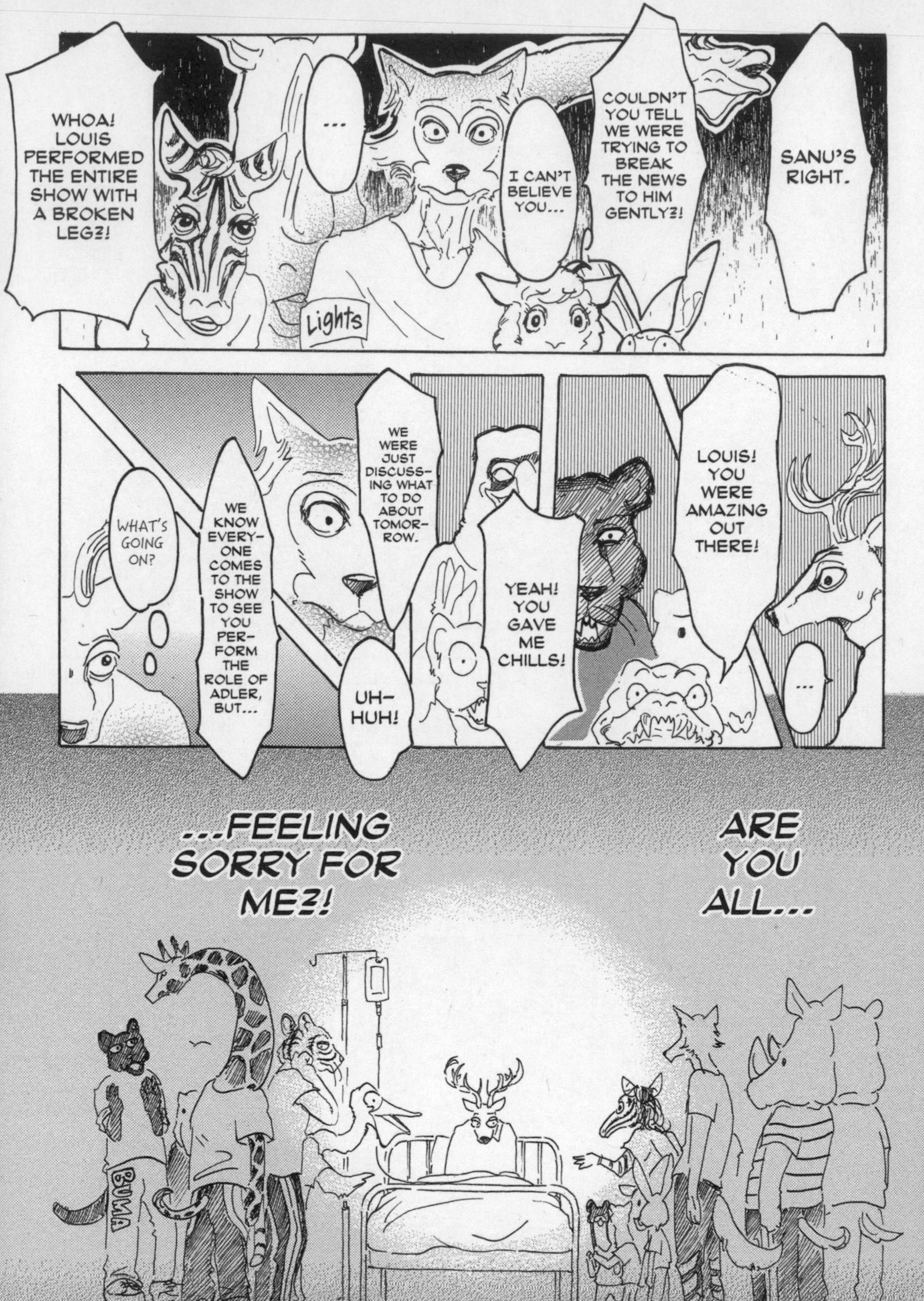
SANU'S RIGHT.
COULDN'T YOU TELL WE WERE TRYING TO BREAK THE NEWS TO HIM GENTLY?!
I CAN'T BELIEVE YOU...
...
Lights
WHOA! LOUIS PERFORMED THE ENTIRE SHOW WITH A BROKEN LEG?!
LOUIS! YOU WERE AMAZING OUT THERE!
...
WE WERE JUST DISCUSSING WHAT TO DO ABOUT TOMORROW.
YEAH! YOU GAVE ME CHILLS!
UH-HUH!
WE KNOW EVERYONE COMES TO THE SHOW TO SEE YOU PERFORM THE ROLE OF ADLER, BUT...
WHAT'S GOING ON?
ARE YOU ALL...
...FEELING SORRY FOR ME?!
BUMA

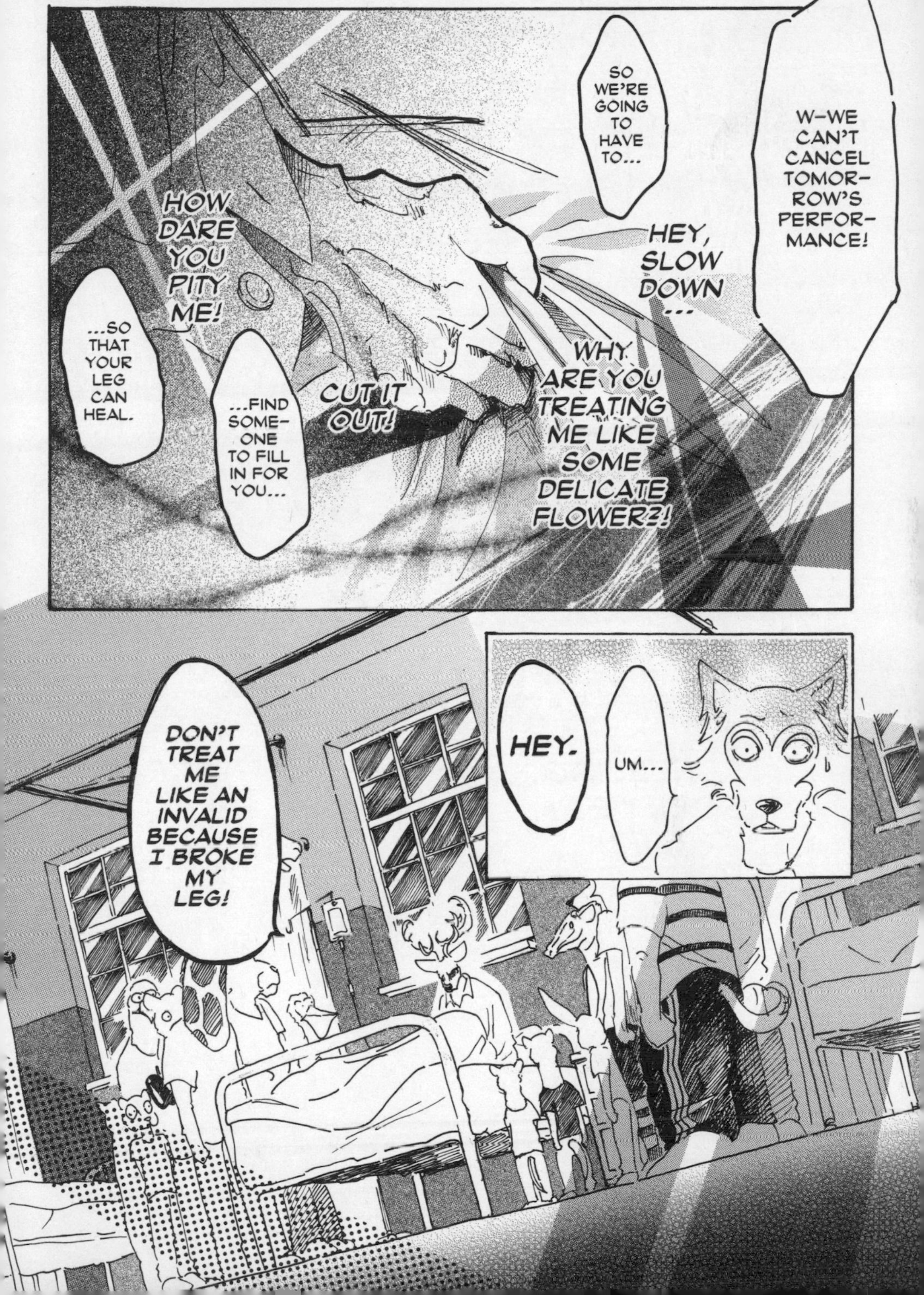
W-WE CAN'T CANCEL TOMORROW'S PERFORMANCE!
SO WE'RE GOING TO HAVE TO...
...FIND SOMEONE TO FILL IN FOR YOU...
...SO THAT YOUR LEG CAN HEAL.
HEY, SLOW DOWN...
WHY ARE YOU TREATING ME LIKE SOME DELICATE FLOWER?!
CUT IT OUT!
HOW DARE YOU PITY ME!
UM...
HEY.
DON'T TREAT ME LIKE AN INVALID BECAUSE I BROKE MY LEG!

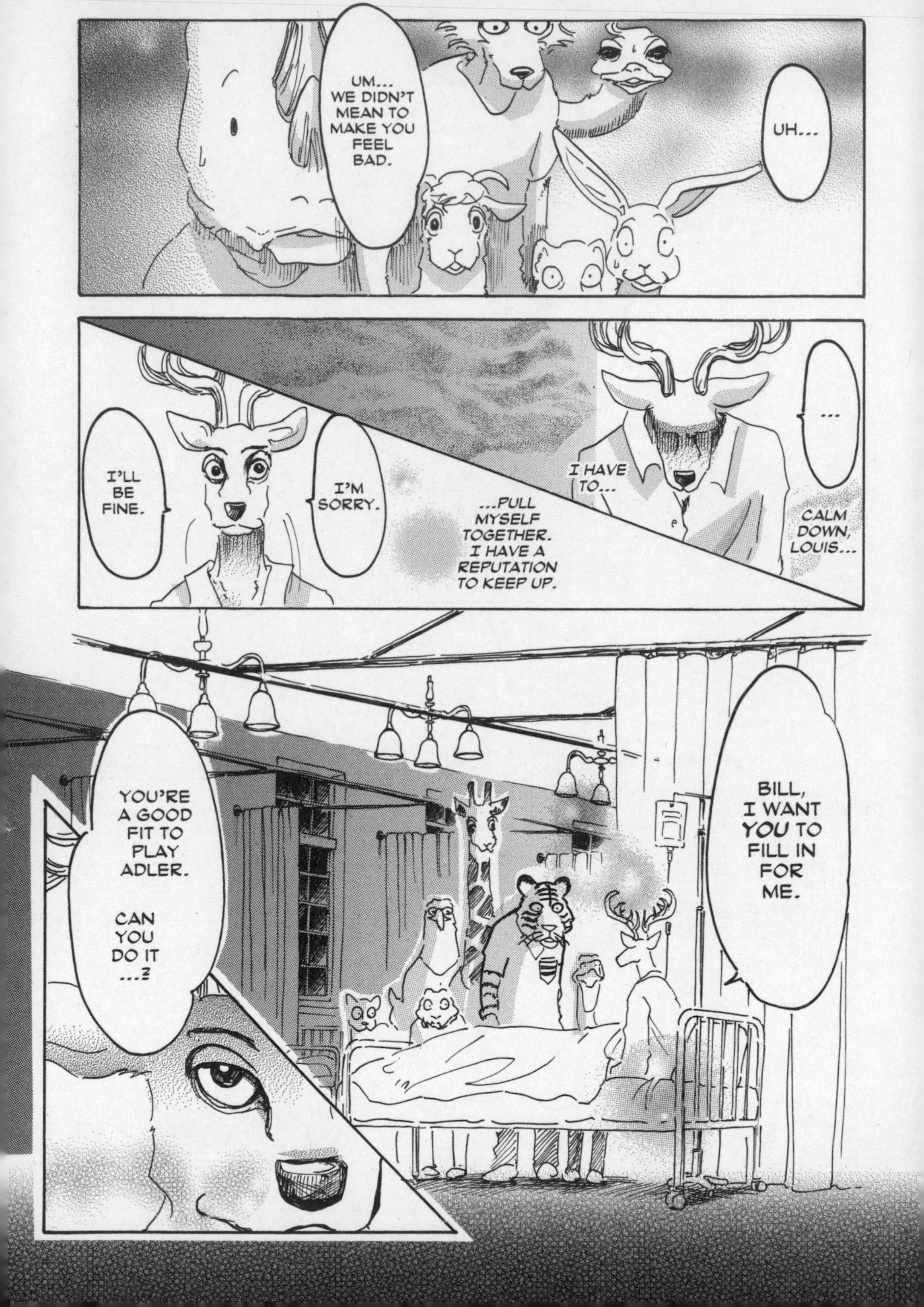
UH...
UM... WE DIDN'T MEAN TO MAKE YOU FEEL BAD.
...
CALM DOWN, LOUIS...
I HAVE TO...
...PULL MYSELF TOGETHER. I HAVE A REPUTATION TO KEEP UP.
I'M SORRY.
I'LL BE FINE.
BILL, I WANT *YOU* TO FILL IN FOR ME.
YOU'RE A GOOD FIT TO PLAY ADLER.
CAN YOU DO IT ...?

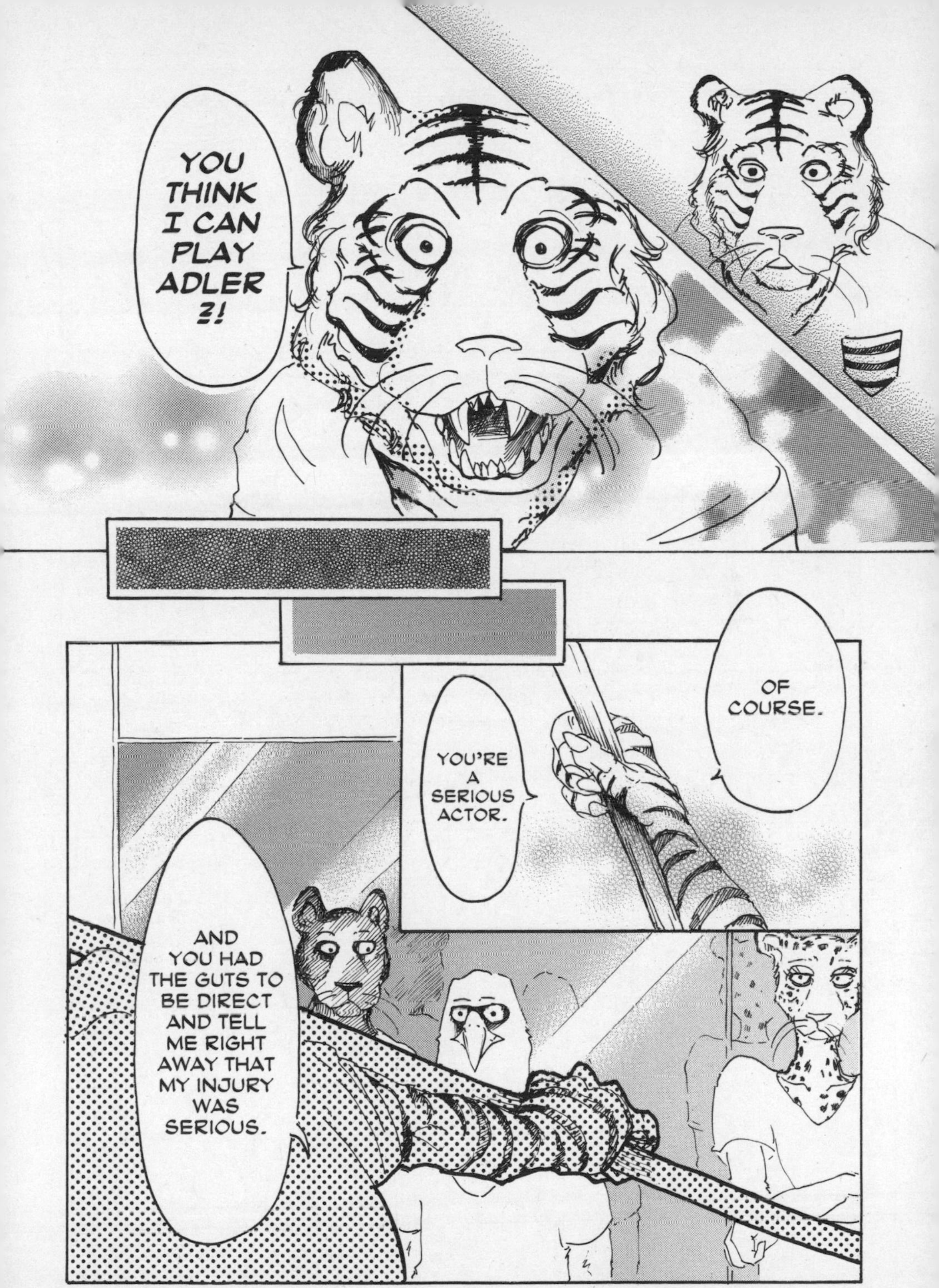
YOU THINK I CAN PLAY ADLER?!
OF COURSE.
YOU'RE A SERIOUS ACTOR.
AND YOU HAD THE GUTS TO BE DIRECT AND TELL ME RIGHT AWAY THAT MY INJURY WAS SERIOUS.

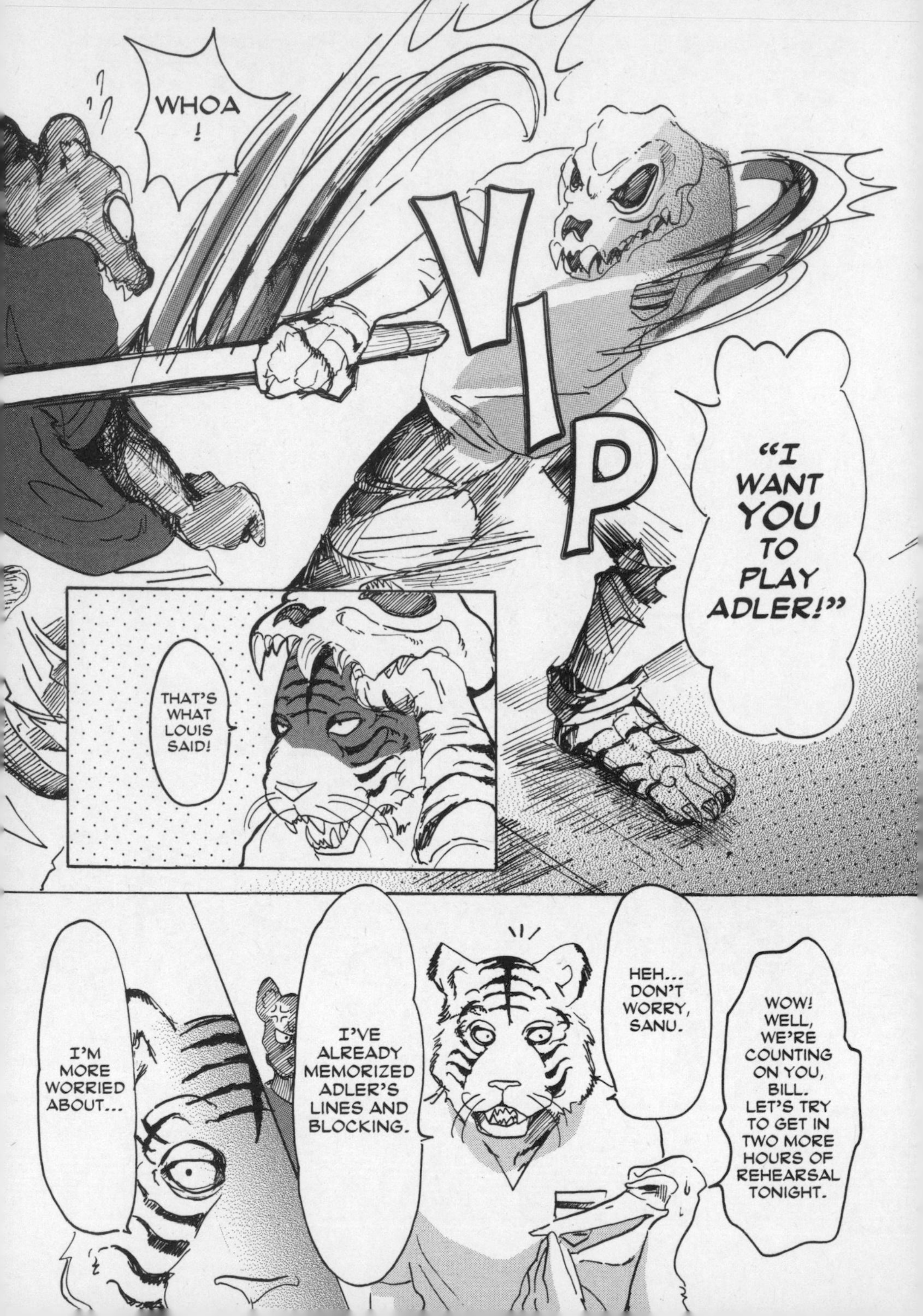
"I WANT YOU TO PLAY ADLER!"
VIP
WHOA!
THAT'S WHAT LOUIS SAID!
WOW! WELL, WE'RE COUNTING ON YOU, BILL. LET'S TRY TO GET IN TWO MORE HOURS OF REHEARSAL TONIGHT.
HEH... DON'T WORRY, SANU.
I'VE ALREADY MEMORIZED ADLER'S LINES AND BLOCKING.
I'M MORE WORRIED ABOUT...

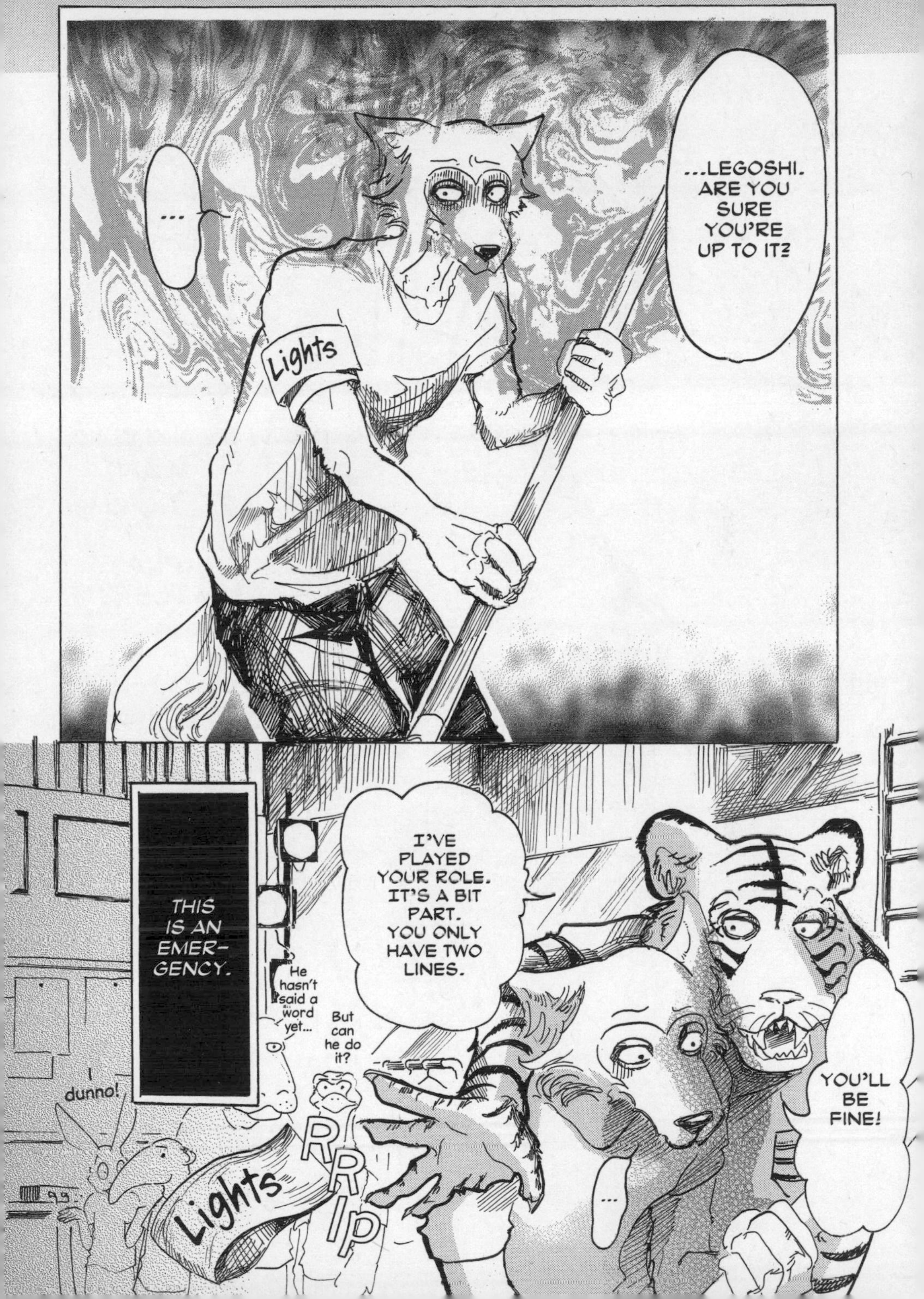
...LEGOSHI. ARE YOU SURE YOU'RE UP TO IT?
...
Lights
I'VE PLAYED YOUR ROLE. IT'S A BIT PART. YOU ONLY HAVE TWO LINES.
YOU'LL BE FINE!
...
RRRIP
Lights
But can he do it?
He hasn't said a word yet...
THIS IS AN EMERGENCY.
I dunno!

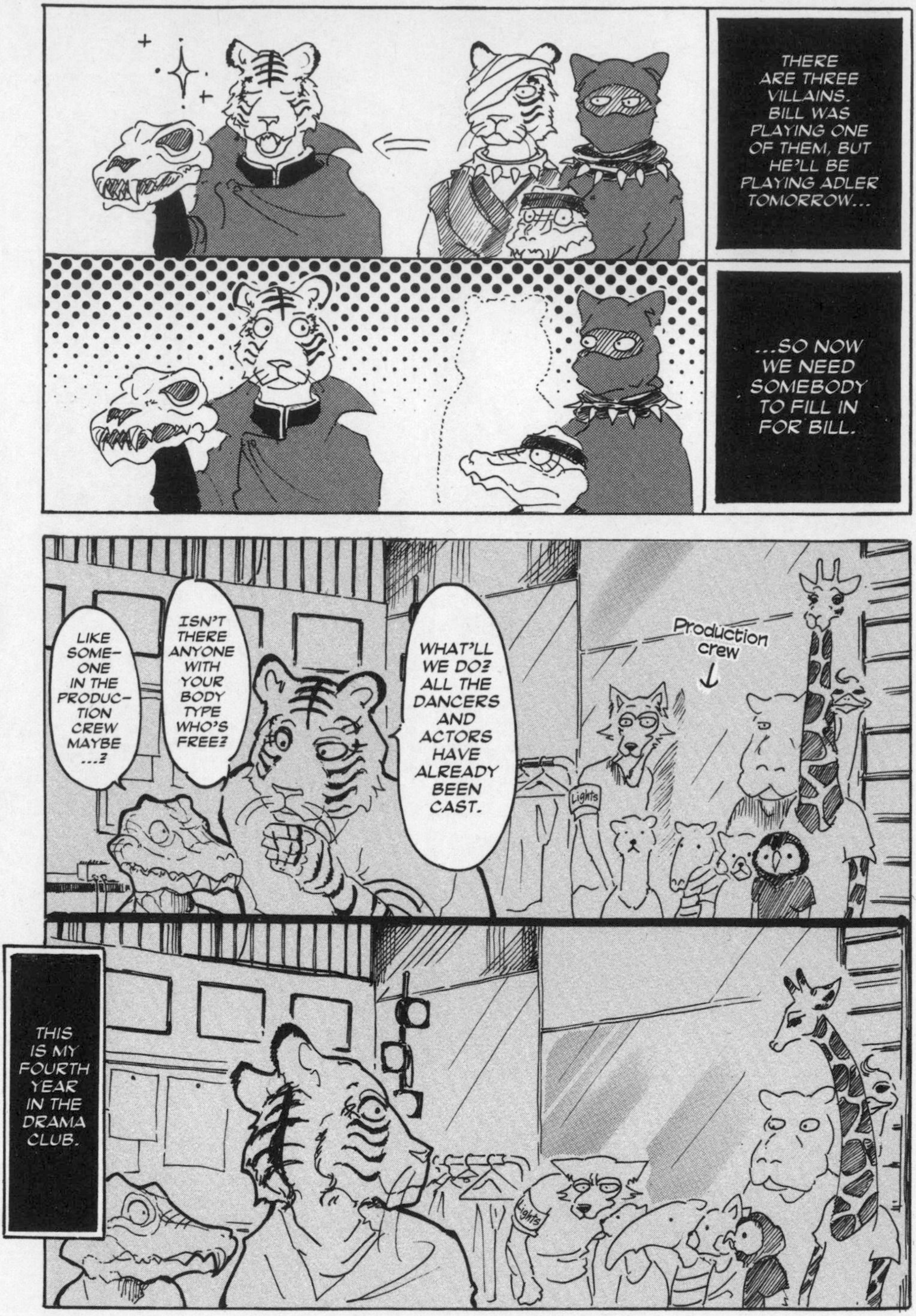
THERE ARE THREE VILLAINS. BILL WAS PLAYING ONE OF THEM, BUT HE'LL BE PLAYING ADLER TOMORROW...
...SO NOW WE NEED SOMEBODY TO FILL IN FOR BILL.
Production crew
WHAT'LL WE DO? ALL THE DANCERS AND ACTORS HAVE ALREADY BEEN CAST.
ISN'T THERE ANYONE WITH YOUR BODY TYPE WHO'S FREE?
LIKE SOMEONE IN THE PRODUCTION CREW MAYBE ...?
Lights
THIS IS MY FOURTH YEAR IN THE DRAMA CLUB.
Lights

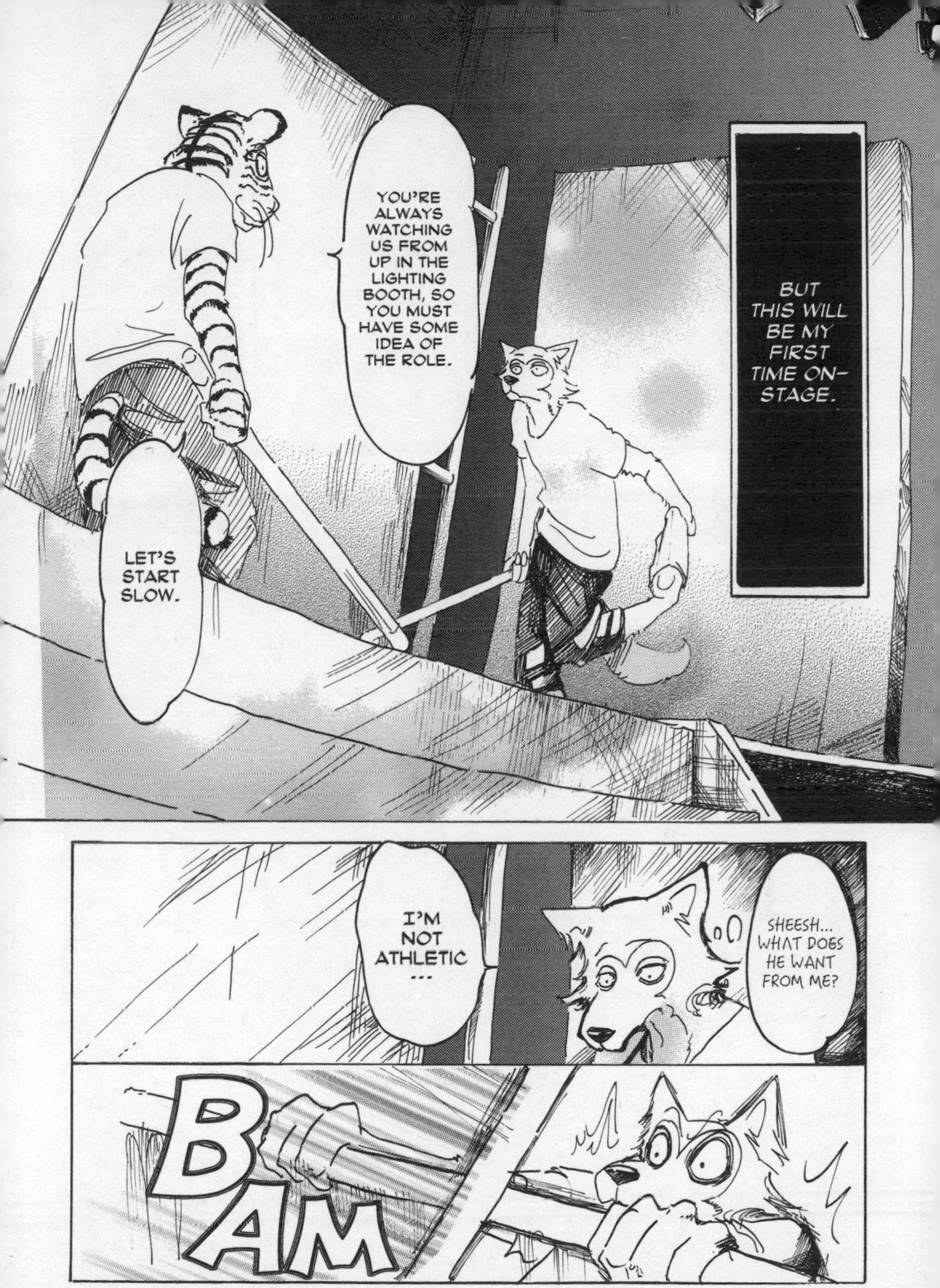
BUT THIS WILL BE MY FIRST TIME ON-STAGE.
YOU'RE ALWAYS WATCHING US FROM UP IN THE LIGHTING BOOTH, SO YOU MUST HAVE SOME IDEA OF THE ROLE.
LET'S START SLOW.
SHEESH... WHAT DOES HE WANT FROM ME?
I'M NOT ATHLETIC...
BAM

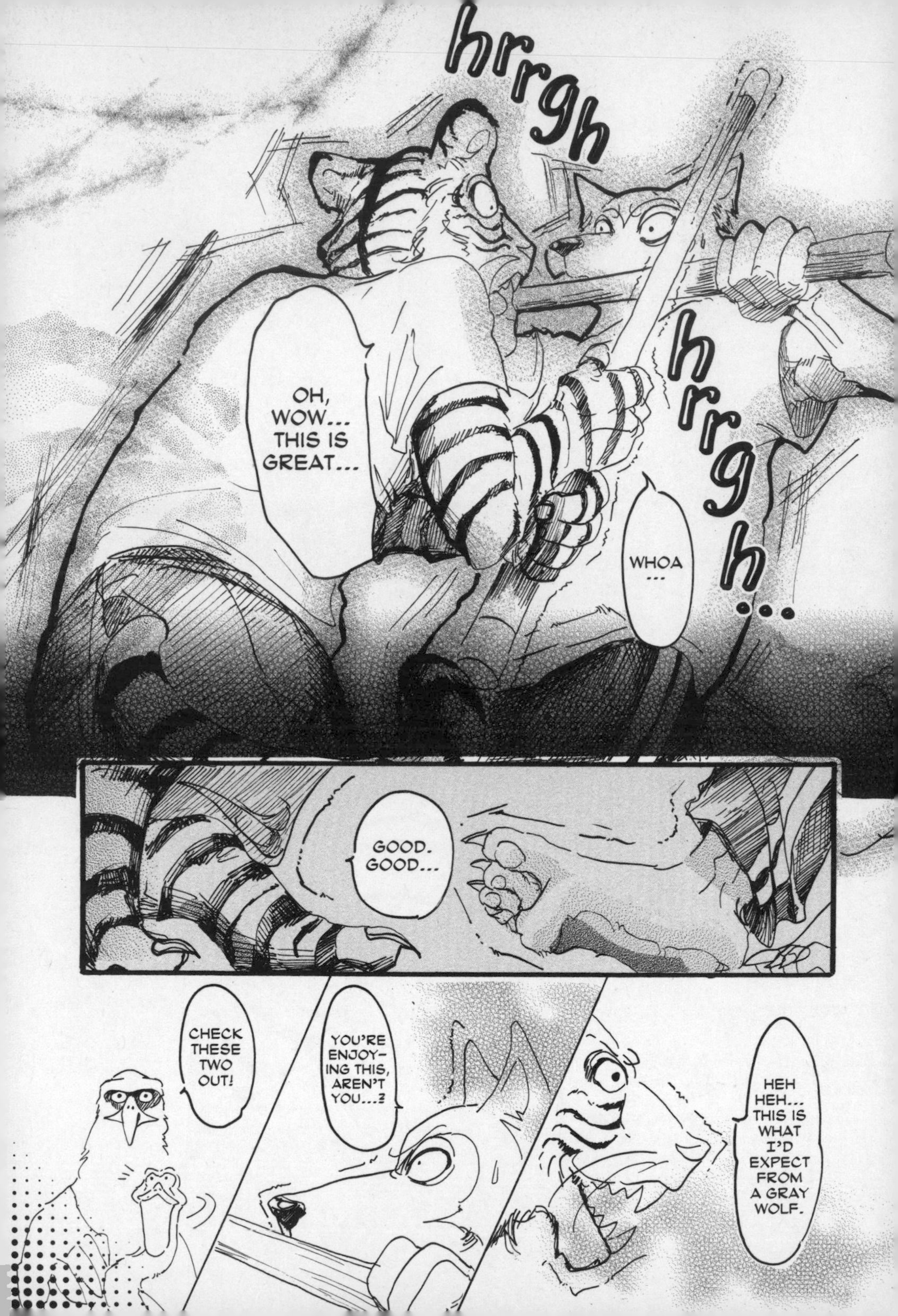
hrrgh
hrrgh...
WHOA...
OH, WOW... THIS IS GREAT...
GOOD. GOOD...
HEH HEH... THIS IS WHAT I'D EXPECT FROM A GRAY WOLF.
YOU'RE ENJOYING THIS, AREN'T YOU...?
CHECK THESE TWO OUT!

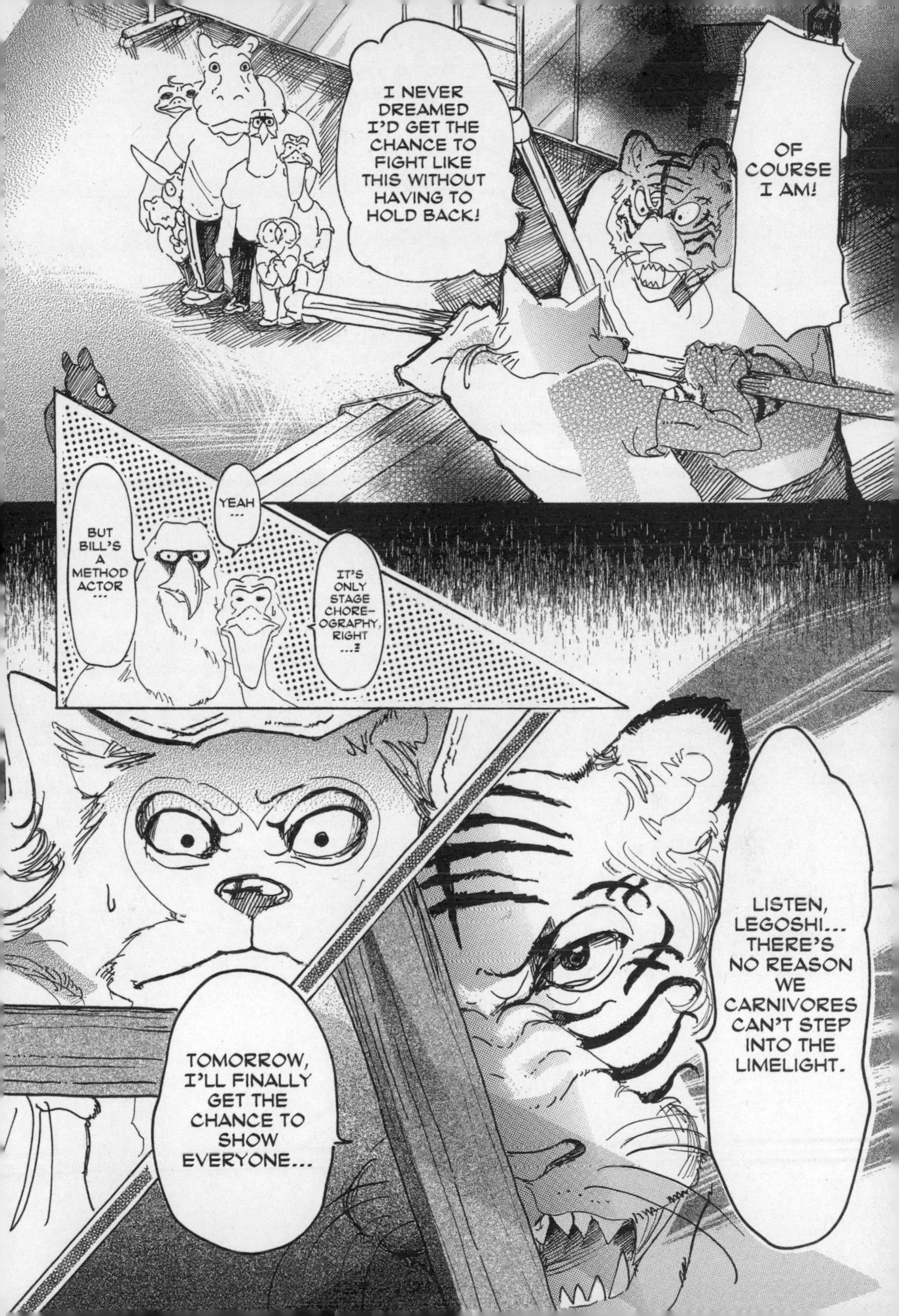
OF COURSE I AM!
I NEVER DREAMED I'D GET THE CHANCE TO FIGHT LIKE THIS WITHOUT HAVING TO HOLD BACK!
IT'S ONLY STAGE CHOREOGRAPHY, RIGHT...?
YEAH...
BUT BILL'S A METHOD ACTOR...
LISTEN, LEGOSHI... THERE'S NO REASON WE CARNIVORES CAN'T STEP INTO THE LIMELIGHT.
TOMORROW, I'LL FINALLY GET THE CHANCE TO SHOW EVERYONE...

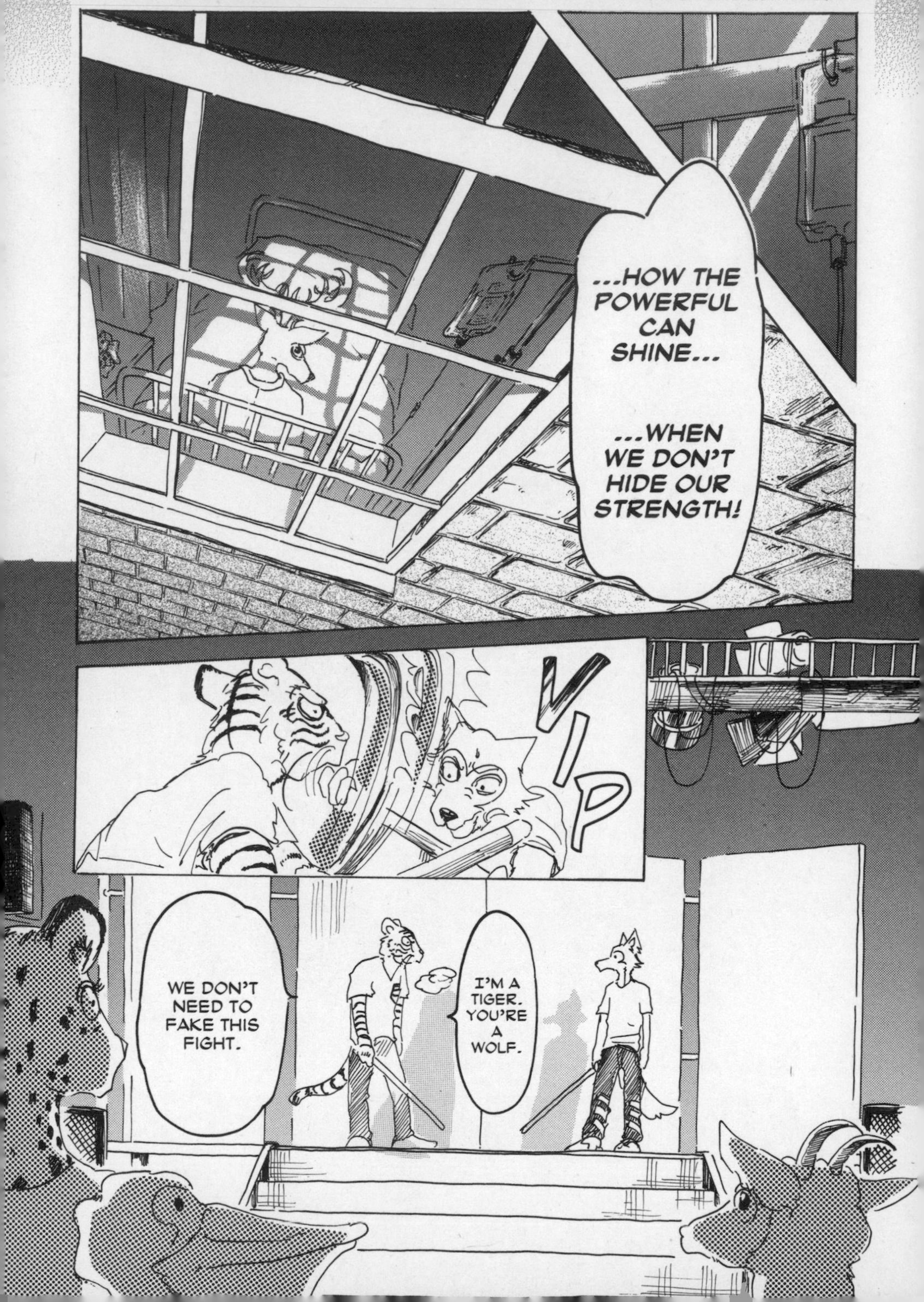
...HOW THE POWERFUL CAN SHINE...
...WHEN WE DON'T HIDE OUR STRENGTH!
VIP
I'M A TIGER. YOU'RE A WOLF.
WE DON'T NEED TO FAKE THIS FIGHT.

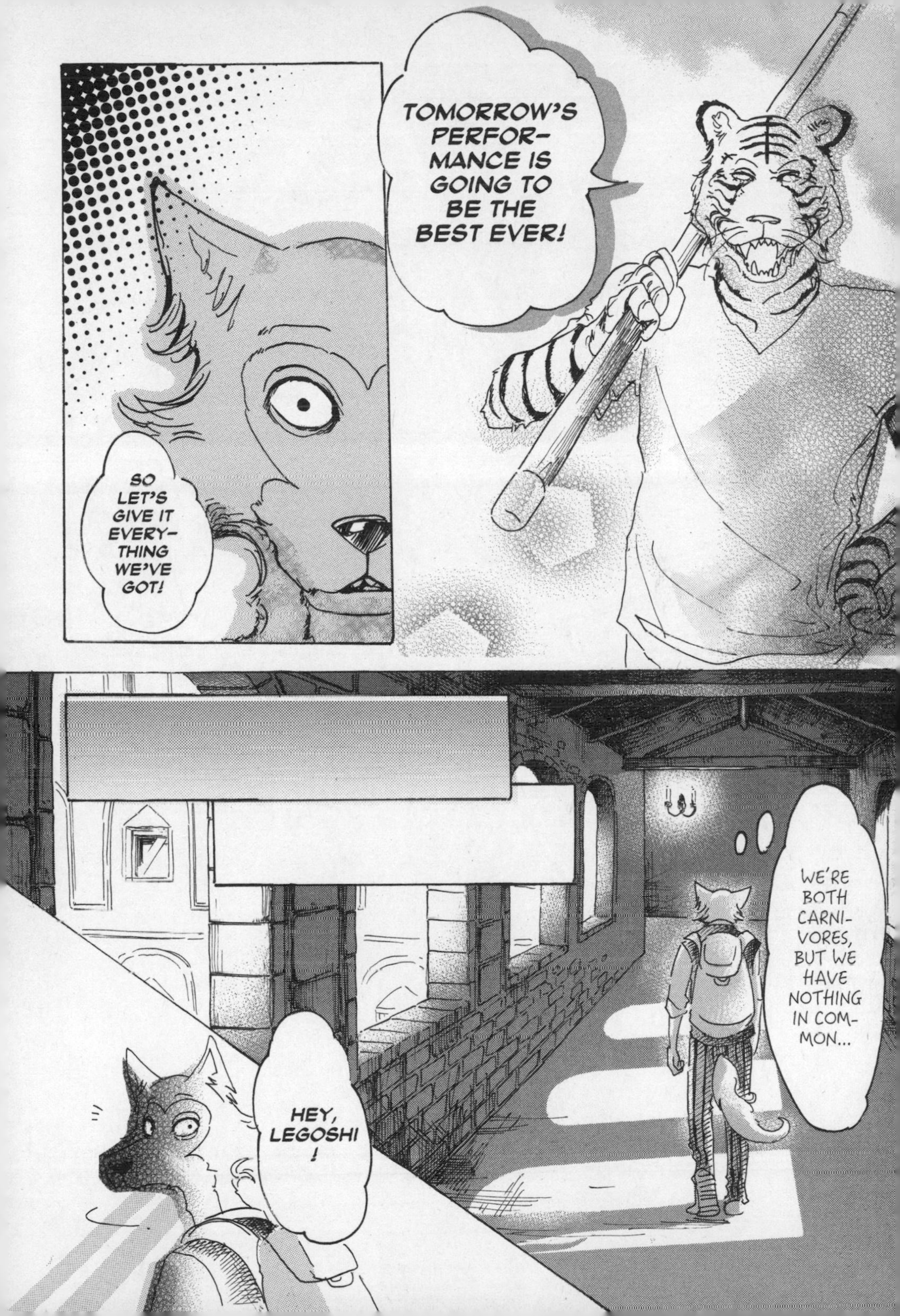
TOMORROW'S PERFORMANCE IS GOING TO BE THE BEST EVER!
SO LET'S GIVE IT EVERYTHING WE'VE GOT!
WE'RE BOTH CARNIVORES, BUT WE HAVE NOTHING IN COMMON...
HEY, LEGOSHI!

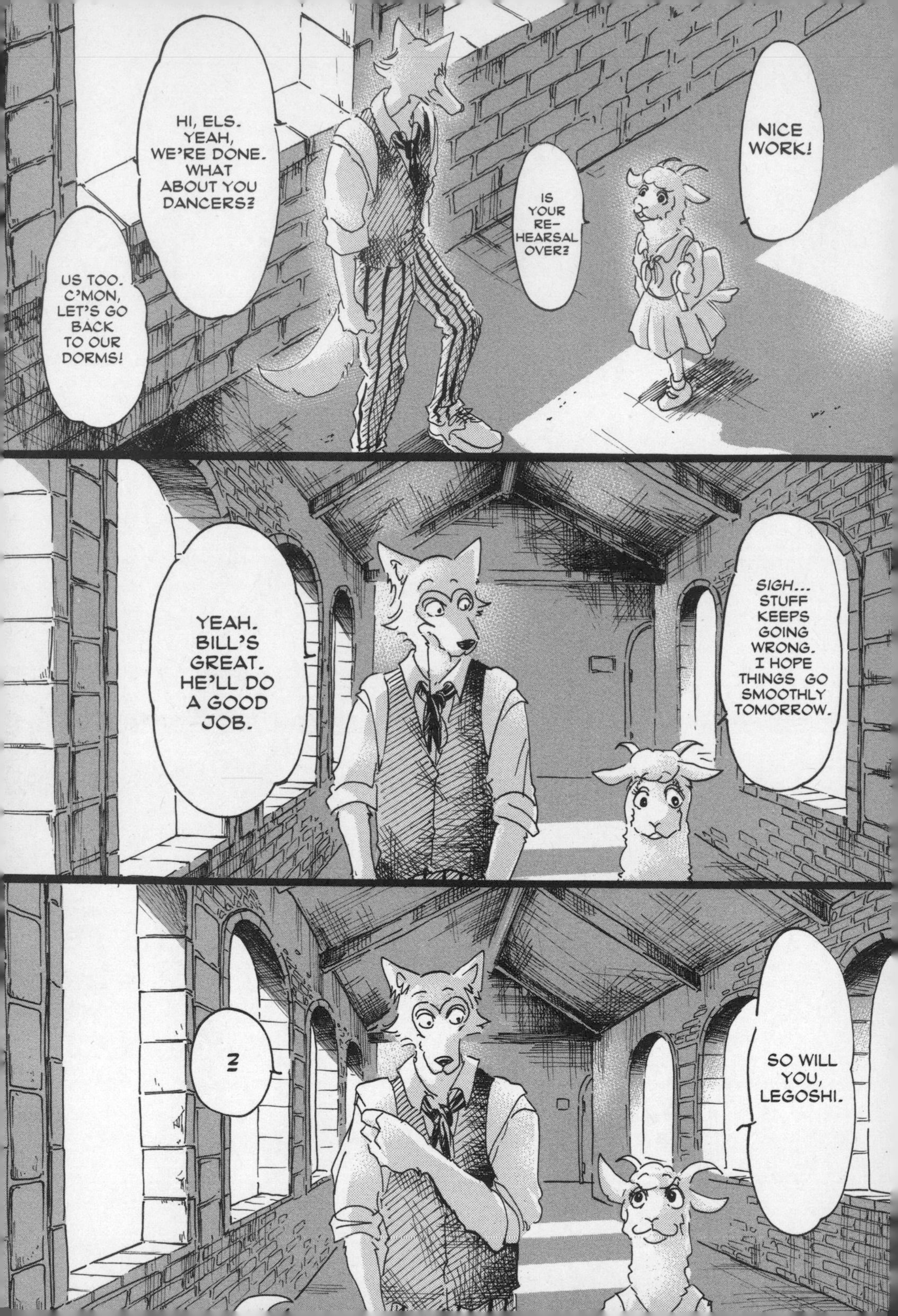
NICE WORK!
IS YOUR RE-HEARSAL OVER?
HI, ELS. YEAH, WE'RE DONE. WHAT ABOUT YOU DANCERS?
US TOO. C'MON, LET'S GO BACK TO OUR DORMS!
SIGH... STUFF KEEPS GOING WRONG. I HOPE THINGS GO SMOOTHLY TOMORROW.
YEAH. BILL'S GREAT. HE'LL DO A GOOD JOB.
SO WILL YOU, LEGOSHI.
?

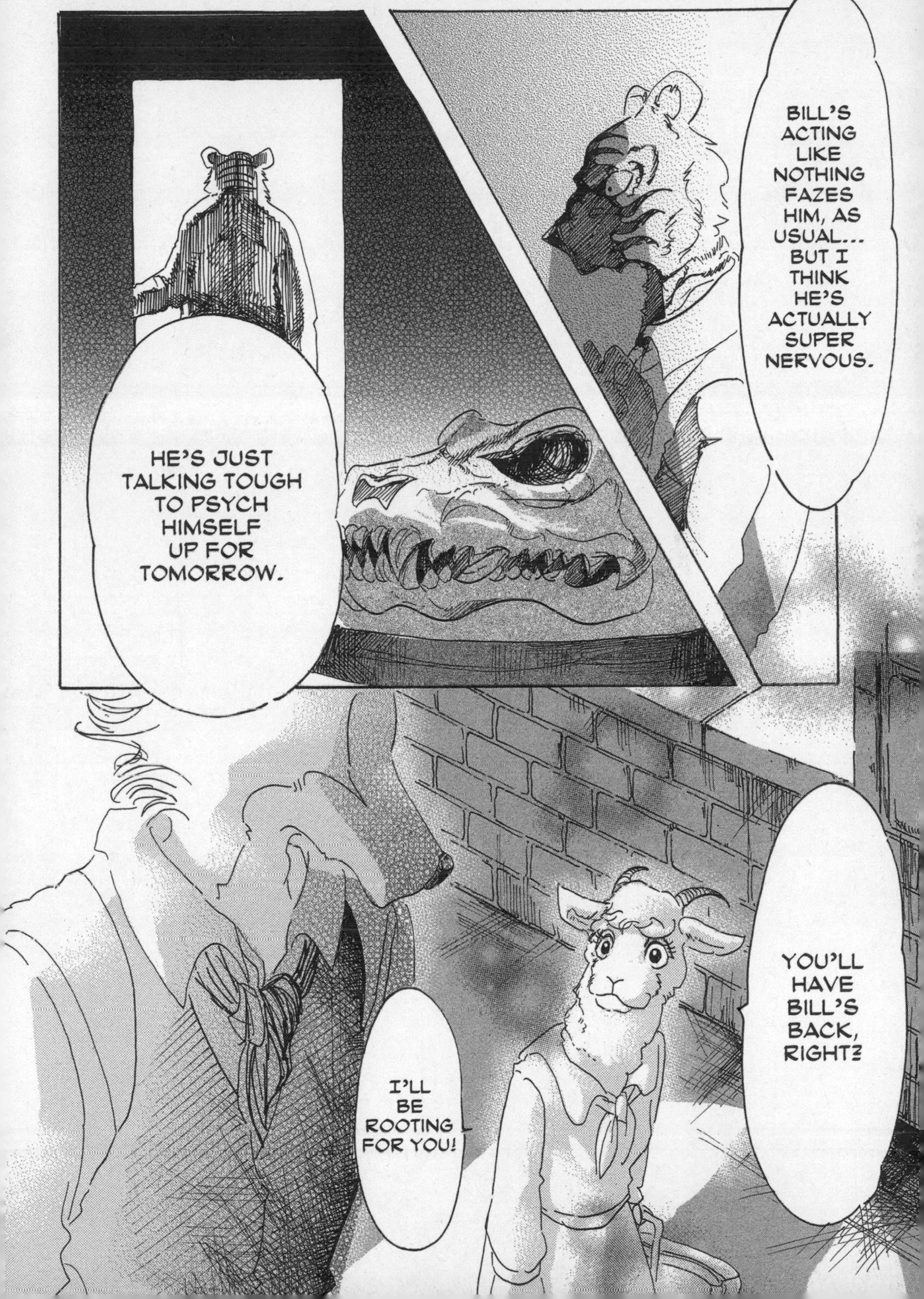
BILL'S ACTING LIKE NOTHING FAZES HIM, AS USUAL... BUT I THINK HE'S ACTUALLY SUPER NERVOUS.
HE'S JUST TALKING TOUGH TO PSYCH HIMSELF UP FOR TOMORROW.
YOU'LL HAVE BILL'S BACK, RIGHT?
I'LL BE ROOTING FOR YOU!

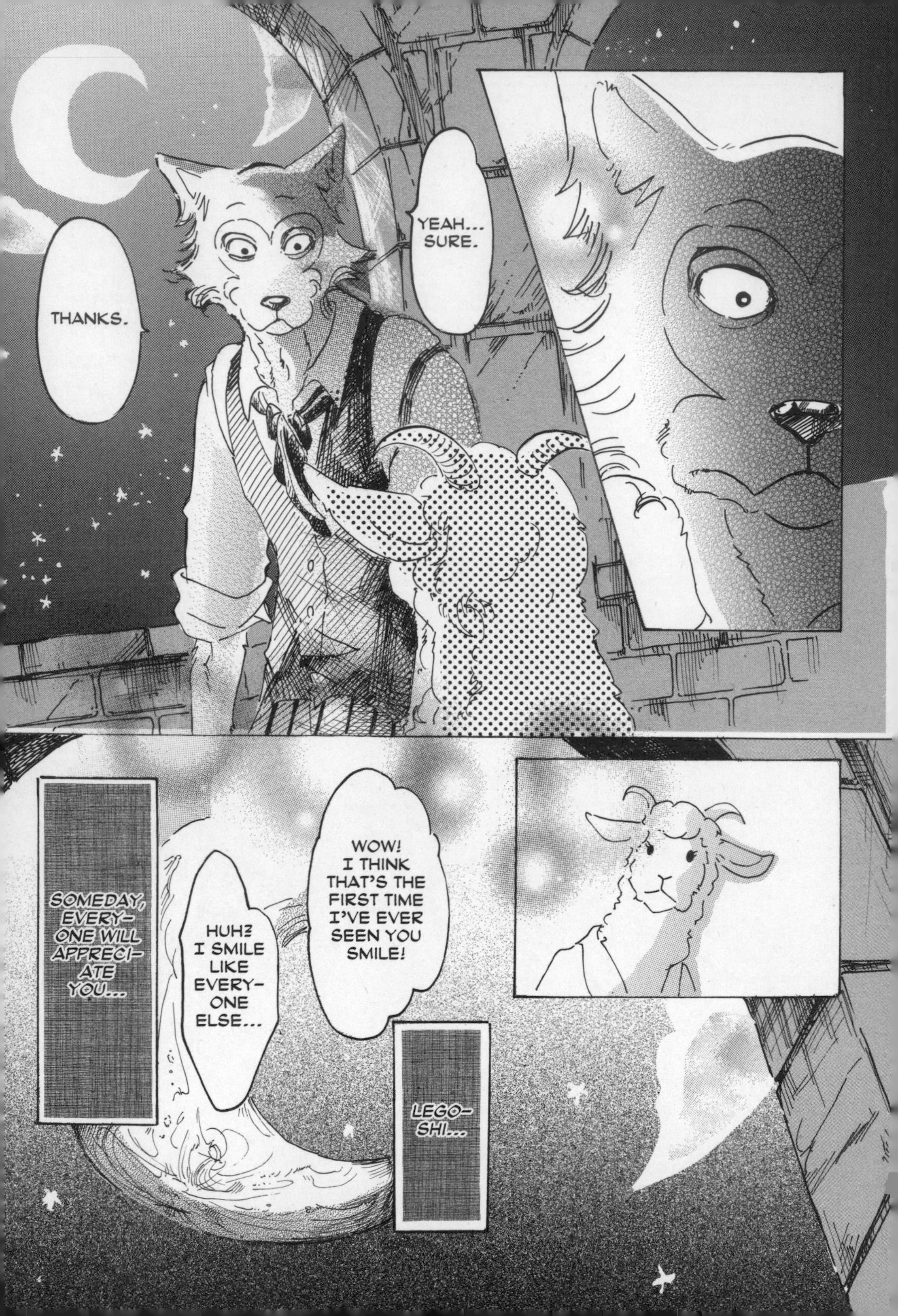
THANKS.
YEAH... SURE.
WOW! I THINK THAT'S THE FIRST TIME I'VE EVER SEEN YOU SMILE!
HUH? I SMILE LIKE EVERY-ONE ELSE...
LEGO-SHI...
SOMEDAY, EVERY-ONE WILL APPRECI-ATE YOU...

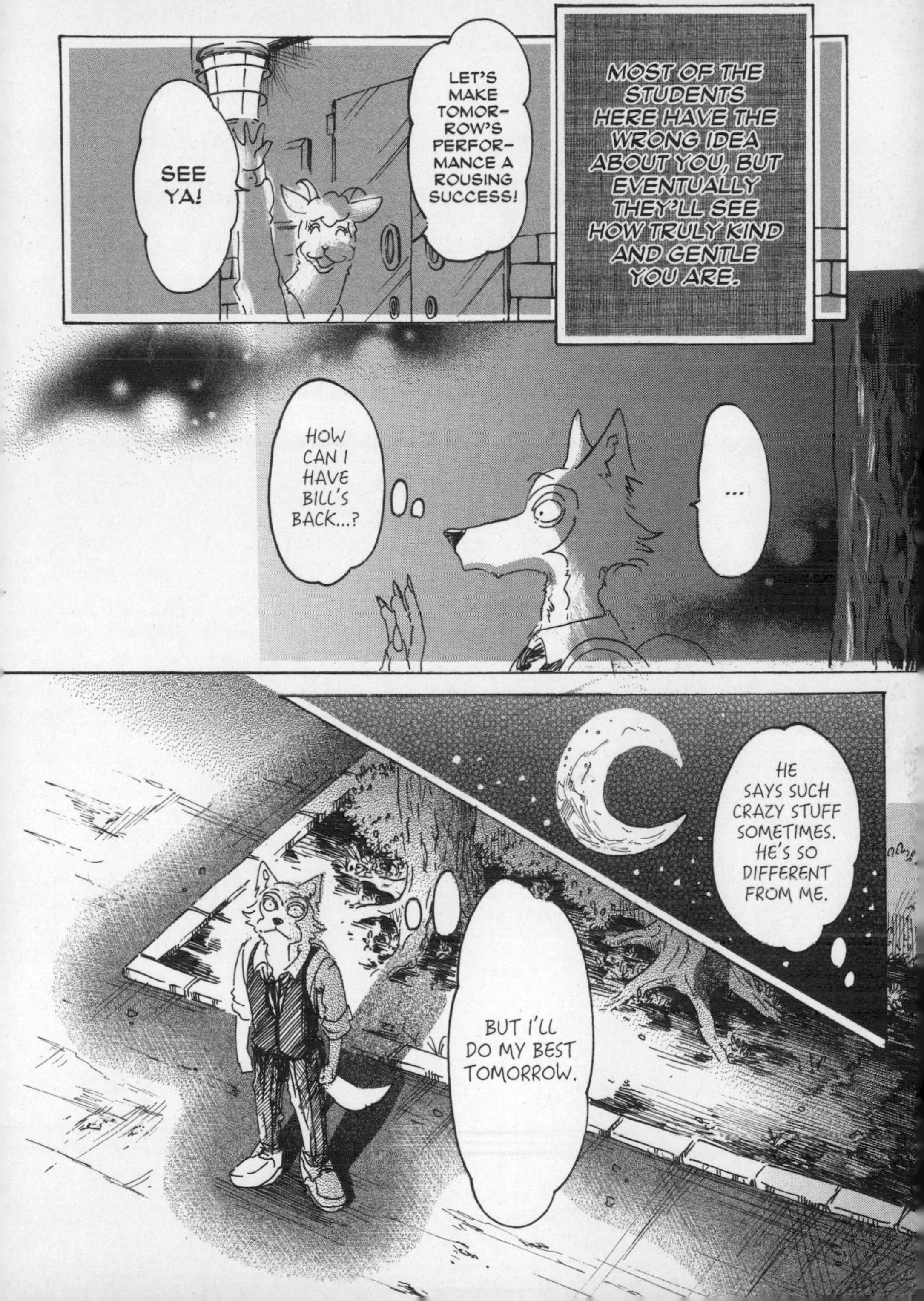
MOST OF THE STUDENTS HERE HAVE THE WRONG IDEA ABOUT YOU, BUT EVENTUALLY THEY'LL SEE HOW TRULY KIND AND GENTLE YOU ARE.
LET'S MAKE TOMORROW'S PERFORMANCE A ROUSING SUCCESS!
SEE YA!
...
HOW CAN I HAVE BILL'S BACK...?
HE SAYS SUCH CRAZY STUFF SOMETIMES. HE'S SO DIFFERENT FROM ME.
BUT I'LL DO MY BEST TOMORROW.

Chapter 14: On the Scent of the Holy Grail

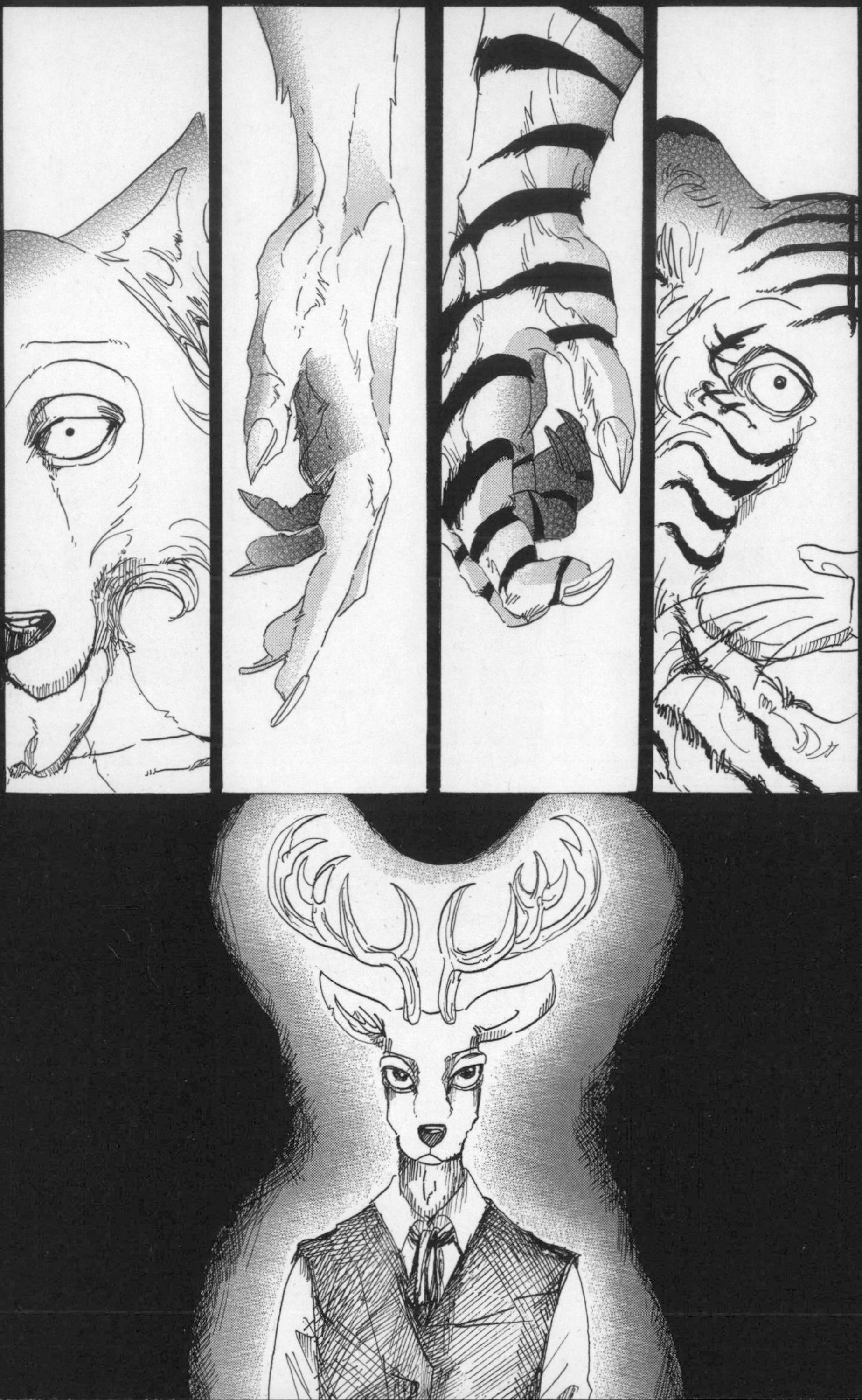

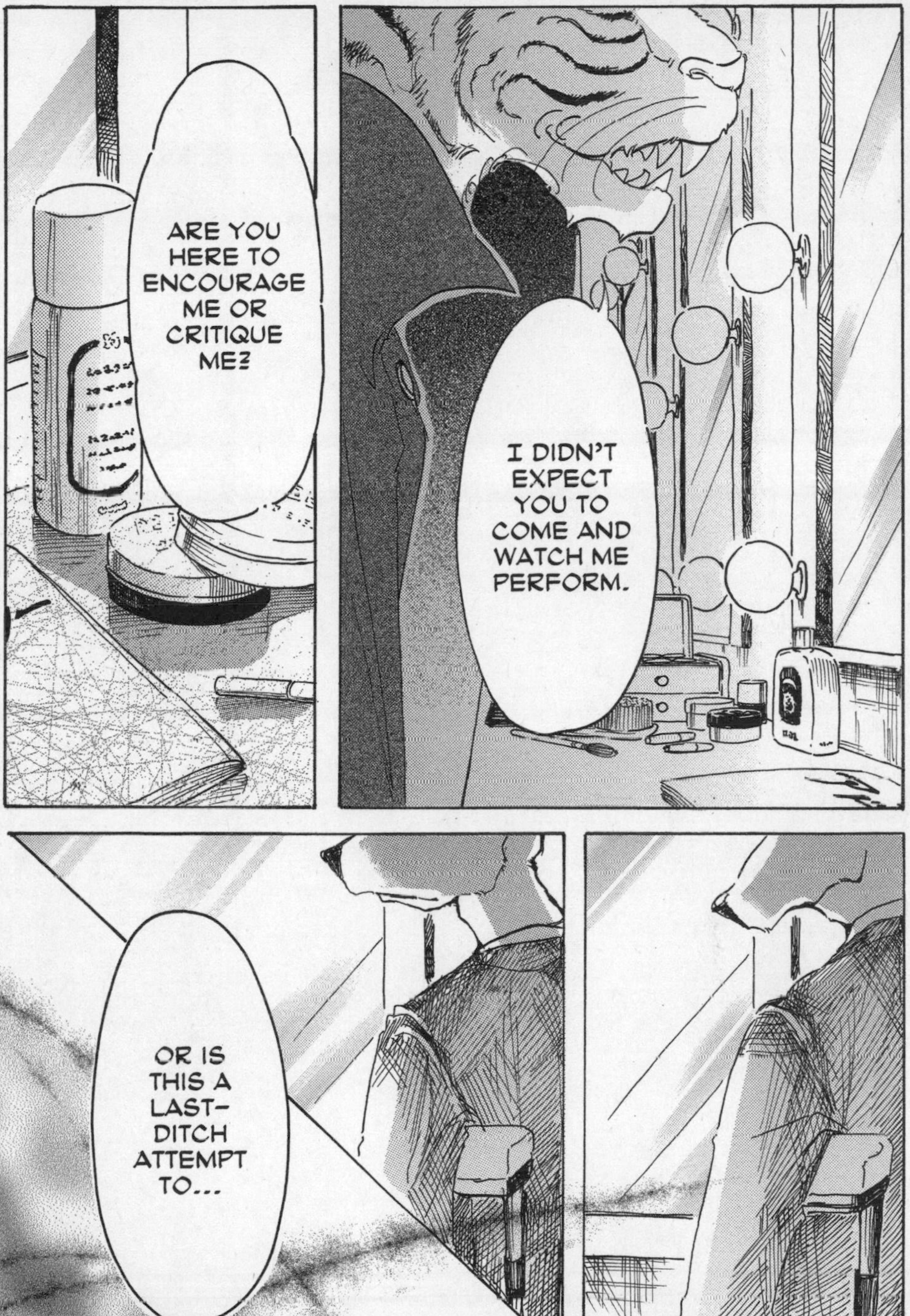
I DIDN'T EXPECT YOU TO COME AND WATCH ME PERFORM.
ARE YOU HERE TO ENCOURAGE ME OR CRITIQUE ME?
OR IS THIS A LAST-DITCH ATTEMPT TO...

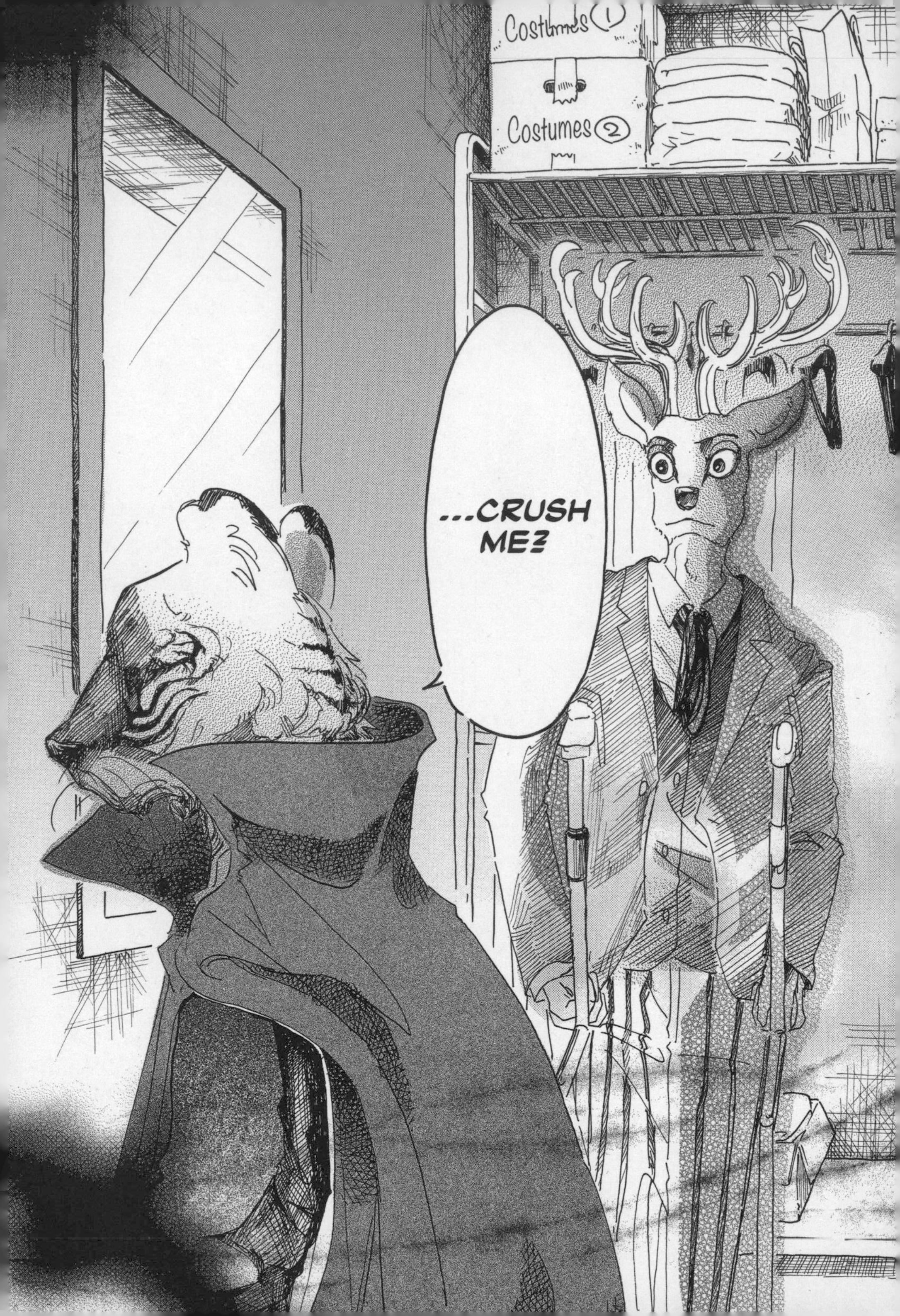
Costumes ①
Costumes ②
...CRUSH ME?

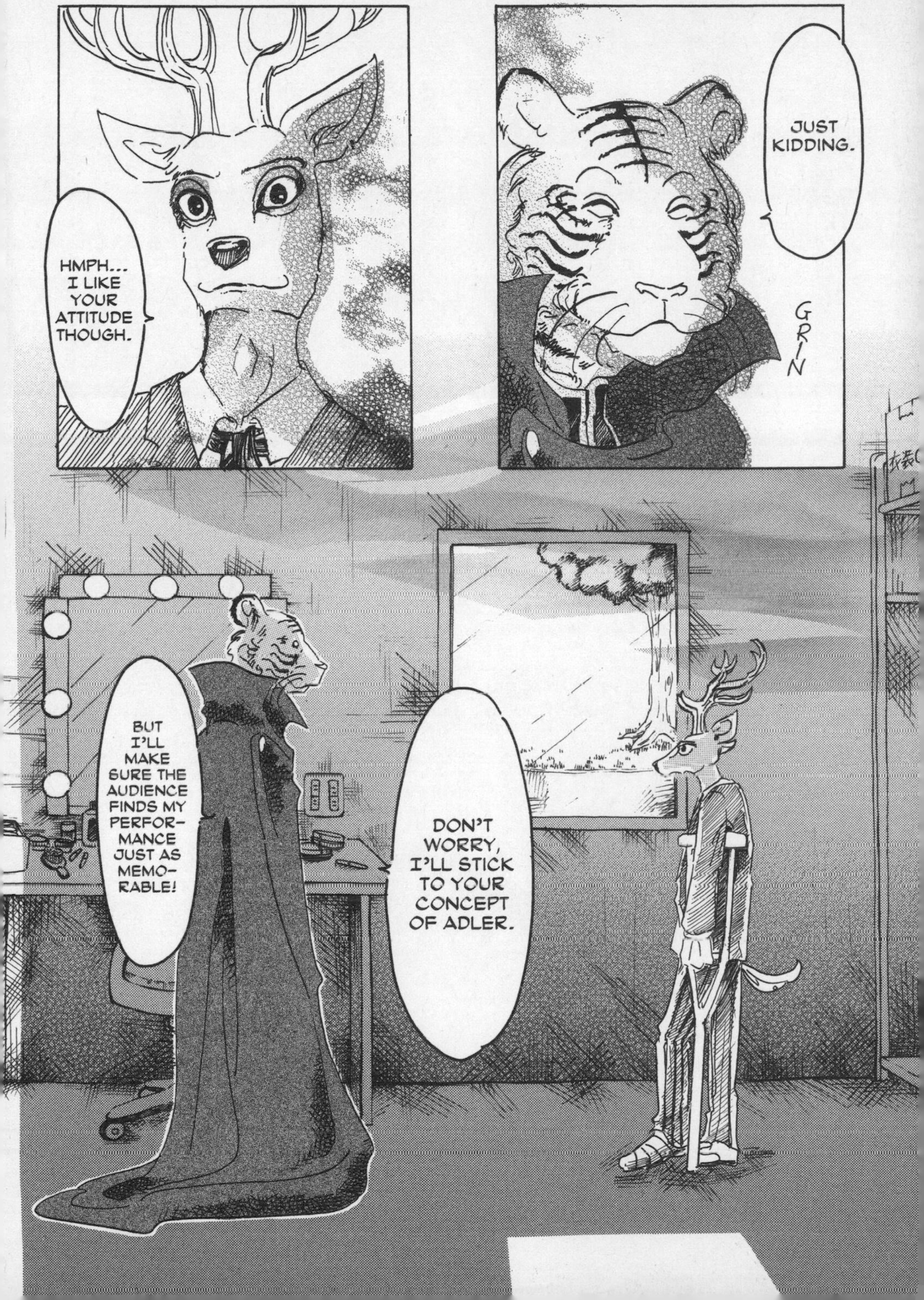
JUST KIDDING.
GRIN
HMPH... I LIKE YOUR ATTITUDE THOUGH.
DON'T WORRY, I'LL STICK TO YOUR CONCEPT OF ADLER.
BUT I'LL MAKE SURE THE AUDIENCE FINDS MY PERFORMANCE JUST AS MEMORABLE!

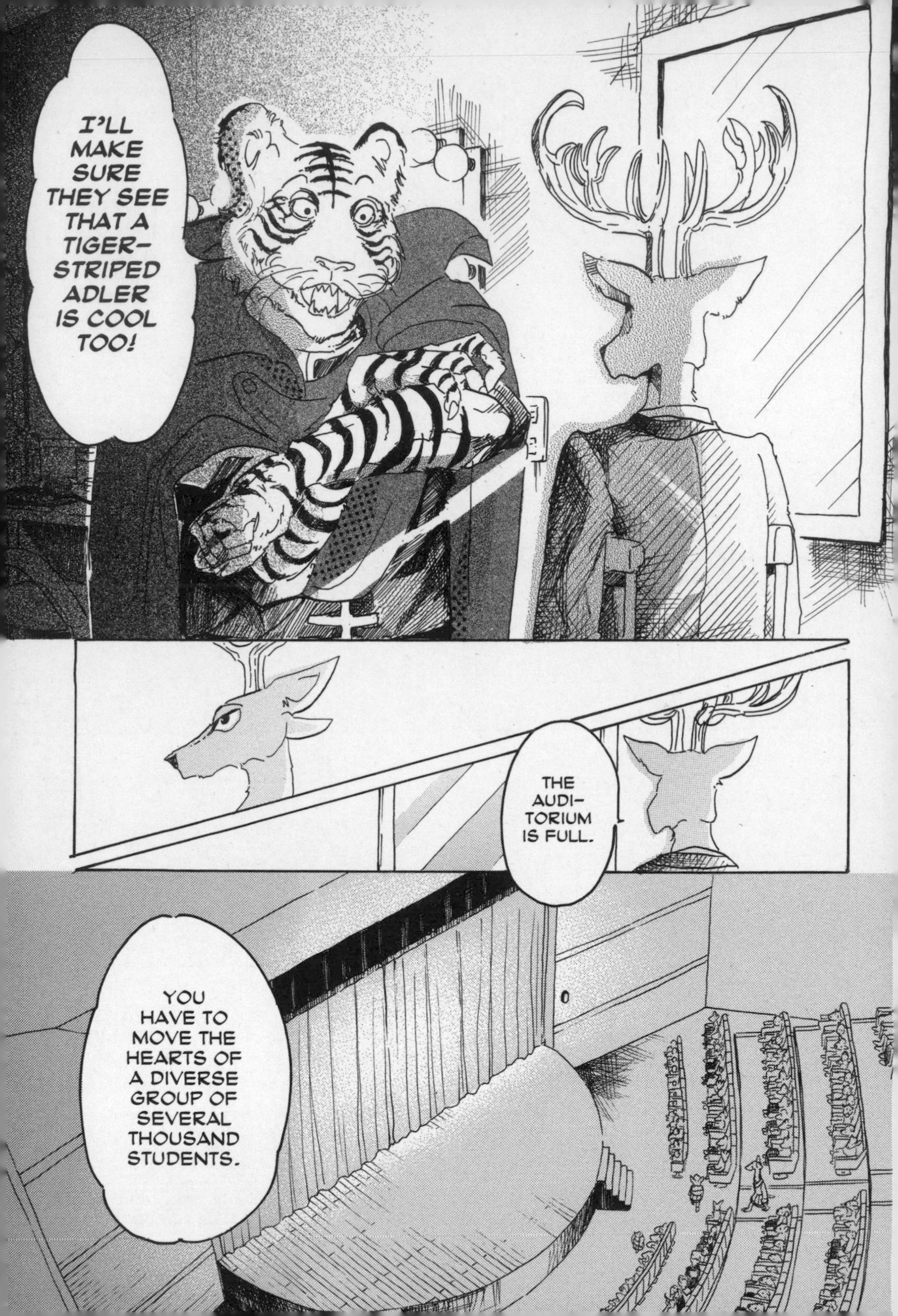
I'LL MAKE SURE THEY SEE THAT A TIGER-STRIPED ADLER IS COOL TOO!
THE AUDITORIUM IS FULL.
YOU HAVE TO MOVE THE HEARTS OF A DIVERSE GROUP OF SEVERAL THOUSAND STUDENTS.

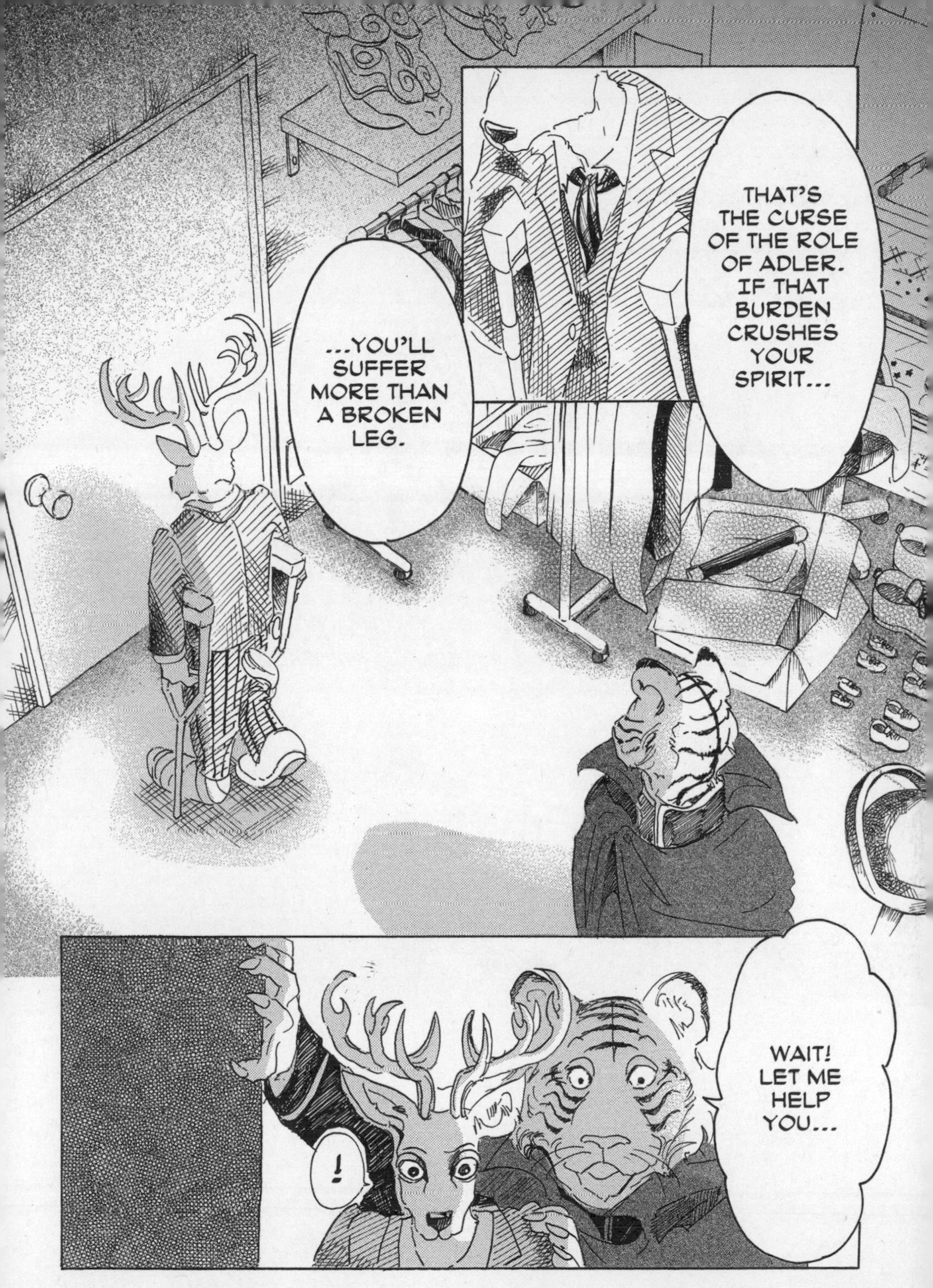
THAT'S THE CURSE OF THE ROLE OF ADLER. IF THAT BURDEN CRUSHES YOUR SPIRIT...
...YOU'LL SUFFER MORE THAN A BROKEN LEG.
WAIT! LET ME HELP YOU...
!

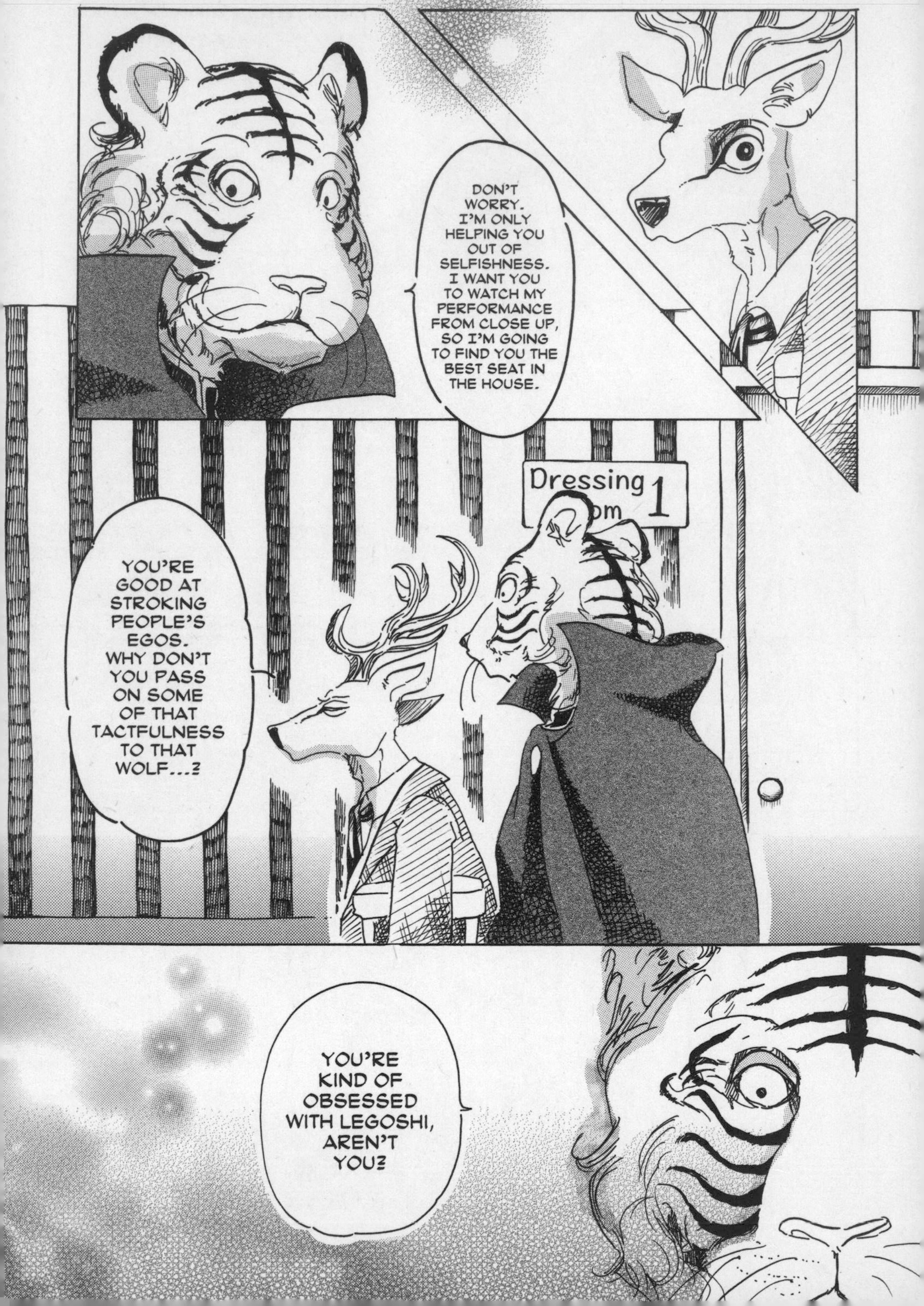
DON'T WORRY. I'M ONLY HELPING YOU OUT OF SELFISHNESS. I WANT YOU TO WATCH MY PERFORMANCE FROM CLOSE UP, SO I'M GOING TO FIND YOU THE BEST SEAT IN THE HOUSE.
Dressing
1
YOU'RE GOOD AT STROKING PEOPLE'S EGOS. WHY DON'T YOU PASS ON SOME OF THAT TACTFULNESS TO THAT WOLF...?
YOU'RE KIND OF OBSESSED WITH LEGOSHI, AREN'T YOU?

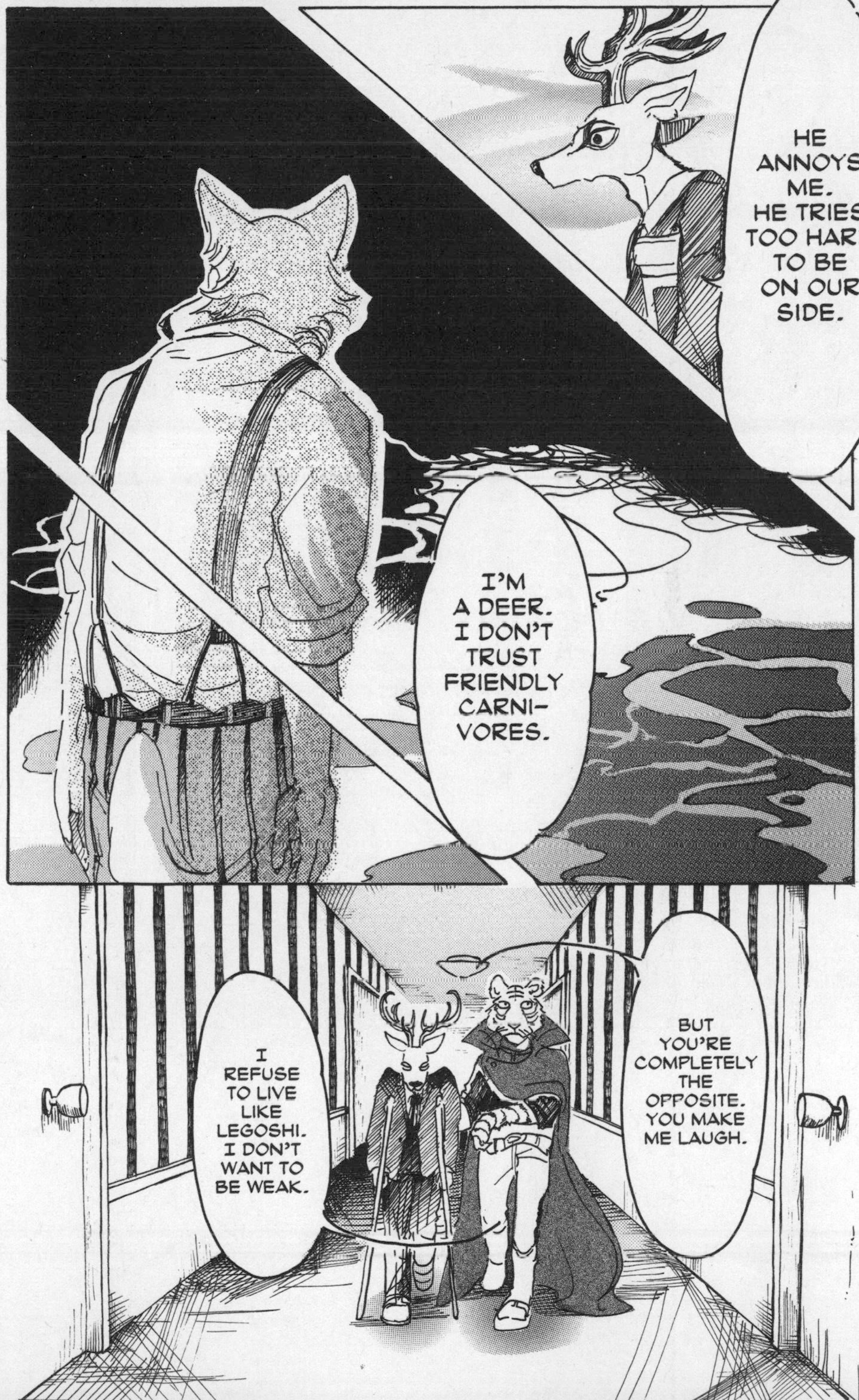
HE ANNOYS ME. HE TRIES TOO HARD TO BE ON OUR SIDE.
I'M A DEER. I DON'T TRUST FRIENDLY CARNI-VORES.
BUT YOU'RE COMPLETELY THE OPPOSITE. YOU MAKE ME LAUGH.
I REFUSE TO LIVE LIKE LEGOSHI. I DON'T WANT TO BE WEAK.

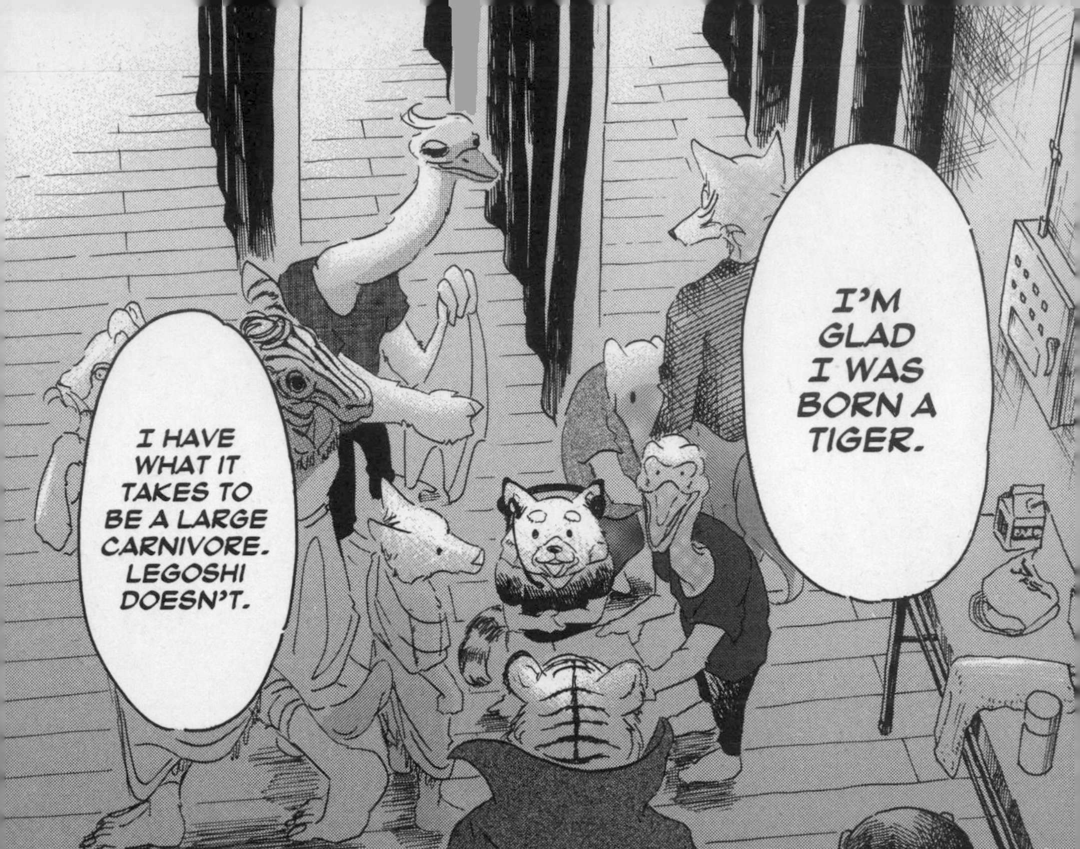
I'M GLAD I WAS BORN A TIGER.
I HAVE WHAT IT TAKES TO BE A LARGE CARNIVORE. LEGOSHI DOESN'T.
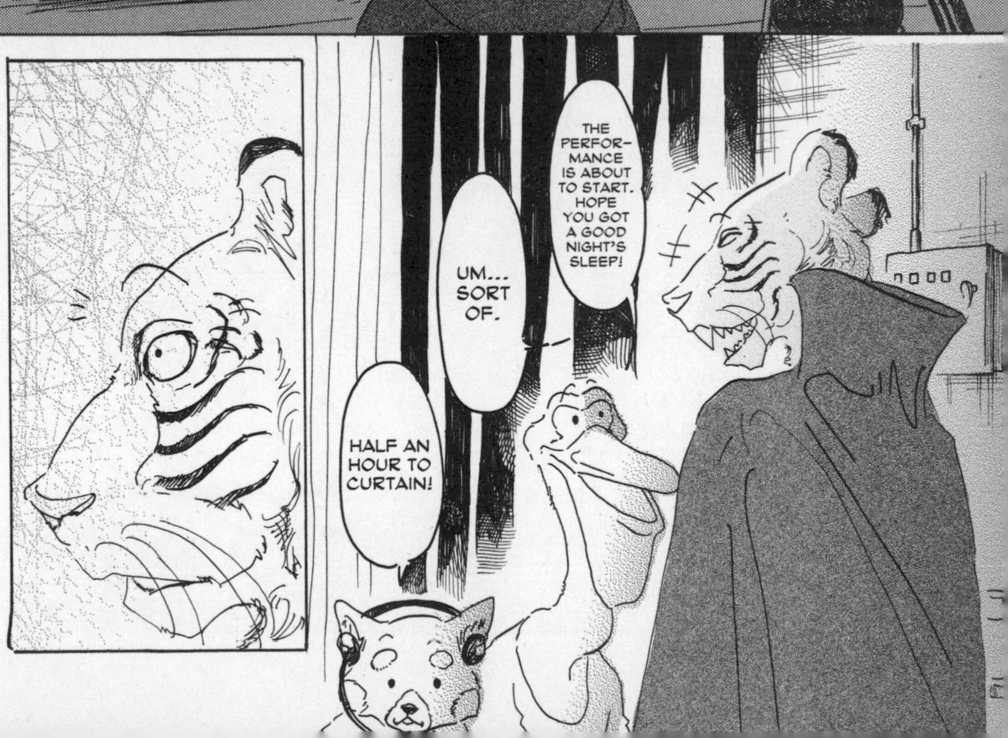
THE PERFORMANCE IS ABOUT TO START. HOPE YOU GOT A GOOD NIGHT'S SLEEP!
UM... SORT OF.
HALF AN HOUR TO CURTAIN!

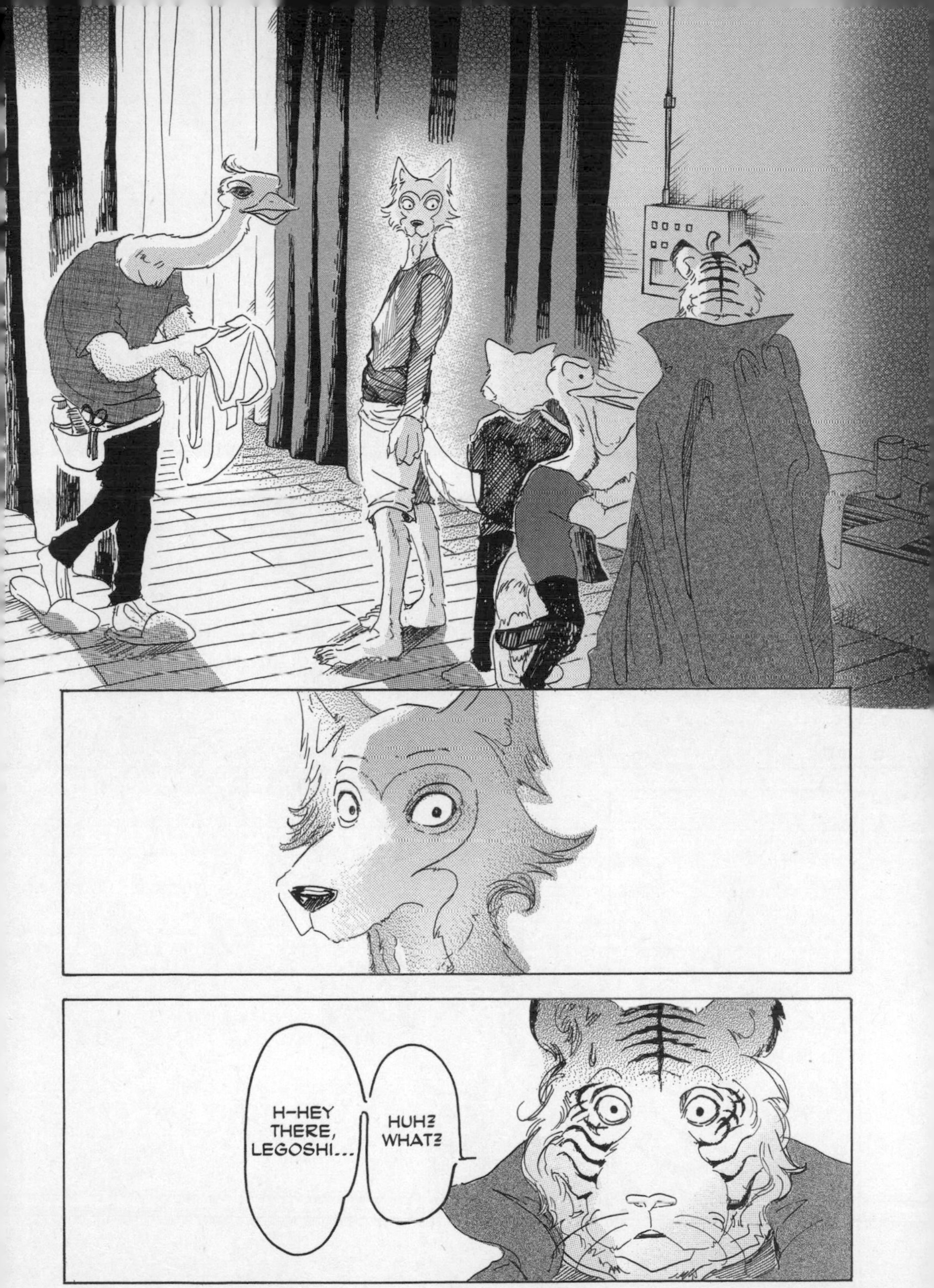
HUH? WHAT?
H-HEY THERE, LEGOSHI...

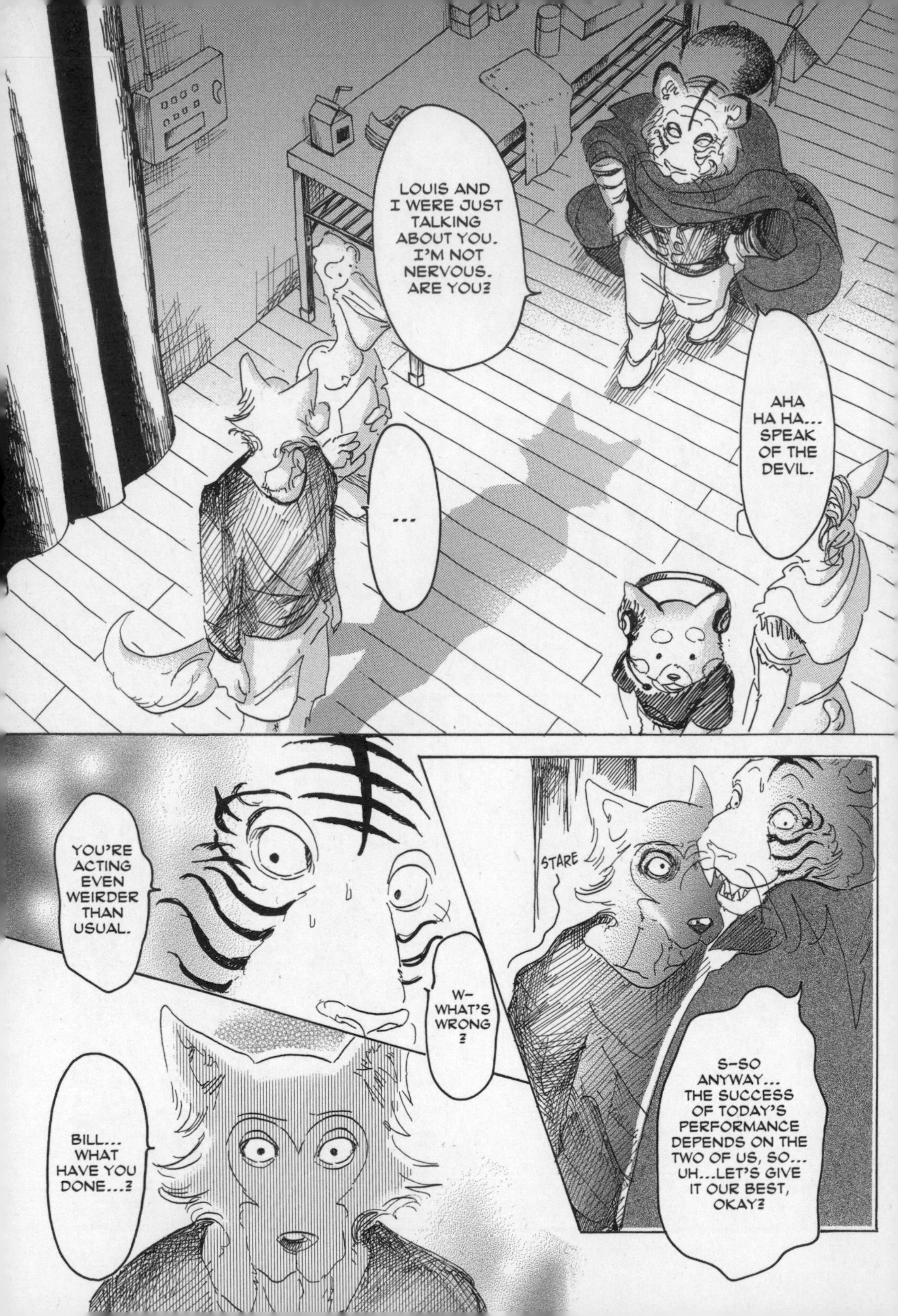
AHA HA HA... SPEAK OF THE DEVIL.
LOUIS AND I WERE JUST TALKING ABOUT YOU. I'M NOT NERVOUS. ARE YOU?
...
STARE
S-SO ANYWAY... THE SUCCESS OF TODAY'S PERFORMANCE DEPENDS ON THE TWO OF US, SO... UH...LET'S GIVE IT OUR BEST, OKAY?
YOU'RE ACTING EVEN WEIRDER THAN USUAL.
W-WHAT'S WRONG?
BILL... WHAT HAVE YOU DONE...?

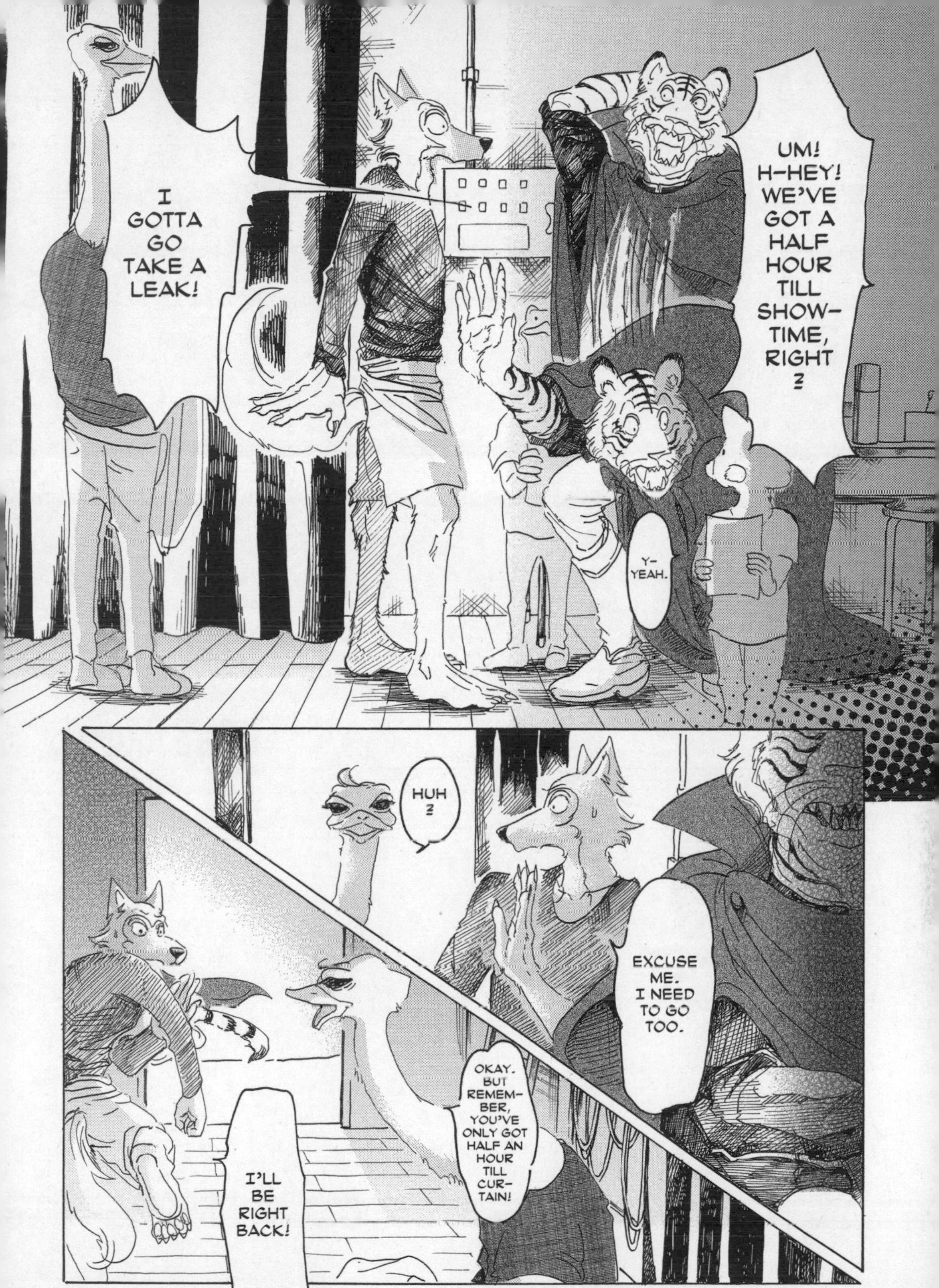
UM! H-HEY! WE'VE GOT A HALF HOUR TILL SHOW-TIME, RIGHT?
I GOTTA GO TAKE A LEAK!
Y-YEAH.
EXCUSE ME. I NEED TO GO TOO.
HUH?
OKAY. BUT REMEMBER, YOU'VE ONLY GOT HALF AN HOUR TILL CUR-TAIN!
I'LL BE RIGHT BACK!

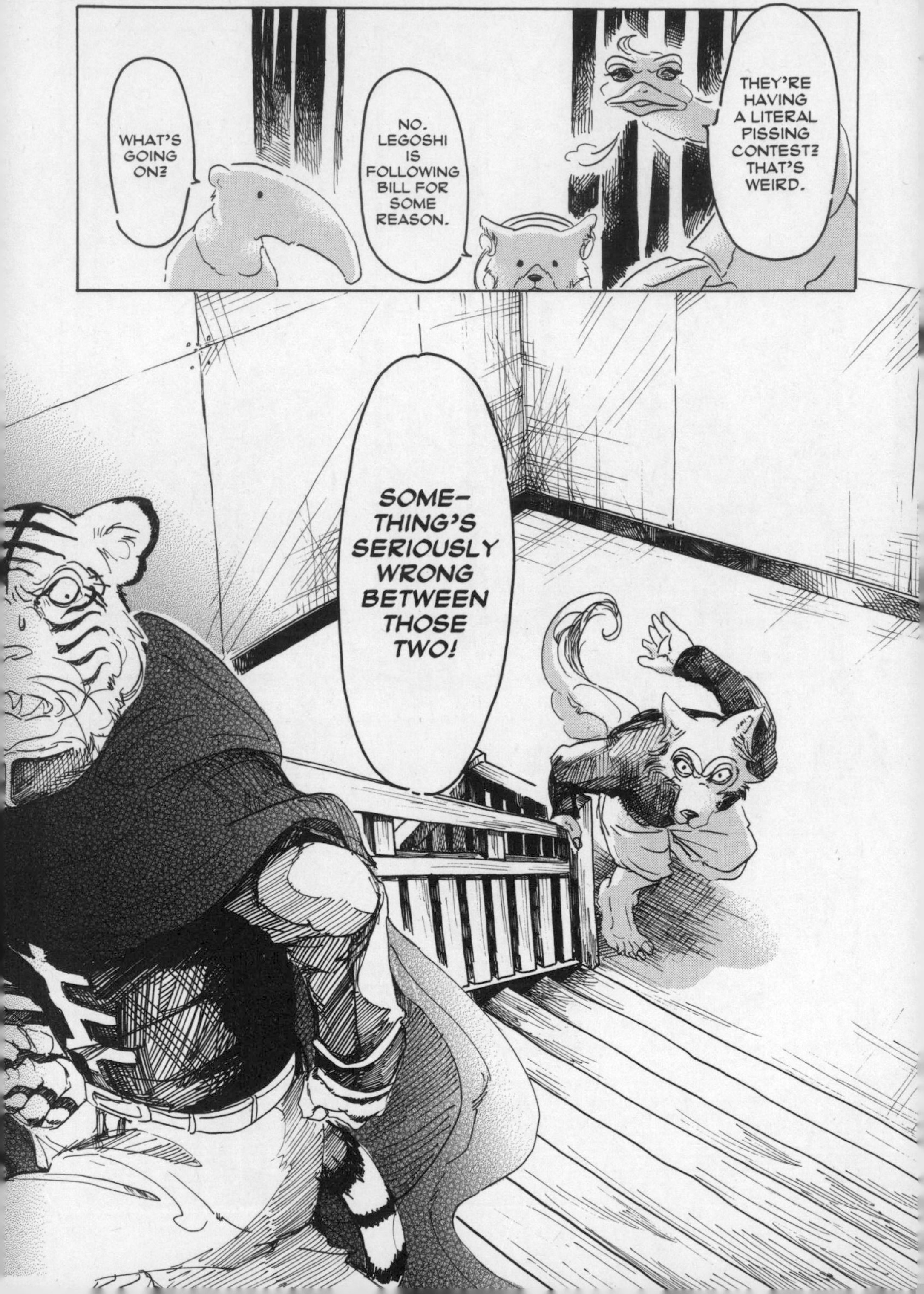
THEY'RE HAVING A LITERAL PISSING CONTEST? THAT'S WEIRD.
NO. LEGOSHI IS FOLLOWING BILL FOR SOME REASON.
WHAT'S GOING ON?
SOME-THING'S SERIOUSLY WRONG BETWEEN THOSE TWO!

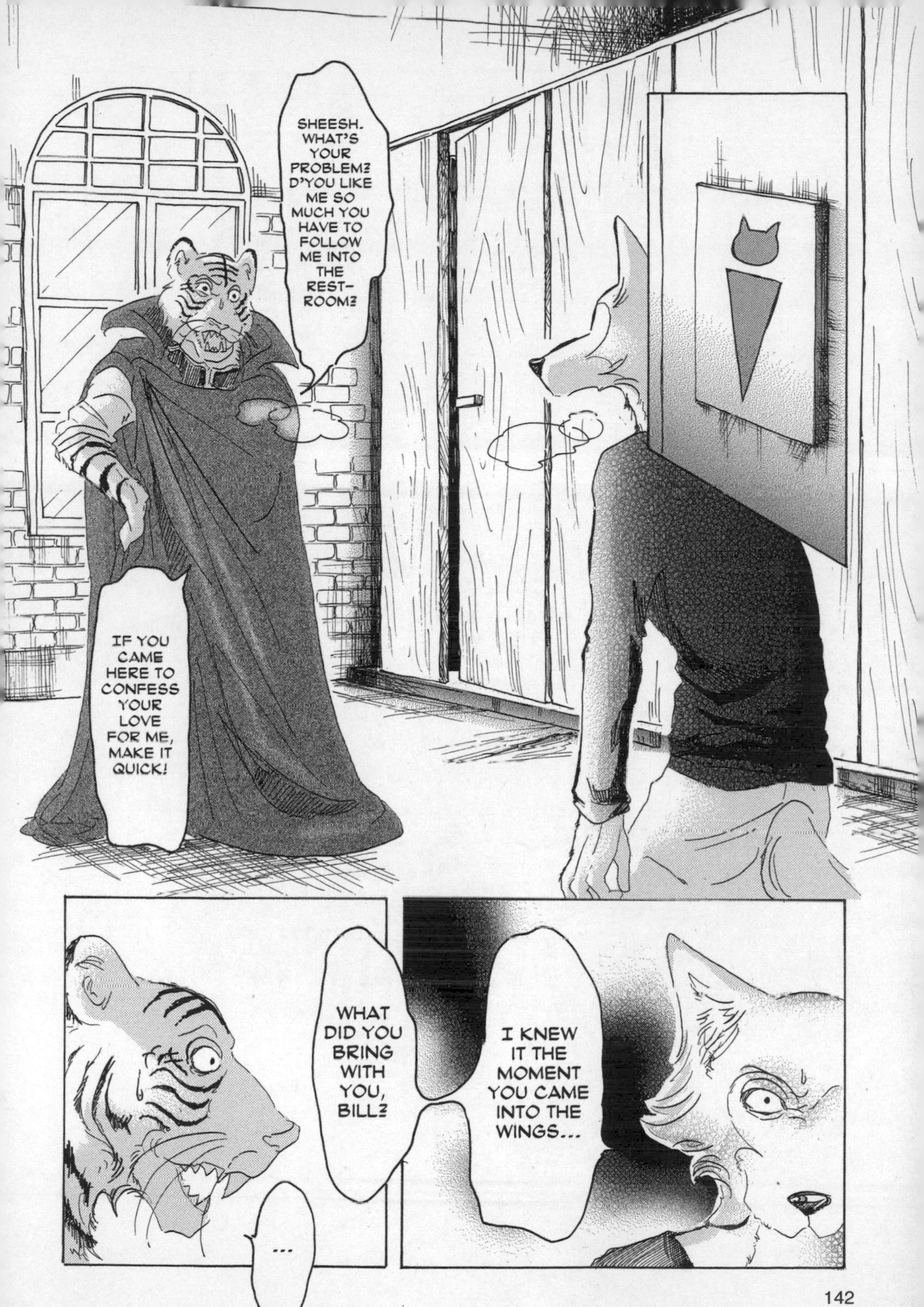
SHEESH. WHAT'S YOUR PROBLEM? D'YOU LIKE ME SO MUCH YOU HAVE TO FOLLOW ME INTO THE REST-ROOM?
IF YOU CAME HERE TO CONFESS YOUR LOVE FOR ME, MAKE IT QUICK!
I KNEW IT THE MOMENT YOU CAME INTO THE WINGS...
WHAT DID YOU BRING WITH YOU, BILL?
...

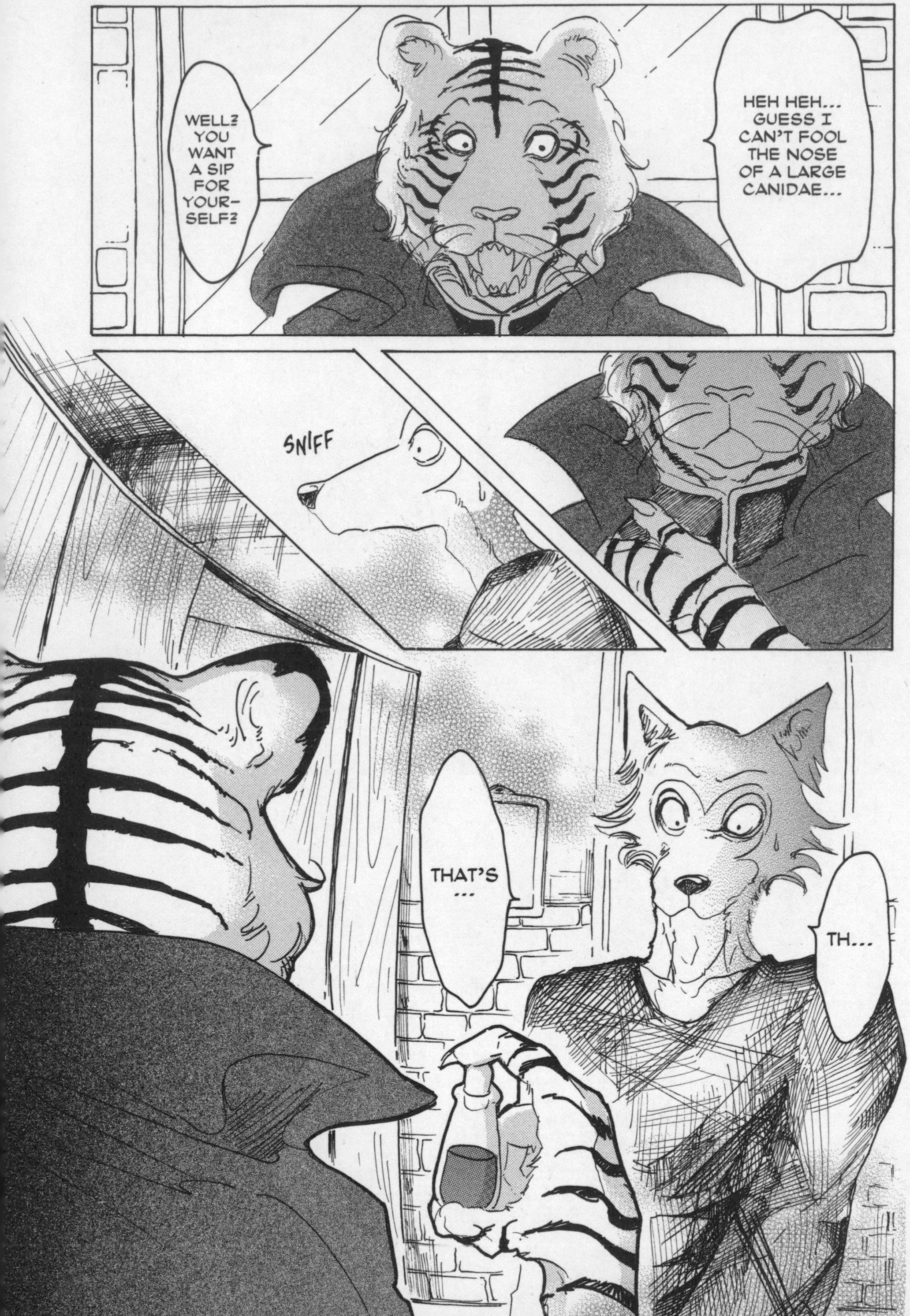
HEH HEH... GUESS I CAN'T FOOL THE NOSE OF A LARGE CANIDAE...
WELL? YOU WANT A SIP FOR YOUR-SELF?
SNIFF
TH...
THAT'S ...

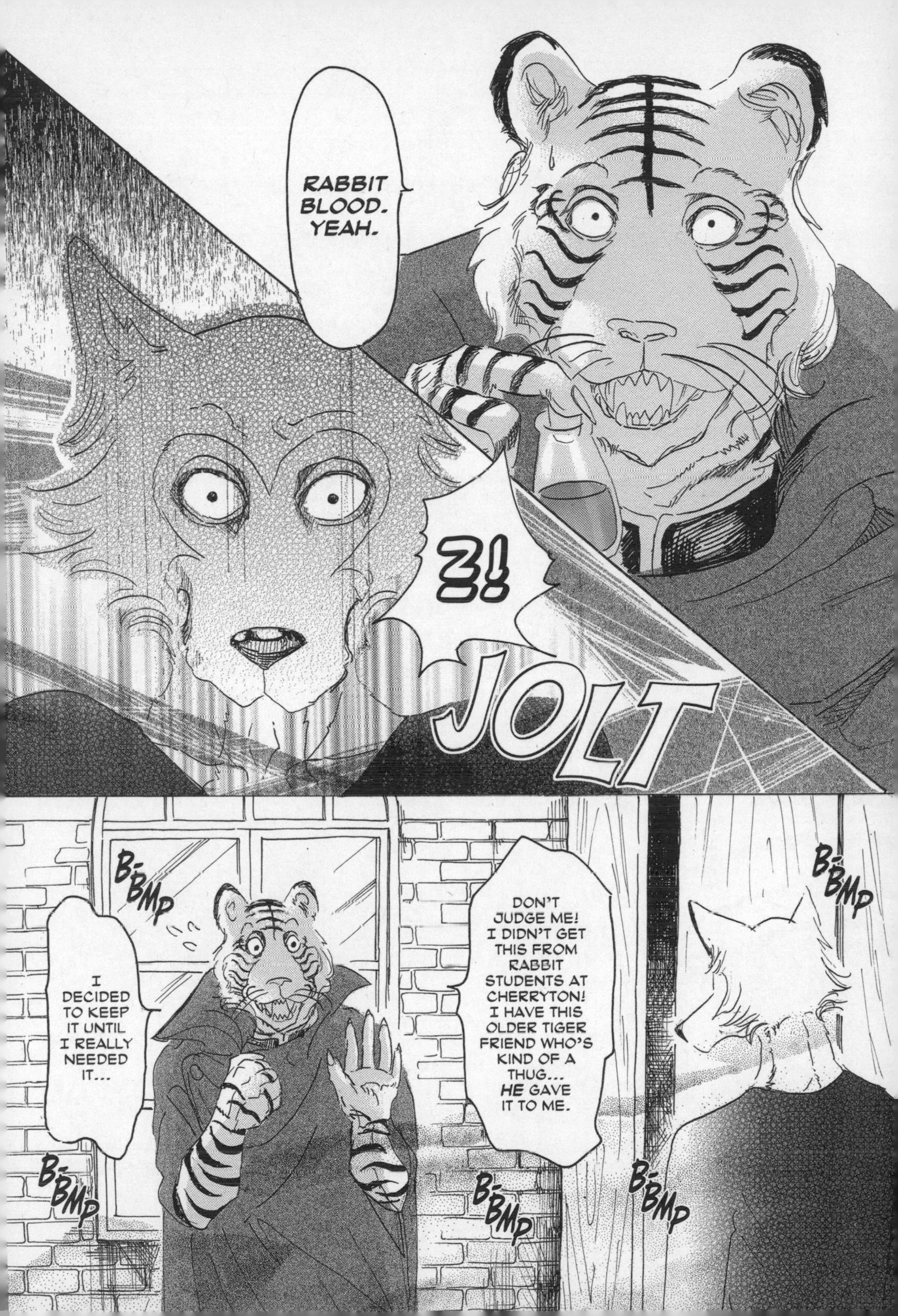
RABBIT BLOOD. YEAH.
!!
JOLT
B-BMP
DON'T JUDGE ME! I DIDN'T GET THIS FROM RABBIT STUDENTS AT CHERRYTON! I HAVE THIS OLDER TIGER FRIEND WHO'S KIND OF A THUG... *HE* GAVE IT TO ME.
B-BMP
I DECIDED TO KEEP IT UNTIL I REALLY NEEDED IT...
B-BMP
B-BMP
B-BMP

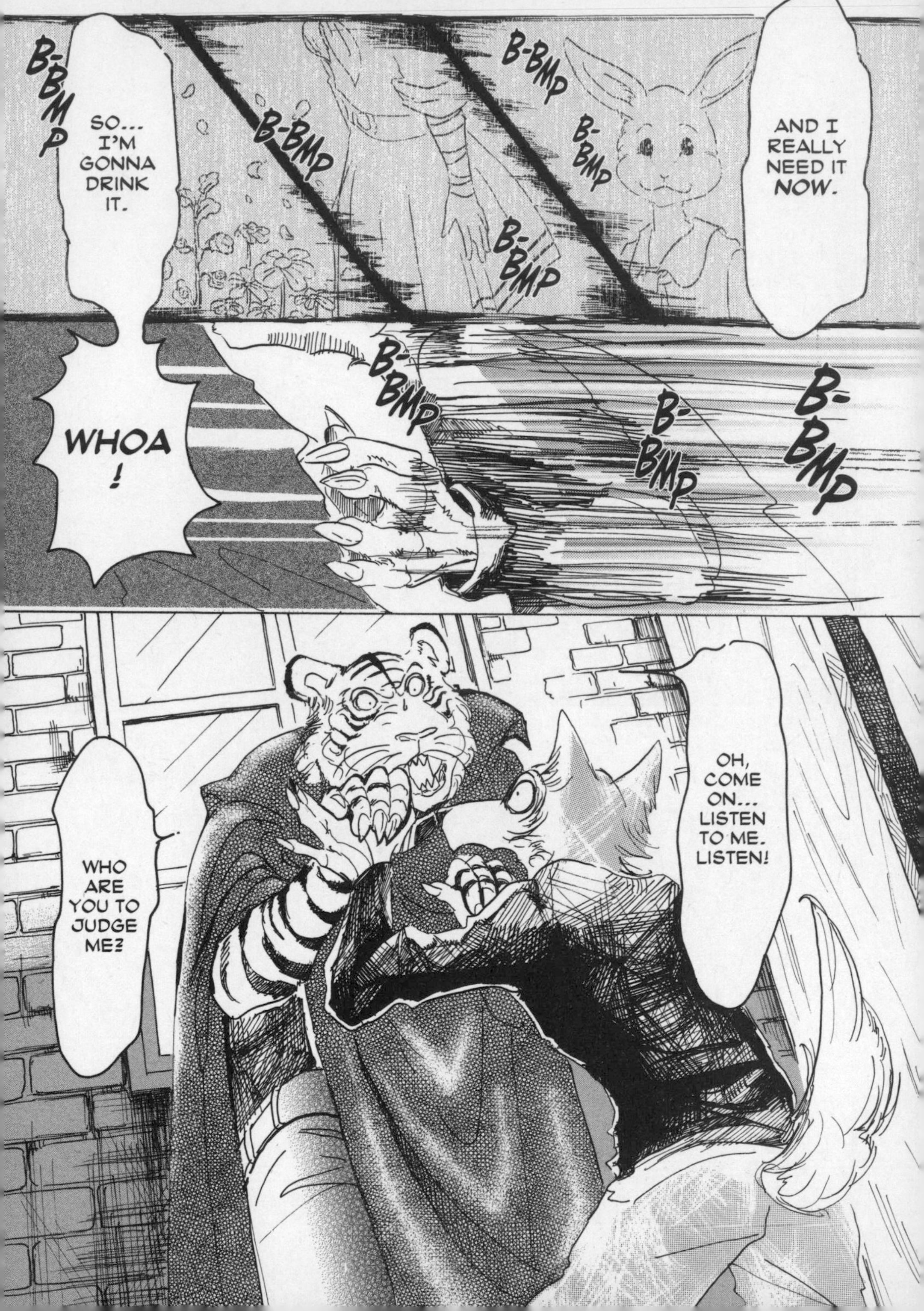
AND I REALLY NEED IT NOW.
B-BMP
B-BMP
B-BMP
B-BMP
SO... I'M GONNA DRINK IT.
B-BMP
B-BMP
B-BMP
B-BMP
WHOA!
OH, COME ON... LISTEN TO ME. LISTEN!
WHO ARE YOU TO JUDGE ME?

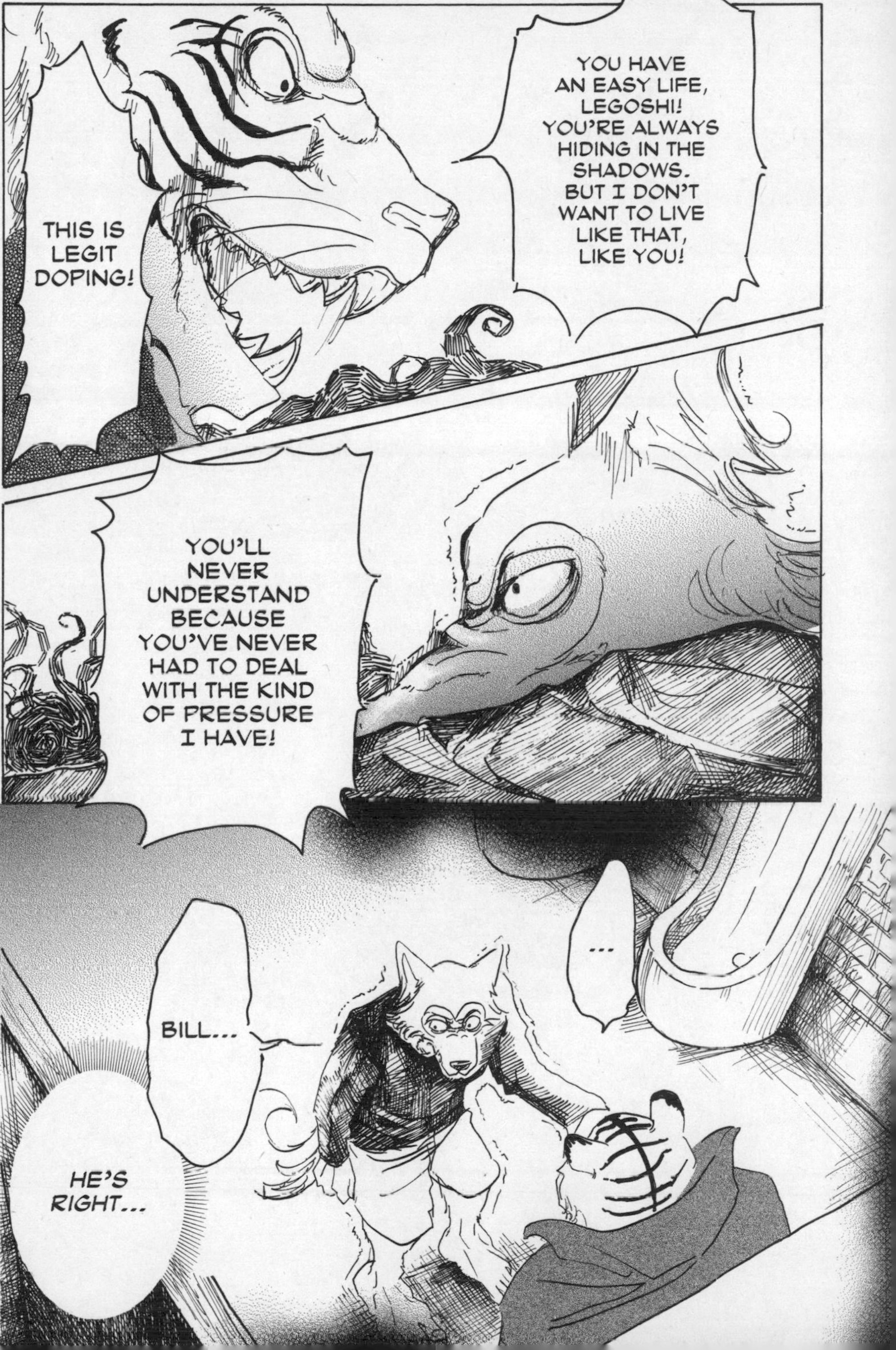
YOU HAVE AN EASY LIFE, LEGOSHI! YOU'RE ALWAYS HIDING IN THE SHADOWS. BUT I DON'T WANT TO LIVE LIKE THAT, LIKE YOU!
THIS IS LEGIT DOPING!
YOU'LL NEVER UNDERSTAND BECAUSE YOU'VE NEVER HAD TO DEAL WITH THE KIND OF PRESSURE I HAVE!
...
BILL...
HE'S RIGHT...

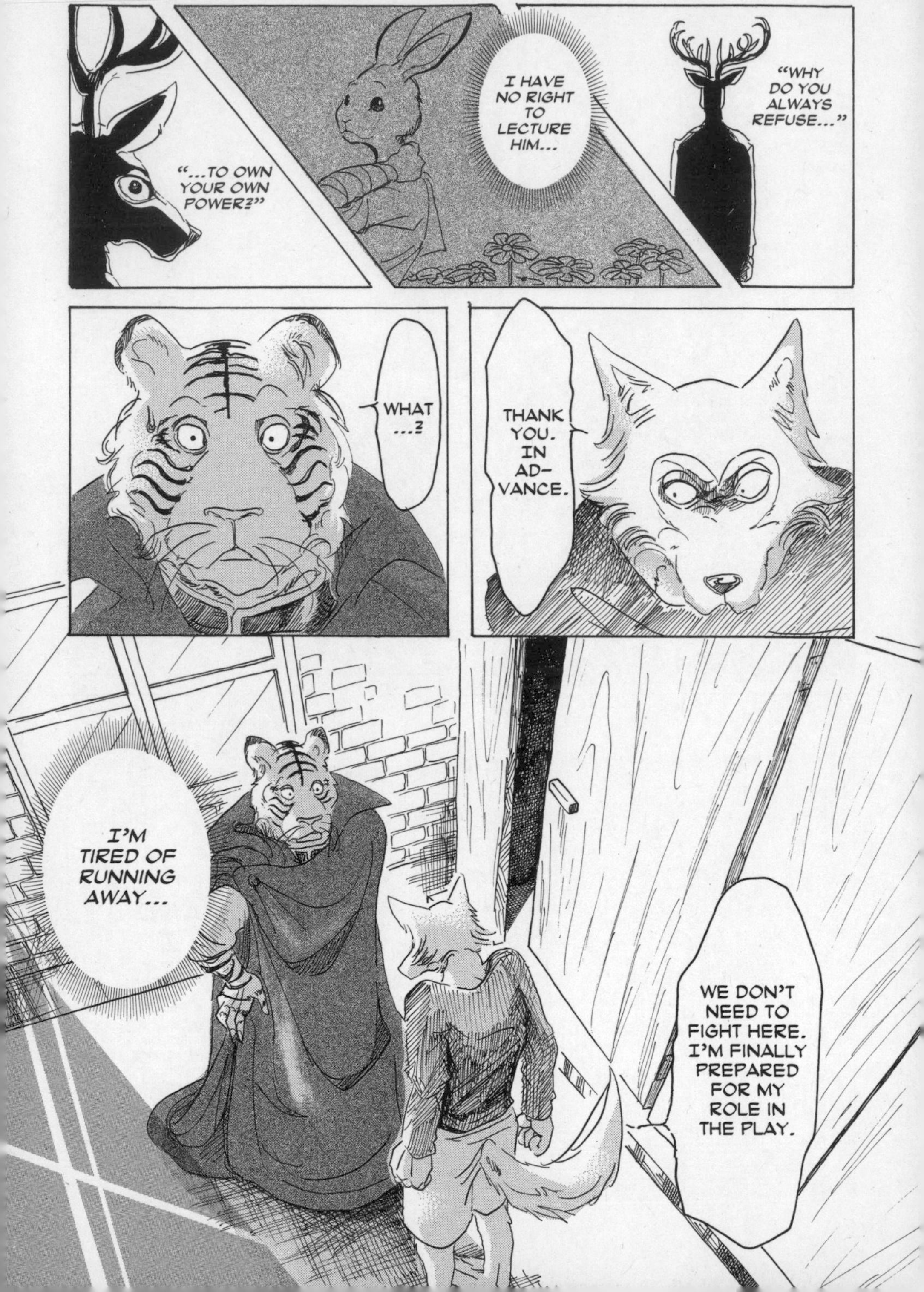
"WHY DO YOU ALWAYS REFUSE..."
I HAVE NO RIGHT TO LECTURE HIM...
"...TO OWN YOUR OWN POWER?"
THANK YOU. IN AD-VANCE.
WHAT ...?
WE DON'T NEED TO FIGHT HERE. I'M FINALLY PREPARED FOR MY ROLE IN THE PLAY.
I'M TIRED OF RUNNING AWAY...

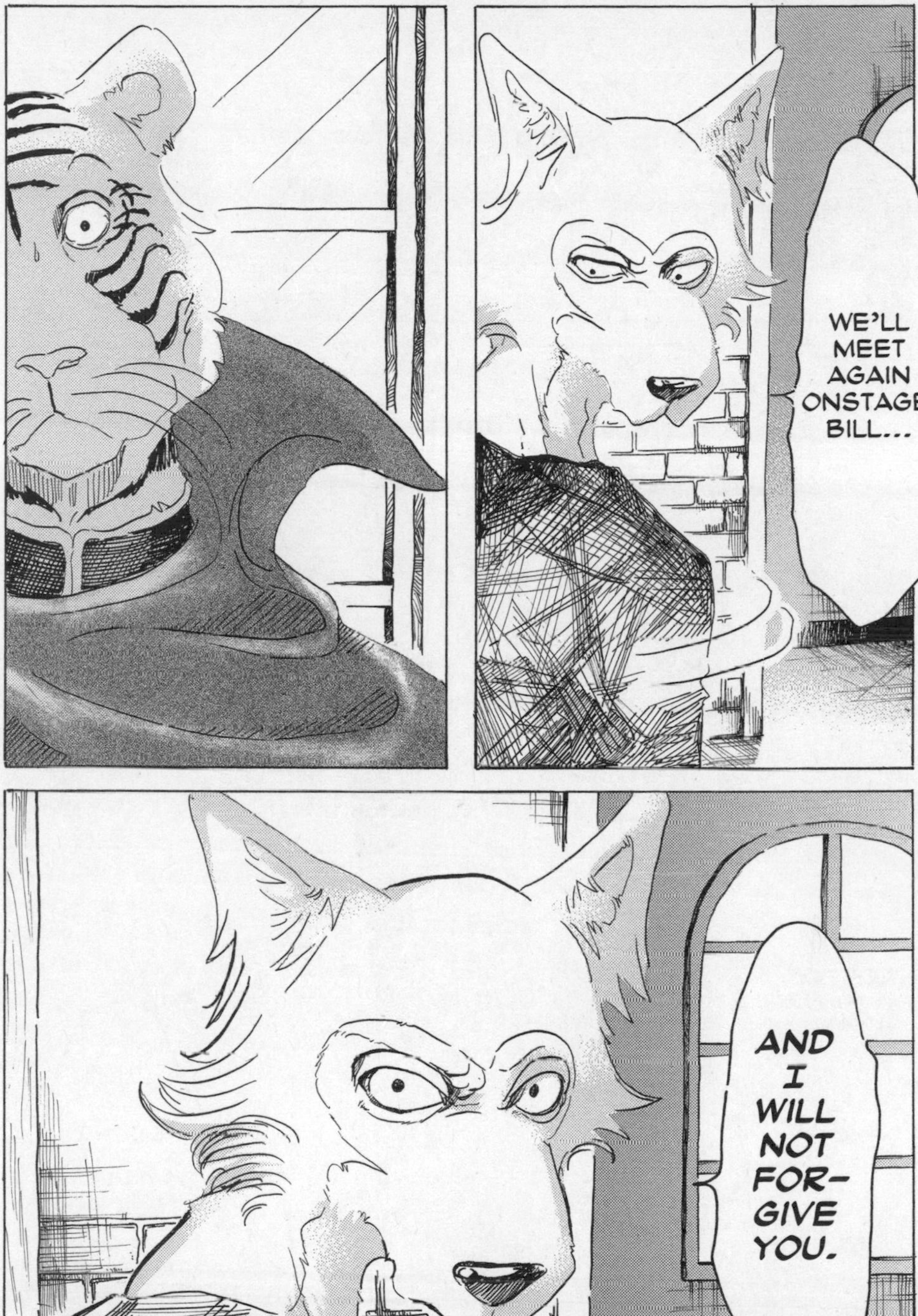
WE'LL MEET AGAIN ONSTAGE, BILL...
AND I WILL NOT FOR-GIVE YOU.

Chapter 15: Camaraderie

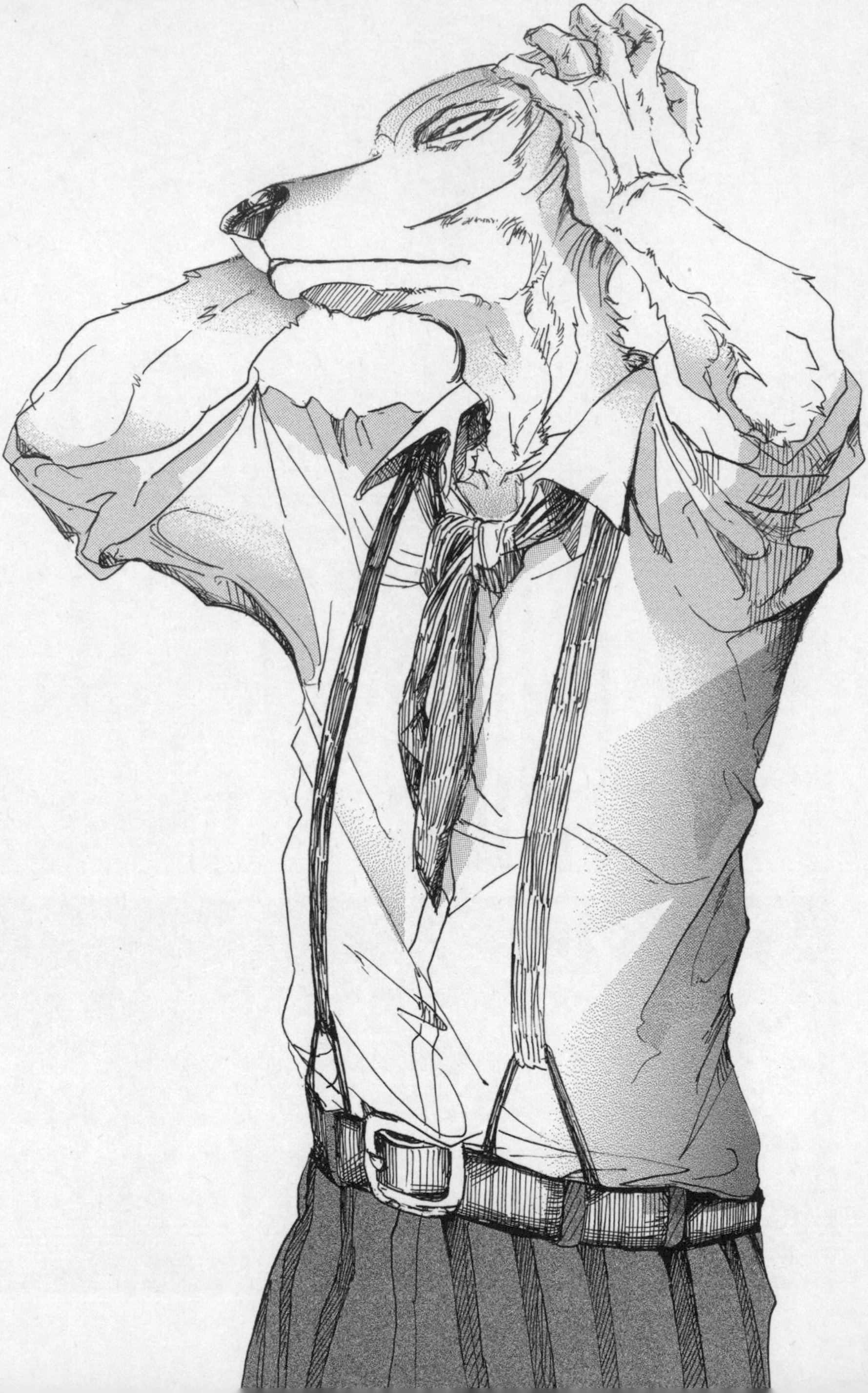

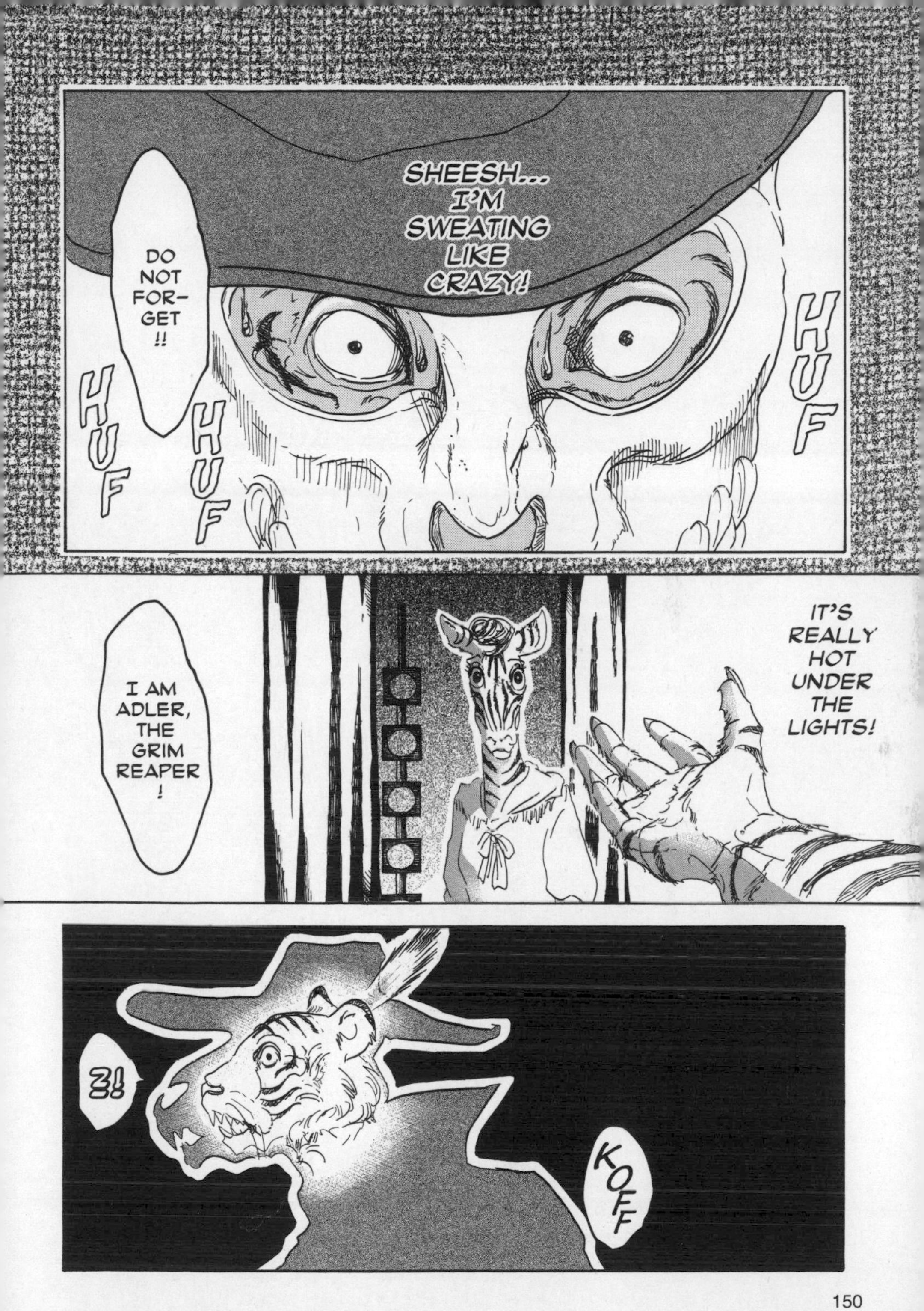
HUF HUF
SHEESH... I'M SWEATING LIKE CRAZY!
DO NOT FOR-GET!!
HUF HUF
HUF HUF
IT'S REALLY HOT UNDER THE LIGHTS!
I AM ADLER, THE GRIM REAPER!
KOFF

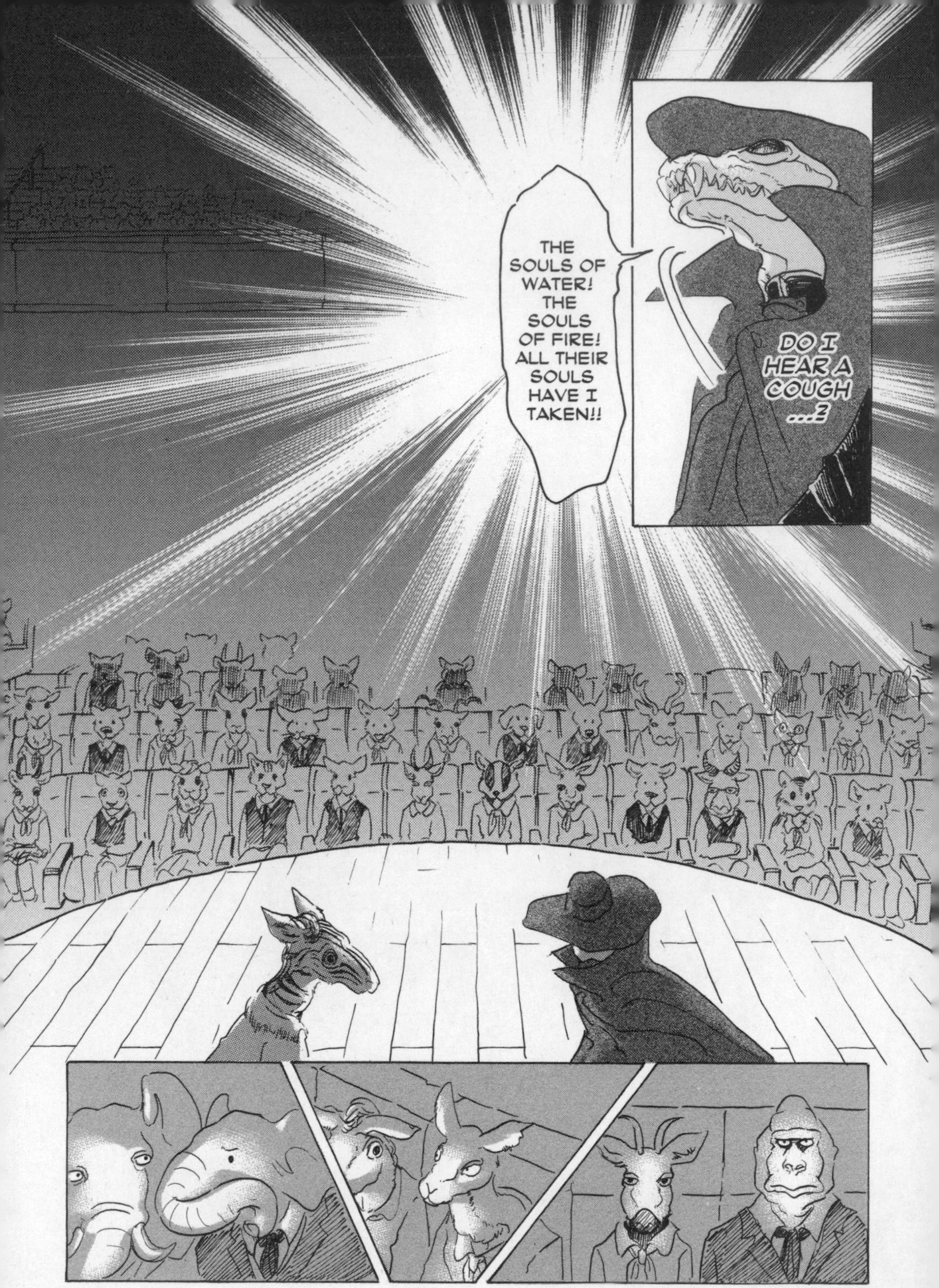
THE SOULS OF WATER! THE SOULS OF FIRE! ALL THEIR SOULS HAVE I TAKEN!!
DO I HEAR A COUGH ...?

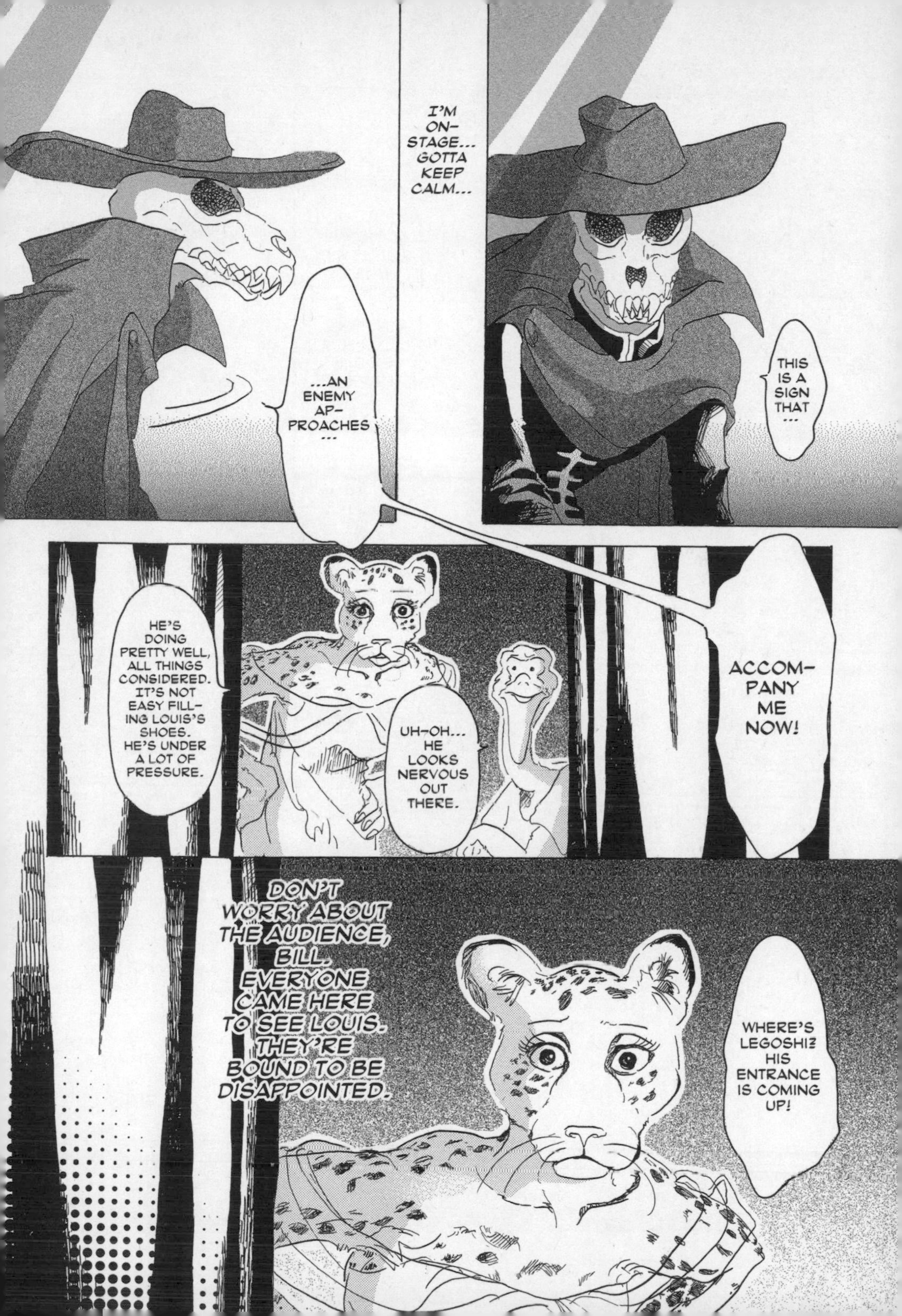
I'M ON-STAGE... GOTTA KEEP CALM...
THIS IS A SIGN THAT...
...AN ENEMY AP-PROACHES...
ACCOM-PANY ME NOW!
UH-OH... HE LOOKS NERVOUS OUT THERE.
HE'S DOING PRETTY WELL, ALL THINGS CONSIDERED. IT'S NOT EASY FILL-ING LOUIS'S SHOES. HE'S UNDER A LOT OF PRESSURE.
WHERE'S LEGOSHI? HIS ENTRANCE IS COMING UP!
DON'T WORRY ABOUT THE AUDIENCE, BILL. EVERYONE CAME HERE TO SEE LOUIS. THEY'RE BOUND TO BE DISAPPOINTED.

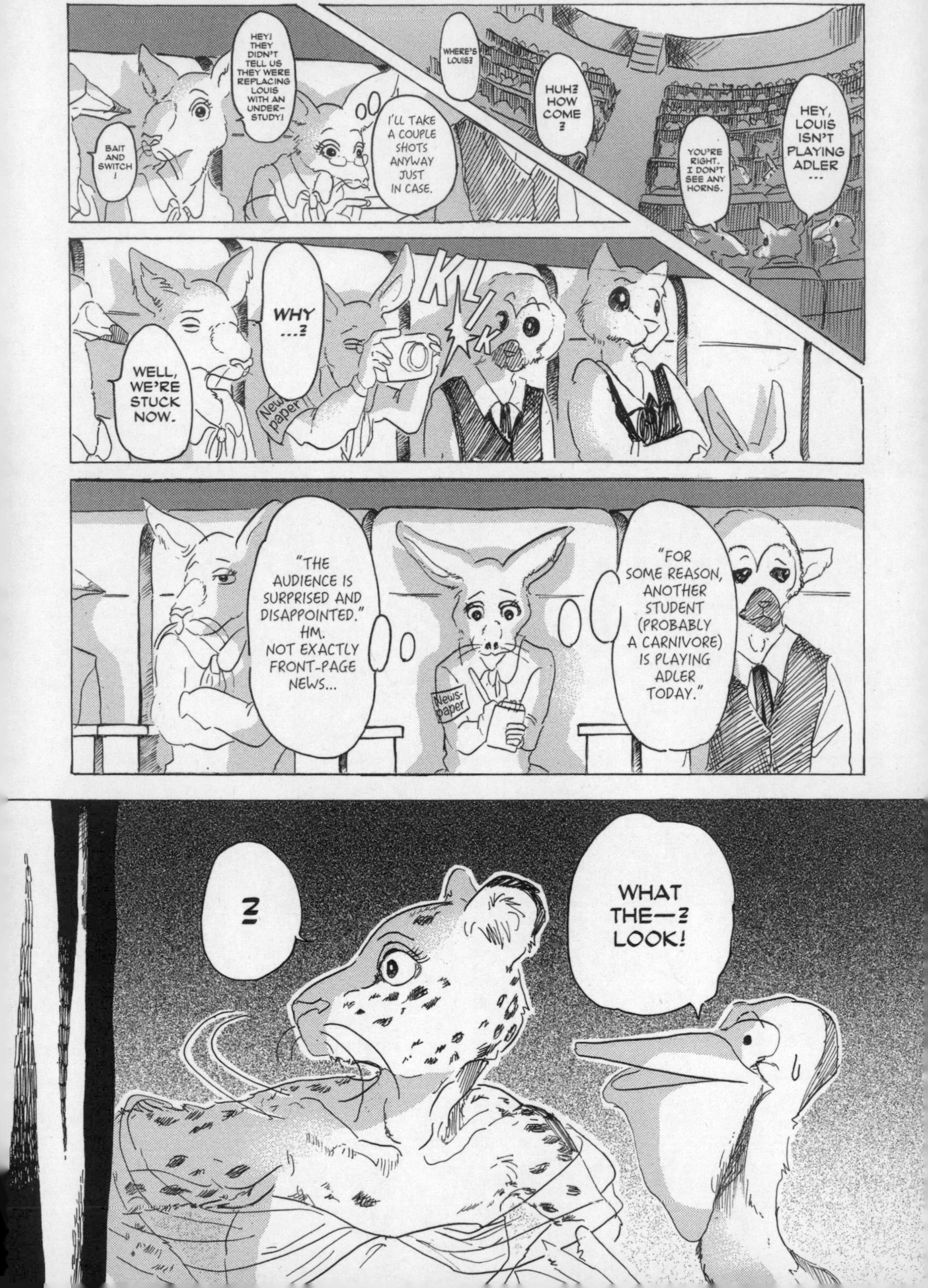
HEY, LOUIS ISN'T PLAYING ADLER ...
YOU'RE RIGHT. I DON'T SEE ANY HORNS.
HUH? HOW COME?
WHERE'S LOUIS?
HEY! THEY DIDN'T TELL US THEY WERE REPLACING LOUIS WITH AN UNDER-STUDY!
I'LL TAKE A COUPLE SHOTS ANYWAY JUST IN CASE.
BAIT AND SWITCH!
KLIK
WHY ...?
Newspaper
WELL, WE'RE STUCK NOW.
"FOR SOME REASON, ANOTHER STUDENT (PROBABLY A CARNIVORE) IS PLAYING ADLER TODAY."
News-paper
"THE AUDIENCE IS SURPRISED AND DISAPPOINTED." HM. NOT EXACTLY FRONT-PAGE NEWS...
WHAT THE—? LOOK!
?

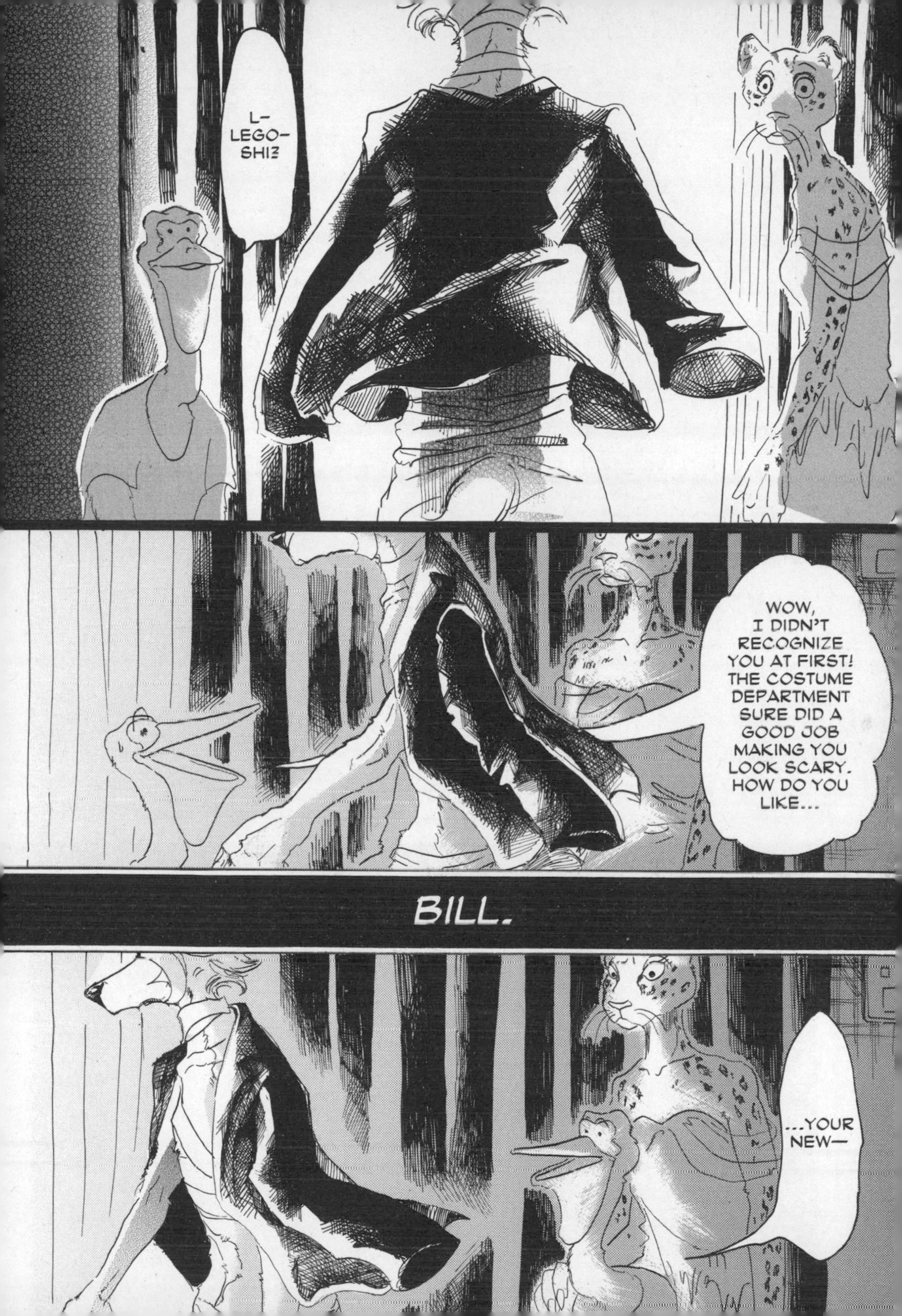
L- LEGO- SHI?
WOW, I DIDN'T RECOGNIZE YOU AT FIRST! THE COSTUME DEPARTMENT SURE DID A GOOD JOB MAKING YOU LOOK SCARY. HOW DO YOU LIKE...
BILL.
...YOUR NEW—

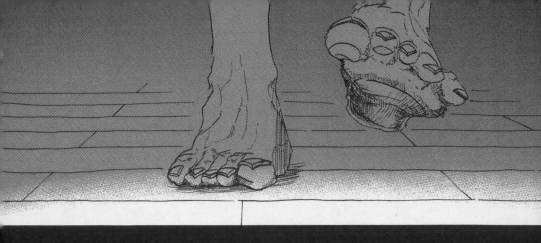

IF YOU INSIST ON...
...DRINKING THAT RED BLOOD AND CALLING IT LEGITIMATE DOPING...
YOU HAVE AR-RIVED, OH DEVIL!!
...THEN SHOW ME HOW POWER-FUL IT'S MADE YOU.

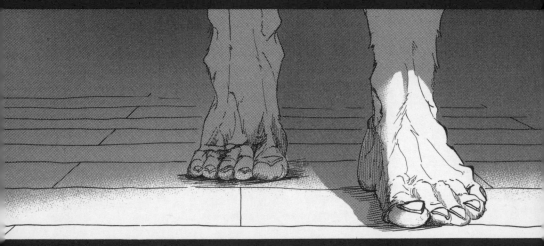

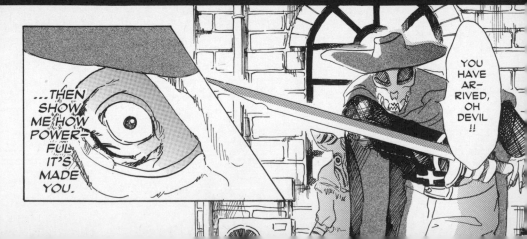

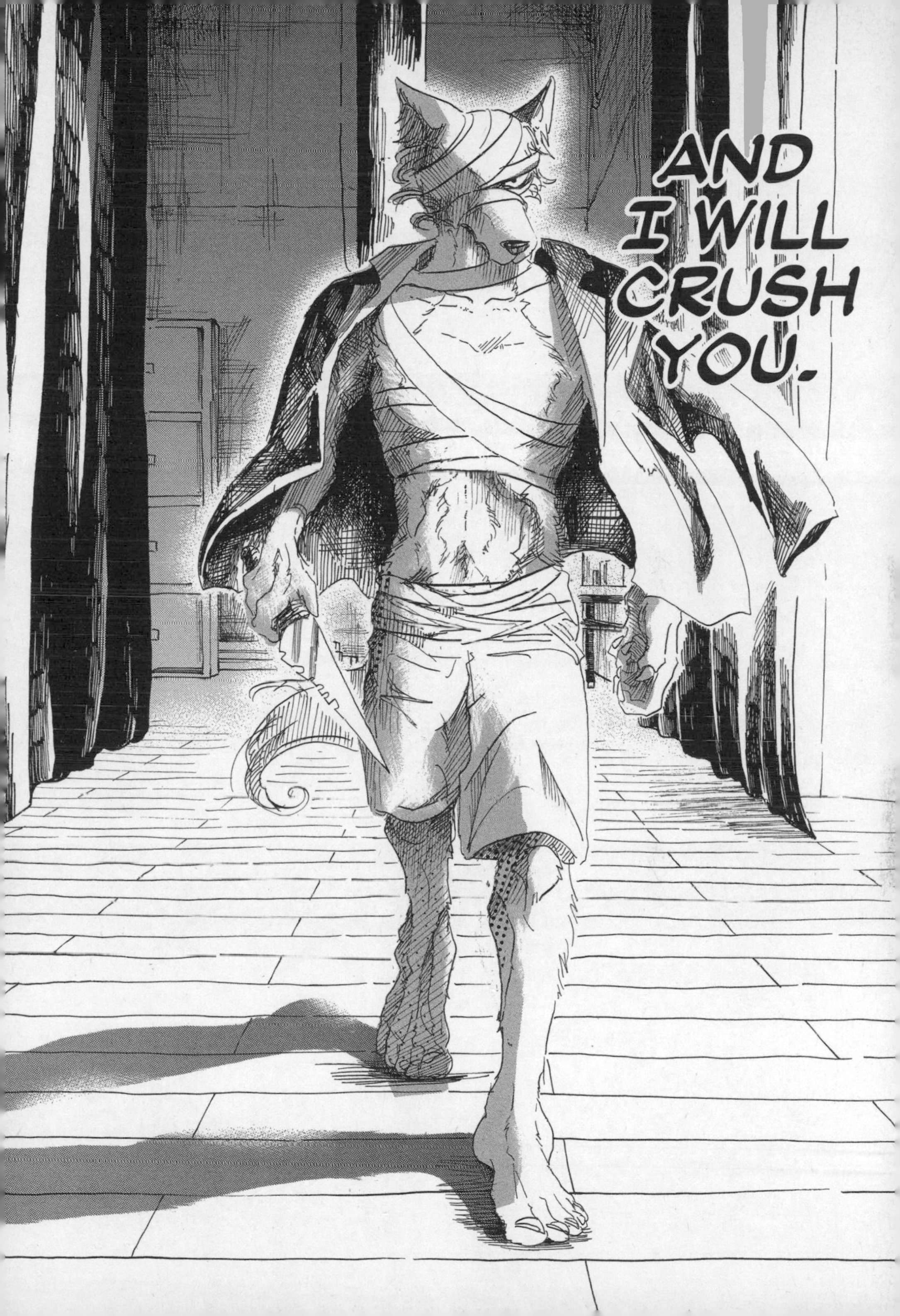
AND I WILL CRUSH YOU.

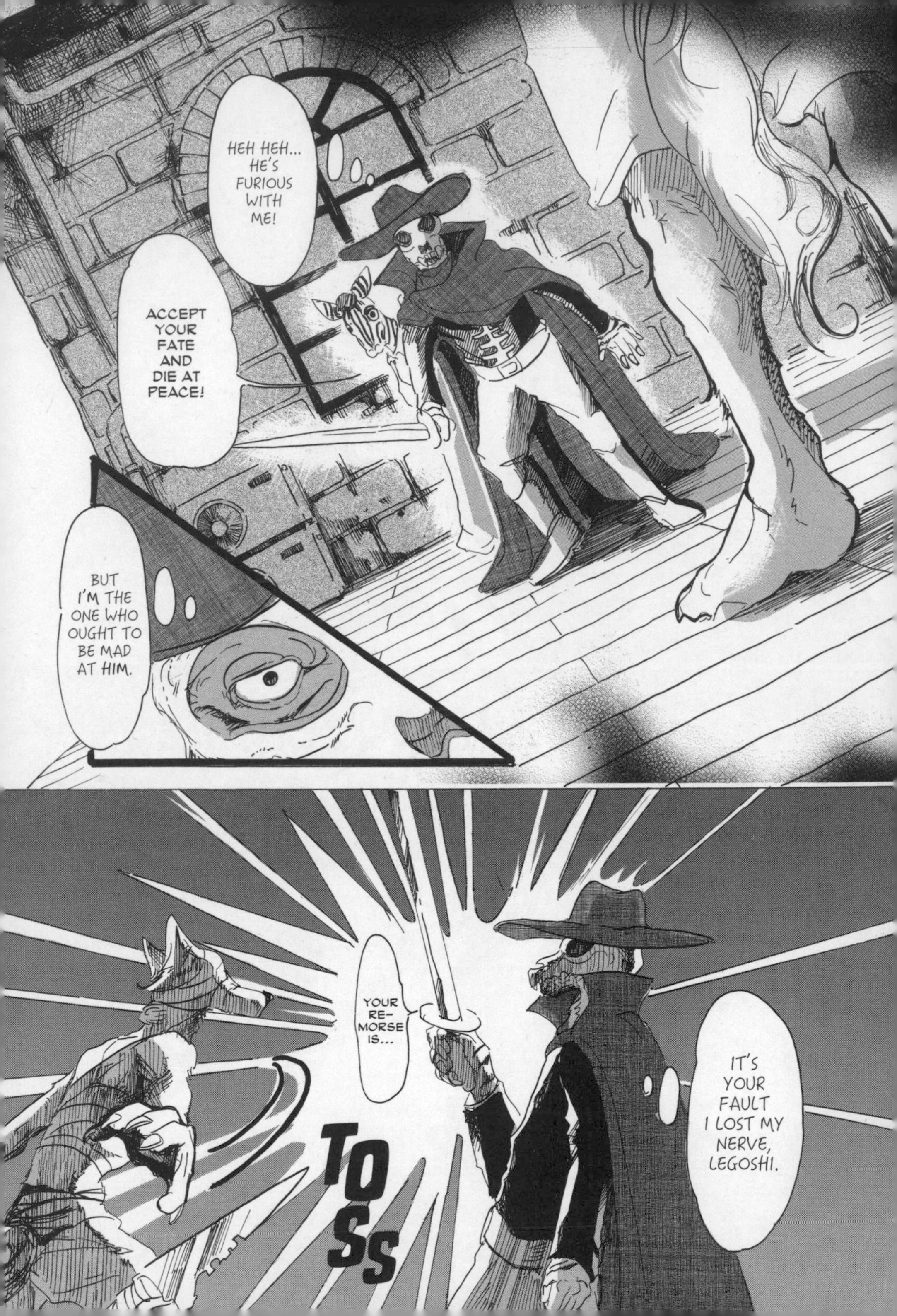
HEH HEH... HE'S FURIOUS WITH ME!
ACCEPT YOUR FATE AND DIE AT PEACE!
BUT I'M THE ONE WHO OUGHT TO BE MAD AT HIM.
IT'S YOUR FAULT I LOST MY NERVE, LEGOSHI.
YOUR RE-MORSE IS...
TOSS

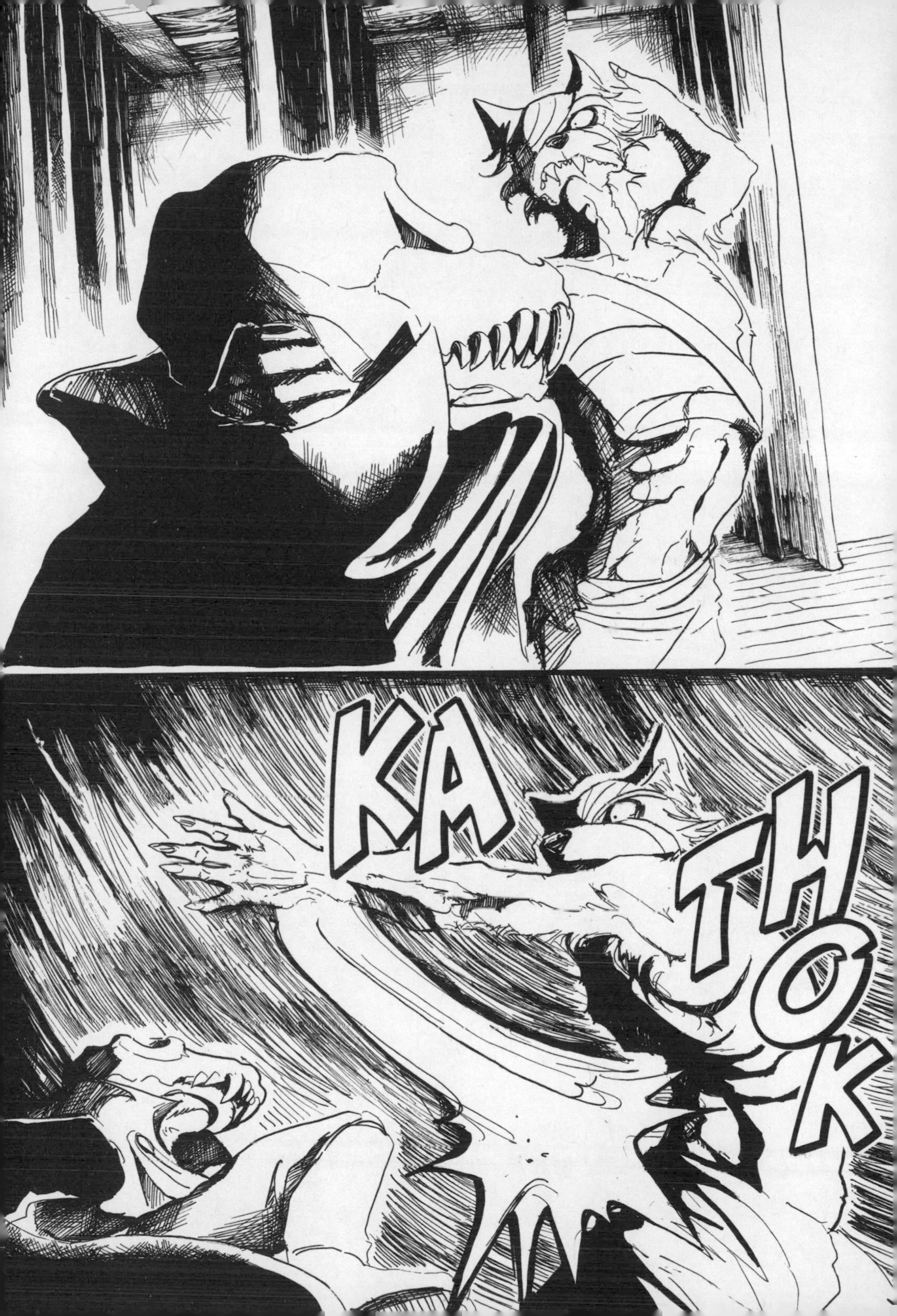
KA THOK

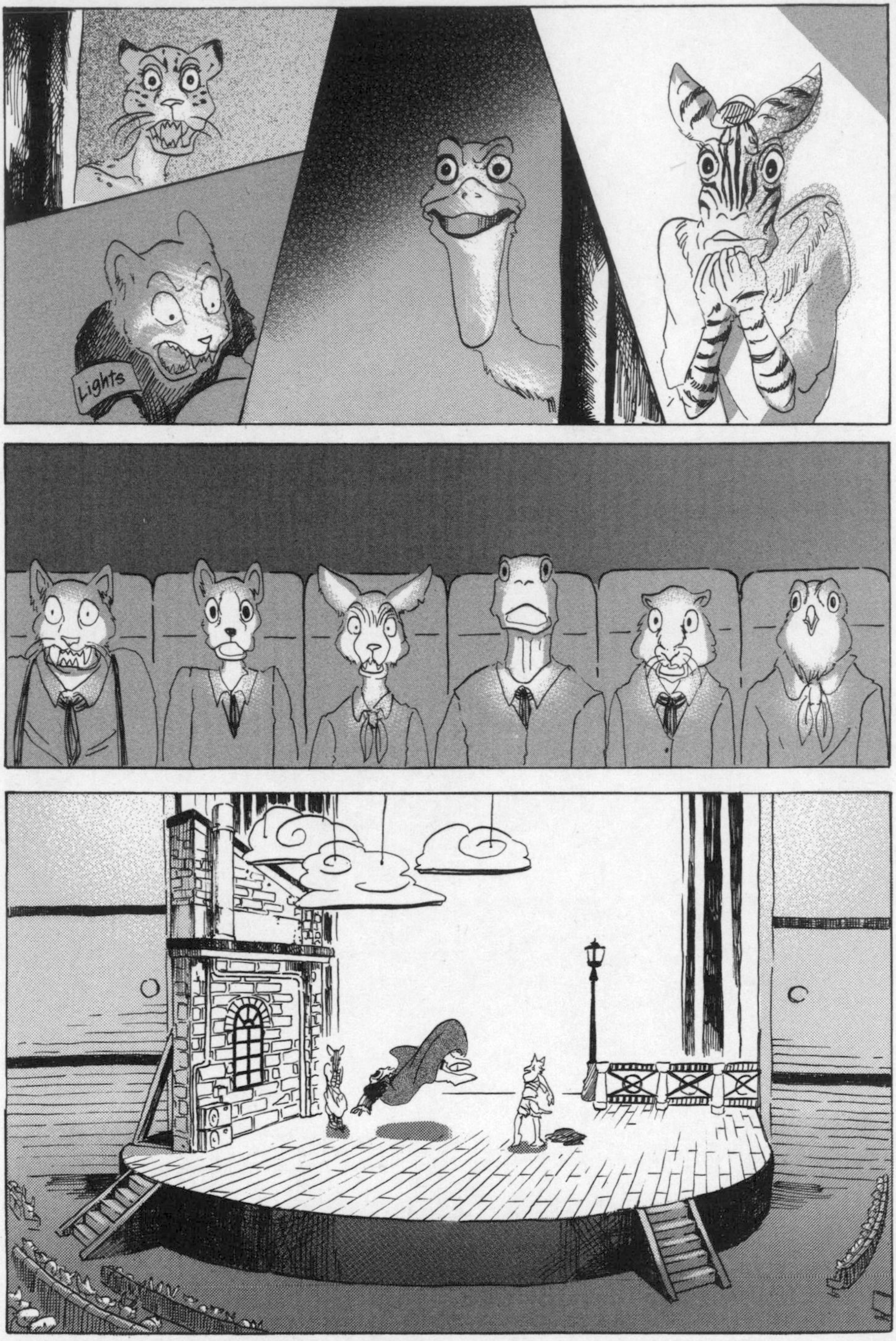
Lights

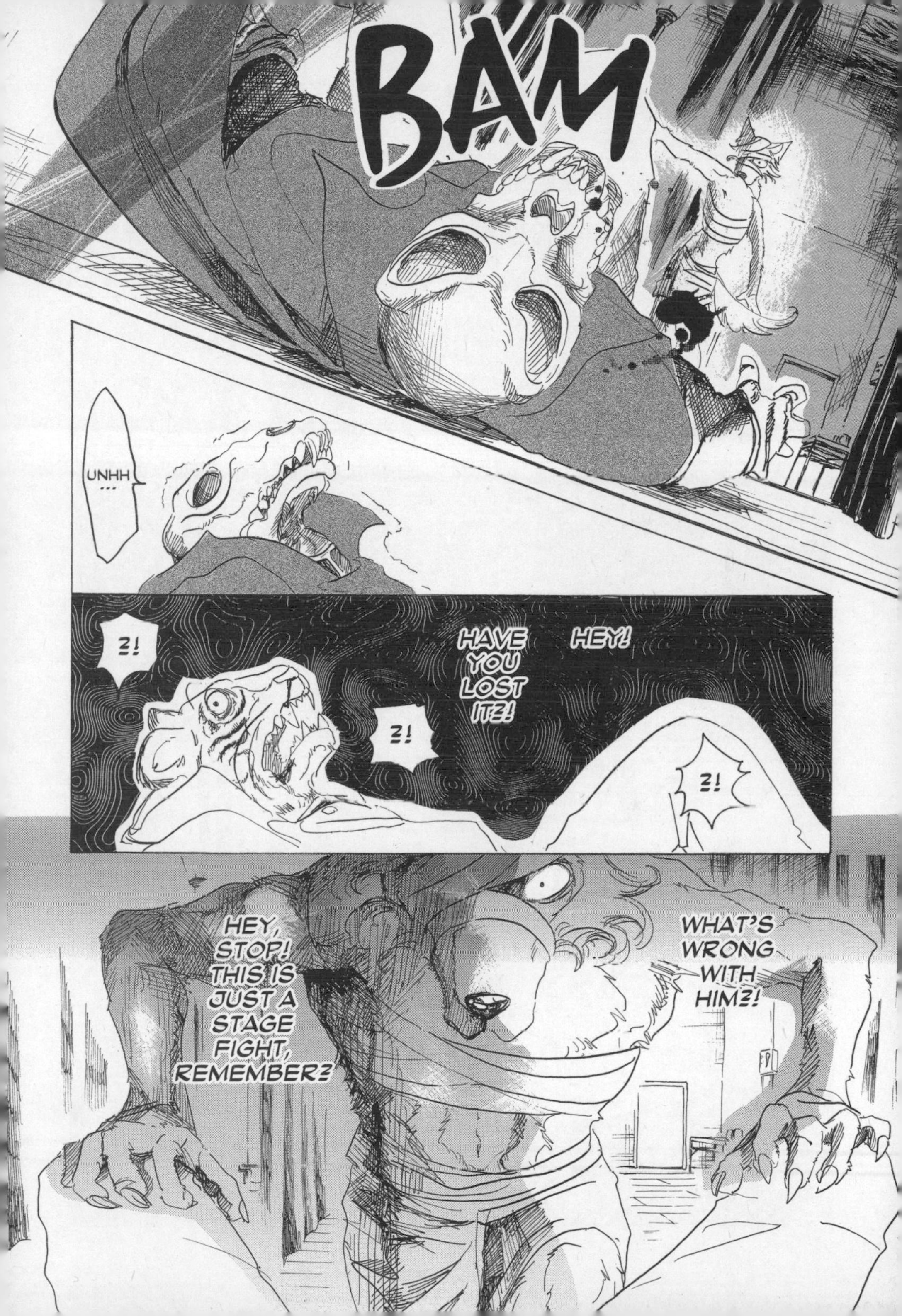
BAM
UNHH...
?!
HEY!
HAVE YOU LOST IT?!
?!
?!
WHAT'S WRONG WITH HIM?!
HEY, STOP! THIS IS JUST A STAGE FIGHT, REMEMBER?

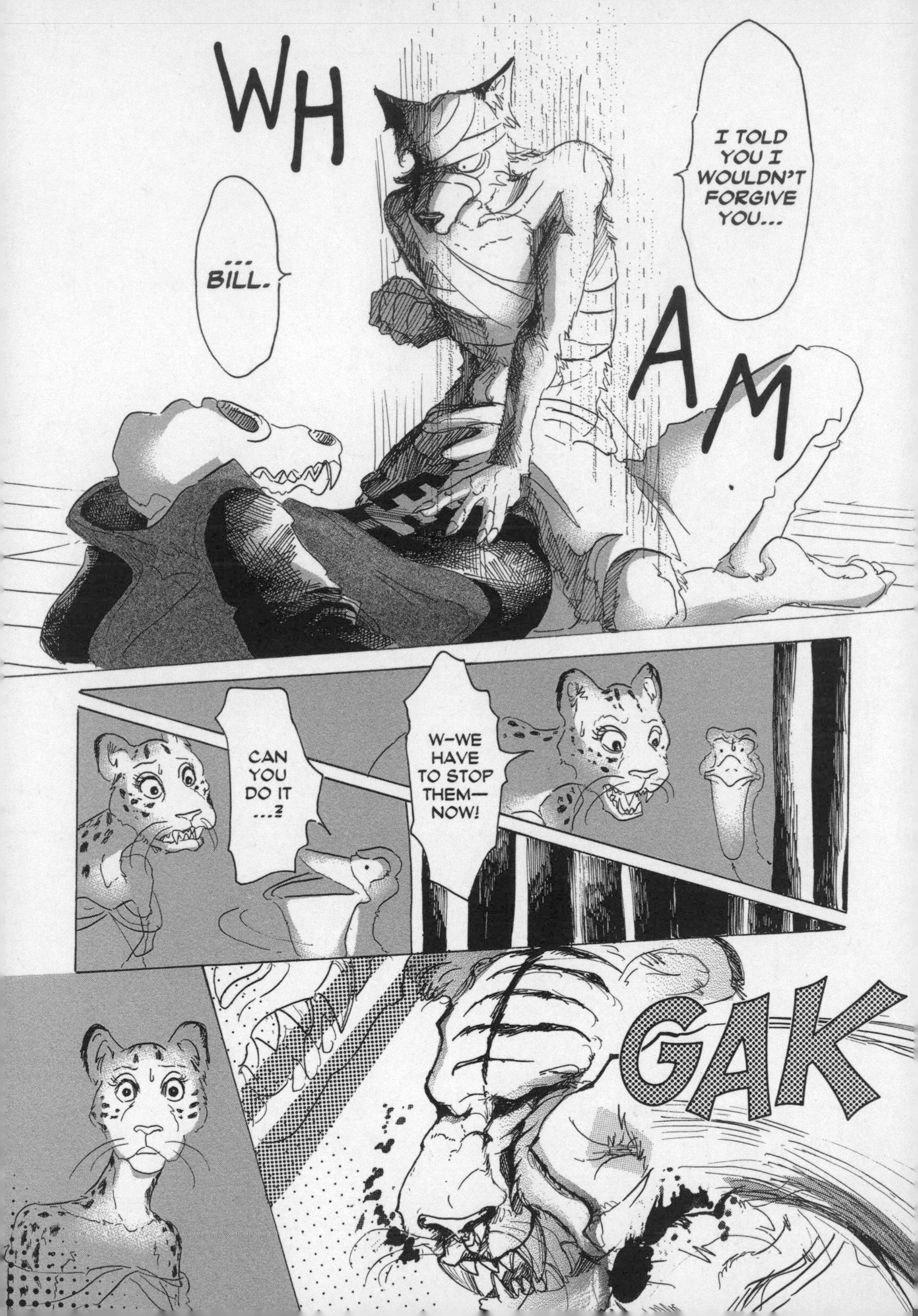
I TOLD YOU I WOULDN'T FORGIVE YOU...
WHAM
...BILL.
W-WE HAVE TO STOP THEM—NOW!
CAN YOU DO IT ...?
GAK

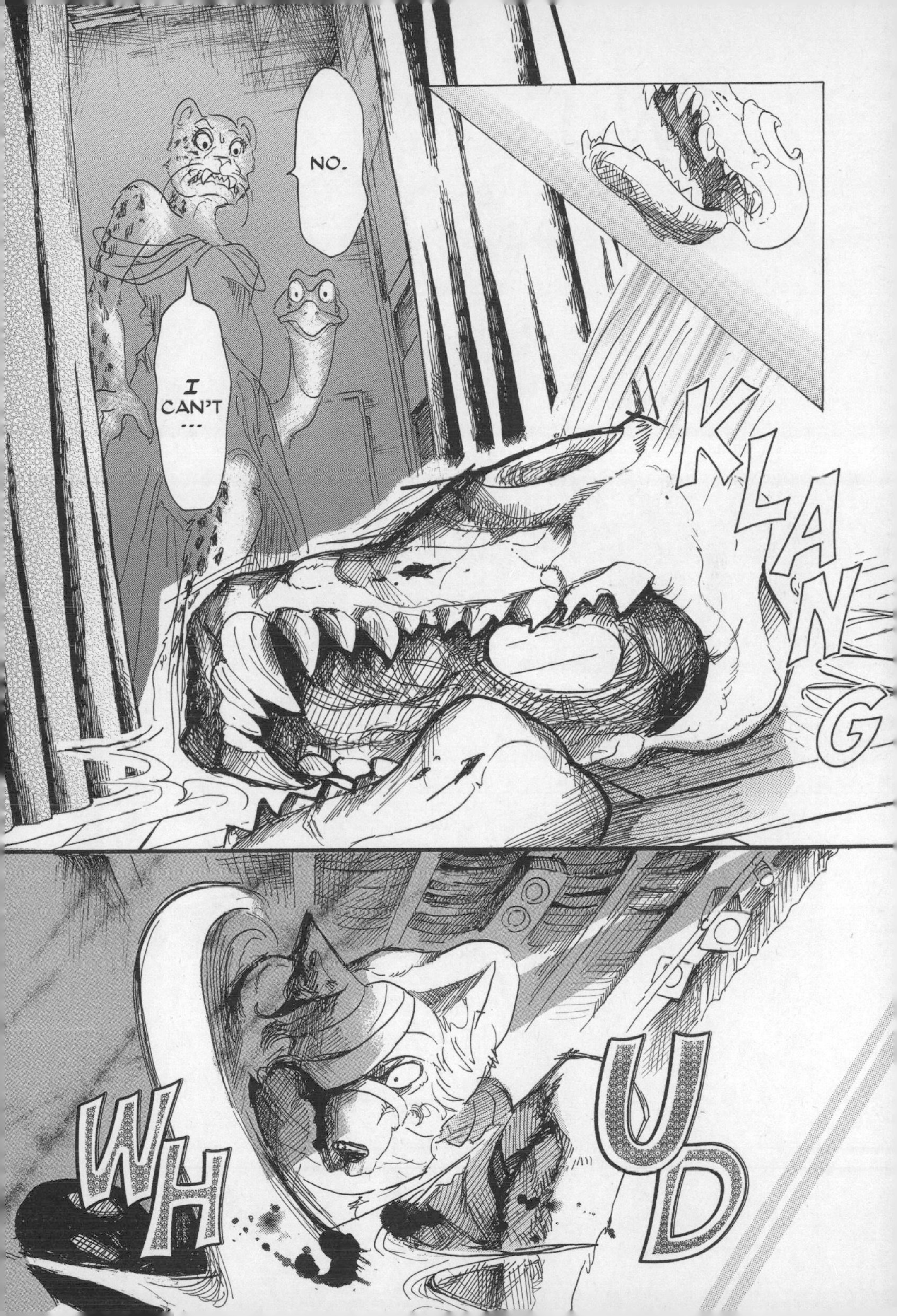
NO.
I CAN'T ...
KLANG
WHUD

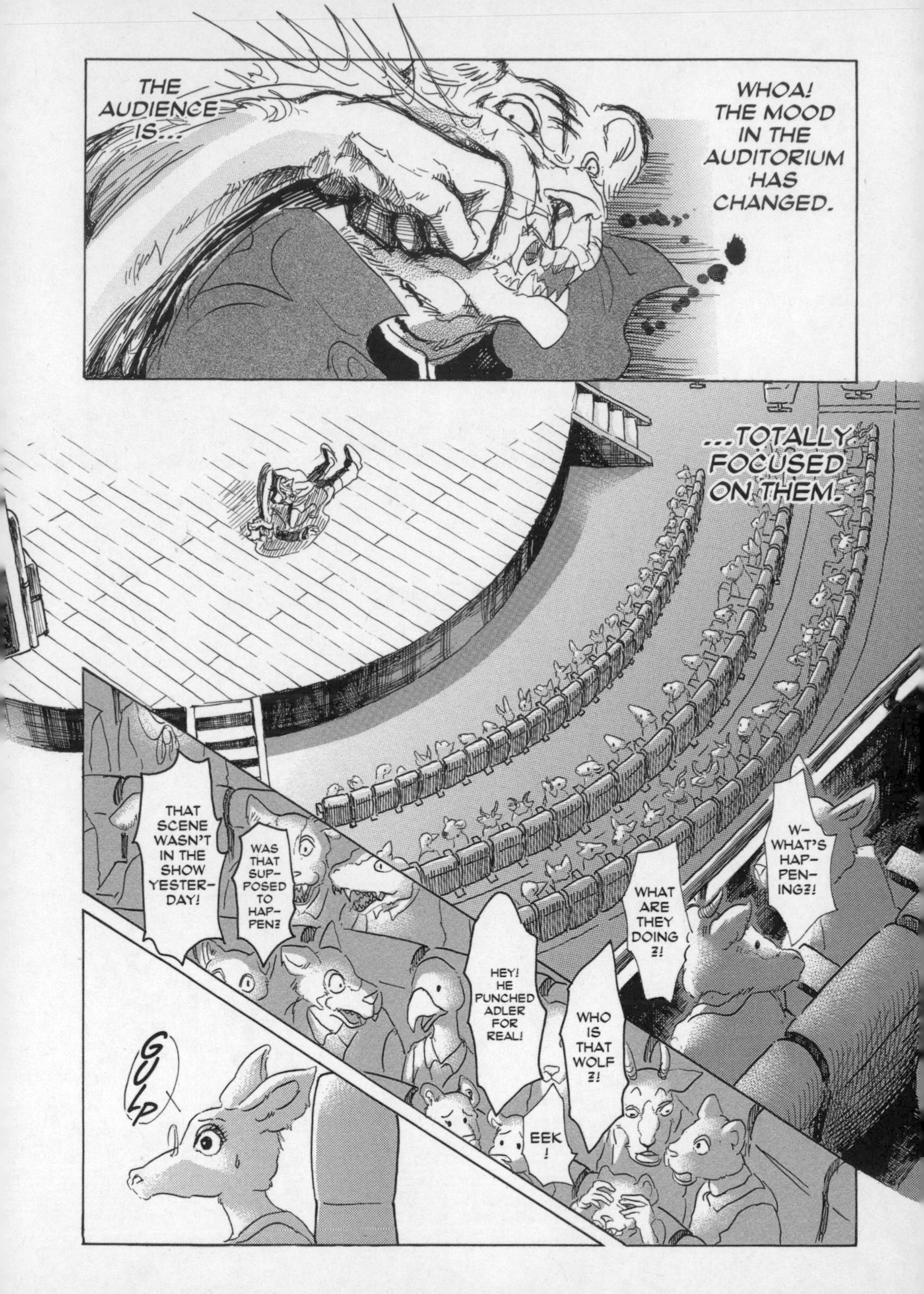
WHOA! THE MOOD IN THE AUDITORIUM HAS CHANGED.
THE AUDIENCE IS...
...TOTALLY FOCUSED ON THEM.
W-WHAT'S HAPPENING?!
WHAT ARE THEY DOING?!
WHO IS THAT WOLF?!
HEY! HE PUNCHED ADLER FOR REAL!
EEK!
WAS THAT SUPPOSED TO HAPPEN?
THAT SCENE WASN'T IN THE SHOW YESTERDAY!
GULP

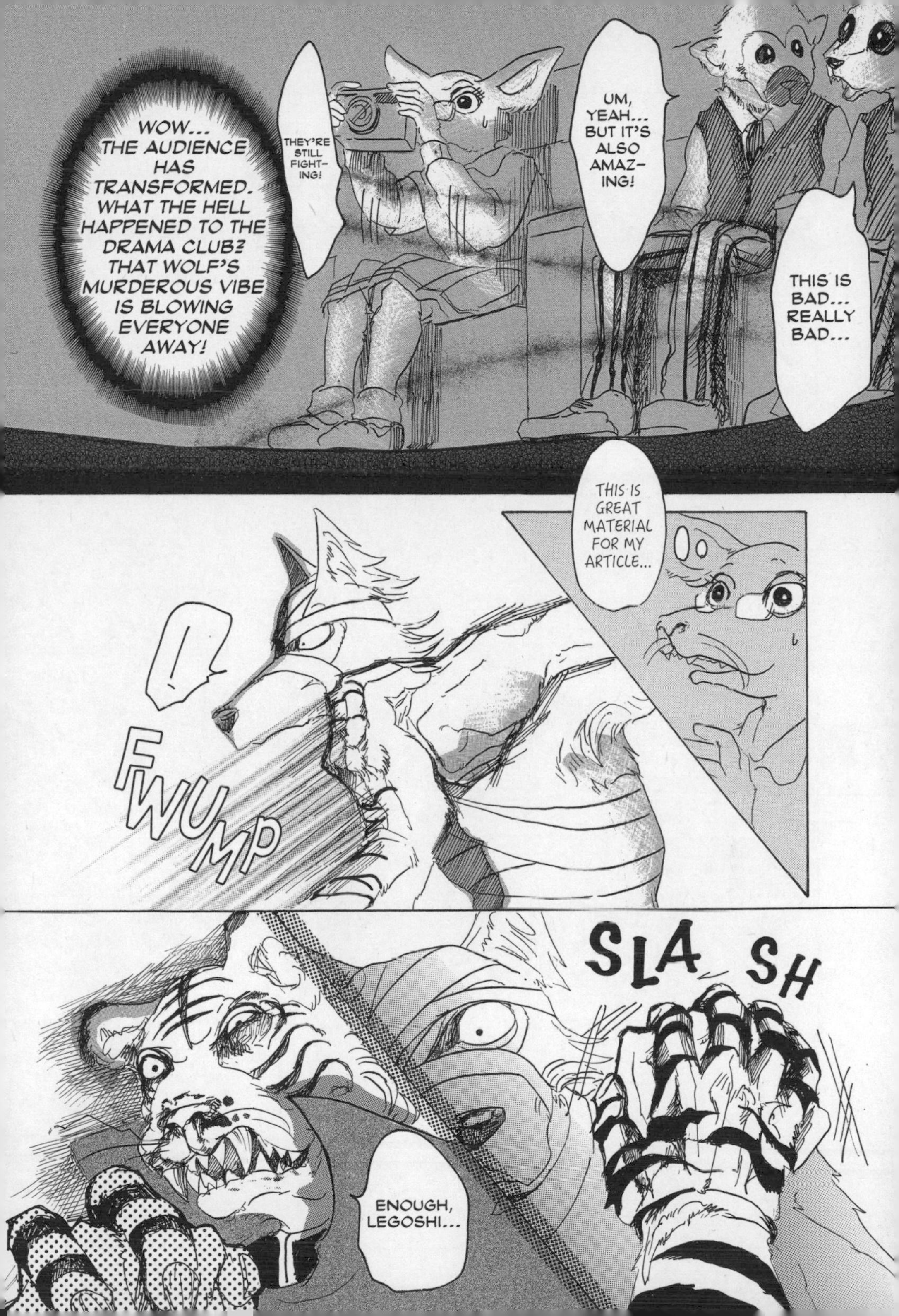
THIS IS BAD... REALLY BAD...
UM, YEAH... BUT IT'S ALSO AMAZ-ING!
THEY'RE STILL FIGHT-ING!
WOW... THE AUDIENCE HAS TRANSFORMED. WHAT THE HELL HAPPENED TO THE DRAMA CLUB? THAT WOLF'S MURDEROUS VIBE IS BLOWING EVERYONE AWAY!
THIS IS GREAT MATERIAL FOR MY ARTICLE...
!
FWUMP
SLA SH
ENOUGH, LEGOSHI...

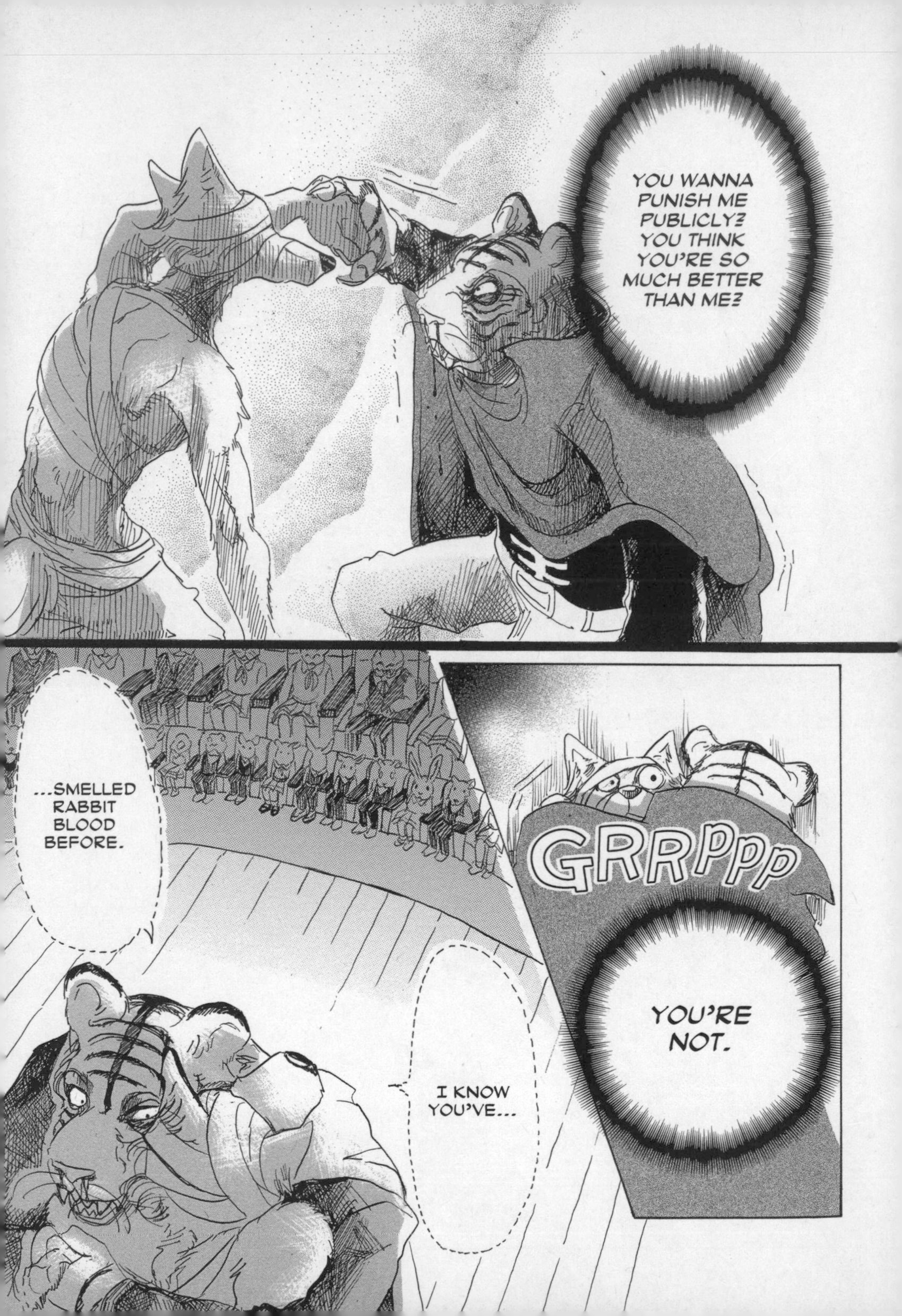
YOU WANNA PUNISH ME PUBLICLY? YOU THINK YOU'RE SO MUCH BETTER THAN ME?
GRRPppp
YOU'RE NOT.
I KNOW YOU'VE...
...SMELLED RABBIT BLOOD BEFORE.

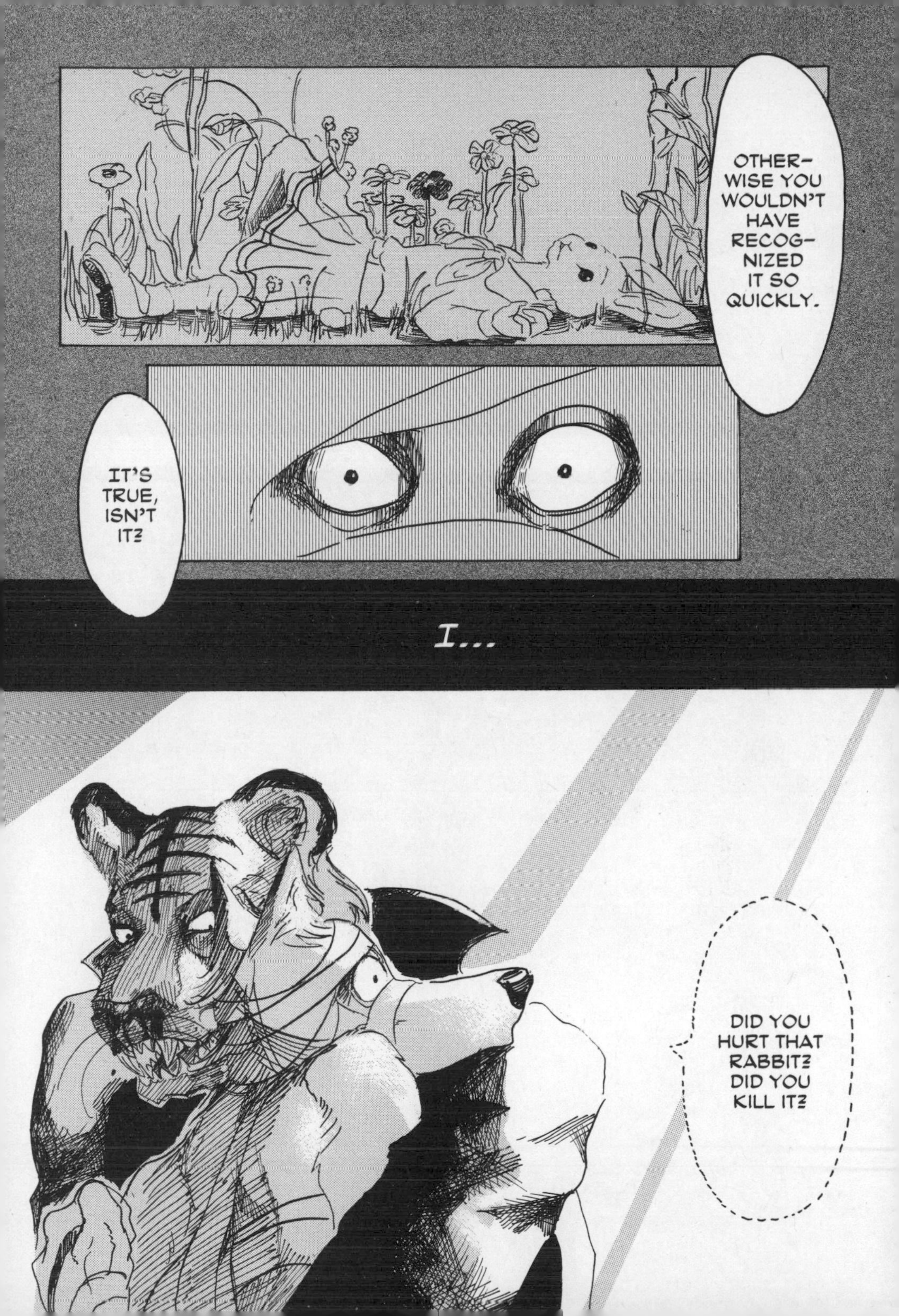
OTHER-
WISE YOU
WOULDN'T
HAVE
RECOG-
NIZED
IT SO
QUICKLY.
IT'S
TRUE,
ISN'T
IT?
I...
DID YOU
HURT THAT
RABBIT?
DID YOU
KILL IT?

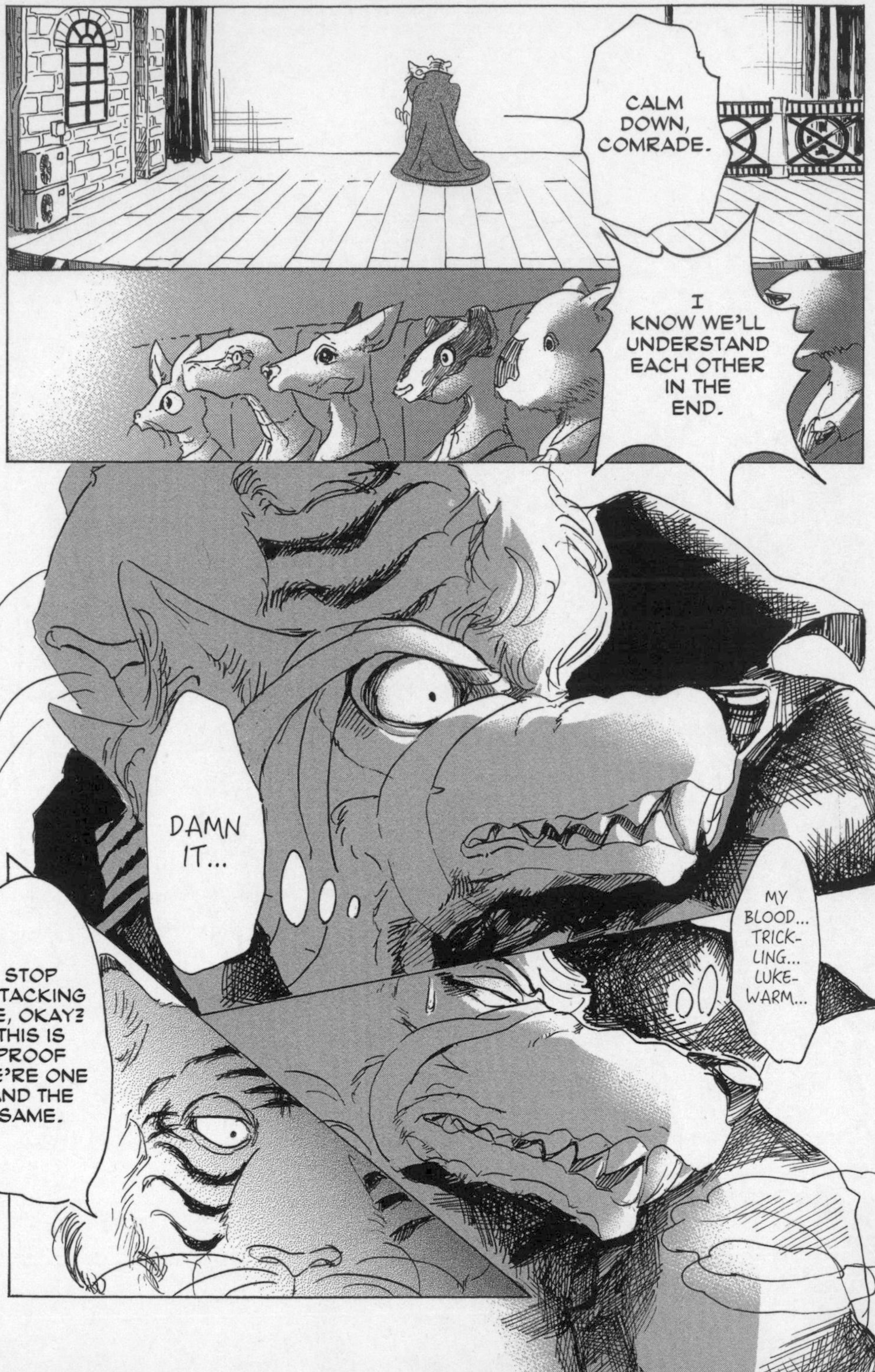
CALM DOWN, COMRADE.
I KNOW WE'LL UNDERSTAND EACH OTHER IN THE END.
DAMN IT...
MY BLOOD... TRICK-LING... LUKE-WARM...
STOP ATTACKING ME, OKAY? THIS IS PROOF WE'RE ONE AND THE SAME.

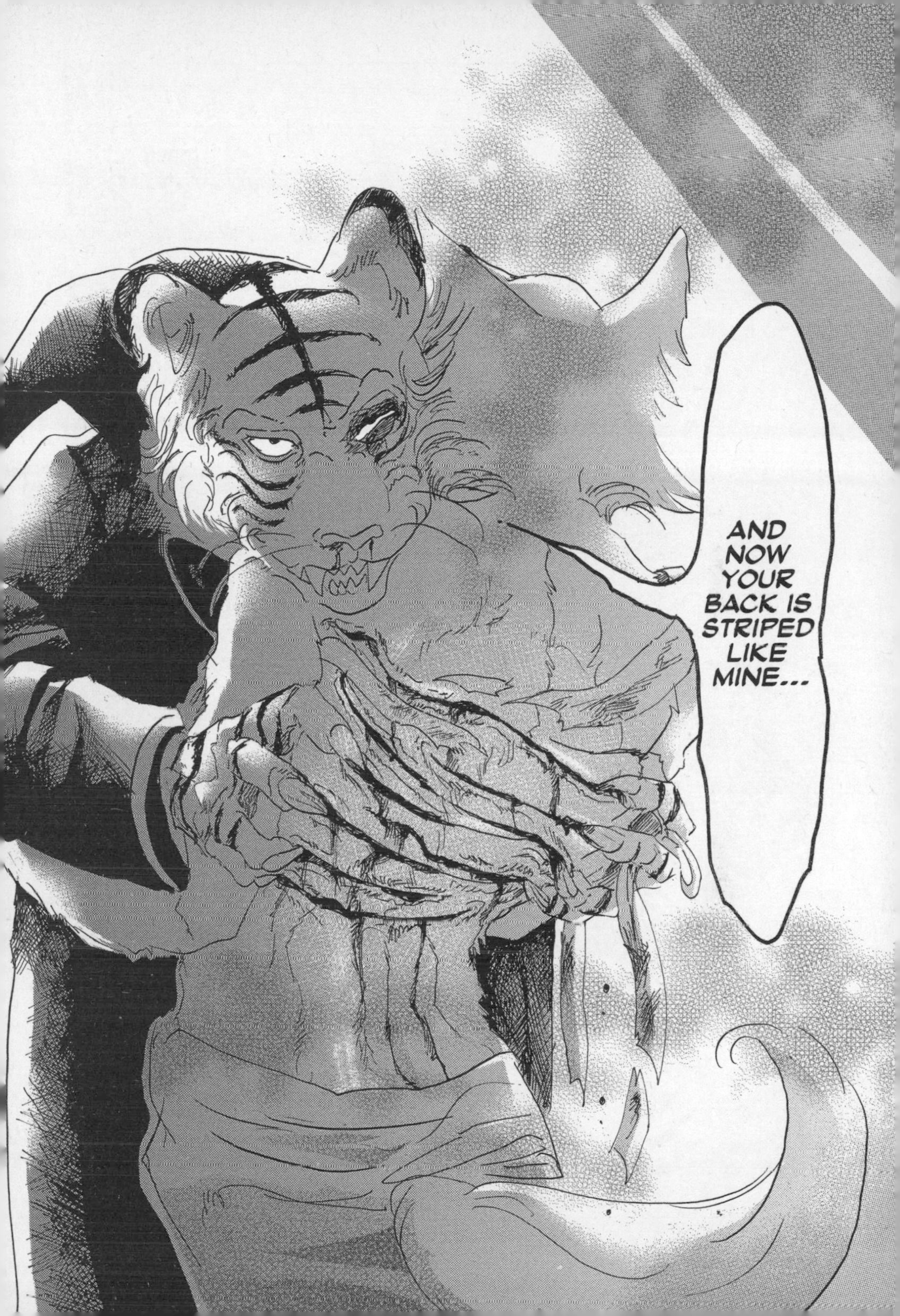
AND NOW YOUR BACK IS STRIPED LIKE MINE...

Chapter 16: Scorching Punishments

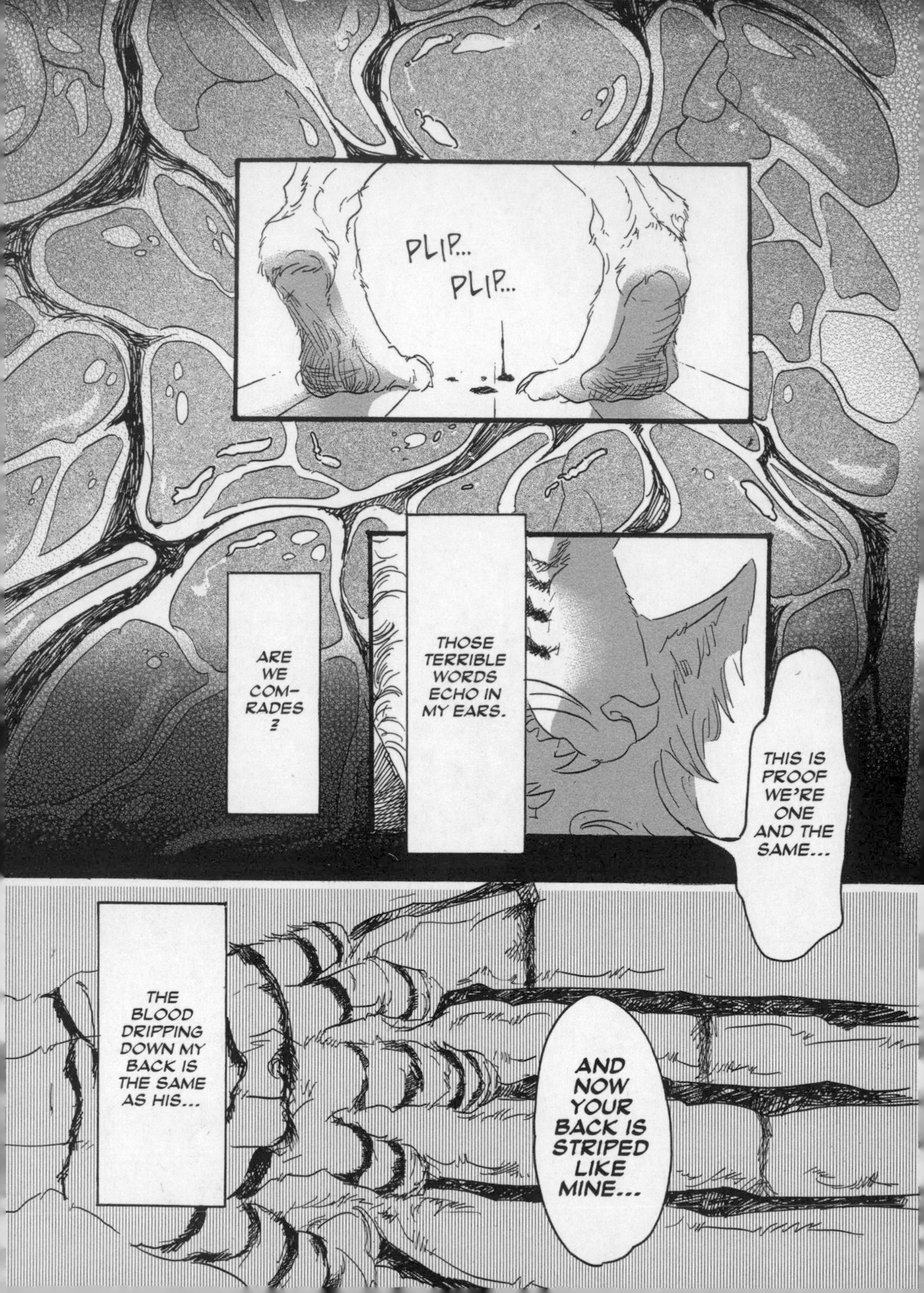
PLIP...
PLIP...
THOSE TERRIBLE WORDS ECHO IN MY EARS.
ARE WE COM-RADES?
THIS IS PROOF WE'RE ONE AND THE SAME...
AND NOW YOUR BACK IS STRIPED LIKE MINE...
THE BLOOD DRIPPING DOWN MY BACK IS THE SAME AS HIS...

Chapter 16: Scorching Punishments

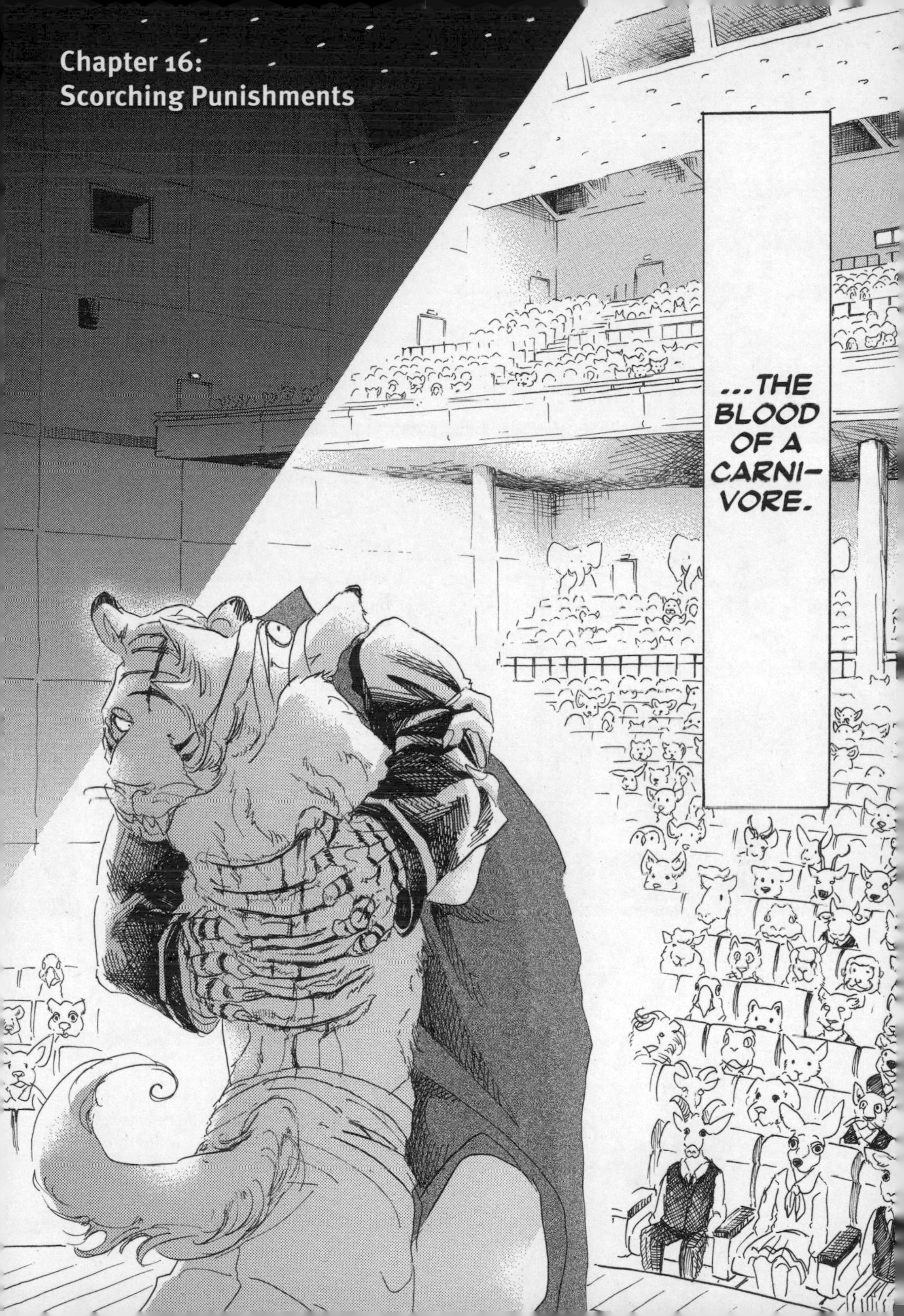
...THE BLOOD OF A CARNI-VORE.

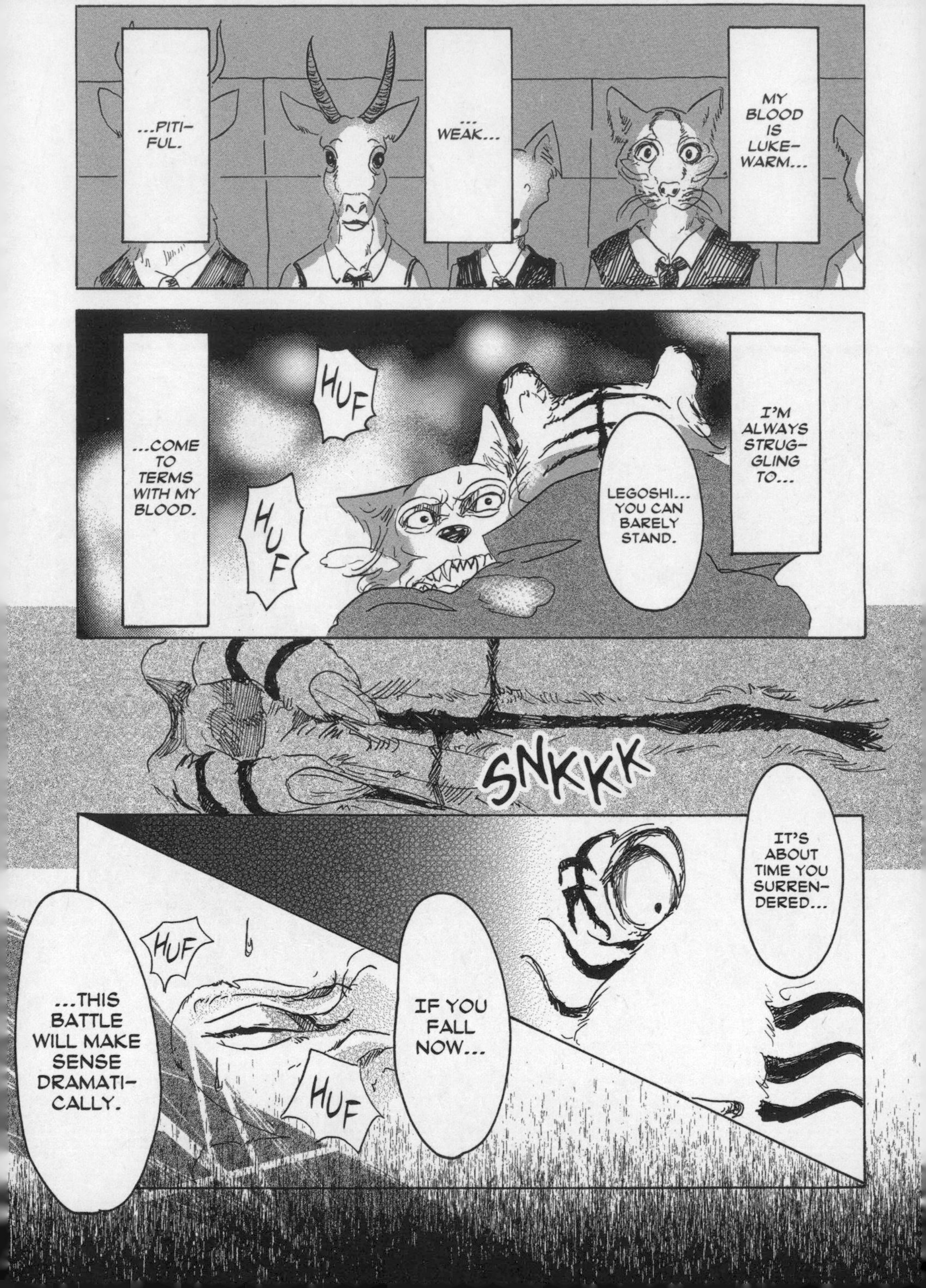
MY BLOOD IS LUKE-WARM...
...WEAK...
...PITI-FUL.
I'M ALWAYS STRUG-GLING TO...
LEGOSHI... YOU CAN BARELY STAND.
HUF
HUF
...COME TO TERMS WITH MY BLOOD.
SNKKK
IT'S ABOUT TIME YOU SURREN-DERED...
IF YOU FALL NOW...
HUF
HUF
...THIS BATTLE WILL MAKE SENSE DRAMATI-CALLY.

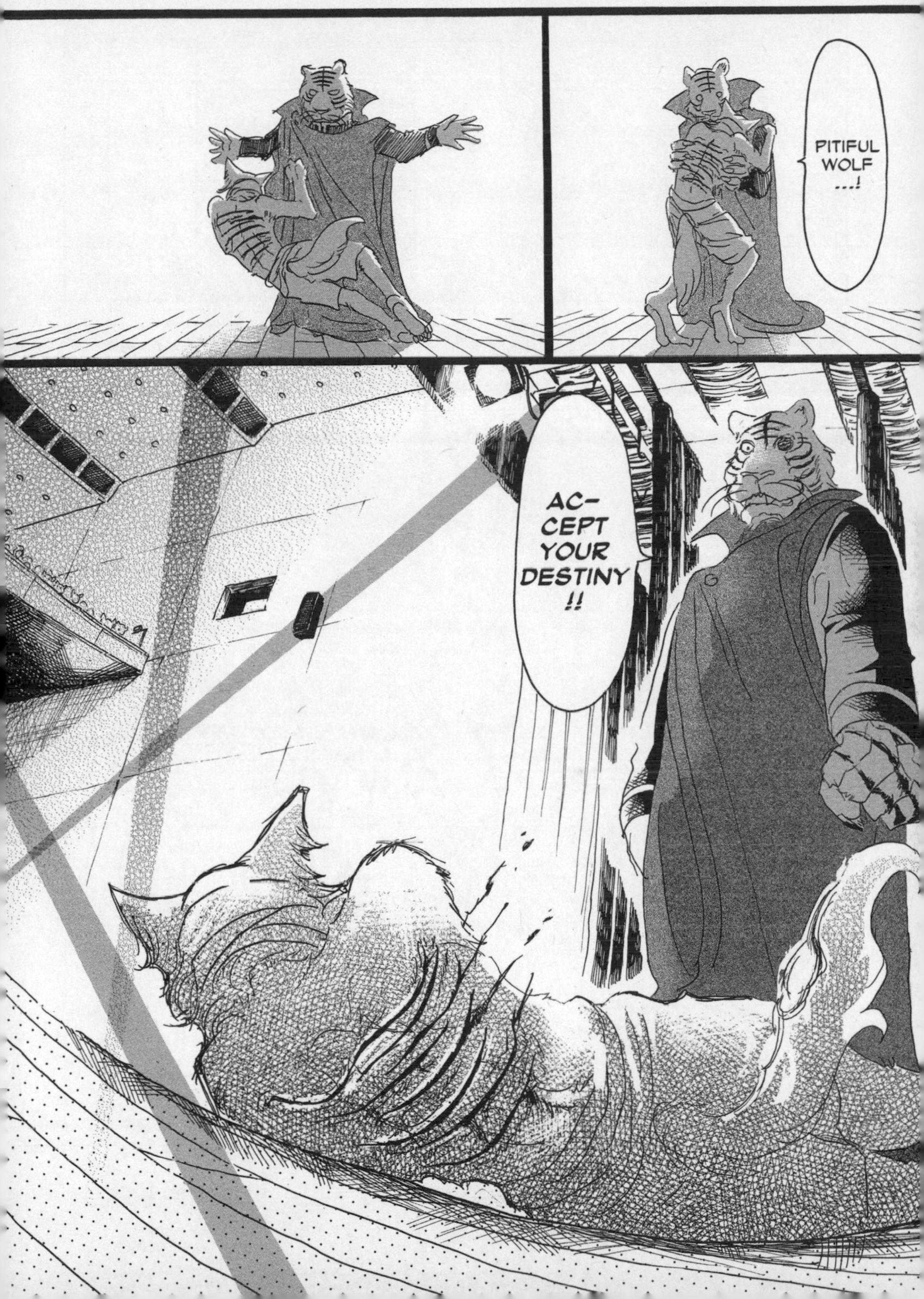
PITIFUL WOLF ...!
AC-CEPT YOUR DESTINY !!

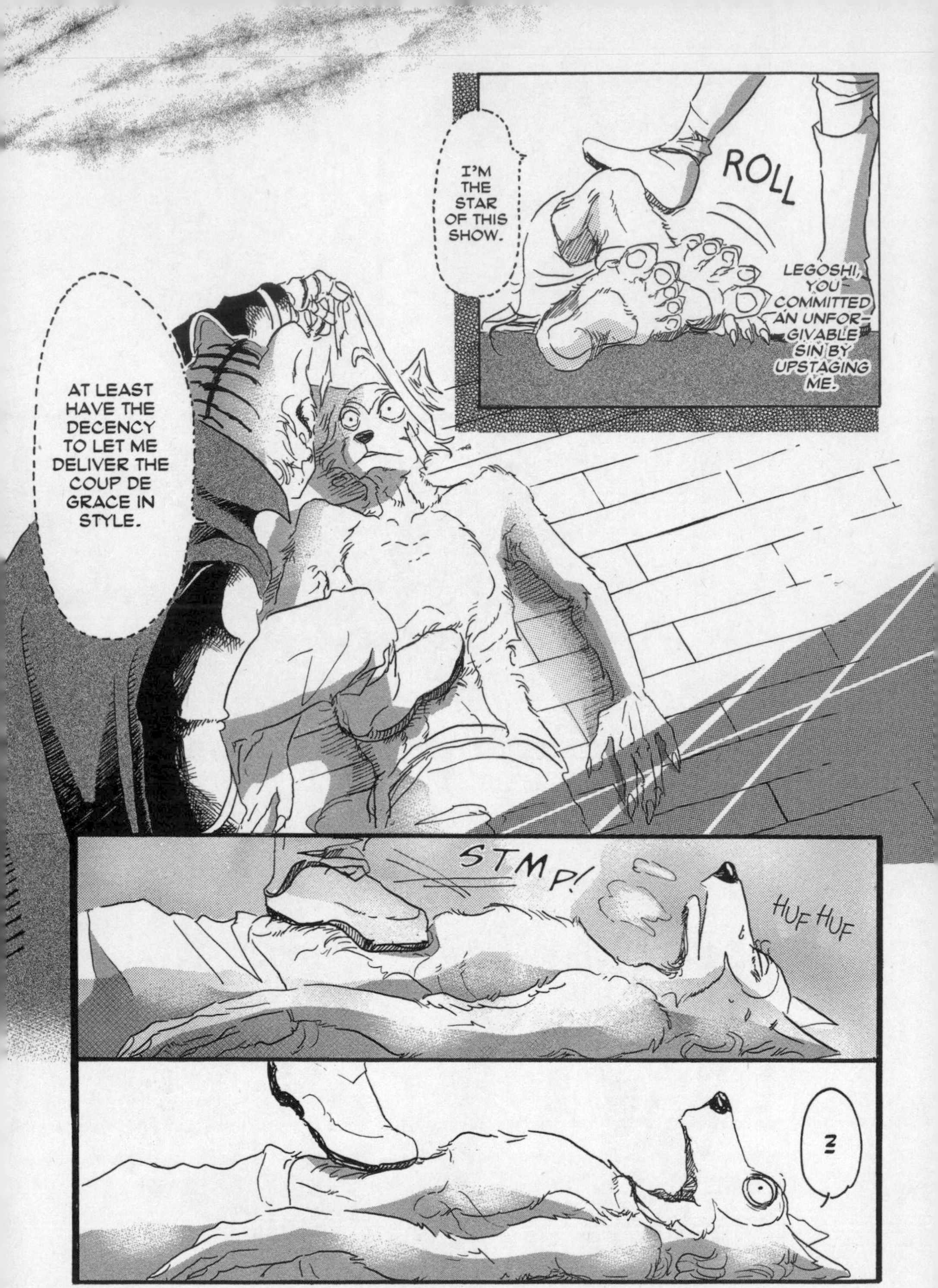
ROLL
LEGOSHI, YOU COMMITTED AN UNFORGIVABLE SIN BY UPSTAGING ME.
I'M THE STAR OF THIS SHOW.
AT LEAST HAVE THE DECENCY TO LET ME DELIVER THE COUP DE GRACE IN STYLE.
STMP!
HUF HUF

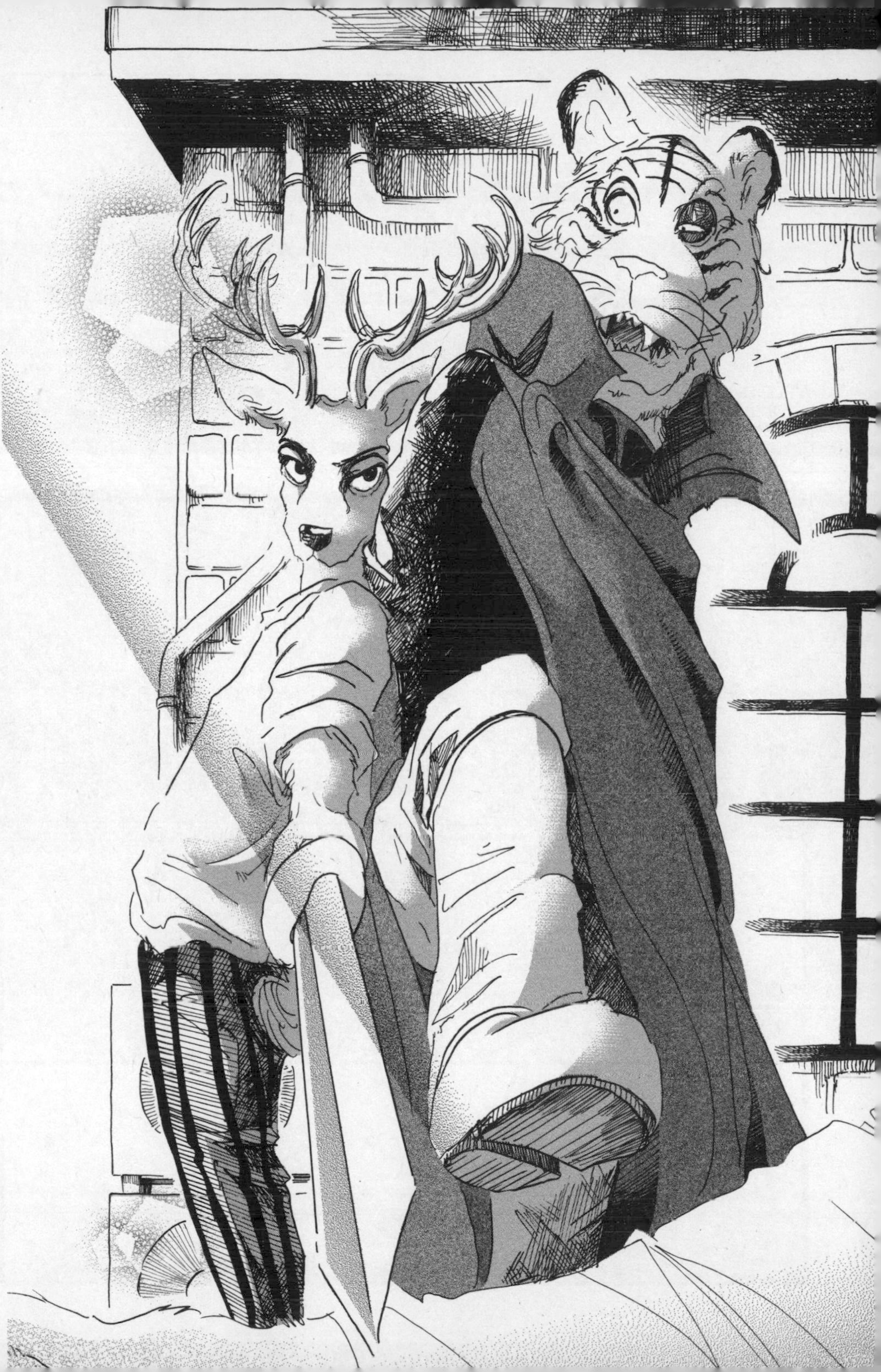

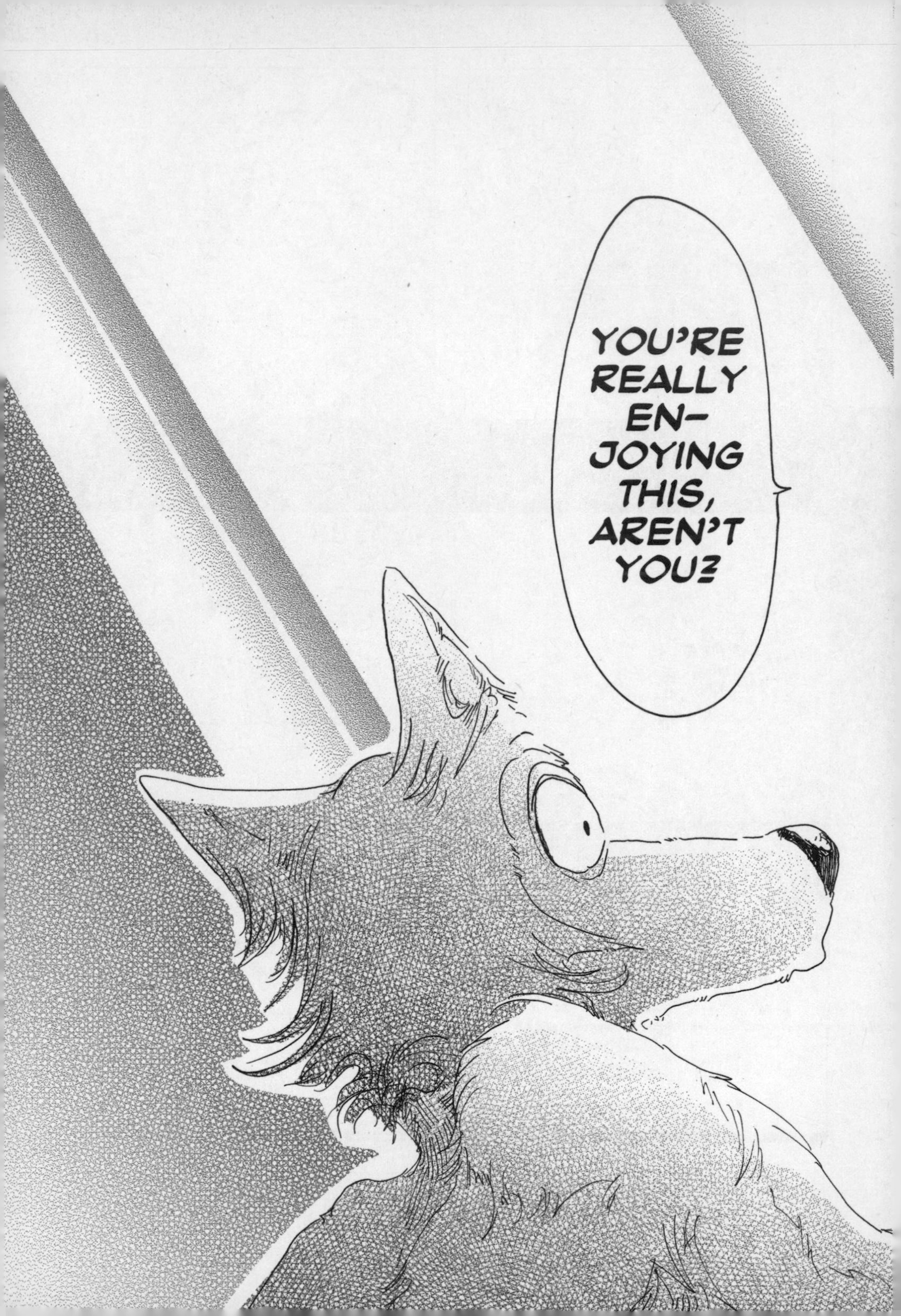
YOU'RE REALLY EN- JOYING THIS, AREN'T YOU?

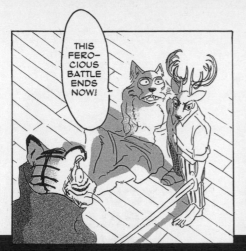

THIS FERO-CIOUS BATTLE ENDS NOW!

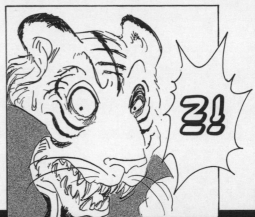

Z!

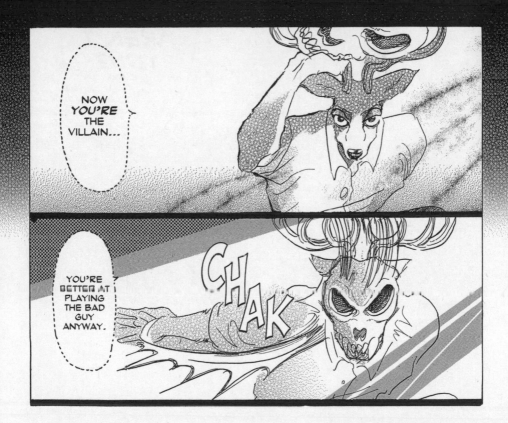

NOW *YOU'RE* THE VILLAIN...

YOU'RE BETTER AT PLAYING THE BAD GUY ANYWAY.

CHAK

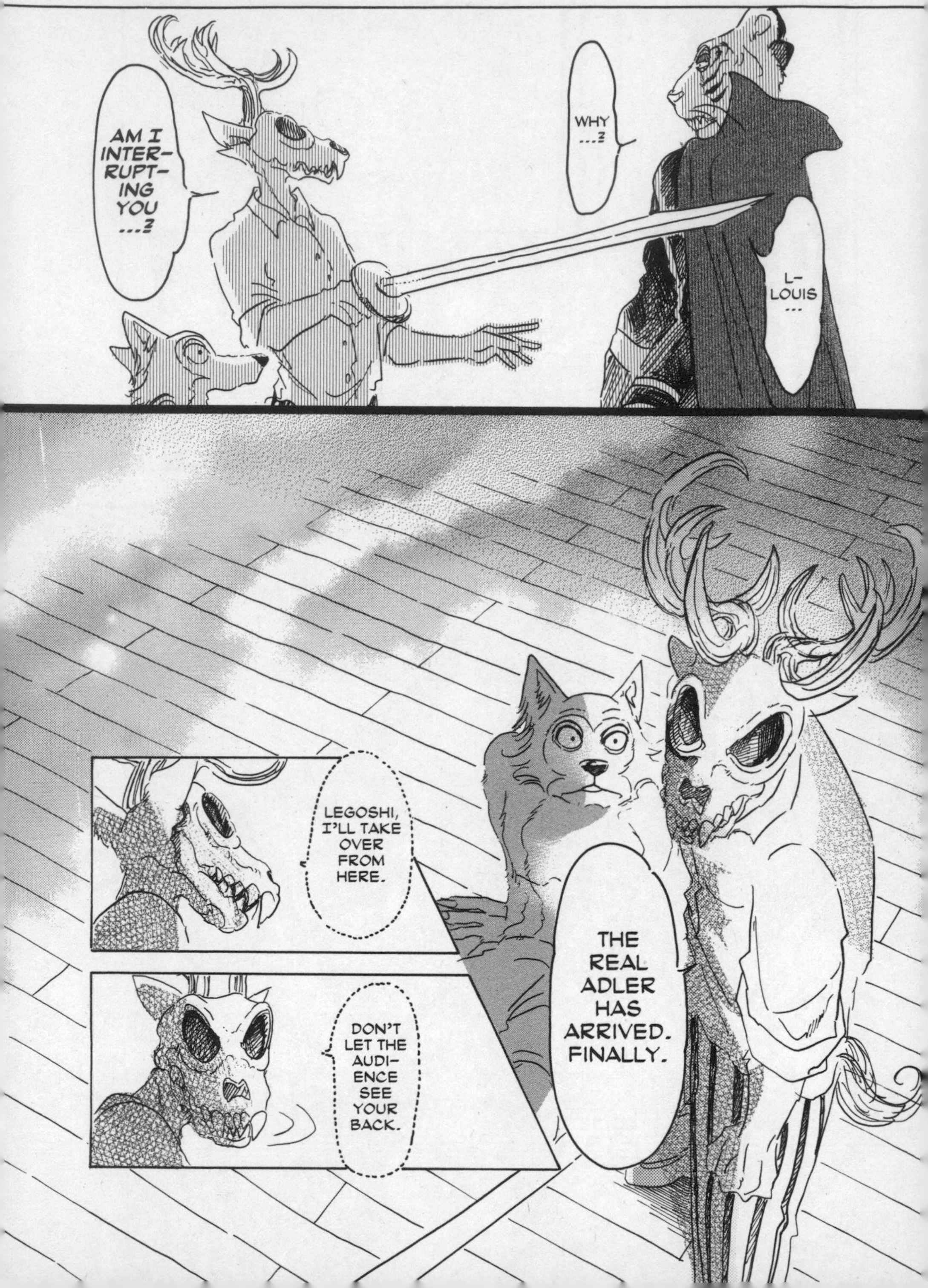
WHY ...?
L-LOUIS ...
AM I INTERRUPTING YOU ...?
THE REAL ADLER HAS ARRIVED. FINALLY.
LEGOSHI, I'LL TAKE OVER FROM HERE.
DON'T LET THE AUDIENCE SEE YOUR BACK.

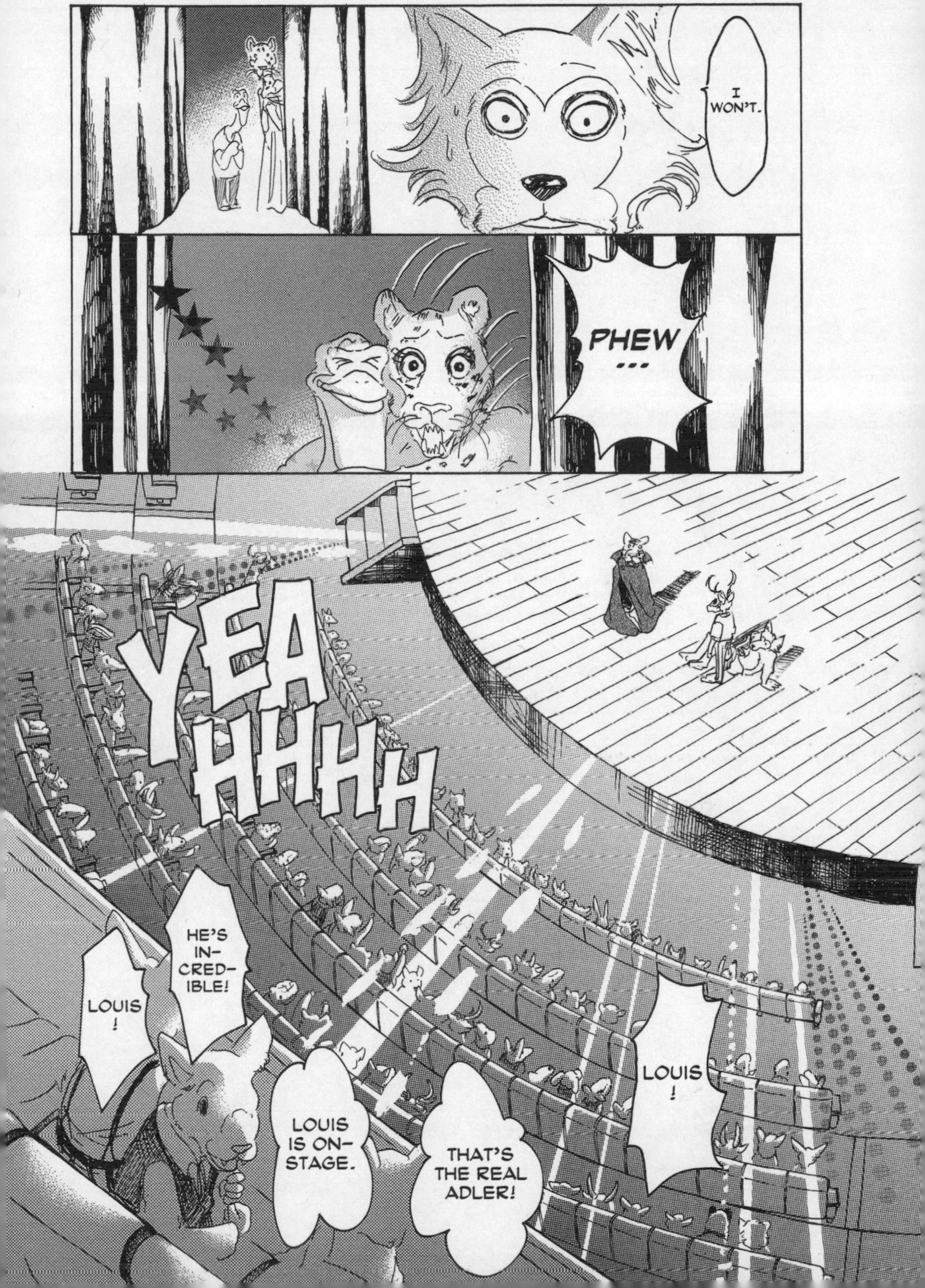
I WON'T.
PHEW ...
YEAHHHHH
LOUIS!
THAT'S THE REAL ADLER!
LOUIS IS ONSTAGE.
HE'S INCREDIBLE!
LOUIS!

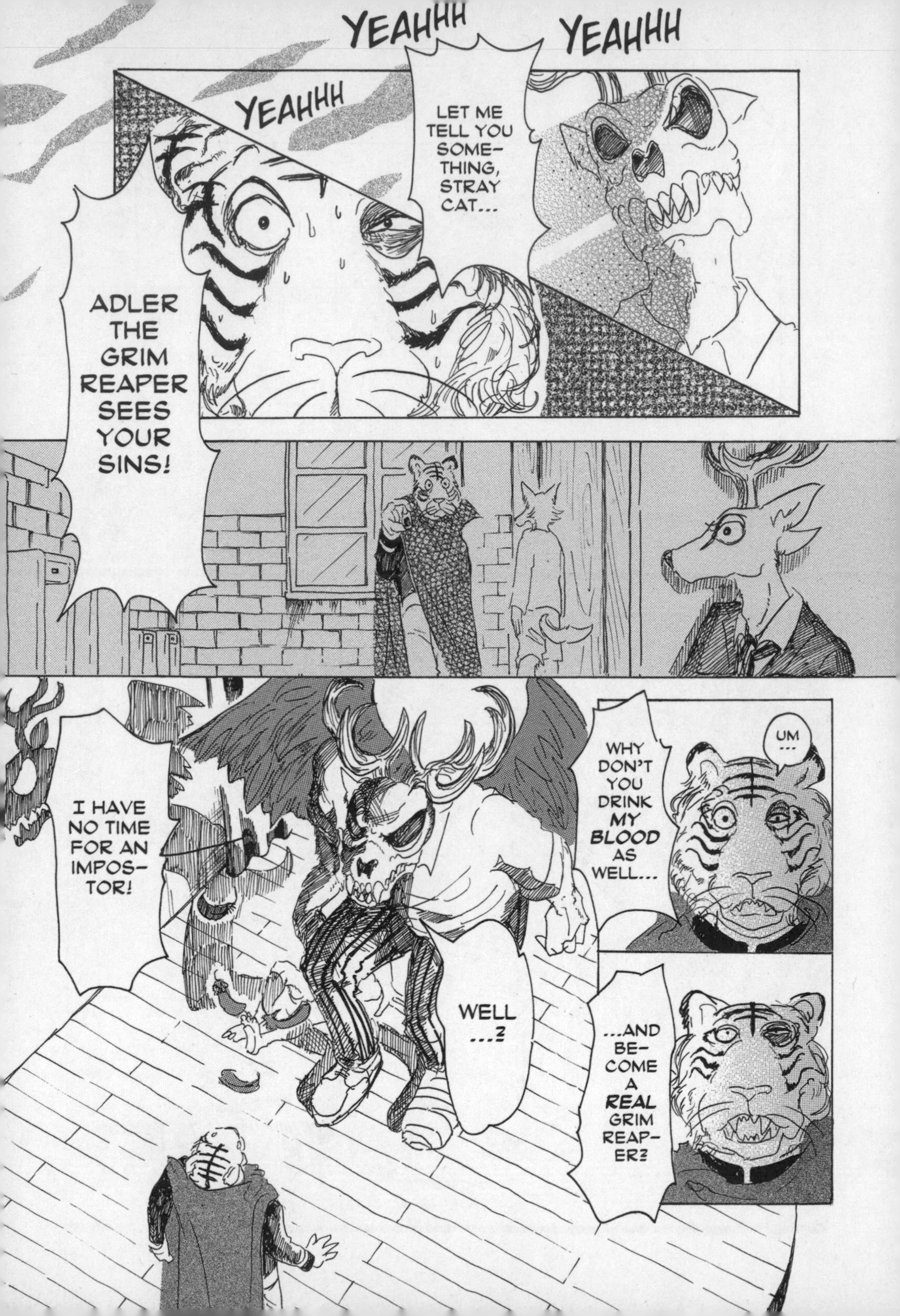
YEAHHH
YEAHHH
LET ME TELL YOU SOME-THING, STRAY CAT...
YEAHHH
ADLER THE GRIM REAPER SEES YOUR SINS!
UM ...
WHY DON'T YOU DRINK *MY BLOOD* AS WELL...
...AND BE-COME A *REAL* GRIM REAP-ER?
WELL ...?
I HAVE NO TIME FOR AN IMPOS-TOR!

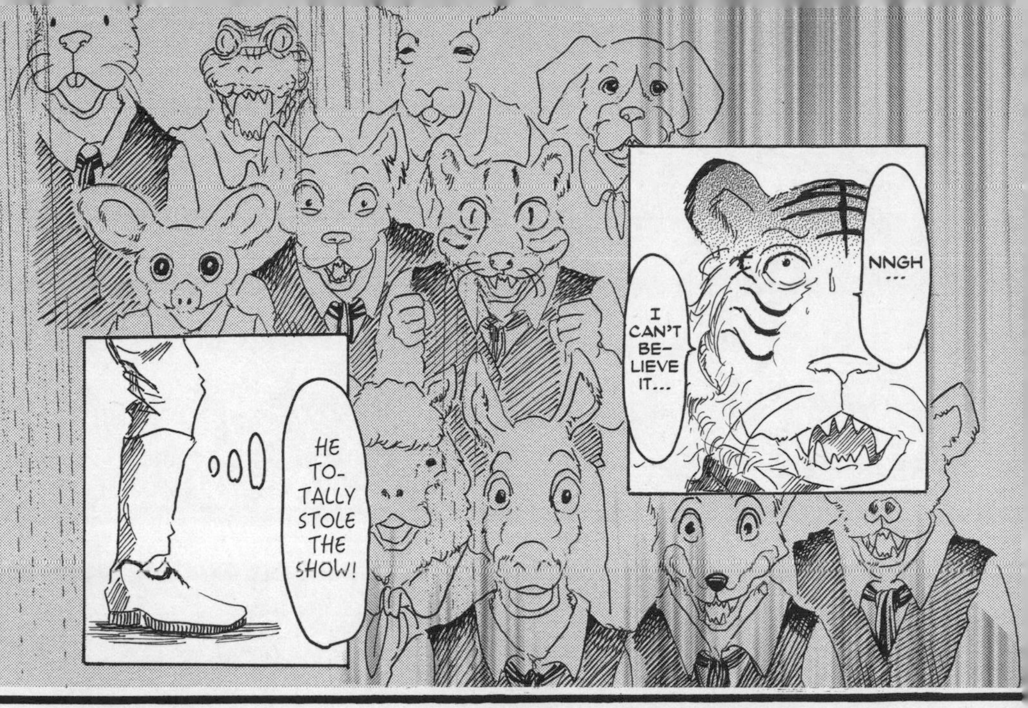
NNGH...
I CAN'T BE-LIEVE IT...
HE TO-TALLY STOLE THE SHOW!

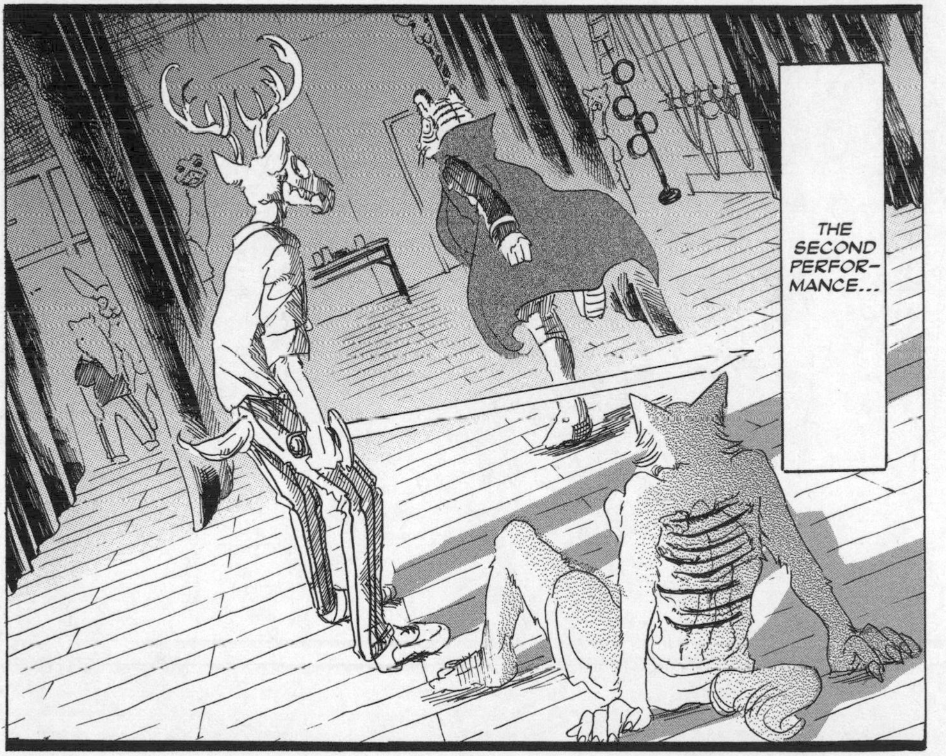
THE SECOND PERFOR-MANCE...

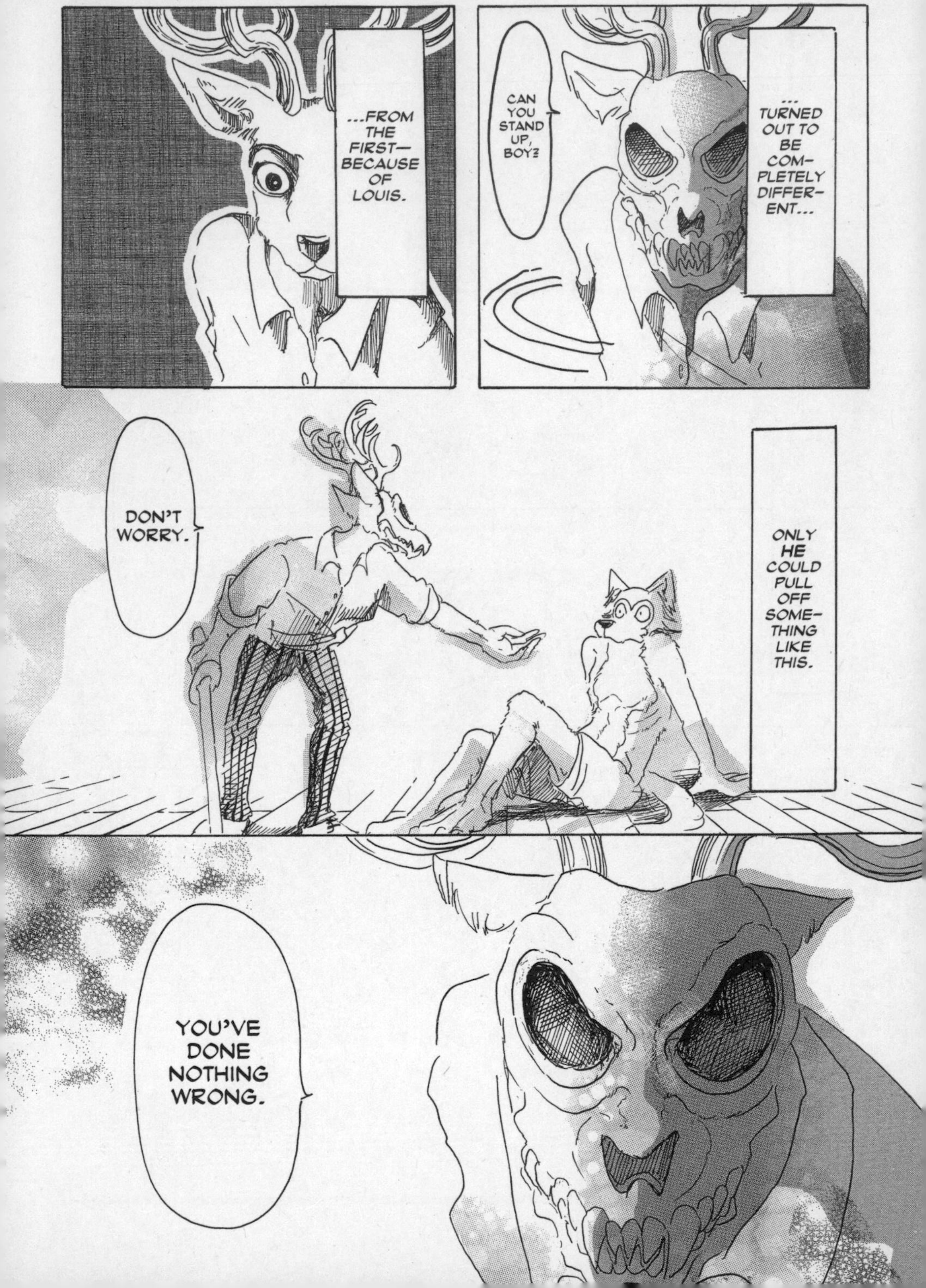
...TURNED OUT TO BE COMPLETELY DIFFERENT...
CAN YOU STAND UP, BOY?
...FROM THE FIRST—BECAUSE OF LOUIS.
ONLY HE COULD PULL OFF SOMETHING LIKE THIS.
DON'T WORRY.
YOU'VE DONE NOTHING WRONG.

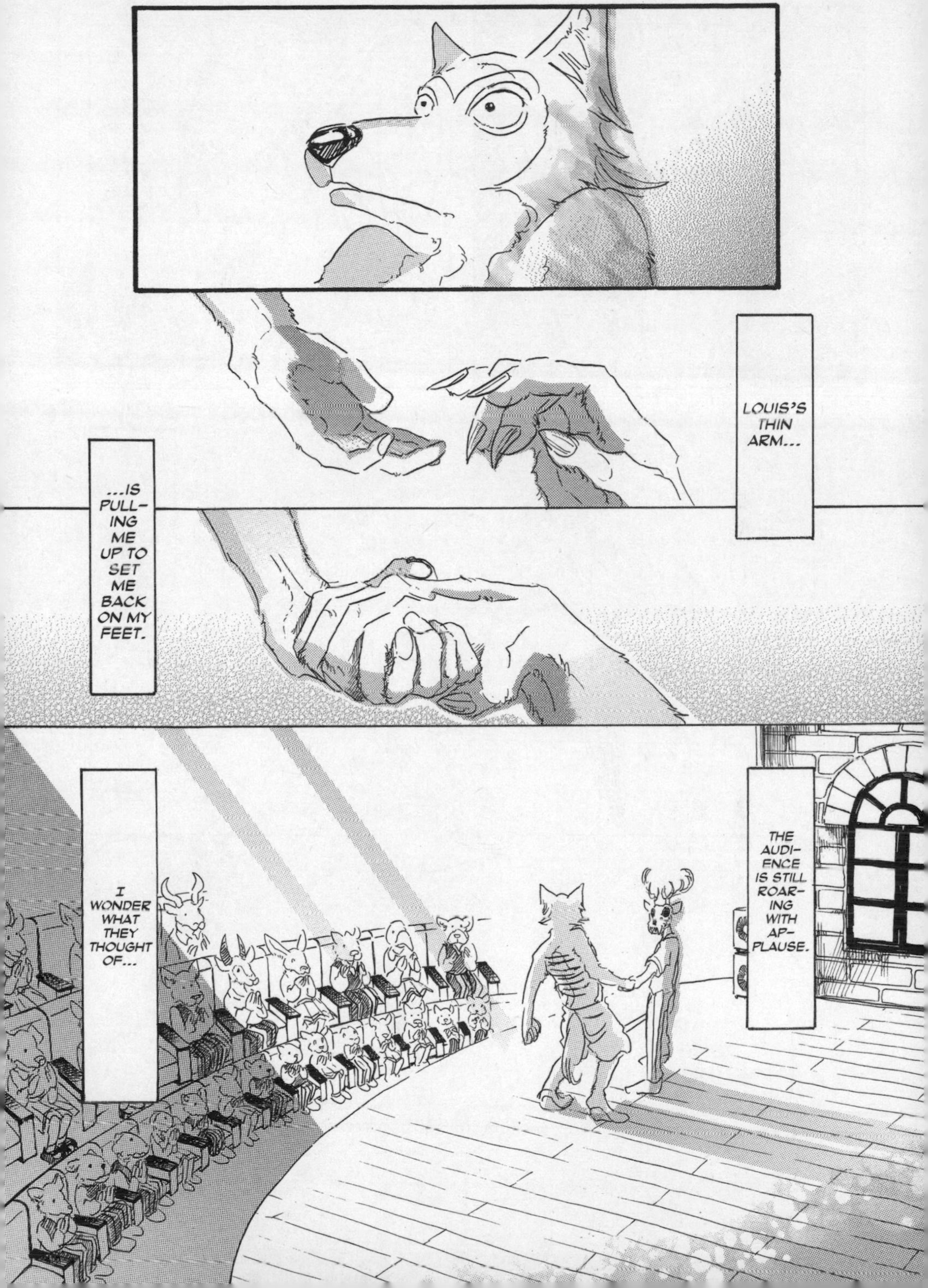
LOUIS'S THIN ARM...
...IS PULLING ME UP TO SET ME BACK ON MY FEET.
THE AUDIENCE IS STILL ROARING WITH APPLAUSE.
I WONDER WHAT THEY THOUGHT OF...

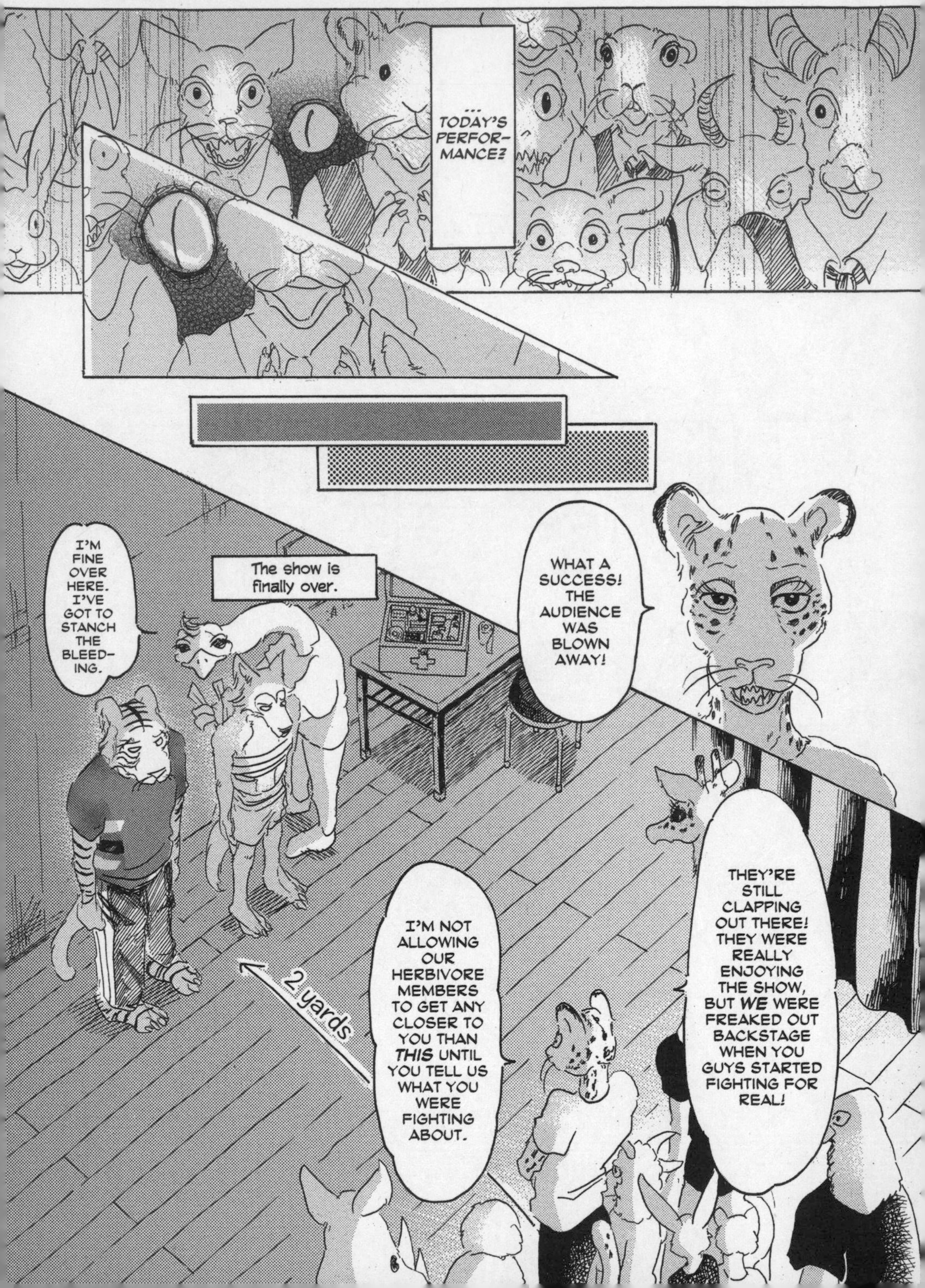
...TODAY'S PERFORMANCE?
The show is finally over.
WHAT A SUCCESS! THE AUDIENCE WAS BLOWN AWAY!
THEY'RE STILL CLAPPING OUT THERE! THEY WERE REALLY ENJOYING THE SHOW, BUT *WE* WERE FREAKED OUT BACKSTAGE WHEN YOU GUYS STARTED FIGHTING FOR REAL!
I'M NOT ALLOWING OUR HERBIVORE MEMBERS TO GET ANY CLOSER TO YOU THAN *THIS* UNTIL YOU TELL US WHAT YOU WERE FIGHTING ABOUT.
2 yards
I'M FINE OVER HERE. I'VE GOT TO STANCH THE BLEEDING.

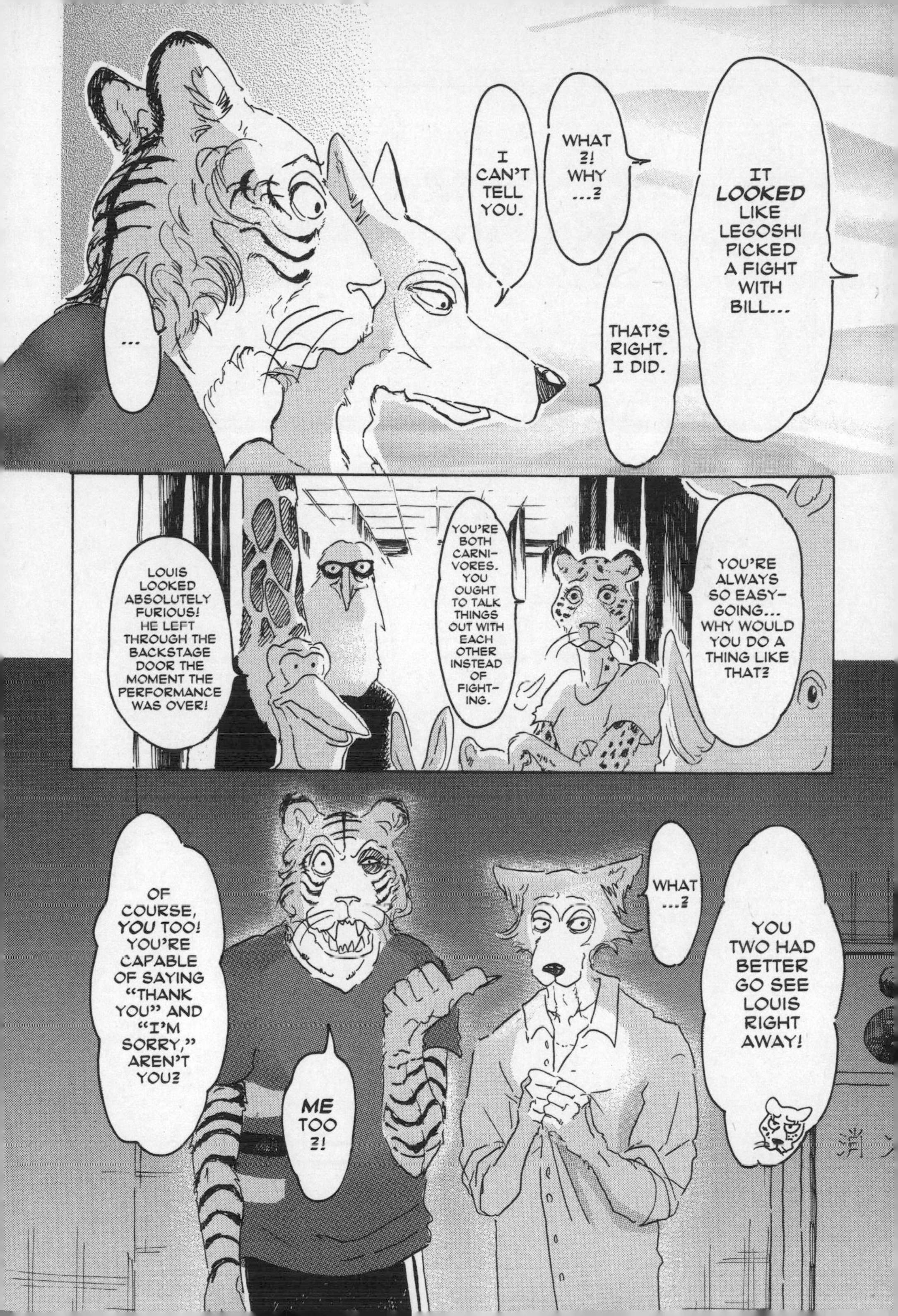
IT LOOKED LIKE LEGOSHI PICKED A FIGHT WITH BILL...
THAT'S RIGHT. I DID.
WHAT?! WHY...?
I CAN'T TELL YOU.
...
YOU'RE ALWAYS SO EASY-GOING... WHY WOULD YOU DO A THING LIKE THAT?
YOU'RE BOTH CARNIVORES. YOU OUGHT TO TALK THINGS OUT WITH EACH OTHER INSTEAD OF FIGHTING.
LOUIS LOOKED ABSOLUTELY FURIOUS! HE LEFT THROUGH THE BACKSTAGE DOOR THE MOMENT THE PERFORMANCE WAS OVER!
YOU TWO HAD BETTER GO SEE LOUIS RIGHT AWAY!
WHAT...?
OF COURSE, YOU TOO! YOU'RE CAPABLE OF SAYING "THANK YOU" AND "I'M SORRY," AREN'T YOU?
ME TOO?!

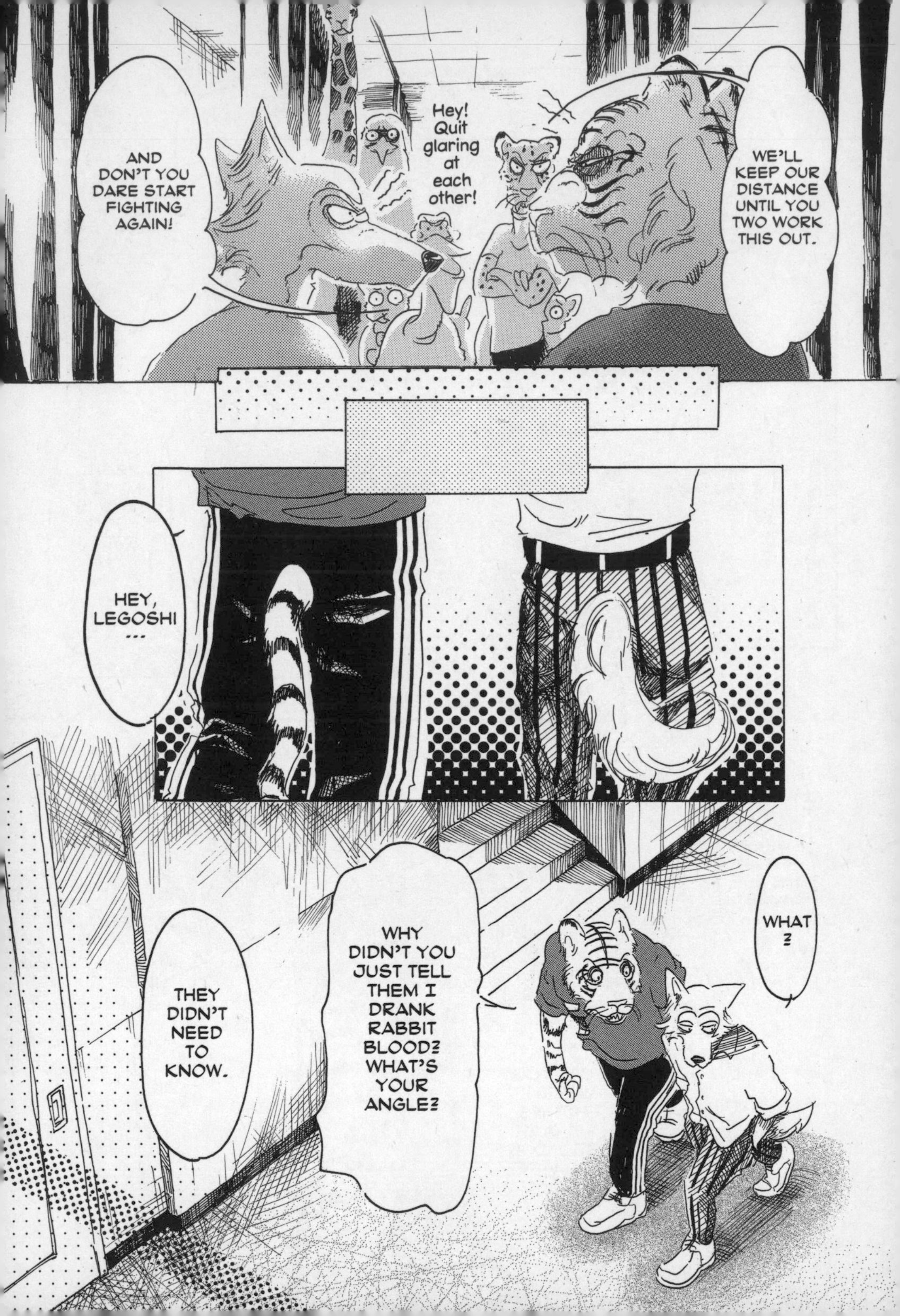
WE'LL KEEP OUR DISTANCE UNTIL YOU TWO WORK THIS OUT.
Hey! Quit glaring at each other!
AND DON'T YOU DARE START FIGHTING AGAIN!
HEY, LEGOSHI ...
WHAT?
WHY DIDN'T YOU JUST TELL THEM I DRANK RABBIT BLOOD? WHAT'S YOUR ANGLE?
THEY DIDN'T NEED TO KNOW.

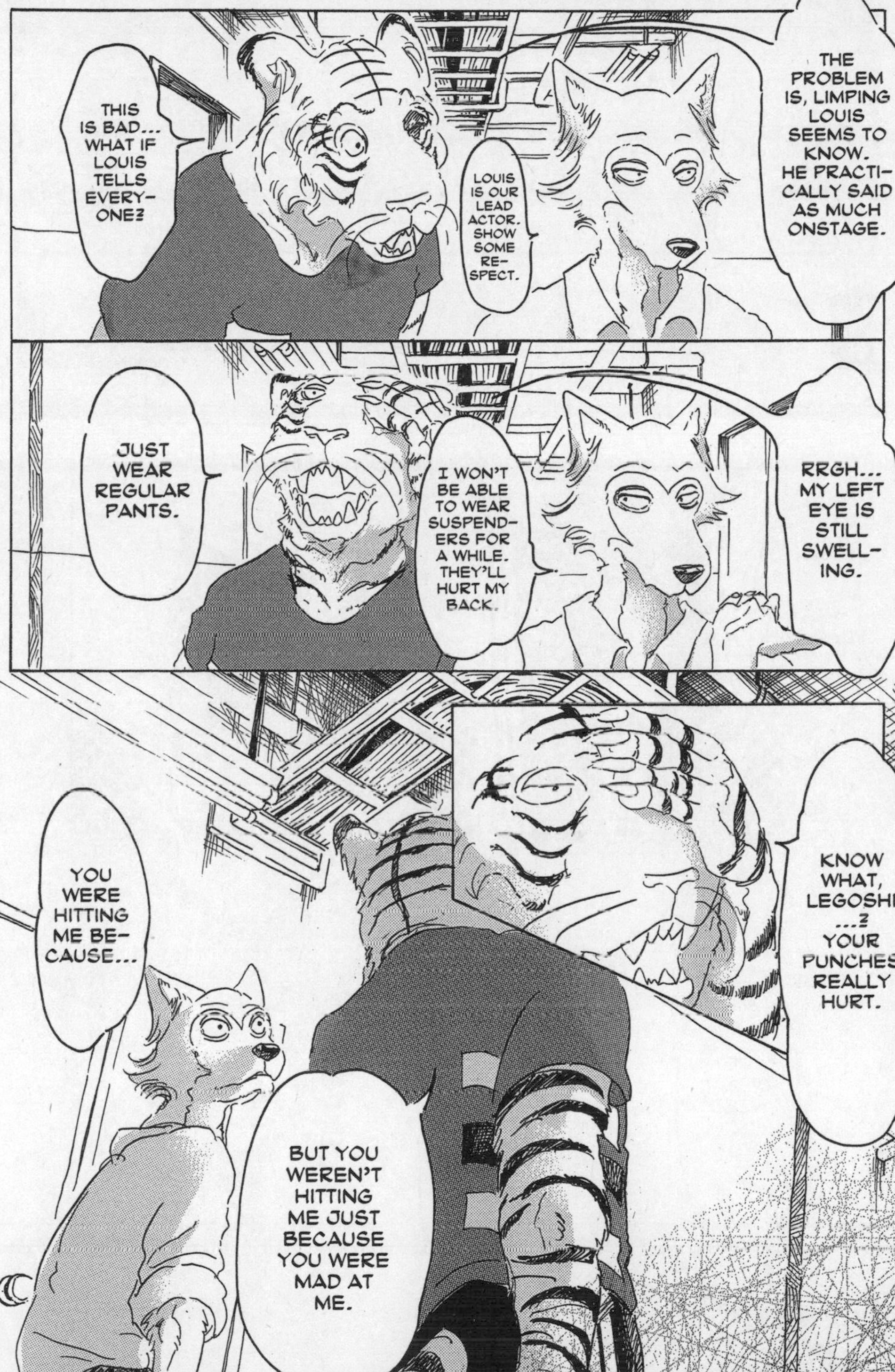
THE PROBLEM IS, LIMPING LOUIS SEEMS TO KNOW. HE PRACTICALLY SAID AS MUCH ONSTAGE.
LOUIS IS OUR LEAD ACTOR. SHOW SOME RESPECT.
THIS IS BAD... WHAT IF LOUIS TELLS EVERYONE?
RRGH... MY LEFT EYE IS STILL SWELLING.
I WON'T BE ABLE TO WEAR SUSPENDERS FOR A WHILE. THEY'LL HURT MY BACK.
JUST WEAR REGULAR PANTS.
KNOW WHAT, LEGOSHI...? YOUR PUNCHES REALLY HURT.
YOU WERE HITTING ME BECAUSE...
BUT YOU WEREN'T HITTING ME JUST BECAUSE YOU WERE MAD AT ME.

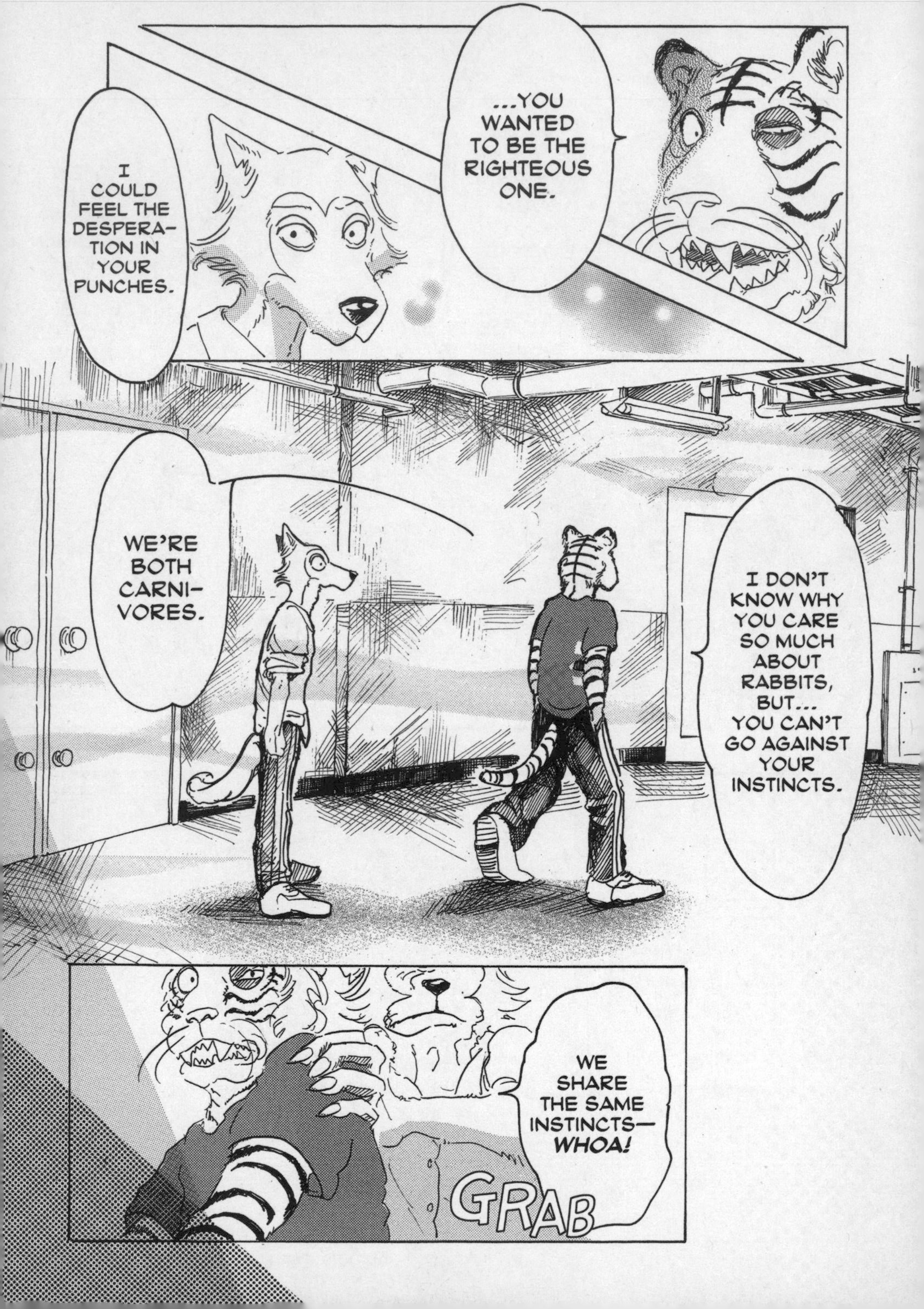
...YOU WANTED TO BE THE RIGHTEOUS ONE.
I COULD FEEL THE DESPERATION IN YOUR PUNCHES.
I DON'T KNOW WHY YOU CARE SO MUCH ABOUT RABBITS, BUT... YOU CAN'T GO AGAINST YOUR INSTINCTS.
WE'RE BOTH CARNIVORES.
WE SHARE THE SAME INSTINCTS—*WHOA!*
GRAB

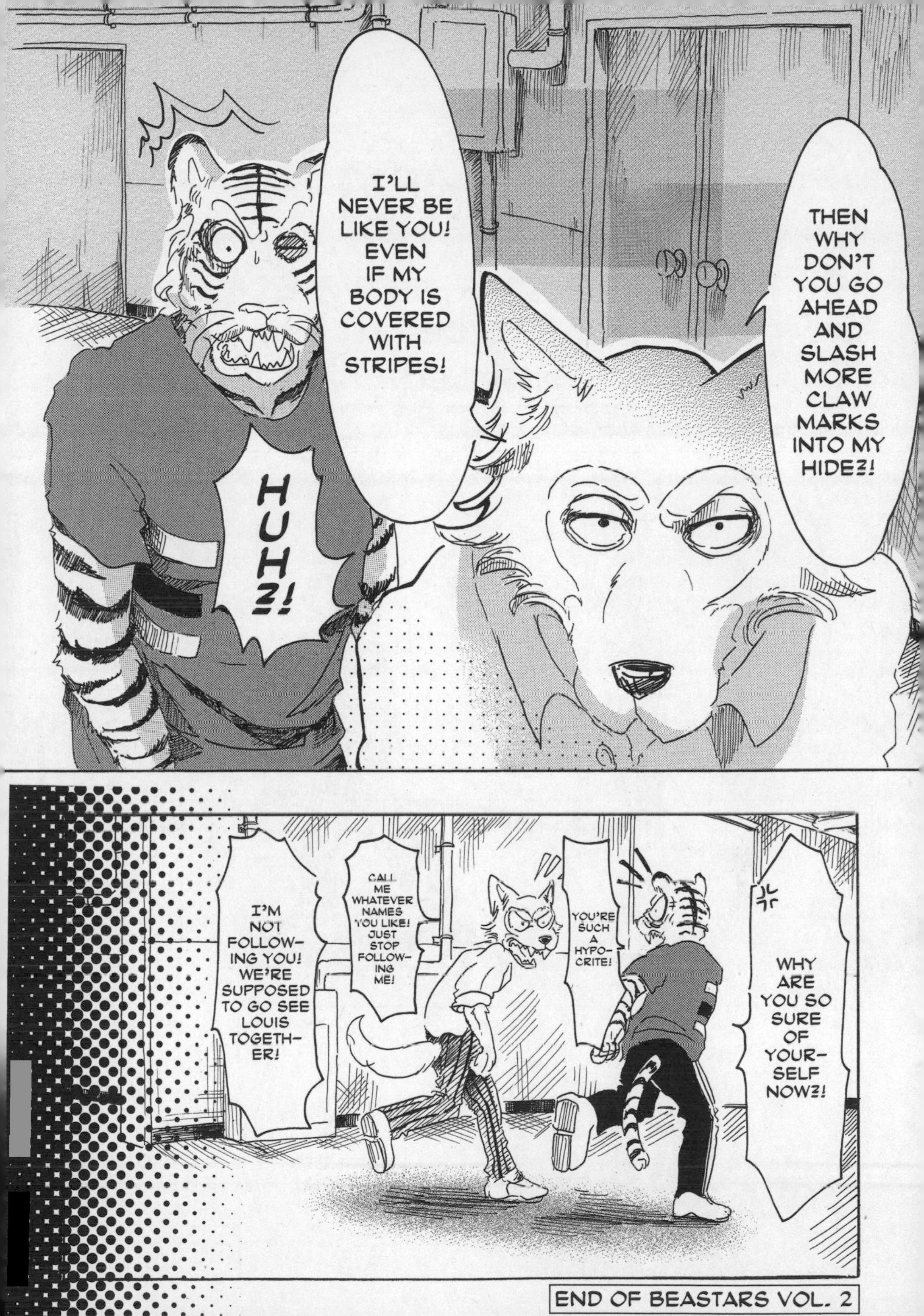
THEN WHY DON'T YOU GO AHEAD AND SLASH MORE CLAW MARKS INTO MY HIDE?!
I'LL NEVER BE LIKE YOU! EVEN IF MY BODY IS COVERED WITH STRIPES!
HUH?!
WHY ARE YOU SO SURE OF YOUR-SELF NOW?!
YOU'RE SUCH A HYPO-CRITE!
CALL ME WHATEVER NAMES YOU LIKE! JUST STOP FOLLOW-ING ME!
I'M NOT FOLLOW-ING YOU! WE'RE SUPPOSED TO GO SEE LOUIS TOGETH-ER!

END OF BEASTARS VOL. 2

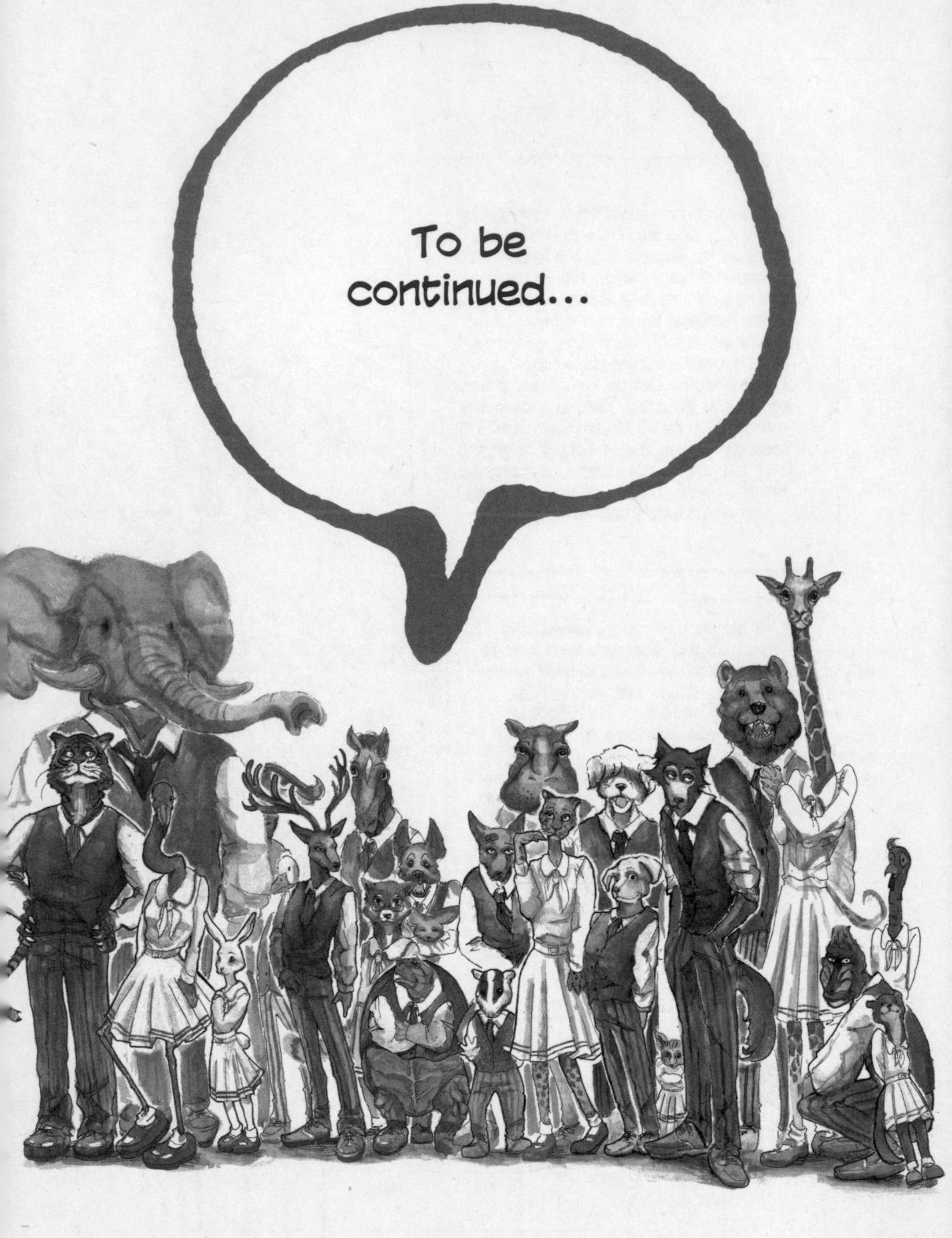
To be continued...

Louis

Character Design Notes

Louis's role

Louis is the most difficult character for me to draw. (It's not difficult to draw his exterior, but it's difficult to portray his interior, his emotions.) Legoshi and I have a lot in common, but I get nervous trying to depict Louis because it's the opposite with him. When I see Louis's vulnerable side, I feel a lot closer to him. Then I find him easier to draw. He's a character I need to treat with special care. I'll keep giving him the special treatment until the day I can completely expose his true self. That's what I'm hoping to accomplish, anyway. (*grin*)

The origins of his name and character design

I chose this name because it sounded like someone who comes from a wealthy, distinguished family—like a king... I've consciously designed Louis so he's the complete opposite of Legoshi.

Louis is a typical handsome guy. He's stylish and always has good posture. (He definitely doesn't want others to perceive him as small.)

He always wears a suit jacket. Maybe he thinks that someone is always looking at him.

How does he get into his clothes?

Clothes made for deer have quite a bit of give to them. They are made of extremely stretchy fabric so they can stretch them over antlers.

PROFILE

LOUIS (AGE 18)
MALE
ARTIODACTYLA
CERVIDAE (RED DEER)
BIRTHDAY: MARCH 29
ASTROLOGICAL SIGN: ARIES
BLOOD TYPE: A
HEIGHT: 5 FT., 6 IN.
WEIGHT: 117 LB.
LIKES CELERY

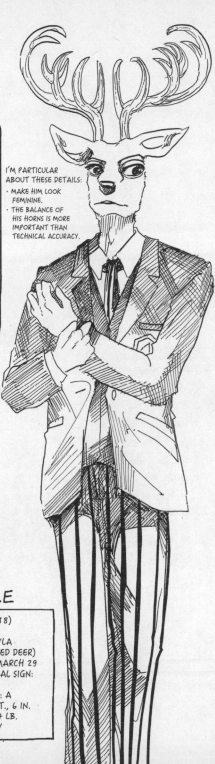

I'M PARTICULAR ABOUT THESE DETAILS:
· MAKE HIM LOOK FEMININE.
· THE BALANCE OF HIS HORNS IS MORE IMPORTANT THAN TECHNICAL ACCURACY.

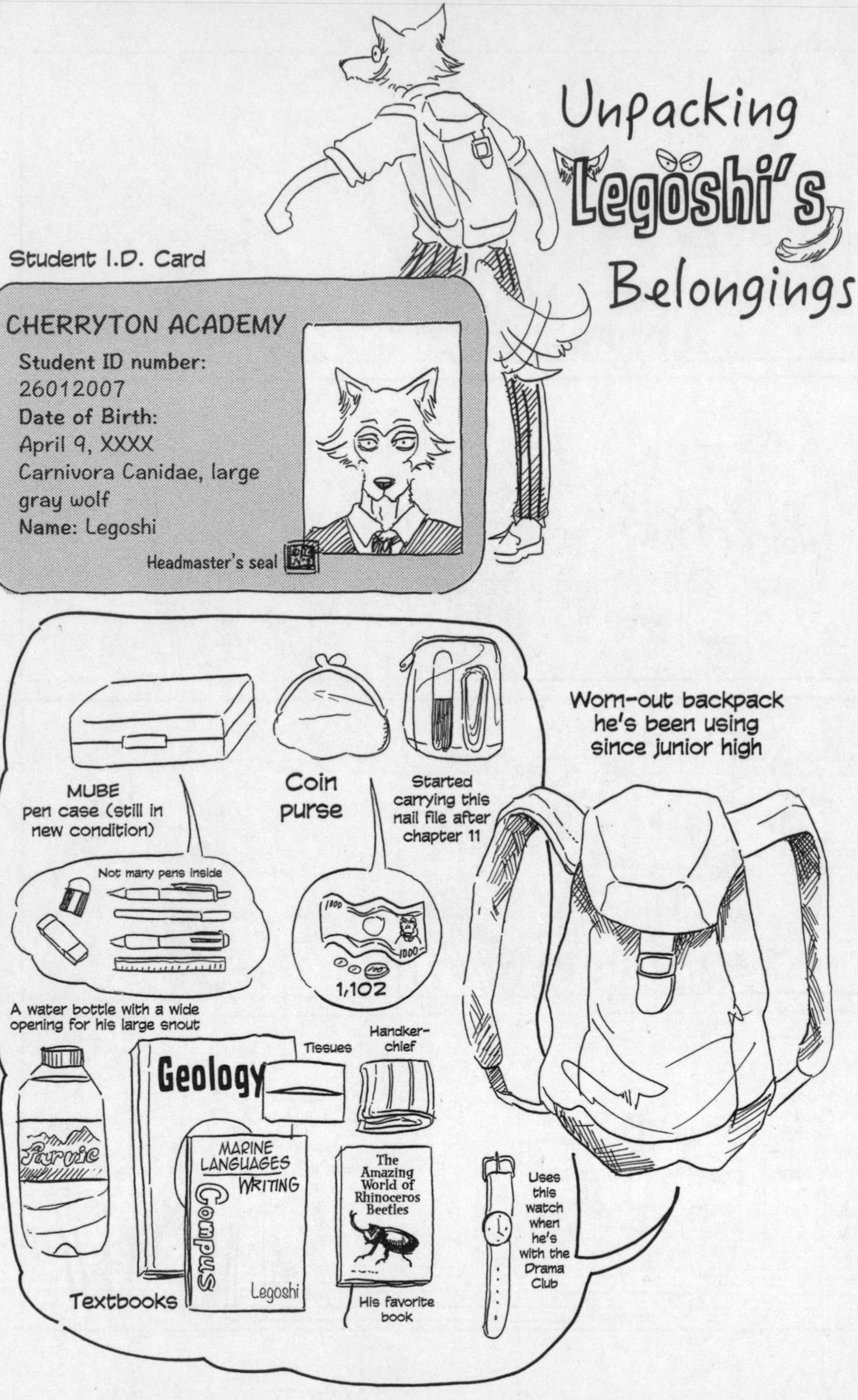
Unpacking Legoshi's Belongings
Student I.D. Card
CHERRYTON ACADEMY
Student ID number: 26012007
Date of Birth: April 9, XXXX
Carnivora Canidae, large gray wolf
Name: Legoshi
Headmaster's seal
MUBE pen case (still in new condition)
Not many pens inside
Coin purse
1,102
Started carrying this nail file after chapter 11
Worn-out backpack he's been using since junior high
A water bottle with a wide opening for his large snout
Geology
MARINE LANGUAGES WRITING
Compus
Legoshi
Textbooks
Tissues
Handker-chief
The Amazing World of Rhinoceros Beetles
His favorite book
Uses this watch when he's with the Drama Club

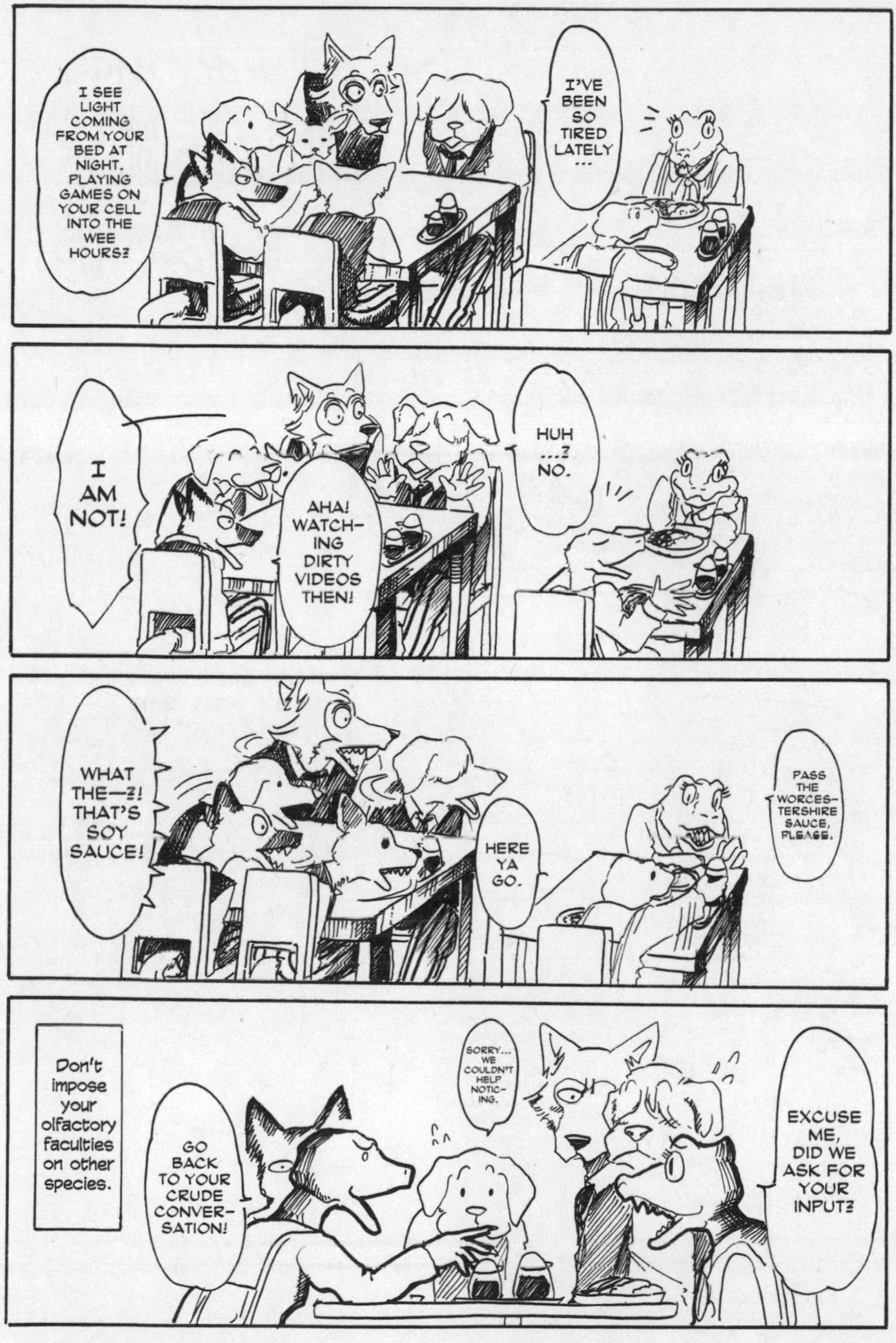
I'VE BEEN SO TIRED LATELY...
I SEE LIGHT COMING FROM YOUR BED AT NIGHT. PLAYING GAMES ON YOUR CELL INTO THE WEE HOURS?
HUH ...? NO.
AHA! WATCHING DIRTY VIDEOS THEN!
I AM NOT!
PASS THE WORCESTERSHIRE SAUCE, PLEASE.
HERE YA GO.
WHAT THE—?! THAT'S SOY SAUCE!
EXCUSE ME, DID WE ASK FOR YOUR INPUT?
SORRY... WE COULDN'T HELP NOTICING.
GO BACK TO YOUR CRUDE CONVERSATION!
Don't impose your olfactory faculties on other species.

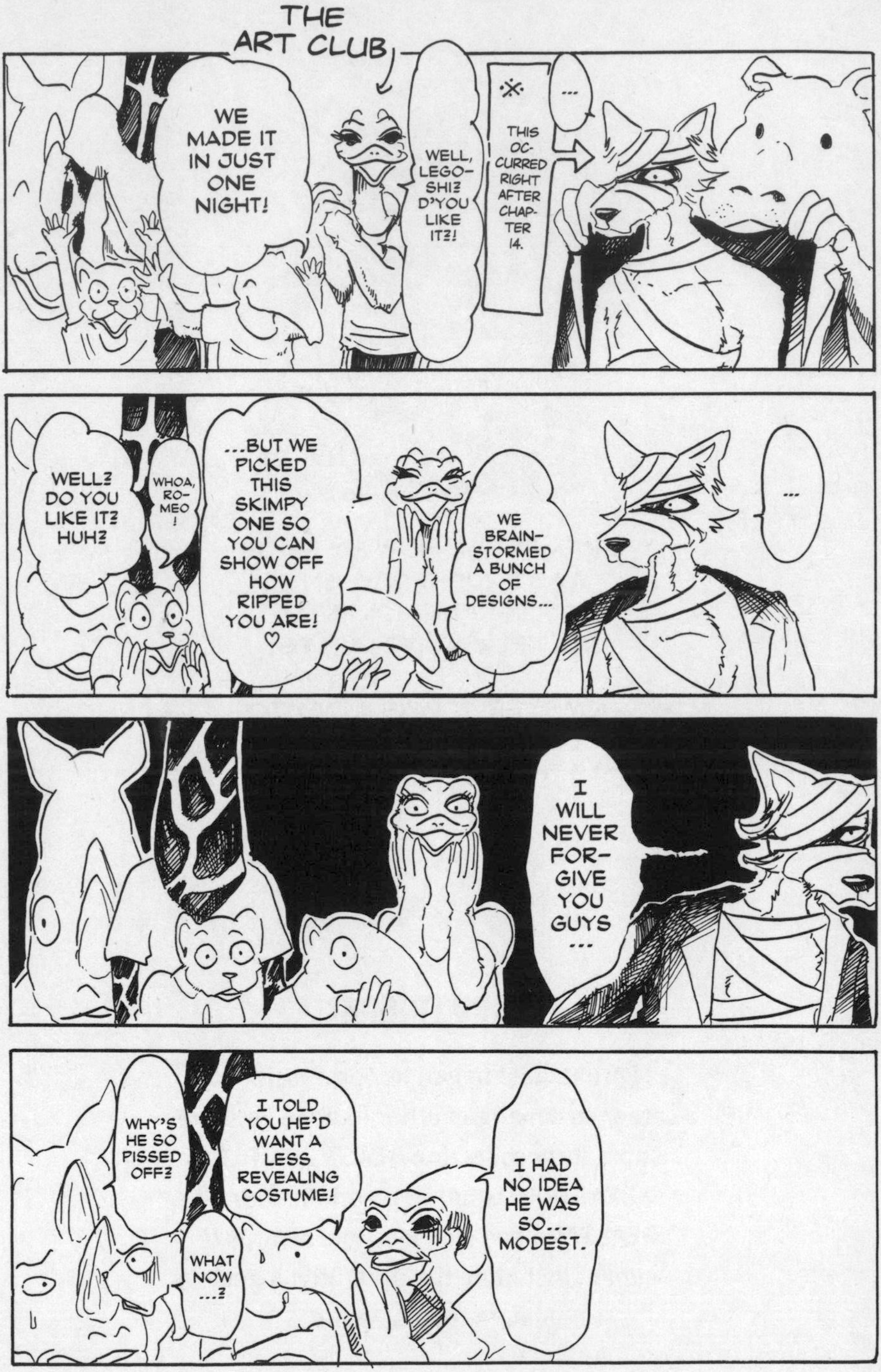
...
※ THIS OCCURRED RIGHT AFTER CHAPTER 14.
THE ART CLUB
WELL, LEGOSHI? D'YOU LIKE IT?!
WE MADE IT IN JUST ONE NIGHT!
...
WE BRAINSTORMED A BUNCH OF DESIGNS...
...BUT WE PICKED THIS SKIMPY ONE SO YOU CAN SHOW OFF HOW RIPPED YOU ARE! ♡
WHOA, ROMEO!
WELL? DO YOU LIKE IT? HUH?
I WILL NEVER FORGIVE YOU GUYS...
I HAD NO IDEA HE WAS SO... MODEST.
I TOLD YOU HE'D WANT A LESS REVEALING COSTUME!
WHY'S HE SO PISSED OFF?
WHAT NOW...?

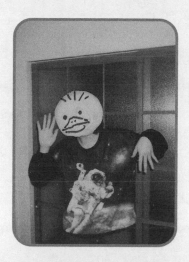

I REMEMBER HOW MY PRIDE
WAS CRUSHED WHEN I
COULDN'T MEMORIZE MY
MULTIPLICATION TABLES.

HOWEVER, IT WAS A DAY TO
CELEBRATE BECAUSE THAT
WAS THE MOMENT I BECAME
AWARE OF MY EGO!

PARU ITAGAKI

Paru Itagaki began her professional
career as a manga author in 2016 with the
short story collection **BEAST COMPLEX**.
BEASTARS is her first serialization.
BEASTARS has won multiple awards in
Japan, including the prestigious 2018
Manga Taisho Award.

BEASTARS

VOL. 2
VIZ Signature Edition

Story & Art by
Paru Itagaki

Translation/Tomoko Kimura
English Adaptation/Annette Roman
Touch-Up Art & Lettering/Susan Daigle-Leach
Cover & Interior Design/Yukiko Whitley
Editor/Annette Roman

BEASTARS Volume 2
© 2017 PARU ITAGAKI
All rights reserved.
First published in 2017 by Akita Publishing Co., Ltd., Tokyo
English translation rights arranged with AKITA PUBLISHING CO., LTD. through
Tuttle-Mori Agency, Inc., Tokyo

Printed in the U.S.A.

Published by VIZ Media, LLC
P.O. Box 77010
San Francisco, CA 94107

10 9 8 7 6 5 4 3 2
First printing, September 2019
Second printing, December 2019

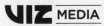 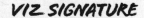

viz.com   vizsignature.com

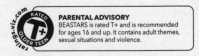

COMING IN VOLUME 3...

It's time for the Festival of the Meteor, which honors the world's dinosaur ancestors. While helping to decorate the town, gray wolf Legoshi runs into dwarf rabbit Haru and finds he is still inexorably drawn to her. Is it a crush or bloodlust? Is it her or any small animal? Relationships are complicated for carnivores—their bird classmates lay the eggs they eat, and some desperate herbivores even sell their body parts on the black market. Then, when Bengal tiger Bill is tempted to buy a piece of forbidden meat, he tries to convince Legoshi to join him...

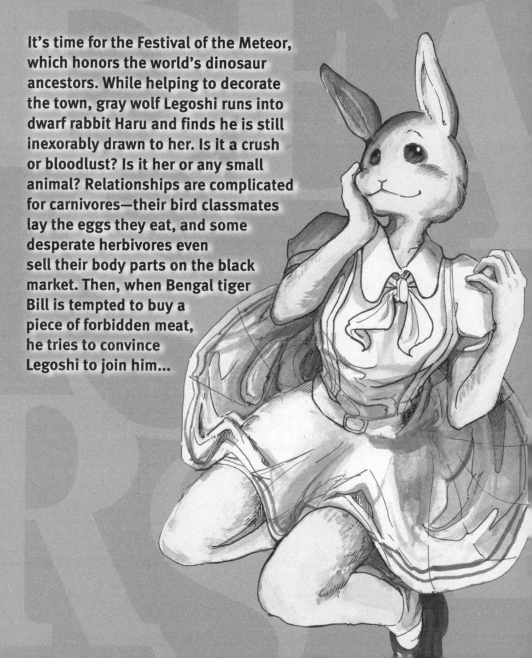

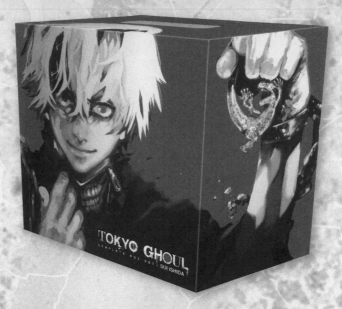

TOKYO GHOUL

C O M P L E T E   B O X   S E T

STORY AND ART BY **SUI ISHIDA**

KEN KANEKI is an ordinary college student until a violent encounter turns him into the first half-human, half-Ghoul hybrid. Trapped between two worlds, he must survive Ghoul turf wars, learn more about Ghoul society and master his new powers.

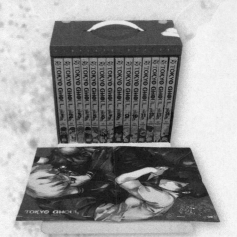

Box set collects all fourteen volumes of the original *Tokyo Ghoul* series. Includes an exclusive double-sided poster.

COLLECT THE COMPLETE SERIES

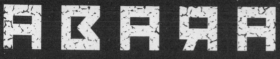

ABARA
COMPLETE DELUXE EDITION
TSUTOMU NIHEI

A visually stunning work of sci-fi horror from the creator of **BIOMEGA** and **BLAME**!

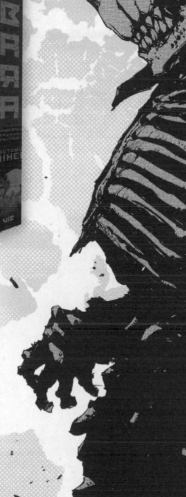

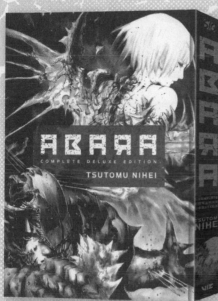

A vast city lies under the shadow of colossal, ancient tombs, the identity of their builders lost to time. In the streets of the city something is preying on the inhabitants, something that moves faster than the human eye can see and leaves unimaginable horror in its wake.

Tsutomu Nihei's dazzling, harrowing dystopian thriller is presented here in a single-volume hardcover edition featuring full-color pages and foldout illustrations. This volume also includes the early short story "Digimortal."

RATED T+ OLDER TEEN

VIZ

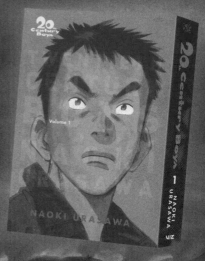
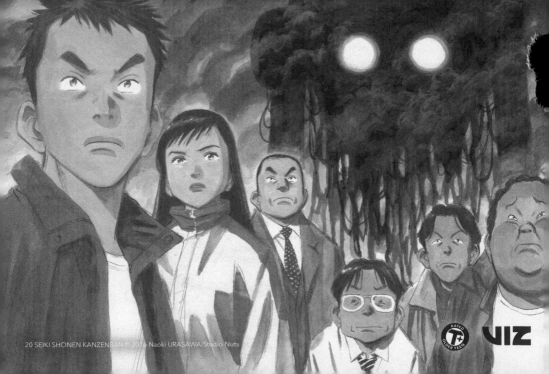

This is the last page.

BEASTARS reads from right to left
to preserve the orientation of the
original Japanese artwork.

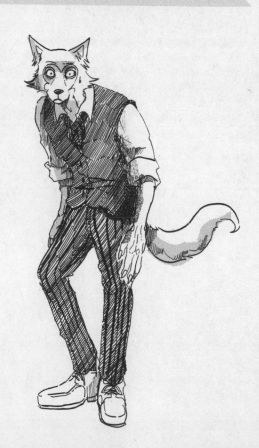